The Witch and the Clown

Two Archetypes of Human Sexuality

ANN and BARRY ULANOV

CHIRON PUBLICATIONS • Wilmette, Illinois

Printed in the United States of America

Book design by Lauretta Akkeron

Library of Congress Cataloging in Publication Data

Ulanov, Ann Belford.
   The Witch and the Clown.

   Bibliography: p.
   Includes index.
   1. Sex role. 2. Archetype (Psychology)
   3. Sex (Psychology) 4. Identity (Psychology)
   I. Ulanov, Barry. II. Title.
   HQ1075.U52 1987   155.3   86-21628
   ISBN 0-933029-07-1

FOR ALEXANDER
Lover of Clowns and Witches

ACKNOWLEDGMENTS

We are grateful for the interest and support of many people in the long process of bringing this book to completion, not the least of them those who responded so warmly to the lectures and workshops we conducted over a number of years on *The Witch and the Clown*. In gatherings brought together by Jungian groups and others, by training institutes and related organizations in San Francisco, Los Angeles, New York, Pittsburgh, Westport, Montreal, Toronto, Ottawa, Zürich, and London, people shared experiences, voiced concerns, offered insights which greatly supported and extended our understanding of the archetypes of witch and clown. We are grateful, too, for the generous support of Union Theological Seminary, in the case of Ann, and years ago of a Guggenheim Fellowship for Barry, which made possible research in areas central to this undertaking. We are thankful to Staley Hitchcock once again for making clean typewritten copy of mottled manuscript pages and to our friend, colleague, and publisher Nathan Schwartz-Salant for his graciousness and understanding.

A.U.
B.U.

Contents

We should never forget that in any psychological discussion we are not saying anything *about* the psyche, but that the psyche is always speaking about *itself*.

—*C. G. Jung*

I The Archetypal Witch and Clown

Who

What is the psyche saying to us through the archetypal images of the witch and the clown? Who are these figures? Where do they appear? How do we deal with them? Why do witches turn up at all? What causes us, from childhood on, to be so fascinated by them, so eager to hear tales about them? Why does the witch persist in our imagination as a figure of archetypal dimension, more magnificent than maleficent?[1] Why does she not retire gracefully from our central stockpile of images, now that we have come to understand that the witch-cults of the past were almost certainly the inventions of pseudo-history? How can we hold on to her as an image far more positive than negative when we think of the persecutions of women by those who believed in the monstrous fantasy of the witch-cult? Why is she not simply a quaint figure from a variously distant past, a pathetic one, even a tragic one? Why does she remain so appealing to us? Why does she still possess something that could be described as grandeur? There are many reasons.

The persistent witch of our imagination is full of secret knowledge, powerful spells, hidden ambitions, cackling revenge. What a relief she offers women trapped in dubious definitions of goodness! What permission she gives us—to feel rage and envy, to accept our wishes to defeat others while triumphing ourselves! What license there is for us in her ability to turn her enemies into toads! How appealing to turn those who hurt us into slimy things—not to have to debate them, or out-argue them, but so effectively to silence them!

The archetypal witch arouses many reactions in us, whether she is presented in her benevolent everyday form or her threatening nightmare form, to use two traditional witch categories.[2] We are curious about her knowledge of uncanny things. We may feel aggressive toward her, want to outsmart her, burn her in our fantasies, defeat her wily plots. We may fear her dread powers even as a mere fantasy figure, apprehensive lest she cast an evil spell on those we love. We may disapprove of her as she coldly defies all human values and lives outside human society. Yet we marvel at her too. She is a fairy-tale figure who with her white magic can bestow upon us a protean tinder box, an invisible cloak, all sorts of secret treasures. Although she often appears as a remote old crone beyond the reach of human convention, in her youthful form her seductive beauty continues to bewitch us.

The witch commands response from all ages and interests. Children have always loved to hear of her in fairy tales. They still revel in her appearances in

1

comic-book and television versions, where she appears sometimes as a charming magician in everyday life, sometimes as a nightmarish villain. The Cat-Woman of Batman days was a combination of the witches, an ambiguous mixture of good and bad, a plotter of evil who sometimes occasioned good results. Such a figure evokes a fearful delight in young audiences.

In the women's movement one group decided to champion the witch, taking the letters of her name to identify its cause: Witch's International Terrorist Conspiracy from Hell. Their manifesto supports all the witch qualities of the female that patriarchal society proscribes. It lauds aggressive women who reject playing a supportive role to men, and who eschew feminine gentility as well, screeching and bellowing their rage rather than swallowing it or masochistically directing it against themselves.

The image of the witch that survives from the centuries of the witch hunt, especially the sixteenth and seventeenth centuries, is a projection that can well exercise an aroused feminist. A terrifying conspiracy was foisted onto actual women in many different times and places, uniting a cunning intellectuality and a maddened animality, each more diabolic than the other, and both ascribed to pacts with the Devil. As we know, that projection was used to hound and to persecute women, to outlaw them, to torture them, to kill them. So strong was the power of the witch image to summon up all the qualities that various communities, usually religious, found hateful or alluring, that ordinary scruples were easily overridden in pursuit of the witch.

It is not insignificant that the assiduous hunt of the witch-woman reached its peak in the sixteenth and seventeenth centuries. In a time of burgeoning intellectuality and the development of a philosophy of scientific investigation, persecutorial demonology achieved its greatest triumph. The persecutors were not simply ignoramuses and bigots who had achieved power. Among them were men like the philosopher of law Jean Bodin, whose *Démonomanie des sorciers* of 1580 was a handbook for judges used in the trials of sorcerers. A hundred years later the English divine Joseph Glanvill wrote *Saducismus Triumphatus*, which pleased even so considerable a figure as the Cambridge Platonist Henry More with its analysis and condemnation of witchcraft—so much so that More added material of his own to a later edition of the book.[3]

For reasons that we shall hope to make clear in this book, women of unmistakable craft, whether of mind or of body or of both, are not easily tolerated. They are particularly objectionable when they seem to have access to those powers of mind that are sanctioned in only a very small number of persons—exclusively male persons in the sixteenth and seventeenth centuries and before. When the powers are associated with subjects and positions reserved by church and society for a designated few, the affront is intolerable. Having apparently broken the sacred law intellectually, these women could be imagined to have done so in every other way as well—could be, would be, must be. Surely they are consorts of the Devil. They must be understood to have done every foul deed that persons constrained by law or belief from doing themselves can imagine another doing—and secretly wish to do themselves. Thus the fullness of the projection which resulted in witch hunts in earlier times. Thus the significance today of the question, Who and why the witch? In order to answer this question, we must focus on a symbol of forces so potent within us that they can utterly distort our perception of reality and turn us into persecutors and murderers, alive with prejudice, with sexual perversion, with blood lust—at least in our imaginations.

Witch figures still turn up in our dreams as images of malevolence and destruction. Two different women's dreams offer chilling examples. In the first, "A cat and a rabbit are marrying, only it is wrong. An evil woman has cast this spell. Other animals behind the scene try to do in this evil woman. They succeed. The result is that cats marry cats and rabbits marry rabbits."[4] The dreamer said of this dream that the parts of the cat and the rabbit were not exactly wrong, just terribly mismatched to make a monster. The cause of the monstrous mismatching was the witchy woman who represented "energy in chaos." The essence of this woman's evil was her ability to make confusion, to twist energy into chaotic expression, stealing it from the dreamer's chosen direction. As the dreamer put it, "She works to confuse; that's the nature of her, and I lose my sense of direction about who I am. I cease to be my own self, and then I get the parts of me all mixed up."

The second dream, also a woman's, is more complicated.

I have a sudden overwhelming impulse to make a drawing. The idea is to represent the aura of people, not just to represent them literally. I know exactly what I want to do—to represent each person, a sort of cloud of delicate striations and crosshatchings in pencil. The tension and excitement of the drawings will derive in part from having overlapping patterns—presumably to represent relationships between people. I am very inspired . . . and go to work with great industry, concentration, and excitement. I have some trouble achieving the subtlety I'm striving for, but I have confidence that if I work at it long enough I will be able to pull it off. I find the grain of paper that helps give my picture added texture.

But then, as I'm losing a little confidence, I become aware of a person who is extremely obstructive, who completely breaks down my sense of identity. Her eyes glow red. It's as if ugly reality were breaking through and destroying my creative vision. There is real fear, almost nightmarish, and I feel completely stalled. Yet I realize I must go on with the drawing if I am to have any existence at all separate from this figure.

The dreamer said of this figure, whom she referred to as "the red-eyed witch," that she had the "power to contaminate and make timid and second-rate; bad will conquer good. She is so full of blood that her eyes are red; she is full of power and capable of destruction. Here I want to create out of a loving impulse, out of my true feelings, not what I should do but out of where my heart is. Her effect is like a magnet sucking everything into it." The dreamer felt she was brought to confrontation with this witch figure every time she wanted to create (which was almost constantly, for she was an artist). She said that when she openly owned her desire to create, then the witch figure was there, " . . . waiting for me. I'm brought to confrontation with her and something will be missed if I by-pass her. The red-eyed witch is the worst side of myself, full of anger, but also wanting something for myself."

Thus it is that the witch configures something essential—energy in one dream, an aggressive creative force in the other. We cannot simply repudiate all that these archetypal manifestations configure unless we are willing to lose access to the tremendous energy and power they galvanize. The witch image depicts the force that arises when women want to create themselves and from themselves in ways other than biological reproduction. The witch's positive effect is to be found here in her very negativity. She may occasion something strongly positive to happen in a woman, if the woman neither avoids the archetypal figure nor is overcome by her. We will return to this insight later.

What of the clown? In sharp contrast to the witch's musty brews of nature's leftovers, filled with bat's wings and frog's eyes, stirred up in rusty old pots in a hovel by a crone in dingy garments, the clown bursts happily onto the scene. He comes in costumes of vivid color, in circus hurly-burly, in slapstick surrealism, in swoops of laughter. Most people would say that he is the opposite of the witch. Whereas the witch cackles and flies away from human concerns, apparently not giving a rap for dependent needs, hurt feelings, or anyone else's wishes, the clown arouses all of our human feeling. He makes us laugh until we cry, and then cry until his next performance sweeps us back into laughter. He makes us feel superior when we foresee the outcome before he does, as we do, say, with a figure about to slip on a banana peel or to receive a custard pie smack in the face. Then he personifies all our worst and most hidden feelings of inferiority. He alone is left out of the group that stands around laughing at him. He is the touching, sad one, wistfully wanting to belong, to do his own impressive feat to scale the heights and rescue the stranded cat that belongs to the beautiful girl—yet he always bumbles and staggers, and fails miserably. The ladder wobbles; one of its legs is too short. Then the rungs snap, and the clown comes crashing down as the cat nimbly jumps into its mistress's waiting arms. They go happily off, leaving the clown a sad, sorry figure, bruised and foolish-looking. But just as we plunge with him into hopeless despair, up goes the clown's balloon and we are off again in high-spirited antics, seeing how silly it was to take our failure so seriously.

Unlike the witch, the clown alternates between destruction and restitution, between wreckage and reparation. In slapstick films and their modern counterparts, no one pays the bill for the apartment that lies in ruins as a result of all the clowning. No one is permanently hurt from the banana-peel accident; no one has to clean up all the pie, whether on a face or on furniture and walls. By the next scene the apartment is reconstituted; the bones and tables are mended; the banana is in place again; the custard is piled high once more.

Clowns get started in smaller spheres of life, too, and in firmly fixed ways. In a third-grade class, one boy reported about his friend Sam. Sam could not throw a ball. Instead of learning, he "fell down in a funny way every time the ball came to him." Clowning covered up Sam's clumsiness and embarrassment and came to substitute for his learning a skill. Clowning turns up in people's dreams with the same rigid masking effect. A man dreamt that he was told a young man had died: "He had been crossing the street, looking at a woman, and had been hit by a car. I said, 'Sounds like he got broadsided.' People laughed and said, 'That's pretty good.'" The witty remark masks what happens to nervous young men who look too hard at women, while at the same time giving the dream figure an amusing identity in relation to the others with whom he spends his life. He wins their appreciation rather than their criticism. The dreamer himself commented that this was the way he siphoned off his aggression, turning it into humor.

Another example gives a glimpse of what problems arise when the masks of clowning substitute for identity. The clown evokes a feeling of pleasure in us, but where is the clown's own feeling? A man in a therapy group shared his troubles with the other members, but did it in such a funny way, with such charming stories, that all were reduced to helpless laughter or sympathetic tears. He won their appreciation and their exited anticipation to hear more. Group members found his ardors delightful—he counteracted their depression and made it possible for them to laugh at their own problems. They found him tender and warm. He made them aware of their weaknesses, but in a way that enabled them to accept what heretofore they had scorned in themselves. Not until weeks passed did the group come to realize that though he had reached them, they had not reached him. They could not find him behind his antics, could not see his own real face behind the many masks he wore. Increasingly they felt anger at him for so successfully eluding them, and found themselves wanting to attack him in order to penetrate his disguises. They began to see that the clowning that touched their feelings also acted as an effective defense against his own.

Sometimes the clown and witch motifs weave together in one person's psychology. A man who knew he clowned to keep people at bay said he feared women who took an interest in him as a man. Such a woman would invade him or swallow him up, he said. "I'm a clown and she's a witch and she takes me in and destroys my clownness."

Like the witch, the clown turns up in many areas as a figure of fascination. Worldwide, in very different societies and cultures, audiences treasure their comedians. They admire their performances in circuses, film, radio and television, theaters and nightclubs, and laugh at their jokes, puns, routines, their words and costumes, their use of pies and cannons, make-up and props. These figures are alloted a special place in our lives as chroniclers of nation and culture. The films of Charlie Chaplin and Buster Keaton and their slapstick contemporaries, of W. C. Fields and the Marx brothers, of Bing Crosby and Bob Hope, and of Peter Sellers, summarize a whole epoch, stretching from World War I to Viet Nam.[5] The misery and joy, the only too believable frustrations and not quite credible triumphs of six or seven decades, fall into place in routines as sharply defined as the painted laughter or melancholy on a clown's face.

Why

The witch and clown figures are vivid to us as intensifications of what ordinary people feel, as extreme exaggerations of primordial human qualities. They supply us with images of what clearly belongs to the sexual identity of a woman or a man, but is usually left out of the conventional pictures we carry around with us. They are, however, altogether human figures—not gods or goddesses, but human beings like the rest of us, identifiable with particular parts of an unmistakably human identity that they shape into their own peculiar wholes, intensifying and caricaturing themselves as they do so.

The witch figure bodies forth a primordial intellect and power in the female that strongly differ from conscious rationality and ambition. Her intellect and power are more nature-bound, more centered on interior life, issuing from unconscious sources, defying logic and causal sequence. She stands apart from the human community, and brings to it new combinations of familiar ingredients. She challenges, she frightens, she inspires. Her intellect, if claimed, issues in wisdom. Her power, if owned, exudes the strength that accompanies truth. She depicts the contrasexual element that belongs to female identity, something split off, rejected, even scapegoated as disturbing, alien, "not feminine."

The witch is an archetypal picture of the masculine element within feminine identity, of that opposite sexual dynamism that belongs to the feminine personality.[6] She is an easy butt for grudges, a made-to-order container for blame, even in emancipated societies far removed from witch-diviners, witch-hunts, witch-trials, and executions. There she stands, always in an exaggerated pose, a caricature of what society and culture call masculine, of power, intellect, logic, precision. Even more challenging, she embodies these elements in her own peculiar feminime way. Thus her logic is one of association, not of cause and effect; her precision, one of focused intensity, not conceptual clarity. Her power is that of nature's secret life, not society's; her intellect, that of the unconscious, not of reason. She personifies an issue faced by all women, one way or another: how to integrate this contrary sexual dynamism, with all its unmistakable masculine characteristics, within a feminine identity.

For women, the witch is a major missing piece of sexual identity, a culturally elaborated piece, even in its most exaggerated and caricatured forms. In her negative guise, the witch offers a picture of a woman possessed by the masculine elements in her. The witch is masculine in appearance, with whiskered chin and strident manner. She shuns the traditional female roles of helpmate and hearth, supporter of the dependent and needy. She goes after her own power and power over others. She wants secret knowledge and the craft to use it for her own ends. She wants weapons that will force others to do her will. She thrusts her ambitions at us. She must be acknowledged as a superior being, whose purposes others cross at their peril.

Having given up torturing witches, society can still use the exaggerated negative portrait of the witch to keep women from deviating from the norms of conventional femininity, threatening them by suggestion. You see, this is what happens! You become a witch! The threat makes a woman suspect her intensity and the original power of her mind as the causes of any difficulties she suffers in trying to relate to others. She herself may look upon these gifts with distrust.

Unlike the clown, the witch finds no audience eager for what she knows or brings with her. Others may want to use her power, but reject the woman herself. They may even try to steal her power before banishing her. She stands as a threat to society that society arms itself against. Instead of helping her to deal with her disproportionate energies—outsized, far beyond what is thought to be normal for female identity—society forces itself on the woman's psyche, offering to her perceived imbalance a new and different imbalance of its own in the lures of social causes and social strictures. The causes lure her to identify with her energies, the strictures to repress them. Her imbalance is worked on by an accruing social pathology. Most of what is thought of as a witch's negative effect on her environment is really the environment infecting her. The environment ascribes to her powers that are altogether outside the conventional definition of female—a trafficking between the seen and the unseen, the determination and skill to color outside the lines drawn by social custom and constraint. That is her crime—not consorting with the devil, not embezzlement of the emotions, not rape, not cannibalism of children. She poses a danger because she enjoys contact with the hidden secrets of nature; she knows things, she goes after things. But her human environment is spell-fixated and blames its spell-binding power on the witch as if it were entirely her doing, whereas in fact her scapegoat role, designed by the community, is clasped in a secret handshake by the whole community.

The clown figure embodies a different set of primordial emotions, all the feelings that are outlawed by the fixed conventions of masculine identity and the society that fixes them in place. The clown plays fool to the hero, the effeminate one to the manly, the unsettled maudlin one to the composed leading man. With his ass's ears or coxcomb, he thrusts the obscene into the realm of the genteel, the raucous into the sober. He is a loud psychic aberration in the midst of a soft, calm normality. Lurking on the borders between the attractive and the grotesque, the wise and the foolish, the clown brings chaos into an ordered society, reversing its hierarchies, seeming to inject madness into sanity. But unlike the witch, he is usually loved by his audiences, or if he is disliked, he continues to bring people close to him to watch his show, to stand around fascinated even when they feel repelled. His mixing of sexual categories, ordinarily so threatening, proves more amusing than anything else. Is he a man or a woman? Infant or parent? Lecher or timid lover? Is he strong enough to escape all the wreckage he causes, or a victim whose slightest plan must disintegrate?

Through the painted face of a circus clown, or the fixed, deadpan expression of a Buster Keaton, or the raised-eyebrow expectancy of a Groucho Marx, he shows no clear relation to feeling, yet he and all his brothers can arouse every kind of feeling in us. He bodies forth the archetype of feeling defended against, a feeling that is discovered or aroused in others by the clown but always masked in himself. Thus he depicts the dissociated or rejected female element in a man's personality that is really part of his masculinity.[7] Because he rejects it in himself and because society outlaws it as not acceptably masculine, this feminine part of the masculine appears in exaggerated form in clowning, as if to mock what it rep-

"[H]e depict[s] the dissociated or rejected female element in a man's personality which is really part of his masculinity."

resents. The feeling is there, but it is defended against. The feeling properly is part of a man's personality, but convention labels it as feminine. When it is so dissociated from the masculine, it must parade itself before us in effeminate guise. The clown depicts this joke on sexual identity by arousing feeling in others while resisting it in himself, threatening the stereotype of the male as strong, firm, clearminded, self-confident, and decisive, with his wobbly, weak-kneed, woolly-minded tentativeness, with his soppy melancholy, and twittery, obscene guffaws.

Why do the witch and the clown remain so strongly alive for us? Because they are archetypes and as archetypes act as indomitable resources against a stereotyping that straps actual men and women into preformed sexual identities and will not let them loose.

No one likes to be reduced to stereotypes, even verbal ones. Most of us, especially women, are revolted by the sexual stereotypes. The most reductive ones define men as strong and tightlipped, never showing feeling, and women as soft, never going openly after power. Women lack intellectual power; men, feeling. These wooden simplifications should enrage us; many of us are committed to changing these demeaning, persistent typologies.

We make the commitment, all right, but then we stumble. A feminist student confesses how she felt caught. She thought she abhorred the image of a man as strong, hard, unemotional, a sort of eternal cowboy defending against feelings by a show of toughness. Yet when her own boyfriend broke down and cried and showed his own dependent needs, she felt turned off, repelled sexually, as if he were a big baby. She resented being turned into a mother—another frightening stereotype, to which her response was stereotypical. Many male students verbally agree with feminist causes and support the full assertion of women's rights, yet they withdraw from forming intimate relationships with the very women whose rights they support publicly. One says, "I get awfully tired of all that arguing. Words, words—a constant harangue."

We must go back and look again at the stereotypes and the whole apparatus that takes shape around them, not simply to reject or to accept them, but to understand how they arose and what might have been their function. With that understanding, we may be able to take intelligent advantage of the unparalleled opportunity provided by the late twentiety-century revolt against received sexual categories. Jung's insights may prove helpful here. For against those stereotypings that would divide up sexual and psychological characteristics in Chinese menu fashion—women get anything in column A; men, anything in column B—Jung asserts that the whole person is a contrasexual person. No woman is simply female; she also has, within her own psychology, dynamic impulses, symbolic images, and carriers of energy that reflect every sort of association with the masculine. The converse holds true for the male. No person of either sex knows who he or she is without conscious assimilation of these opposite sexual sides of himself or herself, however, formed—culturally, physiologically, whatever.

This is our task today: consciously to recognize and affirm the opposite sides of our personalities. We must do this not in some simple-minded, general way that will merely entrench the stereotypes, but in the very special concrete terms of our own persons. Enough of what this means for mankind or womankind. What does it mean for me, for you, to say, I am a woman who comes to terms with what is masculine in me, or, I am a man who knows his own feminine side? It is a two-step process. While we are recognizing this other side, which introduces us in the most intimate terms to living with otherness, we need to integrate it, to link it up with every part of ourselves, to fold it in, to interleave it with everything we know in our conscious identities as men or women.

The two-step task has, in turn, two aspects that can be artificially separated for purposes of analytical clarity. In fact, as we live these parts of ourselves, they blend, and it is precisely the blendings, highly complex mixtures of traits and experiences, that distinguish us as persons and produce the infinite and fascinating varieties of the human. And so we must persist in seeing that there is no single concept of "man" or "woman" that sums up all of us. There are simply *all of us*, concretely here, there, in the flesh. No formulas. No blueprints. No equations. We abstract from the living process these two aspects: seeing the opposite sides, the contrasexual parts, and knitting them into our dominant sexual identity as male or female.

The anima and animus, Jung's words for the contrasexual archetype in a man's and a woman's personality, operate within the human psyche to mediate unconscious contents—always characteristic of archetypes—to our conscious egos.[8] They make it possible for us to include those contents in our day-to-day lives, to assimilate them to our conscious adaptation. What happens then is that the contrasexual parts of our psyches get joined up and mixed in with our dominant sexual identity. A man becomes more of himself as a man; a woman, more of herself as a woman. In this schema, anima and animus link us to our larger self, that center of opposites in the psyche. The conscious result is to be more fully and more recognizably female or male.

The archetypes of witch and clown are points of entry for the outlawed opposites within us, the archaic energies of sexuality and spirit which so urgently cry to be assimilated to the collective world of ego values, to everything we share with others of existence and purpose. This is a chance for the taming of the animals, the funneling of the wind, the reclaiming of the land from the sea, as we reflect the full range of primordial life in our own lives.[9] We contribute to *being* itself when we set ourselves to face and to deal with our own particular version of the witch and the clown complexes.

In this light, we can see the extraordinary relevance of the witch and the clown archetypes to our contemporary situation. Collective stereotypes leave out great chunks of human identity that belong to men and women. The witch and clown figures supply them. The witch personifies what the stereotyped image of woman omits: her primordial intellectual capacities, her drive, her inordinate power. The clown personifies what is omitted in the stereotyped view of man as the achieving sex. The clown shows us the bumbler, the vulnerable fool, the feeling-centered man, pinned in a web of relatedness to the animate and inanimate life around him.

When these archetypes are constellated in a given person's psychology, the effect, if recognized and openly assimilated, is to add vital missing parts to one's sexual identity. A woman who faces the witch force in herself—a force that bludgeons her into confusion and sucks her energies into the unconscious—sees the necessity to take strong, firm hold of her own power and to devote her energies to her primary needs. Power lived this way will not sabotage any genuine desire in her to give herself to those she loves. But she must recognize that her wish to give to others cannot substitute for holding to her own individual ways. The artist of our second dream knew instinctively that her ambition to create had to include the awareness of the negative force that opposes creation.

A man who turns himself around and looks courageously into the mirror of his own clowning finds there all the vulnerability, the hopeful illusions, the playful creation of images and symbols that he had previously projected onto others. He acquires a new capacity to hold his own feeling and give birth out of its creative strength. In a way, each sex acquires the symbolic power of the opposite one: the woman, a phallic thrust; the man, a containing womb. But the woman remains a woman. She is not a transexual, not an undefined sexuality, not with a phallus pasted onto her in place of her own organs. Rather, she is a woman containing within herself her own feminine version of phallic thrust and potency. The man remains male, not substituting the receptivity of the feminine organs for his own—a misguided effort, if he were to make it, that could only result in a caricature of a man, an effeminate male. He finds his own version of feminine receptivity within his masculine identity, his own version of woman's interior holding capacity.

But this is only half the process. The other half, the essential half, and in our opinion the revolutionary one, is to integrate into full consciousness the contrasexual capacity newly won from the unconscious and hence full of the marks of the unconscious. We find it primitive, impersonal, and compulsive because we are still identified with it. A woman truly comes to hold within her own containing space her own kind of power and intellect, which it would not be incorrect to characterize as virile. A man comes to forge a firm link to the feminine capacity within himself to hold vulnerability and his too-much-exposed feelings in a protected interior space. If we stop half way, we get a man-woman, like the haranguing woman who repels intimacy, or a woman-man, like the infantile man who at best evokes maternal responses. Each is altogether incapable of the vibrant, tough, yet pliable contacts between the contrasting othernesses of a man and a woman. Jung calls this mid-point the hermaphroditic stage, a place only half of the way toward the fullness of selfhood:

> The hermaphrodite is usually the symbol that precedes individuation; it precedes the creation of the valuable center, or the precious diamond. That is why it still indicates an unsatisfactory state, as is shown by the pictures in the alchemistic books; the being with two heads represented there is too monstrous, it represents no absolute liberation from the pair of opposites. The reconciling symbols should be something entirely new and detached; in it the opposites should be overcome; otherwise it is not a reconciling symbol. The hermaphrodite shows man still torn asunder, he is only on the way to completion, to all rounded-ness.[10]

In our time, we speak of this hermaphroditism in terms of the popular image of androgyny. How appealing it is to envision a new order of human persons, neither male nor female, liberated from all constricting stereotypes, possessed of all the advantages of both sexes. But all too often, this unisexual ideal offers no guidelines for the practical working out of human identity by real persons, who, like it or not, are male or female. What happens is either a regression to a presexual stage, a sort of return to pre-oedipal times when sexual differentiation has not fully occurred, or, as Jung describes it, getting stuck in the hermaphrodite stage as a kind of man-woman or woman-man monster, like the alchemical drawings of a person with two heads. Thus a girl student signals to her boyfriend to open to his feelings, and then trounces him as nothing but a little boy when he does. She cannot yet find her way to harmonize both sides of herself; one keeps replacing the other. She lives the parts sequentially, never simultaneously. Thus a male student supports his woman friend in her assertion of her own power, but avoids meeting her in any intimate situation. He cancels what he promotes, and cannot simultaneously accept having at his disposal both contrasting capacities, to support receptively and to penetrate. Stop-start, push-pull. And so we go on, hurting and confusing each other.

The witch provides good examples of this stultifying process. There is the woman who finds herself harboring opposite impulses—on the one side, to give lavishly to those she loves, to the point of giving herself away; on the other, to pull everything possible from those she loves down into herself in order to justify her own perceptions of truth. Her struggle is to bring these opposites together in herself, to make room for both sides in her own particular, personal, concrete way. Then there is the bewitched woman who acts out a wild, passionate sexuality, often going to extremes outlawed by the most permissive society, who feels a strong urge toward a stable, permanent, trusting human connection, the very essence of a marriage vow. She must harness both sides of herself or live in desperate incompleteness. She must find her own way to solve the problem that faces so many, that of a yearning toward ecstasy housed in the banal structures of ordinary life. Finally, there is the hag-woman who bursts with energy, thrusting toward the meaning of life. She feels she must live fully before she dies, must somehow find herself in touch with the fires of truth or burn up trying. She must contain this furnace of energy for its positive, glowing, guiding light, and its warmth and power.

None of these women can turn her back on what she knows; nor can she pretend that she has never glimpsed this wide reality. To go back is to amputate some large part of herself. It is to induce a false unconsciousness that can only produce deadly contaminating effects, not only in the woman herself, but in anyone who comes in contact with her. A witch, she eats up her children. A bewitching siren, she puts her own humanity to sleep. A hag, she poisons the atmosphere with her smoldering resentments.

The clown who sentimentalizes and teases his feelings, but never opens to them, also contaminates the atmosphere with a mushy softness that does not further but rather muddies relationship. At his worst, his is a false assertion of feeling that controls others by getting them to take pity on his frailty. He cuts up emotional connections, and his explosions and jerkings between opposing reactions destroy any continuity of sharing. He is bursting with uncontained, unmediated feeling. His only hope is to go forward and claim it, reflect on it, and communicate it to others. To go back to a locked up, feelingless state, associated with the stereoptyped macho man, will only produce ruinous division in himself, resulting in neurosis, and split views of the sexes in society, ending in prejudice and scapegoating.

Just as the witch and the clown images symbolize the missing pieces of our sexual identities, so do they bring essential elements together for us in new intimations of spiritual reality. The altogether human witch and clown figures deposit the spirit in the flesh, showing us the extraordinary in the ordinary, a conjunction which, if not appropriately housed, will distort our body shapes and infect, if not destroy, our psychological boundaries. Here in the witch world is spirit mixed with matter in animal forms, flying rugs, and talking tables. Here in the clown's miraculous escape from endless disaster—in the material forms of falling ceilings, collapsing walls, tumbling staircases that take on a life of their own—is the decisive meeting of spirit and human matter.

The clown collapses the distinctions of I and not-I, of subject and object, in his pantomimes in front of endless mirrors: his own, his audiences', the world's. Watching him, we begin to wonder who is the reflection of whom?[11] Breaking down ego-boundaries, the clown lets in the stream of psychic life that dissolves the discrete I in the seeing eye, his own and ours, moving through the mirror to the flux of being and becoming, touching the Zen idea that seeing into nothingness is true seeing. What we thought was fixed reality is but the play of the phenomenal world, the illusion of personal consciousness, the ephemeral nature of history.[12] Thus the clown leads us beyond discursive reason, symbolizing the values of the suprarational—of the pure heart, the true enlightenment. Ushering us into that space beyond space, we come to entertain different views of what is illusory and what is real. We join the juggling act, to juggle and be juggled. Thus Jesus's silence before Pilate and before the soldiers who mocked him as a fool. Jesus as clown takes us through the mirror to its other side, where what was thought to be foolish is shown to be wise.

The witch, too, lures us into another dimension of thought and feeling operating in all of us, a magical level where we participate in each other's lives, linked by the unconscious principles of similarity, contiguity, and *pars pro toto*. Drawn into the field of energy derived from the archetypes, we feel the identity between like and unlike things. We learn that contact may mean contagion, that a part of a person or thing may stand for the whole, that injury to one in a group may inflict injury upon all.[13] Thus the witch and the clown make evident a kind of spiritual connection that exists collectively among us, one never exhausted by any one individual's efforts to integrate it. The witch never changes into the good fairy godmother. The clown never leaves the arena to sell insurance or raise a family.

The witch and the clown both stay on the borders of human community, persisting in their otherness to mark the nearness of otherness to community. These archetypes are personifications of a large human collectivity, not a mere gathering of personal problems. They set us tasks to work at together. How can the missing or lost energies of the feminine be found again and welcomed back? How can the banished emotions of the male be given full entry into our lives? How can we be reconnected to our primordial roots?

In the collective situation, we find that if we make connection to our archetypal selves, to our centers of psychological identity, we can no longer keep going back and forth as we have been doing, never landing with all of ourselves or in all of ourselves. Now we must risk all to achieve all. Our collective sexual models, as collective models tend to do, have shown us the worst and the best of our shared immaturity and incompletely realized humanity. On the worst side, we see in the stereotypes of the sexes a great hatred of the female and of the feminine as they exist in both sexes, the inevitable result of fearing what the feminine represents.[14] We find a corresponding artificial freedom applied to men that confines them to superficial levels of being, lived on the outside only, displacing onto power manipulations their unsatisfied need for self-validation and a sense of being really related to others.

On the positive side, our collective models have shown us the intrinsic human need to grasp consciously the difference between the sexes as representative of creative elements of our being, offering us the means to nurture and promote the differentiation of personal identity. The archetypal elements reach beyond the rational controls of our egos to put these elements at our disposal, not by a series of logical operations or through the systematic moralizing of a superego authority, but through our deepest, darkest, most formidable parts.

Presently we think we are outgrowing these collective models, so we stress the way they hurt and pinch, how lifeless they are, how much a series of rigid, narrow prescriptions they seem to be, how they outlaw great chunks of our being. They seem to be nothing more to many of us than a giant sexist plot. It is just here, at this point of collective and personal transition, that the witch and the clown archetypes make their weight felt. We can see in them the extraordinary resources of the whole world of the archetypes, especially those that go so far to define and fulfill us as men and women.

Where

Where do we find witch and clown archetypes? Everywhere! In ourselves, on the borders of consciousness, and the boundaries of human society. In the witch's case, near the edge of a forest or the bottom of a grimpen.[15] At center stage, the middle of the ring that is everywhere and nowhere, in the life of the clown. In themselves the witch and clown archetypes are a history of the imagination, reflecting a ceaseless combat against sexual stereotypes, even though they have been used sometimes to reinforce the reduction of male and female identity to a simplified typology. Thus they lurk at the borders of what is acceptable socially —alert, always ready to invade (even when utterly misread), eager to crumble the edge of glib definitions, to move into the core of a person's or group's energies to display their eternal power to infect us from their side, the "other" side.

The border areas that remain the locus for these powerful images are danger zones, whether looked at only from the point of view of a reigning collective consciousness, in custom and conventions, or from the point of view of personal ego-stability. They always nag at the status quo. They threaten to erase the boundary lines we usually draw between imagination and reality, consciousness and the unconscious, order and chaos, existence and nothingness. The clown moves more slyly than the witch, stretching toward the figure of Hermes, the great trickster who leaves his herm, his stone, to mark boundary crossings in the psyche, Hermes, the early personification of transition and of multiple dualities in the male identity, who encompasses every possible polarization.[16]

Reaching us through the border areas and boundary crossings in our own psychologies, the witch and the clown mark the encounter of the known and the unknown within us. We are talking about what is sometimes called the borderline condition or the area of transitional space. Thus we find these images turning up to confront us in our dreams and fantasies, in those transitional spaces between the conscious and the unconscious, and in critical moments of passage across borderlines from one state of being to another as we move from infancy to childhood, from adolescence to adulthood, from singleness to marriage or marriage to singleness, from parenthood to old age to death. These archetypal figures meet us, sometimes threatening us in that space of in-between-ness, of not-yet-ness, of coming-to-be-ness, where we are not securely one thing or another. They stand at the borders to show us what we leave out, to compensate us through their imagery for missing pieces in the sexual identities that we are persuaded we must build for ourselves. Thus a little girl can feel a witch's fury smoldering in herself—in direct opposition to the nice, clean, gentle, cooperative girl she has so often been told she must be. She can feel bubbling up in her own mother that same fierce lust to break free, even as her mother is enslaved in her role as good feeder, forced to give all her time and energy to nourshing her daughter. That force that pushes her mother to break out of her enslavement to feeding others, poisons the food she offers her daughter. Both mother and daughter would be better off if this witch force were openly acknowledged as a valid part of their female identities. Similarly, the impulse to clown, to mock the very things we have labored so hard to acquire, may jump up in us just when serious listening to a father's lecture is mandated. The clown archetype acts as a spy, finding behind those manly qualities that are being pressed on a boy or young man the odd foible, the hidden pomp, the vacuous, bereft, dreamy idealism that must be left behind if he is to put into practice all his father is commanding. A man who heard us lecture on this material wrote us afterward to say that a sharp experience of just this point of transition had decided his own fate. His father, a policeman, was forever telling him by word and example to "grow up and become a man." Instead, the son ran away and became a professional clown.

The witch and the clown direct us back in time, through conscious ego-functioning, to the early origins of being. In the case of the witch, it is to the use of power, mind, and spirit in relation to good and bad; in the case of the clown, to archaic emotion. Each archetype comes alive quickly in early childhood, when these fantastic fairy-tale and circus figures strongly symbolize for most children aspects of the unconscious that they struggle to bring to full, coordinated conscious life. The good and the bad breast, the beneficent and the terrible mother take on witchy dimensions. The emotional exaltation of a goodness that will not be overcome by evil is played out in the clown's scenes of mock destruction, where no one really gets hurt or feels irreparable guilt for damage done. We see here the beginnings of "devaluing" that Roger Scruton thinks of as "integral to laughter," a reduction of objects to human dimensions for which he proposes the splendidly apt description of "attentive demolition."[17] There is laughter in the phrase itself.

Thus do we mark the transition from dependence to independence, from a world of self to a world with others, from a world of fantasy to a world of fact. The witch and the clown show us elements that we need to find or to create, to mix together or to take apart, to combine into the elements of our own symbols for a spiritual reality in which we can live and develop concrete identities. These periods of arduous transition recur throughout our lives—in times of loss or of opportunity, of divorce or of marriage, of death, of all those moments when we are given intimations of life's central truths. Whenever our egos are challenged to move across the borders of consciousness, toward what Jung calls the central other world of the self, the world beyond the ego, we experience a sensation of living in an in-between space that we recognize is both essential and threatening to the quality of feeling really alive.

What the witch and the clown can provide for us at these transitional moments depends on the strength of our consciousness. Is it large and durable enough to face archetypal images and not be overwhelmed by them? Those images can provide us with resources of energy that will reach with a clarity we can positively picture into an ahistorical and transcendent world that lies beyond particular biographies and cultures, a world of the primordial sources of the female and the male. But if our egos are too feeble, we may easily be victimized by these same energies. We may fall into identification with the images and find ourselves compulsively acting out the role of witch or clown in the ordinary ego-world of daily life.

Diagnostically, we can see that these witch and clown complexes correlate to the border line condition and to narcissistic personality disorders, respectively.[18] The ego, too feeble to face, digest, defend against, and integrate the witch force, breaks into disconnected parts. The links are broken. We feel the distress of the psyche; all the conjunctions are erased. Nothing connects with anything else; everything in us splits into warring factions, which are all the more exaggerated because they are unmodified by their opposites. The border reaches across a "vast territory," the line of demarcation always moving, never clear-cut or stable, always making "a fluctuating frontier."[19] The sense of unlived life and undischarged excitement so characteristic of the witch figure is deeply felt by a person with none of the clear identifications of self and other that offer stable channels for self-expression and communication.[20]

Similarly, the clown, whose positionless state makes him feel so invalid, so vulnerable, that to achieve any stability he must spend his time running back and forth in the spaces between objects, can be described in terms of the diagnostic category of narcissistic personality disorder. In the center, where substance and I-ness should dwell, lies the dark side of the mirror where the clown can find no reflection of his face. His is exactly the sense of emptiness that besets a person suffering from a disordered narcissism. He seems always to fall into the cracks, into the gaps between objects. He is never securely in being, any more than one suffering the borderline affliction. The compulsion to perform for an audience, to win its feelings and rouse all its responses, to strut and sham and change masks in order to produce admiration, to bedazzle and win wild applause for one's specialness, which is so typical of one caught up in clowning, is the compulsion that overcomes someone suffering from a damaged narcissism.[21] Wounded feeling hides behind the clown mask. Beneath the jolly persona are suffocating shame, humiliation, panic at being nothing in oneself and not really worth notice, much less worthy of wild applause. From the wounded self-esteem floods rage and outrage, all the more importunate because they are impotent to effect real change.[22]

The witch and clown figures both unmistakably direct our attention to the unlived depths of feeling in us. In diagnostic terms, this has to do with our determination to feel alive and real, the product of a healthy narcissism that successfully negotiates the transitional spaces of life, the feeling that results from owning a secure self with stable boundaries, linked up within ourselves and connected to others outside. We look to attain borders that neither encroach on others nor collapse in on themselves.

As an archetypal symbol, the witch arouses antipathy against women who try to combine feeling *and* intellect, feeling *and* power, feeling *and* spirit. In her negative expression, the witch is accused of having no feeling or only poisoned feeling. She receives the projections of feeling that others, out of fear, do not want to own or claim, and she falls into identifying with the fearful contents. She prepares herself for a life of scapegoating, the kind that in earlier centuries led to witch-hunts and trials. In her positive guise, on the other hand, the witch shows a woman of passion pursuing her goals with a fine intensity of emotion, confidently housing her masculine power and intellect in her feminine identity.

The clown embodies a male figure so caught up in the feelings, usually taken to be the province of women, that he is seen as much less than masculine, at best as an amiable fool. Yet in his positive expression, the clown not only opens his audience to emotions at deep levels of experience, but also shows a way to an enlarged male identity, well beyond stereotypes or generalized definition. His is the largeness of a man secure in his emotions, with connection to his contrasexual self that, far from depleting his focus and power to be a male, finds its roots in ancient earth. His masculine identity houses his feminine emotion.

We might ask, then, if the diagnostic categories of borderline affliction and damaged narcissism match the archetypal symbols of witch and clown. If the interchangeablility of the diagnostic categories matches that of the two symbolic figures, why not use only the categories and forget the images that drag us into fairy tales and the world of the primordial in a constant regression? The answer is important. The categories do not exhaust the archetypal symbols. The match is not perfect; it is merely suggestive. Indeed, we could even indulge the fancy that the recent popularity of borderline and narcissistic diagnoses results once more from the emergence of witch and clown imagery in a time of cultural transition and upheaval, when the borders of conventional role definitions for the sexes are under attack. Intense interest in those clinical terms coincides with intense examination of and challenge to sexual stereotyping from every discipline.[23] The clinical categories are only the barely exposed surface of a profound movement of spirit and emotion. The archetypal symbols form a larger background reality for those concepts. These archetypes remain central to our experience today, even when we approach them from the safe perch of diagnostic outlines, recognizing, as we must, that clinical concepts can never match all the reality that archetypes convey, for diagnosis confines itself to pathology. Surely women or men caught up in a witch or clown complex know that illness besets them, but they must also come to learn that these great images cannot be reduced to illness alone.

Through a witch-like frenzy, a woman may feel herself addressed by a left-out part that could change the whole of her. Through a bumbling clown routine, a man may feel himself laying hold of a different kind of truth about what is central to his identity. These archetypes are entry points through which a larger dimension of psyche may be trying to make itself known to us. They are an invaluable complement to diagnostic categories that not only reduce us to abstract terms, but often make us feel irrevocably judged. They tell us what is wrong or missing, at what level of development we remain stuck. The diagnostic code is based on the etiology of a person's development, usually in relation to environmental provision or failure to provide. We can chart at which stage a person's development went awry, in relation to a particular perceived failure of environment. Thus the clarity of diagnostic categories, however severe, helps us by giving a map, so to speak, even while it halts us by defining us in terms of lack. We feel harshly judged, still to be stuck at an early stage when we should be at a late one. How can we move forward out of such deficiency? Even while feeling pain, we should not underestimate the value of an orientating map. In these concepts that describe from a distance what we suffer, we are given needed perspective and clarity. But the task is to live in the newly mapped country, and that means sensing a palpable nearness, a felt possibility, not just hearing a description of what is missing. Enter the archetypes.

Our view is that we must have both image and clinical concept, for the psyche insists on using both languages. Consciousness splits things off into manageable categories abstracted from the melee, even while under the tyranny of projection and omnipotence.[24] But the unconscious speaks to us in images, right in the midst of experience, touching emotion as well as thought—in preverbal and nonverbal feeling, as well as in what rises up into words for us and links itself into logical sequence. Images touch us immediately, concretely, in directly accessible ways. Our bodily instincts are roused when in a dream a witch-figure —what the dreamer called a "primordial woman"—drops into her cauldron a live rabbit and says to the dreamer that she must eat the whole rabbit—fur, bones, guts, ears, and all! Our imaginations are stirred by a pantomiming clown's play with a tuft of milkweed blowing in the air, pulled along by unseen currents, rising up and drifting down. We are teased into questions. Is it nothing, merely a wisp? Or is it everything, the essence of human life?[25]

These images are not arbitrary. They speak to the specific situation of the dreamer or the fantasizing onlooker. Though they are not outlined for us by strict rules, neither are the images chaotic. As Gaston Bachelard writes, the "poetic image—a simple image!—thus becomes quite simply an absolute origin, an origin of consciousness . . . the seed of a world. . . ." And again, "The poetic image places us at the origin of the speaking being."[26] Images offer a space of their own in which we can enter to ponder our next step across the border, to grasp what particular fear made us hesitate, to perceive what possibilities and detours lie ahead. Like all powerful psychic images, the witch and the clown reveal territories marked out by parameters of tasks and pleasures, possible rewards and failures.

Images often turn out to be more practical in the clinical situation than are diagnostic concepts.[27] Concepts remain abstract, never quite fitting an actual person. They offer helpful guidelines, but are harmful if squeezed too hard, like the shoe on Cinderella's sisters' feet. Images are concrete. They arise from an analysand's own psyche, offer an immediate way into the problem, and often disclose, like the witch and the clown, a way through the problem. We directly experience images and their meanings. We explain concepts; their meaning is understood, not experienced. As the major school of depth psychology that takes images seriously, the Jungian school is particularly intensive in its discussion of the split between the archetypal and the clinical dimensions of analysis.[28] Jungians can be divided along the lines of this split—whether one is more biased toward the

"[A] witch-figure . . . drops into her cauldron a live rabbit and says to the dreamer that she must eat the whole rabbit—fur, bones, guts, ears, all!"

symbolic or the clinical; whether, at one extreme, one is wafted upward into a never-never land of archetypes, losing sight of the patient, or at another extreme is so sunk in the clinical travail of transference and countertransference that any meaning larger than the persoanl interaction gets lost.

We stand against these extremes, because the split is falsely conceived. Both extremes reduce wholes to parts. The experiences of archetypal energy, emotion, and behavior patterns come to us in our most subjective selves and in our encounters with others. "Symbolic" and "clinical" are not divorceable qualities. We get at the fullest meaning of transference and countertransference only by understanding what it is that arranges us in relation to others. As we shall see by a case example, a witch's spell that threatens a man comes right only when the women with him in group therapy allow themselves to experience the effect of the spell on all of them, and permit their reactions to open new routes for the man. Equally, casting a female clown in the scapegoat's role does not take place in the abstract. People find that they want to make a clowning woman into a scapegoat because her impenetrability makes them so angry. Through transference and countertransference reactions, or through almost any subjective reaction, we can connect with archetypal depths; they may make themselves known to us as more than mere personal responses. Through the archetypal images constellated in a specific clinical situation, we enter a new territory. The means of entry is personal experience, but where we arrive is a country larger than our personal memories.

Witch and clown images differ significantly from each other in different times and cultures, but they always possess and define problems in ways that surpass any one age's obvious capacities. Thus we are put in touch with otherness—other people, other times, other points of view, other values. Thus do archetypes transcend our personal limitations, expanding them, working through them, never hopping over them or disregarding them. We may know that in a given year or a given century, people dealt with witches with horror or with reluctant delight, with persecution or shamefaced emulation, which may give us some small idea of how to address our own feeling of being bewitched. But we can only take such a feeling in hand by groping our way toward it, growing a connecting link to that other way different point of view. The narrow ego-world is transcended bit by bit and simultaneously confirmed. We grow beyond it by using it. Thus the familiar objection that focusing on archetypes takes us too far beyond the level of personal conflict falls flat. For it is in fact only through conflict that we discover how concretely to get hold of archetypal resources. Similarly, the objection that concentrating on clinical procedures removes us from the indeterminate resource of archetypal power proves false. Only through idiosyncratic clinical adventures, each peculiar to its own analytic pairing, does an indeterminate archetypal resource take determined shape and effect.[29] The combination is not an additive one, in which archetypal perspectives are added to clinical procedures or clinical grounding is added to archetypal realities. It is mixture, interpenetration, a whole cloth. How then do we proceed to chart the archetypal images of witch and clown?

How

The psyche speaks about itself in symbol. That is our human way of creating internal order and bridging our inside and outside worlds, bringing together person and society, present and past. The impulse in us to make symbols is our creative way of reaching what lies beyond us, of making accessible to us distant regions to which symbols point.[30] The witch and the clown archetypes introduce us to new lands, some rich, some poor, some puzzling, provocative, forbidding, or inviting. Our method is to go right to those lands, to explore them intensively, tirelessly. This means, wherever possible, going into everyone's and anyone's experience of the witch and the clown and trying to see how these ancient archetypal images live in us now.

No matter which archetypes we choose, this method will give offense to someone, because it does not offer safe historical distance, the reduction to diagnostic conceptualization, or any comfortable methodology, be it literary, sociological, or anthropological. Instead, the psyche of the reader will be pricked by a witch's spindle, or yanked, nose first, into a clown's ring—lifted from a spectator's anonymity into open and vulnerable participation. The safety of separating walls is dissolved. Our purpose is to connect with the life of these symbols, to connect them firmly to our lives, making their every side available to all sides of our lives.

For readers unacquainted with or resistant to the life of the psyche, this method may seem threatening. We do not keep the distance usually offered by familiar hermeneutic procedures, seeing witches only, say, in feminist terms, as products of political, economic, or social institutions that oppressed women; or limiting them, say, to literary significance in less complex eras than our own; or investigating them as anthropological phenomena in cultures of the kind that used to be called primitive; or contrasting the differences thrown up by history between the witches of the Middle Ages or the early Renaissance and those of the persecutions and trials of the sixteenth and seventeenth centuries, or between the clown of the king's court or the ancient village and the clown of the modern circus or radio, television, or film. Nor do we begin with contemporary classification systems of mental disorder, insisting on approaching these figures as signs of borderline or narcissistic problems.[31]

All of these approaches and procedures are illuminating in some way, but we are after values they do not often touch. In seeking them, we must cross the borders of each of the hermeneutics, those named and others. For readers who want material bundled into tidy categories, measurable ratings, clear trends, with all the good things they bring, our methods may prove daunting or uncomfortable, for we proceed as best we can with the archetypes, from the organizing power of the symbol. Thus we move across the dividing lines, as archetypes insist we do, between present and past, individual and group, health and sickness. We aim to explore the lands they open that speak to our personal sexual identities as men and women, and, if need be, our changing identities in the particular time in history in which we write.

What is the psyche telling us now through the witch figure of the masculin-ized female? In her bewitching, sexually powerful persona, she displays force, purpose, and plot, taking direct routes to what she wants—all qualities that have long been associated, even if superficially, with the masculine. What is the psyche telling us now through the figure of the clown, sharply delineated in every way except that of sexual identity? What do these archetypal figures say to us in our time, so bent on redefining sexual identities, so ardent in its challenging, upset-ting, and rejecting of accepted classifications of what can be included and what must be excluded?

We are saying that these figures still speak directly to us and about us. We see that they do so in the actual experiences of people, who feel gripped by spells, frenzies, intrigues, or persecutions, which they often identify with witches. We see it in others, caught in the vortex of compulsions to joke, to clown, to rag, to jazz, to parody, to puncture their lives and their worlds. Clinical material opens the way into our own experience of these extraordinary symbols, still active in our own lives, whether we are patients, analysts, people in or outside the analyti-cal process, trying to discover the particular pattern of our own identities.

The method used here accepts the fact that there is no safe distance from the great power and lasting effect of these symbols. Once we are drawn into them, we are bound to experience them and to evaluate anew every other experience where we have known what might be construed as the spell of the witch or the madness of the clown. This is not an historical survey, but an entering into our own history. It is not very different from investigating a diagnostic category or concept, such as the aforementioned borderline or narcissistic conditions, except that the way of blocking out and filling in the terrain is through a symbol or an image, not a concept. We propose to treat symbols as expressions of the psyche speaking about itself. That means we shall hear those expressions and see those images, to enter the land to which they point, making subjective connections to the objective reality they describe. Our procedure is related to Gadamer's under-standing of "historia" in his *Truth and Method*. He calls it "a totally different source of truth from theoretical reason." It is, he says, "what Cicero meant when he called it the vita memoriae" in his *De oratore*. "It exists in its own right be-cause human passions cannot be governed by the universal prescriptions of rea-son. In this sphere, one needs, rather, convincing examples. . . ."[32]

The fact that we almost always experience the witch as female makes us ask, as we examine her history in Gadamer's sense of the word, what qualities enter into feminine identity through her timeless archetypal imagery. Because many tales show men in battle with witches, we must touch on what happens when a man experiences the feminine in the witch guise. The fact that the clown is almost always male leads us to ask what qualities address male identity through his archetypal imagery. In a less pressing way, because female clowns have also been with us—more and more in recent years—we also touch on what it means to women who get caught up in clowning compulsions and who experience the masculine as clown.

These two archetypes speak to and of human sexual identity in urgent terms, sharply portraying what is usually left out of conventional definitions of male and female. As they show us the underbelly, the opposite side of our sexuality, they bring us to confront and claim the shadow side of conscious, collective ego-identity. They show us how, as these elements are neglected or denied, people founder and collapse. They bring information about what needs to be included to construct the vital bridge from ego to self that establishes our ultimate sexual identity, in all its archetypal splendor, connected at the roots. Though the details may differ for each of us, the tasks are the same. When we are possessed by these images, certain clinical problems inexorably present themselves. In round, negative terms, the witch dramatizes the archetypal struggle of a woman with a masculine element in herself that is taking over her whole ego-identity. Similarly, the clown in negative guise shows the archetypal struggle of a man with the feminine part of himself that is dominating his whole ego-identity. If the negative power of each archetype can be said to reverse the usual scheme of things, with a woman becoming virile and a man becoming effeminate, redemption consists in reversing the reversal. Then the masculine does not vie with the feminine, but is housed in it; the feminine does not dissolve the masculine, but is housed in it. Both individually and socially, the cure for those caught in the witch or the clown complex is to see them as they are and for what they are, not to try to change them into something else. It is only through that honest way of seeing that it is possible to disentangle the ego from identification with the archetype.

Always, our method means entering boldly into these lands, experiencing life there, then returning to one's own land with a complete change of consciousness. Investigation of the witch and the clown archetypes makes available concrete ways in which a release from stereotyped sexual identities can lead in turn to the largest of sexual freedoms, where one is more fully one's own man or woman. We do not accomplish this by hopping over the distinctions of male and female into a regressive presexuality or into a neither-nor androgyny. Nor do we discover anything significant about ourselves by splitting male and female into mutually exclusive lists of characteristics belonging, each one, only to one sex. We must see and put together the male and female in each of us.

The question is blunt: How, in very specific, concrete ways, do we house the opposite sexual sides of ourselves? This is the question that the witch and the clown archetypes address to us in the most demanding terms our psyche knows. The answer will change us in the shallows and in the depths of our persons, and with us, it will change all those around us and the society which together we share and define.

II The Witch Archetype

We speak of the witch as an archetype, a cluster of images and of emotional and behavioral potentialities of response that operate unconsciously—and therefore autonomously and impersonally—as part of the reservoir of "the objective psyche," as Jung calls it, well beyond the immediate control of ego-consciousness.[1] If witch images or motifs turn up in our dreams and fantasies, or tinge our emotions or our actions toward others, we can analyze their origin in terms of our own personal biography, but only to a limited degree. Usually we sense the influx of such contents into our conscious experience as coming from a non-ego dimension of unconscious process. Characteristically, witch motifs bring with them the breath of the uncanny, the alien, the cold implacability of otherness unwarmed by human values or feeling-ties.

In the analysis that we are undertaking, our first task is to see the witch. In this we are helped by the philosophical approach of phenomenology, particularly Husserl's notion of the "epoché" or "bracketing." This concept describes how we approach a phenomenon with open receptivity: we let a phenomenon present itself to us in its own terms. We bracket off, for the moment, any preconceptions or evaluations we may entertain about the nature of the phenomenon or its significance for us in the practical living of our lives. We look. We listen. We receive. We let the phenomenon speak to us in terms of what we understand subjectively as its "language," its imagery. We allow it to disclose itself as it will.[2]

Our great temptation with the witch figure is to approach her with a utilitarian motive, that is, to see her in order to change her into some benevolent agent who will benefit us because we understand her properly. Here we approach the witch as if she were really a good mother in disguise. But that will not do. A witch is a witch is a witch.

To attend to a phenomenon without doing anything, without having utilitarian motives, is a principal way of allowing the unconscious to exist in us *as* the unconscious. Jung stresses that fact that the unconscious is not some wastebasket to be emptied by consciousness, nor a resource totally at the service of our conscious thirst, nor yet a honey pot into which we can dip our hands to get sweet tastes and pleasing experiences that will nurture conscious life. The unconscious *is*. It is an unmistakable aspect of human life, existing in its own right, demanding to be respected as such. Only when we acknowledge the "right" of the unconscious to exist on its own terms, can we find our way to that attitude whereby our consciousness can be fed, sweetened, or enlarged by unconscious mental processes.

Fairy tales present us with the phenomenon of the witch.[3] Literature and history also offer rich material about the witch, such as Goethe's *Walpurgisnacht* and Joyce's variations on the motif in *Ulysses*, or the historical facts separated from fancy by Norman Cohn. But all of this takes us too far afield in the space of one chapter. What we find there enlarges, we believe, the essential themes that stand out when one examines the witch image found in fairy tales. Principally, these themes are three: a witch's tremendous appetite, her placement at great distance from the human community, and her keen interest in sex and power.

The Voracious Witch

A witch's appetite craves to feed on the human—its blood, its flesh, its soul. The wicked queen in "Snow White" sends forth her huntsman to cut out the heorine's heart and bring it to her. The rejected witch figure in "Sleeping Beauty" inserts her lethal spell into the bloodstream of the young princess when she pricks her finger on the witch's spindle. Images of a related figure in Indian mythology, the goddess Kali, depict a hideous, blood-drenched female, dancing wildly on the bodies of those whom she has slain. The blood she sucks from her victims still drips from her fang-toothed mouth, and stains her garments with its redness.[4]

This major theme of the witch figure—of sucking human blood, feeding on it, drinking it, exulting in it, and demanding it as sacrifice—associates her with what seems to our conscious perspective to be a reversal of the usual flow of life energies. We think of blood nourishing our bodies, circulating through our hearts, giving us life and health. On the contrary, the witch takes blood out of human bodies to feed her own energies. In some rituals she even "demands" the human heart, our central organ of blood circulation and a central symbol of human feeling.

The witch's demand for blood merges with another of her major demands: her insatiable hunger for human flesh, especially for that of children. The witch in "Hansel and Gretel" lives in a tasty cookie house to lure children within her grasp. On the pretext of feeding the children, the witch plans to fatten them up in order to feed herself. Some women, when they give birth to a baby, are surprised to experience a newfelt sympathy for this cannibalistic witch. Though they rarely admit their feelings into consciousness, let alone tell them to anyone else, these new mothers may feel a desire to lick and nibble at their newborn children, taking unexpected pleasure in their edible fingers and plump cheeks.[5] Think how many games we all make up to play with young children that center on this eating theme—for example, "I am a bear and will eat you up!"

In some tales, like "Brother and Sister," the wicked stepmother sends the children off to an ugly fate at the hands of a witch because she wants to hoard the little bit of food remaining to the family in order to feed herself. As in the case of the witch's appetite for human blood, her cannibalism reverses our usual expectations: instead of sacrificing her needs to feed her children like a good mother, this witch-like mother sacrifices the children to feed herself.

Sometimes the witch uses a young victim for nourishment on another level. In the tale "Frau Trude," a little girl's curiosity leads her, against her parents' strong warnings, to poke into a witch's cottage. When the witch questions the girl about what she has seen, the girl naively tells all. For this impertinence of seeing into her own dark secrets, the witch pops the little girl into the fire to provide light and warmth to her old witch bones.

We see again in this tale a reversal of the proper order of behavior. The girl should have depended obediently and trustingly on her parents' knowledge, but she defied them in favor of her own way. Against their better judgment, she went off into the witch's terrain. But when faced with the witch, against whom she needed all her alertness, guile, and self-reliance, the girl reverted to a childish dependence, dutifully answering every question the witch put to her. So much for dependency needs and trust where witches are concerned! To persist in a child-like attitude of undifferentiated, unquestioning dependence on a witch figure leads to trouble. The witch figure does not nurture the girl's growth to enlightened understanding; instead, she uses the little girl to illuminate and warm her own living space. Where a good mother figure gives of herself for her young, the witch figure uses the young for her own benefit.

The witch's voracious hunger extends to the spiritual life as well. Witches had consuming appetites for human souls. In earlier times in countries in Western Europe and Africa, people often projected this witchly hunger onto a good many unfortunate women, who were persecuted, brought to trial, and sometimes even condemned to death. Witches were accused of meeting together to devour their prey through spiritual infection, thus to feed on the souls of their victims. Bodily illness, infant mortality, and crop failure were thought to be physical signs of an affliction sent by witches.[6]

The witch's reversal of the human order shows up here in the spiritual dimension. Instead of receiving a soul from God, witches supposedly stole the souls of their victims; instead of celebrating a Holy Mass on the church's altar, witches were thought to flaunt a "Black Mass" in celebration of the Devil. Instead of regulating sexual instincts, witches were supposed to engage in sexual orgies employing unusual positions and practices; and in contrast to the holy stigmata, witches were supposed to bear the Devil's stigma on their bodies.

One interesting difference between women actually supposed to be witches and the witch figure of fairy tales is the communal nature of the former's activities. According to historical accounts, covens of witches usually consisted of thirteen—a number chosen, it is thought, to parody Christ and his twelve disciples. Despite this communal aspect, the fairy-tale witch usually shows herself to be a lonely, isolated figure, and both the historical covens and the witch figure of literature associate the witch with deserted places far removed from human society.

The Witch as Distant

The image of the witch as remote from the human community translates physical distance into the great psychological space between a witch's mode of existence and that of conventional human beings. The witch who drinks human blood, consumes human souls, and takes human bodies to feed herself represents something so alien to human consciousness and so contrary to what we think of as the "natural" flow of energy, that we perceive her as altogether foreign to human sensibilities. Fairy-tale descriptions of a witch's abode abound in symbols of remoteness. She lives in the depths of a forest, or on the edge of a distant mountain, or at the farthest reach of ocean. Often her house is surrounded by symbols of death: skulls mounted on fence pikes, burnt-out vegetation, and grasping tendrils hanging from stunted trees. Body wastes, bloody refuse, decaying carcasses with noxious gases and fetid smells cling to the atmosphere that surrounds the witch's dwelling. Nothing grows around her. Like the witch in "The Princess and the Pea," only her "garden of woe" is alive, watered by the tears of human grief. The witch lives on the rim of existence, lives on the edge of the known world that borders on chaos or an abyss. She lives in such a place because she is beyond the reach of reason, beyond the normal operations of the human imagination.

The Aggressive Witch / The Sexual Witch

Even from her remote habitation, the witch exerts a fearful power: her spells, invading human consciousness, possess it with frenzied passion or ecstatic rage. The experience of a male analysand illustrates this sort of possession, this feeling of being suddenly, inexplicably bewitched.[7] When this man neglected to sort out his feeling reactions to daily events, in order to excerise a sort of emotional hygiene, his feelings piled up within him, he said, to the point where he became immobilized. If this paralyzed state had gone on too long, he might have been constantly subject to having unexpected seizures of unbearably intense emotion. He sometimes felt possessed as if by a bewitching spell that appeared in various ways. Irrational laughter, for example, would burst out of him at the wrong time and in the wrong place. Another time, he was swept with furious rage in response to a small irritation, so that he needed all his powers of self-control in order not to put his vengeful, violent impulses into action. Or, he felt invaded by a nearly irresistible sexual attraction for some unknown woman he passed on the street. He might, perhaps, follow her for several blocks as he planned ways to engage her sexually; and only when his projection wobbled—and he could see some bit of her human reality—could he consciously regain distance from his feelings of bewitchment.

A witch's spell exerts this anesthetizing effect on our consciousness. Like the heroine in "Sleeping Beauty," we are put to sleep; like "The Little Mermaid," we lose our voice; like the hero in "The Frog Prince," we are reduced to beastly form; like Joringle, we are fixed to one spot; like Faithful John, we turn to stone. Two dream images of a contemporary woman associate her own feelings of "losing consciousness" with a witch-like spell that makes her unable to talk. The first dream image occurred at the end of a long, detective-like dream drama. The dreamer discovers the real villain: "All at once I discovered there is some evil woman in control. I go to confront her. She is asleep. I try to say something, but suddenly I cannot speak. I am under her spell. If only I can speak out I can become free. She is sucking blood from my arm." Two days later, she dreams: "I am asleep and have asked my friend to wake me. He tries, but I go on sleeping. At first I think I am pretending sleep. Then it seems I cannot wake up. I am paralyzed and immobilized. I try to ask him to wake me, but cannot communicate; no words come out."

The witch infects our human values with her alien touch, often aiming to spoil health with a fatal sickness ("Snow White"), friendliness with malice and hatred ("Rapunzel"), human shape with animal forms ("Three Princes and Their Beasts"). A contemporary woman's nightmare depicts the witch figure's poisonous threat:

> *My dog and I are together. I think of my dog as the underdog, instinctive side of me, a sort of alter ego. A middle-aged woman with the same color hair as both my dog and me regards me balefully from the sand-colored wall she leans against. My dog whimpers. The woman gets up and starts stroking the dog, crouching over him. He whimpers in terror. She seems to have paws instead of hands, and seems to be patting him, not hitting him. But every touch of her drips poison. I too am terrified of her, for it is she who destroys, she who envies, she who hates. I go to help my dog, although I know I am mixing with madness and I am filled with panic.*

Unmoved by human values, a witch's mind bears the cold-blooded quality of instinctual life far beneath the warm-blooded values of human feelings. She is not to be educated or reformed or touched by human culture. The closest she comes to human affect is in her irritability, fretfulness, bad temper, and malevolence. She swoops down on her broom to threaten us with revenge, and flies away again out of reach of our earthly stance ("Dorothy of Oz"). Far removed from human influences or concerns, she dwells in a realm of the uncanny where nothing human rests secure.

Lilith, depicted in myths as a night-hag, a hairy monster, or an evil demon who inhabits desert places and inflicts terror by night, manifests this eerie non-human presence that preys on the human person. Some versions present her as Adam's first wife, with whom he begot strange children. She curses Eve's unborn child, who then turns out to be the murderer, Cain. In other versions, Lilith takes the form of a beautiful woman with flowing hair who, like Odysseus's sirens, lures men off their proper course to destruciton. She draws men away from human relationships with flesh-and-blood women, and into her mind-besotting grasp. Her sexuality enchants and bewitches her victims, exerting on them a suck-

"She dwells in a realm of the uncanny where nothing human rests secure." (Goya)

ing undertow, not unlike her blood-sucking and her devouring hunger. In the tale "The Witch in a Stone Boat," the witch pulls the queen down into the underworld to be wife to a giant, while she masquerades in the queeen's place. Toward men the witch acts like a nightly succubus, taking from them their intellectual power and manly vigor. In this guise, the witch associates herself with the vampire who seduces, in order to feed herself on her victim's blood.

In the past, women who received projections of witch imagery were imagined to indulge in fantastic and lascivious sexual practices that employed other body openings than conventional genital congress. Moreover, these sexual encounters supposedly would be confined to no single partner and no containable passion. Rather, they were understood to be orgies of animal lust with any and all partners, human and nonhuman, such as animals or the Devil. It was thought by some that the witches abandoned themselves to sheer instinct, thus achieving unholy ecstasies.[8]

The witch's concern with power mixes with her violent sexuality. She often indulges in tremendous bouts of sexual envy. The witch-like stepmother in "Snow White" plots to kill her rival for the title of "the fairest in all the land." The witch tries to spoil the heroine's beauty by working her to death, as in "Cinderella," or by fixing her sexuality in an inaccessible form by changing her into a bird, as in

"Jorinda and Joringle," or simply by putting her to sleep where she can only dream her sexuality but cannot live it, as in "Sleeping Beauty."

The witch figure competes with the heroine of these stories for feminine preferment and postion in the world. She wants power, and she takes it. Unlike the fairy tale heroine, she does not have it bestowed on her as a consequence of her great beauty or goodness. In "The White Duck," the witch steals the queen's place; in "The Juniper Tree," she murders her stepson in order to secure the fortune for her own daughter. In "The Frog Prince," she imprisons the prince to keep him for herself, rather than let him journey to his princess. In "The Tinder Box," she lies in order to grab the magic box for herself. In "Melilot," she wreaks cruel revenge when the heroes refuse to grant her sole possession of the miraculous river. As ever, she exhibits in her greed her tremendous sucking power; in "Esben and the Witch," she takes the treasure all to herself and hoards it, giving nothing to anyone else.

Yet if the hero or heroine stands up to the witch, matching human wits against her uncanny knowledge, human courage against her threats, or even respectful acknowledgment of what she is with a precise focus on getting what they want from her, she may do an about-face and bestow the secret formula or talisman ("The Frog"). We never quite know how she will behave. We must approach her with attention and caution, seeing her, but still not seeing her too closely; heeding her, and yet sometimes deliberately ignoring her words; sometimes obeying her, sometimes defying her. The witch figure abounds in ambiguity. She will not fit neatly into our conscious estimates of her negative traits. A young woman's dream of a Lilith figure illustrates this mixture:

> *I dream I am speaking to a wise-old-woman figure who is a healer of people on a psychological and physical level. She says to me I am a woman like herself who is in touch with deep levels of the unconscious, a vampire, a Lilith woman. For that reason I can be a healing instrument for others and take out their negativity. I am alarmed in the dream, as I think she is telling me I am a witch. But as she continues I realize that though the names sound bad, the purpose and direction are positive, and so I relax.*

Seeing the Witch

What can we learn of this witch figure? She stands forth as an archetypal female of tremendous power. She personifies the extremes of feminine receptivity, pulling inward, whirling downward, and absorbing into primordial unconscious depths all that is conscious and human. The witch drinks our blood, eats our flesh, devours our souls, draws into herself our sexual energies. She lures us from our known, familiar world into her far country at a great distance from our ordinary concerns. Seeming not to need others, the witch lives apart, never giving, only taking for herself.

All that is clear, and explains why we usually think of the witch as negative, as a source of pollution and violence. She stands for the worst of the feminine, whether manifested in actual women or in the anima. She stands for that sucking intellect associated with women of underdeveloped minds, who drain answers out of their family, friends, teachers, or books, consuming others' ideas, never putting forth any thoughts of their own. She stands for that sucking reality that seduces a man to give himself over entirely into her hands, and mouth, and body, or, in less exotic manifestations, that clinging, cloying sexuality that saps the last ounce of her partner's emotions.

Yet the witch's positive effects are found in this negative sucking action, too; her actual strength lies in her failure to give. She constellates in the anima-character of men and in the egos of women the energies to connect to an unconscious kind of intellectual order, to an unconscious depth of sexual response that supersedes conventional practices, and to an unconscious spirituality as yet undifferentiated from instinct that may give voice to a primordial dimension of human life. She takes energies out of consciousness and pulls them toward the unconscious to forge a link between the two mental systems.

The witch figure embodies in her female presence a different modality of consciousness than the masculine psychology (which belongs just as much to females) that dominates our society. She personifies the rationality of irrational, unconscious mental processes, and the primordial forms of the personal within nonpersonal psychic processes, the spirit within the instincts.[9] Hence the witch remains an archetype welling up from the objective psyche, touching consciousness but never becoming part of consciousness. We all want to be reconnected with the suprarational element that is not to be found in ordinary rationality. The witch is the instinct that pulls us by the nose. To go where the witch leads is to discover that the opposites contain *their* opposites, that the rational hides an irrationality and that the irrational reveals a hidden logic.

The imagery of the witch, outlawed from human community, presents outlawed "negative" sides of the feminine. Yet if taken with any seriousness, the "negative" depths of the feminine begin to disclose unguessed benefits for the modern woman and for the contemporary man trying to come to terms with his anima.

As a first example, take a woman's interest in developing the ego qualities of a good mother, whether or not she is an actual parent, and take a man seeking maternal tenderness and support from his anima. Here the main theme jumps out at us: the witch reversing the usual order of things. To the mother's nurturing womb, the witch shows a devouring maw. Parodying the maternal attitude of helpful support for the helpless, the witch takes advantage of the helpless and dependent. To the mother's feeding breast, the witch brings her own insatiable hunger. Where mothers give out, the witch takes in. Where mothers are feeders, she is an eater. Where mothers support and hold others, the witch drops them into the pit. Where mothers scent themselves with sweet smells of body-warmth, of food and hearth, the witch stinks of a slimy detritus. Where a mother brings life, the witch faces us with death and decay. Where a mother inspires kindly trust in others, a witch calls forth terror and dread. What could possibly emerge as positive from this frightening picture?

The witch figure presents an awesome image of the primordial feminine concerned with herself. Maternal life spends itself like life's blood flowing outward to nourish the souls and bodies of loved ones. In the witch figure, life flows inward and downward to feed the dark recesses of a woman's psyche or a man's anima. Where a woman's maternal instincts support her young as they move out of unconsciousness into conscious identity and transform archetypal energies for use in the human world, the witch figure directs energy the opposite way—out of consciousness into the unconscious, from the human toward the archetypal dimension.

The witch figure's concentration on her own hungers reminds us as women that we must feed ourselves emotionally. If we constantly disperse our energies to conscious plans and in service to others, our unconscious must eventually avenge itself by exerting a regressive pull on those around us. For example, a husband and children must complain that a woman's giving to them smacks of ulterior motives, that she is playing the martyr, that her resentment is eating them alive. Around such women an atmosphere builds that blights growth, withers enthusiasm, and smells of death. Women's witch-like fury in the face of these accusations betrays how deeply they have fallen into a psychic imbalance, how they are caught on a one-way street going in the wrong direction, where nothing flows into them anymore. They feel devoured by family and by responsibilities, drained dry of their life substance.

The witch figure shows us a compensating force. She looks out for herself and fattens her own substance. Her solitary existence gives her time to digest what she has already taken in. She absorbs; she does not need or want instant results. Consenting to this necessary reversal of energy pulls us toward the periphery of our ego-concerns, to what fairy-tale language calls the "dark pools," the "tidal waters," the "depths of the forest" where we can rest.

We rest from the ego-world. We enter a world of purposelessness where we do not have to grow, produce, achieve any goal, or fashion any resolve. Like the witch, but not so determinedly, we putter around cooking up spells, mixing potions, stewing and brewing, ruminating and chewing over. We engage in a kind of emotional meandering, ticking over thoughts or bits of feeling without getting anywhere in particular. Gaston Bachelard calls this the world of "the anima," the world of reverie, a place of drifting and dreaming in an enchanted time where everything slows down and we are swept in and out of desire without compulsion to act, and drawn into reflection without the necessity to come to a conclusion.[10] A psychological force of gravity seems to pull us down into dark, unexplored places, where no words have been. We consent to a kind of muteness and destiny.

To yield to this dark place, to its unspeakableness, to give ourselves up to it, we may recapture an essential organic rhythm of primordial layers of our unconscious processes. This remote place of a witch's domain that we so feared takes on a quality of presence, a breathing presence that takes in and lets out, resting us, removing us from tasks of the "upper world." There, darkness and light alternate in a rhythmic flow instead of cancelling each other. This darkness that we have so feared now shows its other face, its hidden face, as a haven for our world-weary souls. Like the *Deus Absconditus*—the God revealed in darkness —the God that the Pseudo-Dionysus and the author of *The Cloud of Unknowing* write so eloquently about, this presence in darkness exerts on us a healing effect.[11]

We know in those moments, when we are in right relation to the witch archetype, that we are establishing around ourselves an atmosphere of possibility and growth. We do not infect those we love with the regressive pull of our unconscious, nor do we feel wasted by the insatiable demands of others' unconscious needs, because we turn directly toward our unconscious. We accept, as it were, the pull of the witch forces within our psyche. We know that the roots of our consciousness reach deep into the nonhuman, archaic unconscious, deeper than the layers of nature's organic fertility symbolized by the earthmother archetype. The witch archetype makes visible to us the very depths of what is humanly possible, the great silences at the edge of being.

Any one of us who is consciously in touch with the witch archetype can, in effect, retreat to this sparse wilderness and experience what has come to us without acting on it. There we can change our enemies into frogs, eat up our children, cast a spell for our success, gnash our teeth and plot revenge over our failures, both digest and let go of purposes that inform our life. We can make space in consciousness for this other remote life of the unconscious to flow through, a movement that brings with it a sense of the dark recesses of human emotion, the dark recesses of intellect—those intuitions that may inspire speech but are never themselves uttered in words.

Here, remote from human concerns, we may be renewed unexpectedly. For example, our capacity for contemplation may enlarge; we may find we can gaze upon the flow of life, with all its attendant horrors, neither avoiding it by pseudo-maternal sentimentality nor denying it by defensive detachment and coldness. We need less protection. We can eschew that false maternal cheeriness that declares "life is not so bad." Life often is "so bad." What people suffer is unspeakable. Their minds break up in little pieces that get lost and cannot be found again. Their children die suddenly, brutally, or suffer painful wasting diseases. We inflict meanness on each other—lying, betraying, refusing to give. We kill each other. But we need not turn cold or hard in order to survive our own and others' suffering. We need not jump hastily to remove difficulties, satisfying our power motives at the expense of the suffering, and thereby avoiding our fear of looking at the misery of others that stares us in the face.

The witch lives in this gruesome place where nothing grows. She does not shrink from it. If we are consciously in touch with the witch archetype, we may gain energies to connect to what is before us without forsaking our human responses. We do not go over to her realm any more than the fairy-tale witch moves in to stay in the king's realm. We meet her half-way. The energies the witch symbolizes give us the strength to combine our conscious human feelings with the tough implacability of life that she represents. Thus we may come to be able to look more equably at life's suffering and survive what we see, giving what we can, wholeheartedly and warmly, precisely because we do see more unflinchingly what life costs us. A warm, loving hand reaching out from person to person goes a long way to make suffering endurable. Spontaneous laughter among friends goes a long way to balance life's hardship with life's goodness.

The Witch and Sexuality

A second example of the witch's reversal of the usual order of things appears in the witch's interest in sex. She pulls sexuality out of the human realm. She stands in contrast to the kind of sexual partner most of us would like to have or to be. She cares nothing for loving mutuality; the witch knows no sexual partnership. She symbolizes an impulse to shun personal relatedness as entrapping and stultifying. The witch leads away from human life and community into night orgies of chillingly inhuman ecstasies. She lures men off course with her siren voice, pulling them deep into the cold, impersonal unconscious where all conscious perspectives perish. She possesses men's spirits to such an extent that they forsake their humanity, and transmogrify into beasts of lustful drives—a rutting boar, a horny stag, a raging bear. Cold sex, unwarmed by human feeling; impersonal sex, unbounded by human relationship; power-driven sex, unsoftened by human sharing—these are the weapons wielded by the witch woman. Having ensnared her victims, she sucks them dry of their feelings, their patience, and their sensitivity. Then she casts them away like dried-up shells, unmanned, besotted, incapacitated.

As women, if we find our egos taken over by this witch-like sexuality, we find ourselves driven far into a sexuality that is nonpersonal and instinctive. We may find ourselves gripped by an inhuman passion that impels us to give way to a kind of rutting instinct that is without shame and without relationship to our partner. Swept away into acting out a sexual projection, at first we are filled with a driving lust, but afterwards we collapse, deflated, and with a sick, empty feeling of being spent.

Under a witch's evil spells, female sexuality cannot emerge at all, but goes instead into a death-like sleep, like Snow White's or Sleeping Beauty's, that can only fantasize but never fulfill a sexual role. Still more gruesome versions depict the witch as taking a male's phallus for herself, absorbing it into her own body to satisfy her passion. A contemporary male traced his sexual impotence to an underlying fantasy that he would not get his phallus back if he inserted it into a woman's body. Here the witch showed herself as a monster or as a phallic female who castrates men.

Another lethal passion connected with witches turns up as a popular theme in Western culture: the familiar conviction, posing as wisdom, that passionate love cannot survive, that it must inevitably lead to death. The film *Elvira Madigan*, for example, tells the story of a circus performer and a soldier who run away from their work, their families, and their homes to give themselves utterly to their passion for each other. But then winter brings the cold; money and food run out; they cannot go back to their former lives. They blow their brains out. The message? The fate of true passion is death.

Unexpectedly, however, the sexual side of the witch-motif also compensates in a helpful way for our consciously lived sexual life, and suggests ways in which passion can lead to life rather than to death. Like the hungry old hag, this bewitching young beauty also speaks from an out-of-bounds perspective. The energies she represents balance what is for many people an all-too-domesticated or anesthetized sex life, one totally lacking in any uplifting passion. Where sex is one more chore to be gotten through, or simply discarded as unimportant, the witch conveys an image of a demonic sexuality that breaks through old forms, changing them, rearranging them, and opening them to a new spirit.

The extremes of passion that the witch-siren stands for can move sexual meetings past the boundaries of human convention grown stale. Between the one extreme of being caught in a rut sexually, and the other extreme of sheer instinctive rutting, lies a different kind of sexual experience that mixes human and trans-human passion, personal and impersonal arousals of instinct to such a degree that we feel all parts of us are gathered together in our need to be intimate in a personal way and our hope to be flung out of ourselves.

At the very least, the motifs of bewitchment betoken energies that lure us away from constricting personas that force us to play demanding roles, that force us to repress our sexual instincts, and instill in us the fear that if we follow them we can only die like the Elvira Madigans of pop culture. Often our heavy-handed emphasis on "personal commitment" and the security of a "permanent relationship" in our sexual lives crowds out any possibility of consenting to an ecstasy that exalts us. Yet the fleeing from committed relationships in order to be "free" and "adventurous" soon pales as we discover that we have failed to take account of our loneliness, of our desire for a lasting human intimacy, or our need of a warm, loving interaction with another person who is special to us and to whom we are special. The most rousing orgies are pretty cold stuff in comparison to the fires of human love.

The demonic spirit of sexuality that threatens to disintegrate our ego-world may unexpectedly consolidate it in new terms. The new terms are open terms. Instead of battening down, closing gates, locking all the doors once we have found some mode of sexual life or a suitable partner—all ego-attitudes that make marriage a fairly dull business after a few years—we leave spaces and holes through which this impersonal, untamed, erotic, witch-like intensity can reach us. This is not open marriage, or bisexuality, or group sex. This is an ego-attitude that, though defined, is not complete in itself; though firm, is not closed; though durable, is not dense. Like a house with many windows, a tree with roots deep in the soil, a sea with no definable bottom, our ego stays open to another dimension of existence. We do not swap our personal world for this nonpersonal dimension, any more than a witch figure ever remains the king's wife or the hero's partner. She comes and goes on her own terms; she touches us and disappears. Her terms are not our human terms.

By consenting to her existence as *hers*, without trying to make it ours, our ego-processes mix with these deeper, unconscious, impersonal processes. These archaic energies find some outlet, not by blasting our ego-world apart, nor by totally displacing it, but by filtering through the spaces we leave open.

The Witch and Distance

We have learned from the first interpretive theme of the witch phenomenon that unsuspected benefits accrue to us from the witch's reversal of the normal flow of things. The second theme follows directly: the witch draws positive qualities out of us from her negative position just *because* her position is negative. The witch's distance exerts unexpected positive effects on our familiar world. The witch then appears as the mysterious woman who brings with her the breath of the altogether uncanny. She speaks for the nether world of unseen forces, indefinable purposes. When she comes near us, our hair fairly rises on our necks. She brings a sense of an unspeakable dimension into our world of words.

In the face of what the witch represents, terror grips our human hearts. We feel plunged into an awful context of ghostly happenings—where trees talk, sticks rise up and beat people, and severed hands set about to do her bidding—events not only beyond our control, but exceeding our comprehension. Moreover, this type of witch-magician cares not a rap for our conventions and our needs for safety. She stirs up storms that invade whole communities of people. She conducts vast collective energies to our very doorstep, and cackles with glee when we shrink in fear. She makes visible the horrible forces of collective life that can run over our little personal worlds, not just natural forces but those of an unseen, untamed spirit world as well. These undirected, unhumanized spirit forces are sharply symbolized for us when ghosts, dead ancestors, gods and goddesses seem to come up to us from the world below. The witch conjures them up right before our eyes. No wonder we want nothing to do with her!

Yet this witch figure, in showing us something of the collective non-ego world, compensates for our tendency to concentrate too singly on the worlds of our conscious making. She stands, so to speak, on the borders of our human perception, pointing to another far country that stretches beyond our clear understanding, vast and broad and silently there, symbolizing unconscious mental processes that exist next to our consciousness, but are still on the other side.

What do we gain from this vision? A sense of perspective, even if it is one that seems to diminish us, for the eerie, non-ego world of unchanneled energies and random purposes of the witch greatly enlarges our understanding. In no way do we hear echoed there our personal needs and hopes; in no way do we see a focused recognition or valuing of our ego life. Yet at the same time, this larger perspective makes us recognize that our ego goals are not the only goals or all the goals of life-processes. We feel ourselves set in the unimaginable dimensions of life in general—organic and non-organic, human and nonhuman, of races and groups of people beyond our personal circle of friends and family. The witch-seer makes *us* see into the proportions of life. She puts us in our proper place, small but focused, puny but personal.

Related to this new perspective, the witch evokes in us a new kind of fear. She makes our flesh creep, our hair stand on end, because she makes us afraid in a way sharply at variance with our familiar, conscious fear in the face of a hard piece of work or a known danger that is before us, that frightens us because its own denominated procedure clearly demands from us a sustained effort to reach a distant goal. We know from experience how enervating such work can be. But the witch personifies a different kind of work that is not clearly nameable, not confinable to delineated steps, not answerable to a precise goal. Hers is the meditative task of mulling, of ticking over. This work conforms to no predictable timetable. We may strain to the limits of our efforts, and nonetheless arrive at no end. Yet, another time, something will come clear in barely five seconds.

What the witch evokes is not fear of a hard task ahead, not any fear that arouses mechanisms of defense or avoidance. She evokes instead a fear that is tremendous and terrifying just because the dimensions of the "work" before us are unknown. We cannot circumscribe "a task" for our egos; we can only meditate over what the witch-image mediates to our consciousness—such questions as, How do we live as persons in the face of the immensity of being? How can we consciously relate to the unconscious?

The witch does not labor to produce a product. She constructs within herself living connection to nonpersonal, unconscious, collective life-processes. Her "work," concocting spells, mixing potions, elaborating secret formulas, symbolizes our "work," improvising personal connection to the awful largeness of being. Paradoxically, the witch may thus release us from a too confining ego-consciousness and, simultaneously, release us into fuller involvement with our conscious lives. Our glimpse of this alien dimension of existence makes all that we associate with home the more precious. The breadth of the uncanny makes the ordinary all the more dear to us. Insight into the nonpersonal realm increases our appreciation for all that is personal. We see more clearly the boundaries and smallness of our personhood. Yet we also see more boldly that our existence together as persons sets the finishing mark for all of life.

In personal feeling, and nowhere else, we find warmth and loving mutuality. In a human face we see the realization of an individual personality looking back at us in recognition of our own personality. The glimpse into the chilling expanse of nonpersonal collective life mediated by this witch-seer sets a proper value on the small but priceless recognition found in the human face.

The Witch and Intellect and Aggression

The witch, in her negative position on the other side of consciousness, draws out of us a level of our intellect and aggression that usually remains unconscious. Inspired by the women's movements of our late twentieth century, many women want to build richer lives for themselves by making new combinations of home and career, and by asserting themselves to discover their own personal styles of doing this, rather than conforming to a stereotyped female role.

The witch figure, with her interest in power and cunning, has something to offer this type of woman. The witch figure constellates female intellectuality and assertiveness in their primordial forms. She embodies intellectual and aggressive energies not yet harnessed into forces with clear human uses. The witch is known, for example, for her secret knowledge, knowledge that clearly surpasses that of ordinary people. She activates other people's use of their intellects, too. The hero or heroine of fairy tales must use very clever ideas to outsmart her.

The witch gives little or nothing away, and scorns a helpless dependency or childish receptivity that waits to be told the answer or shown the way. Yet she appreciates those who rely on their own wits. Faced with heroic action, she sometimes relinquishes a treasured formula or secret answer that earlier she had firmly withheld.

The witch also incites heroes and heroines to make full use of their aggression. To vie with the witch, her opponents must endure serious tests of will that call for all their determination and perseverence. The witch figure often evokes so fierce a hostility that her enemies cry, "Burn her!" Unfortunately, in real life witch hunters have literally acted out this negative aggression against the women upon whom they have projected the witch image. Yet, considered symbolically, the fiery aggression the witch archetype calls up in us might also be a force to help us in the performance of unusually difficult tasks or in mastering the fears that beset us.

Living as we do in a time when many women want to bring their potentialities of assertion and intellect into conscious use, we can even speculate that one reason more women do not excel in the creative arts is their insistence on creating so much out of their consciousness, rather than heeding the primordial contents that the witch symbolizes. Mixing substances and sensibilities into arcane potions, magic apples, talking mirrors, wondrous tinder boxes, the witch takes us to the edge of human perception. She fashions new metaphors and original combinations from familiar substances. There are, for example, women artists who are willing to yield to that level of experience as far as it is possible. These women are willing to look to the far boundaries of the nonpersonal unconscious where the witch stands, and there to develop their creations. The terrible goddess Kali, full of aggression, and howling triumph, also "bestows existence upon new living forms in a process of unceasing generation."[12] Thus there are women who will allow themselves to be consciously influenced by this archaic and all but unconscious level of fructifying creativity within themselves, and they will, as a result, gain energy to bring new artistic forms into existence. Rather than unconsciously identifying themselves as the material of creation and simply living out their creative impulses through the biological reproduction of children, some women paradoxically find ways both to differentiate themselves from their creative material and to mix with it, working it into an art of originality and power in painting, music, dance, poetry, and drama.

The witch figure's remoteness from human concerns accounts for her unexpected compensating effect on women of superior functioning, on men whose animas are well developed, and on those areas in our psyches where we differentiate a function to a superior degree. More and more women now are seeking lives typified by new combinations—of family and career, of childhood and parenthood, of dependence and independence. But if we are successful in bringing our energies into such a variety of uses, we face new problems. We may sometimes be endangered by attaining our ambitions, rather than by failing to do so. Our ambitions are not necessarily misplaced or out of order, but the successful attainment of our ambitions may leave too little space, too few gaps to allow the softer, more hidden aspects of our personality to get through.

Our danger lies not in the old-fashioned caricature of the virile woman, without pliancy of attitude or suppleness of mind, who hates men, fears pregnancy, and shuns passion. Our modern danger hides in our new success as a competent juggler of many "lives." Without realizing it, we may gradually slip into an archetypally-dominated existence wherein we become a contemporary amazon, a "Wonder Woman,"[13] perfect in achievement but slowly losing humanness.

Our life of accomplishment may become so extreme that it clicks along autonomously, everything in its proper place and time, efficient and ordered. Our day may begin to look like a computer program. Even our sexual life must find its appropriate slot in it, as if we were machines due to go in for oiling each week.[14]

Like a series of threads in a giant spider's web, each part of our lives outlines the next part. We assume a compartmentalized character that is dazzling but repellent. Events that disrupt most people's lives—such as having a baby, getting sick, falling in love, or getting fired from a job—we can take in stride, putting them neatly in place in a pre-ordained structure. Women like this may even be in danger of getting pregnant, not out of a desire to become a mother or to produce a baby out of love, but simply to fulfill a fantasy picture of an "ideal woman." The unconscious and unintended effect on our children of such mechanical role-playing can be frightening. The children may conform to our spirit and themselves turn into inhuman little robots, perfectly reasonable and polished in their parts, or they may refuse to adapt and go crazy with frustration and loneliness, messing up their lives, yelling, howling, hitting out at their mother's inhuman perfections.

The man in our life, if this is our way, feels as if he lives alone even though he lives with us. We do everything well, too well, but it is not our excellence that disturbs him; it is rather our indefinable absence from him, our lack of personal connection. We are not there as a human presence. Our primary relation is effected between our egos and an abstract ideal. There is little room for human warmth. We are swept along by the tides of efficient functioning and cannot be found outside of it. We leave no gaps.

Our own feelings, needs, and desires may also be in mechanical juxtaposition with our egos, with no entrance, no spaces to flow in and out of our consciousness for our husband or our children. We seize upon our feelings in order to organize them. The personal idiosyncratic style of being ourselves that belongs to most of us gradually trickles away from this type of life. We really become an impersonal "ideal," or a mechanized version of it, and lose our ordinary human reality. The desolate remoteness from all that is human that clings to the witch figure thus builds up all around us. Like the witch, we may inspire awe, but no one wants to touch us.

To our surprise, the witch figure herself brings us the necessary answer to the exaggerations and distortions of the "Wonder Woman" type. The witch lives far away from human society and knows herself to be not only lonely, but also hungry for human flesh, blood, and warmth. She represents in herself the incompleteness of being without the human aspect that so often characterizes the highly differentiated accomplished woman who has lost sight of her own interior uncertainties and incompleteness. If we fall into this super-functioning to achieve amazonian prowess, we almost always repress our needs for simple human contact. Our sense of not being enough in ourselves goes underground and operates in the unconscious to spur us on to greater and greater achievements that leave us more and more inhuman, more lonely, and more wildly hungry for human company, whatever its imperfections.

By becoming aware of what the witch figure represents, we may come to admit the gaps in our ego-functioning, and to accept our dependence on others. Thus our singleness of being—despite marriage or motherhood—may soften. We may accept the fact that, after all, none of us is complete like some archetypal virgin; rather, we need other people to give us back to ourselves in order that our possibilities may become actualized.

The witch figure also gives us a clue to the ways in which such an accomplished woman needs others' company. She must not, as the price of human love, be forced to renounce her talents and achievements, or to make herself less than she really is. The witch, after all, shares her secrets or treasures only with the hero and heroine who stand their ground and use their intellect and aggression to the fullest. She befriends the hero or heroine who is truly heroic and achieves a stature equal to her own. Similarly, a woman who has attained a high level of psychological differentiation and ego-development, a strong woman who radiates talent and integrity in herself and connects comfortably in a well-differentiated way with the anima of a man, needs to be seen and recognized for all that she really is. She must not be converted into a motherly feeding role, or a daughterly needing role, or a sisterly competitive role. She wants to be enjoyed with pleasure in all she can give and do. She yearns for an abundant reciprocity. She needs to be valued for her strengths, without her softness being overlooked.

Just as the mythological amazons represent women with tremendously virile ego-identities who, nonetheless, had to turn to neighboring male tribes for the fructifying phallus, so the highly accomplished modern woman desires to bring a loving other into the midst of her life. She needs others because she has so much love to give.

Living with the Witch

The witch stands for a remote and archaic level of archetypal functioning. To live with her, we need to develop an ego-attitude that recognizes and respects this non-ego side of our existence. Our phenomenological approach to the witch points to the *sine qua non* of this appropriate ego-attitude: to see the witch as she is and not to try to change her into what we want her to be. A witch figure may offer our ego-consciousness pictures of energies that we lack or need to include in our conscious orientation. But she speaks as herself from a non-ego world; if she instructs us at all, she does so from this alien dimension of otherness.

We must beware of conscripting all that the witch stands for into our conscious goals and ego-directed pursuits. She does not belong there any more than we belong to her world, any more than we could imagine outselves forsaking all that is human to sink into her almost nonhuman existence.

We need to find a delicate balance. We must respect her distance, but still befriend her. We must leave her to live at her own level, and recognize the influence of this archetypal dynamism on our own smaller egos. We must allow the unconscious to exist as itself, unconsciously, yet we must know that it is there.

Giving paradox its free rein turns out to be the appropriate ego-attitude to the witch archetype. We become conscious of the witch as personifying many aspects of the unconscious, and we let them remain unconscious. We can entertain a consciousness of the unconscious. The witch that expresses aspects of the unconscious seems now to observe us from its side, as if unconsciousness itself entertains consciousness of our egos. We attend closely to the witch's presence, yet accept her absence, too; that is, we do not inspect her too closely or press to know her too well or besiege her with our observations. We feel both challenged to the utmost use of our energies by the witch figure, and simultaneously invited into a remote place where we can rest from our ego-concerns. We are released from the rigors of consciousness, while at the same time we are inspired to be at our most alert.

The witch leads us down into an abyss beneath our conscious organization of thought and feeling, an abyss of nonhuman darkness that, paradoxically, sheds light upon us. We see more clearly the limits of consciousness set within our impersonal, unconscious, instinctive life. Rather than crushing us, this acknowledgment of the boundaries of personhood arouses the use of our energies to allow us to live more fully as persons, right to the limits of our potential warmth and humanity. Seeing this non-ego world, letting it flow in and out of our consciousness, makes our egos more porous, less dense and stiff and breakable. Feeling the size and breadth of the uncanny, our egos breathe too, in and out, not identifying with the unconscious or becoming lost in it, not trying to make it all conscious. We are more able now to let the unconscious be itself, and to live more fully in our conscious selves.

"The witch . . . symbolizes the taking of known parts in our world and mixing them with unknown parts to arrive at new results." (Filippo Lippi)

The witch arouses our imaginations to new visions of the nature of the psyche. She personifies energies that connect us with unsuspected unconscious potentialities. She typifies a kind of primordial, feminine, unconscious intellect and aggression that would compensate for the highly developed conscious intellect and aggression that have got out of balance with human relatedness.

The witch challenges us to bring unconscious "order" and "rationality" into their own light. To do this is a radical undertaking, best symbolized tangibly by the demands of women to be fully acknowledged and admitted into all aspects of human society and to be seen as distinct members of the human family in their own right. Little is accomplished by simply adding female members to professions dominated by men and by masculine modalities of approach. Little is accomplished by simply changing pronouns in public speech from "he" to "he-she." Little is accomplished by simply adding awareness of an unconscious mentality to our conscious modes of thought. We do not need an additive approach. Rather, we must penetrate and change the whole.

The radical impact of the witch archetype is that she invades the civilized community. She enters it. She changes it. Moreover, the witch takes the human into herself—its blood, its flesh, its soul. The witch archetype stands for a radical mixing of human categories to make new forms. Although she is represented in primitive, undifferentiated expressions, the witch in fact symbolizes the taking of known parts in our world and mixing them with unknown parts to arrive at new results. Just so, we do not merely add women to a male-centered social structure; we do not merely add insights about the unconscious onto conscious mentality. We should create new mixtures instead, and try to change the whole lump in the course of devising a new leavening process. It is no wonder the witch figure persists in our imagination and fairy tales. She heralds the timeless process of originating, out of the unconscious, new forms of human consciousness and the complex society of endlessly different kinds of people they breed.

III Bewitchment

The most terrifying of a witch's magic spells is her power to sabotage a person's intellectual, sexual, and feeling life. When human sensibilities are so bewitched, then the victim becomes the victimizer. The visual presentation of this kind of bewitchment centers on an alluring female who leads her suitors down, down into murky depths, away from the friendly light of day, away from passion shared and discharged together, into an isolated, alien place of frustration and death. A triumph? Not really, for it is out of her own prior bewitchment that a woman bewitches. A witch is compelled to act with a witch's rhythms, rhythms that are very different from the regulated harmonies of conventional human exchange. The bewitched and bewitching female sounds the dominant theme of the witchy life. Energies are reversed, flowing away from consciousness into the unconscious, from the personal concrete into abstract, archetypal constellation, from groups of people to solitary confinement, and from images of the dream and imagination, rich in symbolic layers, to the univocal flatness of obsessive repetition.

Bewitchment in Literature

Human experience, fable, literature, and mythology abound with examples of bewitchment. Each source contributes a different twist to the theme; each has its own varied and subtle accent. To find shared focuses among the many genres where witches abound, we have selected several literary examples and one well-known fairy tale, "The Twelve Dancing Princesses." Its simple plot summarizes the main features of bewitchment: its effect on the ego-connection of the female to her unconscious, its effect on her sexuality and feeling, and her effect, in turn, upon the men she ensnares. The story ends with the heroine rescued from the bewitched state that involved temporary but utter dependency on the male or on her own animus. This kind of dependency gives a hint of the origin of her vulnerability to the witch's spells that made her a suitable candidate for bewitchment in the first place.

The plot of "The Twelve Dancing Princesses" proceeds as follows: A mystery reigns in the fairy-tale kingdom. The king's twelve beautiful daughters, who in the daytime obediently do everything their father requires, awake exhausted each morning and show new holes in their evening shoes. What have they been doing at night? Why are they so tired? How can they wear out dancing slippers in a night? The king calls for help. Any prince who can discover his daughters' secret will be rewarded by his choice of one of them for his bride. Princes flock to the

45

palace. But the mystery only deepens. The princes themselves disappear! Stationed outside the girls' room at night, the princes vanish by morning, never to be seen again. The princesses, meanwhile, grow more tired and sleep farther into the day.

Finally, a prince comes (in another version it is not a prince but a lowly cowherd), and it is he who solves the mystery with the aid of a good woman with magic powers. In one version of the story she is a "golden lady" who instructs him through his dreams; in another she is a woman who tests him and, finding him good of heart, disguises herself as a tiny feather lodged behind his ear and accompanies him on his mission. In every version the prince obtains from his benefactress a cloak that makes him invisible, and he accepts her counsel not to drink the potion that the sisters offer him when they retire, a liquid that will "freeze his heart and leave nothing but a love of dancing."[1] The youngest sister is selected to bring him a drink, and there is immediate attraction between them —in one version this attraction is the result of their mutual love of flowers.

Made invisible by his cloak, the prince follows the sisters through a trap door into an underground world. They journey first through a wood whose trees boast flowers of silver, then into a forest with golden flowers, and finally into a woodland with diamond blossoms. All the missing princes are waiting by an underground lake, ready with boats to ferry the princesses to a castle across the water. Unseen, the prince enters the boat of the youngest princess. All along she has felt something wrong. Not only did this prince fail to be led into the underground, but he himself has disappeared. On descending the stairs, she felt someone tread on her dress; now she feels the boat to be heavier than usual. Wonderful music sounds across the lake from the castle. The sisters grow excited as they near the far shore, for they long to dance, to spin the night away with their princely partners. The ruler of the hidden world of dance is, in fact, an evil witch, Spin, whose sorcery has secured the princesses' ecstatic allegiance to the world of underground dancing. Now they live only to dance, to spin, in her magical terrain.

As they move through the three forests, the prince breaks off one branch each from the silver, gold, and diamond trees, and hides them under his invisible cloak. Again, the youngest princess hears the rustle of the tree branches and feels alarm, but her sisters mock her fears as nothing but her unruly imagination. In one version the prince-to-be tends cows; in another, he becomes an assistant to the royal gardener in order to be near the princesses and solve their mystery. In the latter, the best known version of the tale, he takes the jeweled branches back to earth with him and hides them, one after the other, on three successive days, in the bouquet of flowers he prepares for the youngest princess. When she looks into her bouquet and finds the jeweled flowers, she grows afraid. She knows that the secret dancing has been discovered. She tries first to bribe the gardener's boy with a purse of gold, but he says his silence is not for sale. She then treats him with contempt, as a mere servant. Still he remains silent. His love for her persists.

Only at one point does he speak to her, saying she must not be afraid, for he will not reveal her secret nor will he force her to marry him and become "a mere gardener's wife."

In another version of the story, the prince who comes from the Kingdom of Flowers makes a fateful mistake while hiding the branches of jeweled flowers under his cloak. He drops a sprig of real flowers that the youngest princess had given him earlier, when she had offered him the transfixing potion. In the underworld, the youngest princess suddenly sees these real flowers lying on the ground. In panic, she calls her sisters. They too sense disaster, for the evil Spin has said they could dance in her underworld only as long as neither real flowers nor real feeling entered there. Even the good fairy, who has accompanied the princess in the guise of a feather, predicts that something terrible is about to happen to him. But just as a great rumbling begins, heralding the approach of Spin, the cock's crow announces daylight, and the difficult night ends. The prince appears before the king next morning with the princesses and discloses their secret, and he proves its truth with the silver, gold, and diamond flowers. The youngest confesses—with relief—and the prince chooses her as his bride. The sisters feel dismayed to lose their nightly dancing, until they hear the prince persuade their father to let them dance in the light of the day with the princes who have now been released from bewitchment.

In the other leading version of the tale, the sisters invite the gardener's boy to accompany them to their dancing world. Because he has listened to the girls' plots while he was invisible in his magic cloak, he knows they plan to serve him the bewitching drink. Out of love for the youngest princess, he agrees to take the drink anyway. But just as he lifts it to his lips, she cries out. Better a gardener's wife, she says, than that he should become bewitched. At that, all the princes are free and offer their own love freely to the other princesses. The spell is broken. Each princess chooses a husband, and they all return to earth.

But even in literature, not everyone who experiences profound bewitchment returns to earth. For example, Faust in Goethe's tale of bewitchment was destined for heaven—or at least what Goethe conceives of as that rarified atmosphere. But unlike the fairy-tale princesses, the movement of Faust is from bewitchment to reality. At the end of Part II of the drama, he is firmly grounded, despite the fact that he is being carried up and away by a chorus of angels and led to supreme understanding by doctors of the Church, phalanxes of angelic intelligences, and Mary the Mother of God. Even at that pinnacle of understanding, the wisdom is communicated by creatures who, for the reader, must always seem earth-bound: a chorus of penitents is given full voice by a series of statements from Mary Magdalen, the Samaritan Woman, and Mary of Egypt, that exemplary whore-turned-holy-woman, who spent forty-eight years in the desert after being turned away from the Church of the Holy Sepulchre in Jerusalem. And just to make sure Faust will really understand, crucial words are given to Gretchen, the innocent girl he seduced in Part I, who has now become the articulate woman penitent of the last scene of Part II: "In this spiritual setting, the newcomer barely knows himself, only dimly senses the new life beginning for him."[2]

Faust has won and lost. Technically, he has lost his wager with the Devil, for Mephisto has finally brought him to the point where he feels pleased with himself and where he is forced to say to the passing moment, *"Verweile doch, du bist so schön"* ("Stay for a while; you are so beautiful"). But the passing moment is not merely a break in the chain of contingencies; it is the moment of passing from world to world. It is not simply that Faust, the jaded intellectual, the impossibly bored polymath of the beginning of the drama, has found a momentary ease and the willingness to stand still. It is *where* he has found that ease that counts —there, where to stand still is to move on; there, where to look for long at a still point is to find the turning world.

Throughout *Faust* the machinery is worked by women. It is in his increasingly dreamlike relationships with Gretchen and Helen that Faust discovers the first outlines of his own lasting identity. Out of the mad and impossibly opaque ceremonies of the several Walpurgis Nights, the rituals of bewitchment during which he is spied on by nymphs, sirens, and witches, emerges his encounter with Helen and antiquity. The witches are "foreign ones," as Mephisto complains, bitter that even he, the devil, does not know where he is, with sudden openings in the ground, valleys turning into mountains, and a general chaos in which it is hard to know whether the devil is more bothered by the turmoil or by the protean female figures who ordain it.

But the sirens—the women—prevail. Their exultant announcement centers Faust in his supernatural environment, in which the governing texture is a highly earthly eroticism.

> Let Eros reign, Eros the source of everything!
> Hail to the sea, hail to the waves
> Crowned with the sacred fire!
> Hail to the water, hail to the fire,
> Hail to this rare adventure![3]

Faust's exterior drama has now become his interior struggle to meet and to come to terms with his anima world. However far Goethe may have been from the language of depth psychology, he understood with remarkable fullness of vision the archeytypal figures, and extracted from his own struggle with them an incomparable pageant with which to explain them. Bewitchment in *Faust* follows the fairytale pattern, though by inversion. Whereas in the fairy tale lucidity comes with the breaking of the spell, in *Faust*, as is almost always the case with classical drama, understanding does not begin until the spell is cast and the ghosts of interiority begin their dance.

The fairy tale about the twelve princesses calls to mind aspects of the experiences of women who have lived in a daze, in a frozen state, paradoxically both present and absent to others, involved in actions but detached as well, with their feelings and thoughts fully available neither to themselves nor to those closest to them. The mark of a witch's spell suggests the most helpful description of a woman's state of being in bewitchment. Like the dancing princesses, Faust, and even the devil for a minute or two, all of us who are ordinary women live reversed lives. Instead of our ego exercising awareness and purpose, it lies as if inert and uninformed. Our ego-capacity for consciousness seems to pour out into the unconscious. We may even suffer from a dogged, nameless fatigue, as if our energies were being inexplicably drained away, or as if every day were thick with a heavy humidity that weighed us down with its torpor. Our egos do not work effectively. We come up against areas of blank space and a whole series of odd new reactions in ourselves, so that it is, for example, as puzzling to those of us who are women as it is to our partner that we cannot respond sexually. We cannot explain it. Our reactions simply disappear and fail to make themselves available, as if they have fallen through a trap door, out of sight and out of reach into the unconscious world below, or have gone adventuring with the devil.

In some areas of our personality we live bewitched, so that we not only disappear from real contact with our own feelings and thoughts and fall away from the persons around us, but at the same time we feel pulled into another world, held fast there, bound in the irons of alien convictions. These strong new ideas are as dense and heavy as lead. Out of our blank moments we are apt to utter such pronouncements as "No man has ever stood up for me!" or "All men let me down!" or, like the princesses in the fairy tale, "I live only to dance!" This combination of unformed and yet literal thinking and feeling proves to be the very devil to escape from. For every time we feel accused in an argument of being too empty, too blank, we turn to these new convictions of ours as proof that it is not so. But we are unaware of the damaging effects of these fixed doctrines, for us as well as for others. Just when we should be working to give our vagueness of thought and memory and perception some force and shape, preformed opinions impose their weight, impervious to fact or person or feeling.

In an argument between a man and his wife, for example, when he presses her about her real feelings for him, she returns nothing but a blank stare. She really does not know. Nor does she know why she does not know. He yells at her in anger about her blanking out, but then she fastens on his angry behavior as their central problem, saying that he is acting like a child and that if he were really interested in her feelings he would not bully her. What she overlooks, however, is that she really does not know her own feelings. What has begun as his angry pursuit and her sullen retreat ends in a cruel reversal, as if she were luring him further and further into her own distant place where his vitality must soon trickle away and her blankness will become his. For now he too wonders if his anger at his wife is not a mistake, after all, and out of place. He feels ashamed, guilty, and above all confused. He is no longer sure that her blankness provoked his anger or that his anger drove her into remote silence. Like one of the bewitched princes, he has lost his place in reality.

Like the princesses with their trap-door to the underworld, the wife has just disappeared into a dissociation. Like one of the unsuccessful princes of the tale, the husband, in trying to get her back, has gone from angry determination into a bewitched state himself—one of utter, confused helplessness. He has failed to bring his wife back to humanity, and has instead lost his own way. This theme of bewitchment and its precise effects is a complex and frightening one.

Spinning of Images: Negative Relation to the Unconscious

The creation and amplification of images is a normal and life-promoting activity of the unconscious that represents instinctive responses and the ways we have to channel them into ego-activity and effective relation to others. The fairy tale shows the reversal of this process, changing it into a negative sort of bewitchment. The princesses leave the conscious world to enter in secret, at night, the unconscious world of spinning imagery. They bring nothing back with them from the spinning, except exhaustion and holes in their slippers. Thus the natural order is turned around. Instead of being energized by unconscious imagery, they are drained by it, and must spend their conscious hours asleep. Instead of images that instruct action and configure future purpose for it, they know only a whirling vortex of dancing sensations that must be concealed from inspection, their own as well as others'. Instead of an ego-standpoint supported by a wide range of unconscious activity linked to it through the imagination, the ego now has holes in it—like the princesses' shoes—blank spaces where nothing exists, spaces that call forth from others an anxious worry, much like the fairy-tale king who knew there was something radically wrong with his daughters.

The figure of the witch, Spin, who casts the spell over these young women, has all sorts of meaning for us. For when unconscious image activity finds no outlet in life, no shaping influence on concrete personality, it spins backward in its own circle, sucking the ego down into the fascinating, whirling dance it makes from its own imagery. This point is driven home by the poignant drama of inmates of mental institutions, who may witness in their dreams and visions the splendors of archetypal imagery, but can do nothing with them. It is not enough that we look at these archetypal dramas. We need to react, to move into the world of personal response and out of the stance of the passive spectator. Our consciousness must receive, and intercede, and relate to the images thrown up by our unconscious. As Jung writes, "unconscious contents . . . cannot work properly unless admitted to consciousness. . . . Otherwise the conscious is not supported, it has no roots, nature assumes a contrasting attitude and even becomes an opponent. Then the unconscious is not interested in man, it simply rolls on in its own cycles, and man is left somewhere high and dry, stranded."[4]

The mistress of such archetypal revels always demands a reaction. Whatever form our inner witch takes, she demands and wins reactions. In Goethe's *Faust* she is not one but a horde of anima figures, wearing every classical identity of bewitchment. In the *Walpurgisnacht* episode of Joyce's *Ulysses,* the longest by far of the eighteen chapters of the book, she is the "massive whoremistress" Bella Cohen, in whose Dublin bordello the witches' rite occurs. Bella is marvelously dressed and painted for 1904 dream bewitchment, "in a three quarter ivory gown, fringed round the hem with tasselled selvedge . . . flirting a black horn fan like Minnie Hauck in *Carmen.* On her left hand are wedding and keeper rings. Her eyes are deeply carboned. She has a sprouting moustache. Her olive face is heavy, slightly sweated and fullnosed, with orange tainted nostrils. She has large pendent beryl eardrops." Leopold Bloom, resident dreamer in Joyce's nighttown, is subdued by Bella's speaking fan: "We have met. You are mine. It is fate." Conquered Bloom confesses: "Exuberant female. Enormously I desiderate your domination. I am exhausted, abandoned, no more young. I stand, so to speak, with an unposted letter bearing the extra regulation fee before the too late box of the general postoffice of human life."

Stephen Dedalus, who opposes energy to Bloom's exhaustion, determination to his abandonment, attempts an ironic detachment in his early appearance in Bella-Walpurga's night. He proclaims the terms of the archetypal drama: "gesture, not music, not odours, would be a universal language, the gift of tongues rendering visible not the lay sense but the first entelechy, the structural rhythm." Are his senses aroused? Well, see what august sanction there is for such a response —even in the greatest masters of the literature, even in the personification of ancient wisdom, Aristotle himself: "We have shrew ridden Shakespeare and henpecked Socrates. Even the allwisest stagyrite was bitted, bridled and mounted by a light of love." But Stephen's irony must collapse, his detachment disappear like Faust's emptiness and boredom. His conscious ironies dissolve into the phantom whirlpool. Irish myth and Irish nymph, the one from an ancient world, the other both ancient and modern, sing him lullabies from inside himself. First with groans: "Who . . . drive . . . Fergus now. / And pierce . . . wood's woven shade?" Then, with murmurs: "shadows . . . the woods. / . . . white beast . . . dim." There is no withstanding the phantoms of the unconscious. Bloom's acquiescence, though spoken in the accents of enervation, shows a more lively unconscious than Stephen's. It is Bloom who stands on guard over the sleeping young man, "his lips in the attitude of secret master." His reading of Stephen's groans and murmurs is something less than prescient, but he has, in his own way, accepted the enchantment of the archetypal world: "swear that I will always hail, ever conceal, never reveal, any part or parts, art or arts . . . in the rough sands of the sea . . . a cable-tow's length from the shore . . . where the tide ebbs . . . and flows."[5]

This sort of fascination with unconscious imagery differs from both the life of dreaming and fantasizing and from a life shared with others. This spinning produces no cloth, no fabric of life-giving fantasy woven around a loved one or a child. It does not even yield a plot, a web of intrigue which at least carries with it some human association or purpose. Instead, because no ego integrates the images spun out by the unconscious, the images merely spin out and spin back like a spider going up and down on its own strand, but with far less purpose.

In the normal way of things, images build up connections to reality from within ourselves and nurture our capacity to make use of what reality offers us. They can lead us back into reality at any time in our lives, so that we are not mere spectators, so that out of need or desire or intelligent use of our feelings, we really participate in the world around us. This positive use of images starts early. In an infant's life, for example, instinctive hunger triggers mental images of what might satisfy it. With what D. W. Winnicott calls a "good-enough mother" who willingly adapts for a time to her baby's nearly absolute dependence on her, a feeding breast or bottle is brought to the infant's mouth just when the hunger impels the infant to cry out for food. The image of the breast is gathered into the baby's fantasies when hunger strikes the next time. An example of what Winnicott calls illusion occurs in the baby's experience of the overlapping of the actual breast's availability with the moment of hunger. The world and the baby fit together like two complementary parts of one whole. On the basis of this kind of illusion of a harmonious matching of images with reality, we create symbols that express the conjoining of inner and outer experiences. Then a mutually enriching interplay develops between our images and what is, in reality, available to us.[6]

Just the opposite state of things occurs in our fairy tale, in much of literature, and in our own lively experiences of bewitchment. The absence of any maternal figure whatsoever in the princesses' lives points up the importance attributed by Winnicott to the mother of the infant. For at first it is the mother loving her baby who adjusts reality to the baby's level; in doling out food and play and quiet in digestible bites that give her infant sufficient experience of the life-giving illusion, she fosters the experience that life flows from inner impulse to outer fulfillment and back again. Without such a mothering experience, we fail to find those moments of illusion that give us hope that we can match up our inner needs with outer persons. We are not capable of gathering our fleeting insights from a book, a painting, or a subtle conversation—and ending with a finished communication to others. Instead, the inner and outer worlds fall apart into two separate halves, each impossibly alone, each walled off from the other. Thus, for example, when we fall into depression, we frequently find we can no longer remember dreams; or if we do, we can make no use of them. The images lie as if dead inside us, as inert and uncommunicative as stones. Our conscious imaginations fall victim to a literalism in which an image no longer reveals layers of meaning, but instead is only itself, and nothing but an obvious surface appearance. We swing into compulsive rituals—playing solitaire, or taking long solitary walks, or smoking and staring into space—that fail to rest us or restore our energies.

The modern theater since Strindberg has been preoccupied with the dilemma of the literalist, who is forced by his single-level fixations into a world of appearances in which nothing but surfaces matter. Even so distant a dramaturgy from Strindberg's as Chekhov's constantly stresses the terrible emptiness of the disconnected solitary. The soldiers sent to the small town of *The Three Sisters,* the sisters and their brother and their suitors—all have nothing but surface reality to cling to and the illusion of the grandest of appearances, life in Moscow, as a vision of a possible future that everything in their present combines to destroy. The returning aristocrats and resident peasants, peasant-servants, peasant-students, and peasant-entrepreneurs of *The Cherry Orchard* show concentration upon dead images, endlessly repeated speeches, and ritualized disconnection made into a high art. No one even attempts to listen to anyone else; each one waits for the other to finish his or her aria—or rather, does not quite wait for the end—in order to jump into a competing solo. Sequence may be evident in these strings of speeches, but more by latent circumstance or the force of shared environment than by anything like the clarity of the conscious involvement of people with one another, or even with significant underlying ideas.[7]

No one has dramatized this flattening of a three-dimensional reality into an appearance of one or two dimensions so well as Jean Genet did in *The Balcony.* There, in that most tortured and most self-proclaiming of whorehouse worlds, customers come to be divested of their prosaic appearances and to be assisted in taking on the trappings of bishop, general, judge, or any other establishment figure. The real chief of police can only play at being chief of police. His sexual impotence is not in the least symbolic. He is what he is not. The implicit judgment is that we are all in danger of reduction to the rituals of appearance, to that sort of acting out over and over again of chosen roles which does not even for a moment grasp the mutli-level textures of existence. Dreams are rejected. *Nothing* is what counts. *Nothing* is what is—the re-enactment a hundred times over of the rituals of appearance.[8]

These actions or inactions fixed in ritual take us away to some other place where we exist as if tethered to a deadening repetitive process. Our egos have been knocked out of play. Gradually our lives are being sapped and taken from us. We become unresponsive to the real life around us, too tired to join in, uninterested, dispirited, cut off from the unconscious as well. We can make no use of what life offers us. Although we seem totally preoccupied with our unconscious drama, like the princesses we have nothing to show for our efforts except fatigue and holes in our clothing.

Described in the archetypal terms of the fairy tale, the lack of a mother leaves the princesses with no here-and-now, personal concretization of the archetypal feminine. The girls see no example of a feminine ego channeling all these unconscious energies and instincts into an adult womanly identity. Their energies are not being delivered into real life, but instead, through the agency of the witch, are being used to pull the girls into an unconscious, ritualized dance that spins on autonomously without regard for human needs or feelings.

The experiences of two women illustrate these points. In one case we see the interplay of the unconscious with consciousness; in the other, the bewitched state where the unconscious sucks life from the conscious. The first woman's much-loved husband died in midlife. Her mourning and recovery took some years, and though she married a second time, she did so believing she could never again love a man with the intensity she felt for her first husband. But gradually, in the second marriage, her need to love and to be loved, her impulse to open herself and pour out her feeling in intimate connection to another, connects with her new husband's actual availability to her and his own desire to love and be loved by her. In psychological terms, a real object intersects with inner need and impulse. As a result, this woman found growing in her heart a great insistent love for this man, a strength of feeling gathering up from hidden recesses of memory, image, and affect until, to her deep wonder, it broke in upon her that she loved him without reserve, thinking him now more marvelous than anyone else and feeling herself unbelievably blessed.

In Jungian terms, lavish archetypal images of the masculine as "hero," "savior," and "soul-mate" stirred within her psyche, to support her finite personal experience of her new husband with powerful collective imagery that seemed to go beyond finitude. But a feminine ego must examine these symbols, and not simply endow a living man with this collective, mythological garb. Otherwise, a woman is in for an inevitable let-down, even savage disillusionment, when the symbolic clothing no longer conceals a merely mortal man. For such ongoing work, a woman's ego needs the help of the animus, which functions to connect her with archetypal symbolism of a wider range than her own personal experience. Rather than make over her new husband into a fantasy god, the well functioning animus informs her ego of associations that mix with her experience of her husband, enriching her relation to him with symbolic amplification, not substituting anything for his living reality. She may feel that in loving her husband, she knows something of the cosmic force of Eros. But she does not expect her husband or herself to transcend human dimensions. Instead, she brings her unconscious resources into her personal feeling for her second husband. Her unconscious emotion, imagery, and instinctive response are activated to flow into the personal dimensions of two people building a relationship. The unconscious finds a portal to the real world through her personal ego, and their relationship constantly gains nourishment as if from an underground stream of great resource.

The second woman who concerns us here knew grief when her first marriage ended in divorce. Her husband had let her down badly. When she met a new man who greatly attracted her, she convinced herself and him that theirs would be a different kind of relationship, full of mutual nurture and powerful love that would bind up the old wounds. For a time this promise of healing began to materialize. Like the first woman, she knew a need and desire to love and be loved, and was delighted by the availability of a real man who loved her in return. But then the flow simply stopped. She wanted him to leave her, so she simply shut herself up against him. The relationship broke up into pieces of hurt and recrimination on his part and sealed-off noncommunication on hers. Here the unconscious did not move into life, but rather sucked the life of the relationship into its own stubborn pattern of refusal. Like one of the princes in the fairy tale, the man felt his reality used up by some underground force in the woman, as if he were serving an unconscious purpose in her that could only sacrifice him to her needs. The relationship was killed; the woman was stupefied, frightened by the ebbing away of the feeling that had initially promised so much. The man felt murderous in his pain at having given so much in hope and love only to find it unreturned, and worse, set aside as if it did not matter at all.

Metallic Flowers: Negative Relation to Feeling and to Sexuality

The bewitched princesses in the tale cannot give themselves either to real feeling or to real persons. Even with each other, their genuine concern is subordinate to an all-powerful need to dance. When the youngest sister reacts with fear to something uncanny in the atmosphere, as, for example, when the invisible prince treads on her dress or weighs down her boat, her oldest sister ridicules her and presses her to hurry so that they will not be late for the dance. When the youngest wistfully longs for real flowers that are soft and fragrant, the oldest retorts that the flowers of silver, gold, and diamond are more beautiful—and besides, they last forever. But that is just the point. The underground flowers stand fixed on the trees, unchanging, unbruised, immortal only in the sense of a static existence. Hard and unyielding, they offer material wealth, but they are not real. One could use them as brilliant and startling ornaments. And of course they would not perish because they do not live and have never lived. They can only gather dust.

A woman whose feeling life has fallen into the unconscious suffers much the same fate as the lifeless gems. She can give the appearance of feeling-reaction, often in a dazzling way, perhaps standing out from other women as more intriguing than they, possessed of a startling presence. But her feelings are not alive, not connected with her real ego-identity. She cannot enter into the real world either of feeling experience or of shared life with others. The unusual promise hinted at remains static—dead, really—without development. She grows older without ever growing up. In middle age, she may carry the image of a faded flower, one who gathers dust without ever blooming. The poignancy of undelivered promises still clings to her, but she has missed her whole life. Those men who sought her, those friends and life experiences that came to her, somehow fell away without exerting any significant impact on her.

A similar fate awaits the sexual life of a woman irretrievably caught up in the spin of the unconscious. Her wishes, impulses, needs, affects, instincts, and ideas all whirl together in a dizzying way, so that she impresses suitors as a woman of power, of "large resources," of "heady effect." For one can never tell what impulse might suddenly detach itself from the central spin and be presented to her partner in an audacious way. She may suggest a madcap trip, or dare the other to trust her completely. For a moment, she may appear to be so appealingly defenseless that she cannot be resisted. Sexually, she may appear to be accessible and generous, or to give promise of a full relationship after her touching shyness is overcome. But nothing holds up. The flowers do not bloom. They are fixed in place with only the appearance of special value; they have no life. The woman may be caught in a masturbatory circle where as both subject and object she is the sole arbiter of sexual exchange and the sole possessor. Even though she may appear to yield to her partner and may even want to do so, the triggers that release her sexual responsiveness lie so completely in her own fantasy and her own hands that she alone knows the right way to touch herself, and her directions to her partner must kill the feeling between them, reducing their hoped-for meeting to a mechanical parody of sexual exchange. Though participating with her partner sexually, she may in fact be withdrawing to a fantasy world to achieve her excitement, thus making a gap through which the real feeling between them will disappear. Her sexuality is confined to some hidden world where neither she nor the fantasy partner nor the real one is really alive. Instead they all play parts in a make-believe drama, the plot of which may literally repeat itself in her mind and parody performances for years on end.

"[T]he triggers that release her sexual responsiveness lie so completely in her own fantasy and her own hands . . . [that] her directions to her partner must kill the feeling between them, reducing their hoped-for meeting to a mechanical parody of sexual exchange". (Hans Baldung Grien)

Sartre has made this same situation political in his drama *Les Séquestrés d'Altona,* translated as *The Condemned of Altona.* The sequestered, isolated condemned are the family of Franz von Gerlach, a far-from-willing German soldier in the second World War. His crushing involvement in the terrors of Nazi success and Nazi defeat has imprisoned him forever in the attic of his family home, where he is unaware of the end of the war, and where he is supported in his mad fantasies by his family. He is looking toward a generation of crab-judges in the thirtieth century to exculpate him as it examines the hatreds and "fatal loves" of his time, which he is recording on tapes in his overhead cage for the judgment of posterity. The terms are political, but the terror is sexual, psychological, and spiritual. One need not dwell on the incestuous relationship with his sister Leni, the edge of incest in his brief exchanges with his sister-in-law, or the not-quite-conscious suicidal urge which leads him and his father to their drive to death in the family car. Franz is Germany, and even more he is France (his name is an unmistakable placard); it is a decade or more after the end of the war, and Franz is everyman and everywoman whose dream of release lies in his or her own fantasies and his or her own hands.[9]

Some years before writing *The Condemned of Altona,* Sartre found himself fascinated by the life and writings and fantasies of Jean Genet—*Saint Genet, Actor and Martyr,* as he called him in the huge book he devoted to him. Not the least of his points of engagement with the dramatic figure of Genet is the spectacle of the criminal Genet, imprisoned, working out his homosexual passions in masturbatory fantasies in which the otherness of those who inhabit his fantasies comes and goes entirely by his choice. The psychoanalyst R. D. Laing sees Genet's own existence hanging by the thread of these fantasy beings. "For Genet, the other is conjured up only to be conjured away, together with himself, in his act of masturbation—and when the spell is ended, there remains only Genet, and yet it is only in virtue of these phantom homosexual essences, distilled into images, that Genet himself exists. 'I exist only through those who are nothing apart from the being they have through me.'" Laing sums up Genet's practice as presented by Sartre: "In the vocation of the unreal presence of the other in imagination, that level of experience that has been termed phantasy is resonated. One finds, therefore, a blend of phantasy and the imaginary whereby it no longer becomes possible to say when an act of masturbation begins or ends. The real blends into imagination, imagination sinks into phantasy, and phantasy becomes embodied in the real."[10]

The reality of the imprisoned homosexual or caged Nazi soldier is no more isolated than that of a woman whose life of feeling has drifted away from consciousness. And all three are no less surrounded by others and otherness than all of us who live in what has been called, with unconscious irony, "the outside world." In each case connections—or disconnections—must be made. Some degree of consciousness must be invoked, even if it is only the consciousness that others bring to their dealings with us, the isolated. Franz's seclusion leads to death, his father's as well as his own. It condemns his family (i.e., the French), who have not dealt with their war guilts, whether justified or not, to an only slightly more willing imprisonment than Franz's own. Genet's masturbatory fantasies eventually become the seeds of his dramas, and make it possible to face the kind of self-destruction that "a blend of phantasy and the imaginary" may lead to, unless one comes to believe that this sort of acting out is all the reality one has and thus willingly reduces otherness to the beckonings or banishings of masturbatory fantasy.

The whirling together of unconscious imagery and affect, of idea and wish, leaves the isolated masturbatory woman feeling no responsibility for the effects of her remarks or actions on other persons. She quite forgets that she has encouraged the other to risk trusting her utterly; she meant nothing serious by the idea of going away together; she does not know where all her sexual reaction, initially so promising has gone off to. It has just vanished, and it simply does not occur to her to feel sorry or apologize, because after all, she has lost it too; it has happened to her as well as to the other. The lack of concrete feeling, of connection between what stirs up in her unconscious and what is given out in her actions, leaves her bewildered at the succession of punishing events. She does not understand how she was drawn into this relationship in the first place—or why it failed. This is her bewitchment. Her ego has been by-passed. The unconscious is breaking through, and she is enacting a projected fantasy with a real man, except for the fact that he is not real to her at all. Like the bewitched princes who provide themselves as partners so that the princesses can dance, this actual man is real only in the way a stage prop is real. He serves a mechanical function.

In psychological terms, the woman may be caught in a preference for projection over reality. The images spinning her into their vortex also spin out of her, attracting others and involving them, so that she then sees the real persons clothed in the images with which she invests them. Whatever parts of the persons do touch her are gathered up into the circles of revolving inner fantasy, so that the persons feed the images, keeping them alive with fresh blood. She dances with a fantasy partner, and the real man provides details and occasions that supply the fantasy with new energy. But the plot, whatever it is, remains the same.

Inevitably, the discrepancies between actual persons and her projections make themselves felt, and her projections fall away, leaving the woman astonished that she was so fascinated in the first place—and what happened to all that feeling, anyway? Even now she feels the chilling effect of the impersonal unconscious when it robs reality in order to find its sustenance. As with the princesses, this pattern may be repeated many times with many men. A tension, an excitement stemming from the fantasy, threads through her perception of an actual man, so that she is not able to desist, but is impelled to repeat the glittering dance of empty promises and thus to insure the disillusionment.

Her body must pay a price. As with the princesses who are worn out each morning, this relentless pattern will in time exhaust her. The sexual excitement never releases a real satisfaction, lived out in ordinary time and space. It remains inaccessible because it is dissociated. Thus the undischarged tension that amasses in her body system may make her a candidate for high blood pressure or some similar disorder. The theme of no-exit that we saw applied to images of the unconscious refers as well to body-energy and sexual currents; they build up but do not go anywhere. The fantasy partner occupies her like an evil spirit, and, like a witch, she in turn possesses the actual man.

At first her relationships promise something precious, just as the symbols of silver, gold, and diamond blossoms convey the impression of a world of great treasures. But like the jeweled trees, her relationships do not live. Her unconscious imagery does not grow into real insights. Her feelings do not reach others. Her sexual stirrings do not deepen into committed relationship. In the tale, the wicked Spin says that she will destroy her secret kingdom if ever a real flower or real feeling appears in it. Thus the witch works to sever the connection between the unconscious and consciousness, trying to secure their permanent separation.

Again, the lack of a mother or adult female figure in the tale proves crucial. Instead of the nurturing of an easy transition from unconscious to conscious, and the production of a confident reliance on an unconscious matrix of support, a negative relation to unconscious material is engendered. Like the precious jeweled flowers grafted onto growing trees, an attitude of materialism is spliced onto a woman's sexual and feeling life. She uses sexual appeal only for power or security. She shows feelings only to gain power or to lure a man into her own unconscious fantasy-life. When he no longer serves such a purpose, she will discard him without any awareness of the cruelty of her dismissal. This impersonal use of another person acts in the woman without her active consent. She appears heedless of the other's pain or hurt because she herself does not feel it. Hence, if the man accuses her of destroying him, she is appalled at the fuss he is making. At this point, she is bewildered—cut off from her own personal center, her own feeling, her own instinctive sexual responses.

The Rescue: Dependency and Vulnerability

As we have seen, all the great riches of the unconscious imagery, of potential feeling, and of sexual giving are frustrated or frozen in a woman afflicted by bewitchment. These riches pile up in her unconscious with no movement into her conscious daily life or relationships. Thus the imagery hypnotizes her and freezes her capacity to make good use of it, either in the process of living or in producing anything creative. Her feelings and her sexuality turn hard and cold. They are reduced to what looks like a cynical, self-serving use. Her body tires from the strain of all this undischarged excitement, and her ego loses its energy and falls into a dissociated state. Nonetheless, one senses in women who fall victim to this sort of bewitchment—as one gathers from the tale of the dancing princesses—that unusual things belong to them, that exceptional possibilities are quite within their range, if only they could find a way to them. The symbols of gold, silver, and diamond point to precious values—though they are located in the wrong place and used for the wrong purpose. There is, for example, the diamond-hard center so frequently employed in mandalas to represent the achievement of indestructible psychic wholeness. And the symbol of dancing points vividly to a capacity for ecstasy, for the joyful use of the body in harmony with other people and with the elementary rhythms of music, where so many celebrate their coming together in every kind of movement. The closeness of the sisters points to the possibility of connection to the collective elements of the feminine; today, however, that connection is often pursued at the expense of individuality.

The extraordinary women who were founders of modern dance in America —Loie Fuller, Isadora Duncan, Ruth St. Denis, Doris Humphrey, and Martha Graham—recognized the capacity of their sisters to express ecstasy, joy, harmony, and other positive states of being. They found in body movement a language that was not merely nonverbal, but was often articulate in ways that words could not be, or that supplemented and extended verbal meanings. Whatever epicene uncertainties may have dogged the performances of male dancers and the movements designed for them, there were few doubts about the stark femininity of the women. Even Fanny Brice's satirical thrust at Martha Graham and Graham-imitators—her black-skirted, crack-kneed jump onto center stage with an exultant cry of "Revolt!"—had about it an underlying quality of feminine warmth and a shy delight in what she was doing and what female dancers' movements permitted her to do. That, in effect, parodied her parody and made it touching to see, and not merely comic. Like the dancers of the fairy tale, the women of the modern dance, at whatever level of seriousness, found some magic collective connection in their movements.

The sentimental illusions provided in such abundance by television daytime serials, and the countless films and romantic novels which they both imitate and inspire, offer a more obvious indication of the manipulative power of this sort of bewitchment. We are led through multiple intricacies of plot, which only barely conceal their synthetic nature, into dramas in which all the tension is manufactured, all the characterization is mechanical, and none of the passion is believable—yet millions accept and believe what they see, and hear, and read. Like the contagion of political movements and carefully orchestrated "causes," these plots and characters ensnare us by pretending to be us, to be our world. No politician or causist is quite up to the candor or wit involved in explaining that he is in politics or espouses some cause for what it can do for him. No manufacturer of sentimental illusion is quite up to the degree of consciousness involved in explaining that what he or she is offering is a magic trick, nothing more than an illusion or a masturbatory fantasy, in which the blends of the imaginary and whatever he or she understands to be reality have got well beyond identification by anyone. We have not yet reached the degree of honesty (if that is what it is) and open self-abandonment where we can have printed on our film titles —and our political notices—the fact that these fantasies are dangerous to our health. And what would it matter, we might ask. Would we not go on fantasizing away our consciousnesses in the face of the warnings, just as we blow our smoke into the surgeon-general's words printed across the cigarette packs?

As the feminist movements stand now, the group often dominates the person. All these splendid possibilities remain only possibilities; the shocking fact is that, as with the princesses, women, are helpless to change things, and if they could make changes, they would not choose to do so. They are unwilling to reveal their own secret, for fear of losing access to the world of dancing. Even though in inadequate form, some real connection to the unconscious remains available to them. The woman caught in this sort of dissociation senses that it is touching some important realm of life—even if it is unconscious and not clearly at her disposal. Even in her detached way, she knows the emblem's lively reality. She recognizes the possibility of living well beyond the ordinary hum-drum procedures of doing laundry, cooking, going to work, and sleeping; yet, she is unwilling to give up the hum-drum routines. The bewitchment, therefore, is forged involuntarily with links of her own choice. What she cannot do is to bring into conscious being the promise of life lived unconsciously. She sees only two choices: to lose it altogether, or to live it in this dissociated way with dangerous consequences to herself. But better the little she has than nothing at all.

Rescue from this state of being can only come from outside herself. In life as in the tale, she is utterly dependent upon an alien agent—one who approaches the same problem from a different beginning and therefore sees it in a way beyond her own vision. This agent functions intrapsychically as the animus. In a shared life, it comes to her through a man's love for her. That she must depend on a man to gain release from her enchanted state is often experienced by such a woman as galling and to be resisted at all costs. Today, with emphasis laid on women's liberation, many women are apt to lose sight altogether of the particularly critical aspect of male-female relationships.

For the nineteenth-century Russian theologian, philosopher, and poet Vladimir Solovyov, everything hangs upon the interdependencies of man and woman. Sexual love—and not merely for protective purposes—counteracts "false existence," the root of which is "impenetrability." In moving together in the binding ties of interdependence, men and women model the ideal relationships of "individual members of a community to one another," and to "the whole of their common spheres—the locality, the nation, and finally the universe." It is for Solovyov necessarily "a relation of intimate union," for which he uses the term *syzygy,* from the Greek word for close union. Properly understood and followed, such "an extension of the relation of intimate union" may perfect the historical process, "gradually destroying false or defective forms of union among men (patriarchal, despotic, and one-sidedly individualist) and at the same time approximating ever more and more . . . to the establishment of a true intimately united (*syzeugetic*) image of this oneness of all mankind."[11]

The image Soloyov holds before us is magnificent. It is also frightening to many of us in its insistence on the dependence of men and women upon each other for the very essence of their lives. For to admit to dependence on the other, we must accept our vulnerability—to the point where we can be touched and changed in our being by what this altogether *other* person says and does to us. The root meaning of vulnerable is "to wound." To be dependent on another means we can be wounded—not just flicked on the skin, but penetrated and made to hurt inside, even to the point of bleeding. We can choose to close up against the hurt or to stay open and take the risk, coming to entrust ourselves into others' loving care. Such trust does not deify either the animus or the anima or an actual man or woman into a kind of infallible god who can and will do no wrong. Rather, the motion of trust conveys an internal shift of ego-control. We yield our need for total ego-management, which in fact is no management at all, but is instead helpless bewitchment. We surrender our defensive omnipotence, where we delude ourselves into believing that we are in charge and know exactly what we are doing. We admit that we do not know what we are doing or how to escape this thralldom to static repetitive fantasy, to inaccessible feeling, to undischarged body tension, to dissociated sexuality. We confess our helplessness as women—if we are women—and, in the light of our new, vulnerable attitude, may come to perceive the help of the animus in a more friendly light and the caring love of an actual man as nothing less than a godsend. Who is this rescuer? What is he like?

Some sense of the male rescuer can be gathered from the metamorphosis of Faust at the end of Goethe's drama. What makes him a rescuer of the female is his tie to the feminine. His transformation has been worked by his connections with the bleak and tragic anima archetype. It is tragic in the case of Gretchen, multi-colored and somewhat comic in the cases of Helen and the nymphs and sirens and other incarnations of bewitchment in *Faust*. But however the connection is expressed, it is there to be seen and understood and even to be participated in by the reader, male or female. To make the connection indelible, Goethe assigns to the Chorus Mysticus those astonishing last eight lines of *Faust* that say so much about the role of woman in man's life, as abiding principle, as anima archetype, as lure toward union. The words are blunt. They are also tantalizing in that they seem to share the mystery they proclaim.

> *Alles Vergängliche*
> *Ist nur ein Gleichnis;*
> *Das Unzulängliche,*
> *Hier wirds Ereignis;*
> *Das Unbeschreibliche,*
> *Hier ist's getan;*
> *Das Ewig-Weibliche*
> *Zieht uns hinan.*

> Everything that changes
> Is only a mirroring shadow;
> The incomplete
> Is here fulfilled;
> The inexpressible
> Is here articulate;
> The eternal feminine
> Leads us on.[12]

The special words of wonder are *Das Ewig-Weibliche,* to which no single translation can do justice. They mean the ever-womanly, the unfailing-wifely, the perfecting-anima, the endless inspiration, as well as the somewhat worn and rather too abstract "eternal feminine." It is woman as motivating force that brings fulfillment and complete expression, where before there was incompleteness and a loss of words. In *Faust,* in a parade of beguiling dramatic shadows, she has symbolic life. She has physical existence. And she has a life within Faust, the man, where she is in some ways the most powerful dramatization that the world's literature offers of the anima archetype.

The rescuing male knows a solid connection to the archetypal feminine in fairy tale and myth, as does Goethe's Faust, who in the last pages of the drama takes on the heroic stature of an epic hero, with the aid of the anima archetype. But more than the characteristics of an Aeneas, or an Achilles, or a Hector, he shows the qualities of a Hindu god or fairy-tale prince who needs time to find the embodied feminine principle in order to complete his heroic task. The prince who tends cows in "The Twelve Dancing Princesses" is called "the Stargazer" by his neighbors. True, he takes care of the cow, which is an animal associated with the female goddess Isis and is considered sacred in the Hindu religion, as it symbolizes, on the animal level, an all-plentiful wholeness. From each part of the cow comes life-supporting products: milk and dairy goods, meat, leather, soap. Yet the cowherd also gazes at the stars, symbolizing an attraction to the archetypal constellation of individual fates in relation to the whole of the universe. Like the princesses, he moves beyond the commonplace here-and-now world and knows the nearness of the unconscious. But unlike them, he easily receives the unconscious into his conscious day-to-day world, and can change it because of what he receives. He remembers his dreams and they change him. He dreams three times of a golden lady who will tell him to go to the castle where he will find and marry a princess.

His shift of occupation from cowherd to gardener suggests a shift of psychic constellation that further elaborates his basic connection to the archetypal feminine. A plant naturally grows out of its own center, unfolding its roots downward and its leaves and flowers upward, nourishing itself from its own seed kernel and the environment on which it depends. Thus, a plant shows its own wholeness, but always in relation to the surrounding world. Like a plant, the new gardener shows sure connection to his roots in the unconscious—he hears their messages and neither identifies with them nor rejects them. In this sense, he symbolizes a woman's well functioning animus, one that is fully capable of liberating her ego from its slavish addiction to the unconscious. He can receive what the unconscious says and carry it to the ego, where reflections upon it can occur and decisions can be made as to whether or not to act on it. This is just the opposite of the bewitched state, where a woman's ego has no choice and wants none, but only asks to be spun around by the addicting cycle of unconscious imagery. The well functioning animus promotes and supports a woman's taking full note of what is happening to her.

In the second version of the tale, the rescuer is a prince from a kingdom of real flowers, again suggesting comfortable relation to the world of natural growth and direct connection to the earth—to its smells, its softness, its cycles of birth and death. He is tested by the good queen of the fairies to see if he is worthy of her help. Disguised as a poor, frail old woman, she begs him for food. He gladly complies and offers to lodge her at the local inn until she feels better. At this display of innocent good will, unadulterated by ulterior motive, the good fairy agrees to help the prince discover the princesses' secret.

In both versions of the tale, the rescuer knows good connection to the unconscious and gladly opens himself to its guidance, especially in its appearance as the archetypal feminine. The image of good feminine support activating the animus is just what is lacking in the girls' psychology. For women who have missed the experience of a good mother or some positive surrogate female, a matching support may come through the love of a man. He may give them their first affirming connection to the feminine depths in themselves. In both versions, the man is also innocent of domination by collective conventions and innocent of selfish motives. His innocent openness is essential. It provides a freshness of response not dictated by worldly values or by a blind acting out of unconscious impulse.

Despite obstacles and warnings, the rescuer voluntarily takes on the task of freeing the princesses, thus coupling his innocence with strong determination. The rescuer, prince or gardener, chooses the hard way because of his feeling for the youngest princess. The gardener's boy simply falls in love with the young girl; the prince gives his heart to her because of her love for flowers. Neither fame nor fortune is the spur; rather, it is the fulfillment of feeling. This is a significant detail, for always in life, as in fairy tales, a man's feeling for a woman makes a decisive difference in the outcome of a bewitched constellation. If he loves the woman for her real self rather than her enchanted self; if he seeks her liberation from fixation simply so that she can be herself, as herself, for herself, rather than to act a hero or to have her at his easy disposal, then the future is bound to be good for both of them. Such relationships falter when the man brings a hidden need—usually acknowledged to himself and unadmitted to her—to have the woman in some way liberate him or heal wounds from past hurts or in some way serve him. The fact is, she will be unable to do any of this until she can find herself, for at this point she does not have any genuine feeling or sexual response or significant support of any kind to give to anyone. He is in danger of feeling that she has tricked him to satisfy her own appetites. His disillusionment and consequent anger may wreck the relationship, if it has not already failed because of her inability to achieve relationship.

The tale shows what sustains a man in his rescuing operation: his genuine love of a woman, which patiently persists as feeling, not as a drive for power, not as a hidden need for himself, but as a generous, sustained feeling that rises from him and flows toward her real self, which he prefers to her dazzling false self. His own conscious connection to the unconscious makes it unnecessary for him to establish the link through her. Out of it he forges strong feeling, which he can then give her. The success of his mission depends on the invisible cloak the feminine figure gives him. With its aid, he can overhear the sisters' plot to undo him in the first version of the tale, and in both versions he is enabled to follow the girls to the underground dance, where he can see for himself what sort of bewitchment has trapped them.

Translated into psychological terms, this invisibility suggests that a man who is involved with such a woman or women must at first keep himself unseen. He must not pour out his heart and hopes and dreams to her on the unconscious assumption that a woman will know what to do with them. She will not. She can only take them as new material for her old repeating fantasies. He must wait and exercise some deception. He must see her without being seen, for that reflects the true state of affairs. She does not yet see him as he is, but only as he may be useful to her. His reality *is* in fact invisible to her. He must accept that and wait, while he sees what she is up against in herself. He must give her what she cannot yet give to herself, let alone to anyone else. He must see her as she is, in her reality and in her bewitchment, stolen away from herself by the fascination of the unconscious. Her energies have been caught in a dissociated state. He must discover the truth, but not let her know what he has found until he knows all that can be discovered about her and can close all the doors to her escape. He must accept that she will deny things, even life, until faced with clear evidence that he knows precisely what impels her and she can hear that he loves her as she is, without all the paraphernalia of the unconscious that she has been hiding behind. The strength of his feeling for her lies in its persistence and sureness. He sees her true self and knows where, when, and how she escapes into unconscious fantasy and dons its masks. He will not betray her, he will not bully her or judge her harshly. He will offer her, instead, a way out which she must take. Otherwise, she will lose him forever. In the first version of the tale, the gardener's boy even volunteers to sacrifice himself if the princess chooses to deny his love and chooses unconsciousness instead. In the second version, the sisters deny what the prince says about where they go at night, even when, to prove it, he shows them the magic branches. But the youngest daughter admits that he speaks the truth, and finds relief in choosing the reality of her feeling for him over the spectacle of unconscious images.

The prince symbolizes what a loving man or a well functioning animus may offer a woman caught in this sort of dissociated state. He reflects back to her a perception of who she really is, rather than who she is when she is caught up in unconscious split-off fantasy, or who she may pretend she is to hide the split. He knows her real self and seeks it out, and she knows that he knows it as well as he knows her guilty secrets. She sees that she is seen by him and that her real self matters to him. Despite her efforts to resist his persistent attentions, through ridicule and contemptuous dismissal, he continues to see through her futile gestures to her real self, the self that feels fear in everything. He is not taken in by her defenses.

If we interpret the prince as the personification of an animus function, we find the same sort of reflecting back between it and the girl, though arranged differently. The animus presents to her ego an image of what it would be like really to be loved for oneself. Such love, such perception of her real self, possesses the power to free her from the spin of unconscious fascination. Through genuine feeling for her real self, her ego is able to choose its own authentic identity. The drama turns on just this point: Will the princess choose the love of a real man who possesses his own freedom, over a fantasy partner she can control? Will her ego choose its own life over immersion in the archetypal dramas of the unconscious?

Whether we take the princess to represent a real woman or a female ego, the severity of the issue remains. For either way she is brought to a moment of choice, a choosing that will occur again and again throughout her life, between her real self and her false self, between an ego related to others in a life of consciousness and an ego identification with the unconscious. This kind of juncture point, where choice is so dramatic, is almost bound to occur sooner or later in analysis, in open or disguised form. In such a moment we choose for or against our neurosis, for or against life. We are no longer so ill that we cannot choose. Analytical work has sufficiently loosened the grip of a complex upon our consciousness that we now know its workings, recognize its sources, have come to experience that small margin of freedom which permits us either to step away from unconscious compulsion or to propel ourselves headlong back into it. It is the old story about choosing not to smoke that next cigarette, not to take the second drug, not to repeat once again the cycle of our addiction, but to remember what has been won through such backbreaking analytical labor. Each time we go with the freedom, it enlarges, and our real self enlarges too. Each time we choose against the hard-won margin of freedom, we veer off from our being and it diminishes.

In the bewitchment tale, the princess must choose to make a reality of what the prince offers. If she denies, and veers off, she apparently defeats him—but really loses herself. If we take the prince as a real man, we learn how much love demands. We cannot have real love, except as our real selves. If we choose our mistakenly defended self instead, our unconscious dissociated self, our pretending self, love leaves us. It has found no entrance, no real person in whom to reside. Thus the man does not finally overpower the woman. He upon whom she has depended now depends on her, awaiting her answer. He pursues her ardently with his feeling and makes her aware of the choice she can make. In this way love is ruthless and demanding, "cold as the grave," as the Song of Songs says. It closes our escape hatches, makes us look at what we are doing and know that we have chosen the way we take, that we cannot hide behind illness, ancient trauma, or our lack of awareness of the consequences. A man cannot force a woman's choice. He depends on her choosing freely. Thus if she gives up her false self, she takes a long step toward her own liberation, toward the love he offers her for who she really is. We see how vastly different this surrender is from what women fear it to be—the capitulation to domination by the male at the expense of their real selves. It is not that at all.

If we take the prince as an animus figure, we see the limitations of the animus and its dependence on the ego. It can mediate unconscious images to the conscious ego, but it can do no more. However, it can step into the ego's place if the ego is not functioning, and perform its mediatory function in another way, this time carrying to consciousness the neglected ego-functions that have fallen into the unconscious, where the animus has found them. In the fairy tale, the animus-prince shows the ego what real feeling looks like, what the ego can freely choose as a way out of its identification with unconscious fantasies. But the ego must itself choose, and choose freely.

Collective Significance

Like most fairy tales, this tale of bewitchment tells us something about the collective sources of a dissociated state and shows us some of the implications of its healing for the human family at large. That the princesses lack a mother and any connection of their own to the archetypal feminine is central to the tale. We can see that with such a lack, a young girl cannot easily establish conscious connection to her feminine feelings and sensibilities and her sexual instincts. Why the princesses lack a mother, the tale does not say. With characteristic absence of sentimentality, the tale does not investigate or elaborate the missing mother, but instead emphasizes what happens to a young woman when she finds herself in such a situation and what she must do to free herself from it. By implication, the tale suggests that we must beware of blaming the past behavior of our parents, fate, traumas, or whatever for our situation, and must concentrate instead on what we can do with this difficult legacy.

We might elaborate, on the basis of a few clues, on the significance of the feminine—both in its absence and its recovery—for the state of the kingdom, that is, the collective shared culture that we may take the kingdom to represent. The absence of a nurturing mother or an adult female model leaves the youngest girl with no easy way into her own feminine identity. She lives her instinctive life underground, like a guilty secret. An atmosphere of embarrassment prevails. Her vitality is missing from the collective scene.

The girl may think she has been well and lovingly nurtured. She may have not merely one, but what seem to be an endless number of adult female models. And still she may be altogether without access to her own emerging identity as a woman. The brilliantly instructive example of this sort of failure, with a fine ironic ending that turns the failure into a kind of oblique success, is that psychological masterpiece of the seventeenth century, the Marquise de La Fayette's *La Princesse de Clèves*. Madame de Chartres, the mother of the sixteen-year-old title character, is a widow deeply attached to her beautiful and intelligent child, who

is "one of the most eligible ladies in France." The mother works to inculcate virtue and to proclaim the marvels of love, but it is a twisted nurturing she offers,
bringing bile to milk:

> She often pictured love to her daughter; she showed her what was agreeable in
> it, the better to persuade her of its dangers . . . she told her of men's insecurity,
> their deceit and their faithlessness, of the domestic catastrophes caused by illicit
> love-affairs; and she pointed out to her, on the other hand, the calm that reigned
> in the existence of a faithful wife, and how virtue gives distinction and dignity to
> one who has rank and beauty; but she showed her also how hard it is to main-
> tain this virtue, save by a certain mistrust of oneself and by a constant effort to
> hold to that which alone can bring happiness to a woman—that is, to love her
> husband and to be loved by him.

Madame de Chartres does everything that a trusted companion, a friend, and
a confidante may do, but very little that a nurturing mother should do: "She
asked her, not as a mother but as a friend, to confide in her all the gallant sayings
that were addressed to her, and she promised to help her to guide herself in
matters that are often embarrassing when one is young."[13] In addition to her
mother, the bewitching young woman has every sort of tutelary friendship and
role model available to her at the French court—two queens, the Dauphiness,
the King's sister, court ladies with every kind of rich experience in the games of
love and with a matching variety of temperament and personality. The advice
comes before and after she marries the well-placed, attractive, and passionate
Prince de Clèves, whom she does not love and will not pretend to love. Her
mother is astonished at her daughter's honesty and at the failure of her heart to
be touched by her husband's devotion. All the world marvels when the Princess
will not yield to the Duke de Nemours, the one admirer who evokes real feeling
in her, either before her husband's death or after. In a narrative made by the
meticulous notation of detail, and a skillful avoidance of melodrama, the Prince
comes to know about the attachment of the notorious womanizing Duke to his
wife. He learns in a famous "confession" scene of the feelings of his wife and at
the same time of her rigorously correct behavior, and the result is a sickness
unto death. He cannot tolerate the simple fact of her feelings; he cannot live, so
strong are his feelings, without really possessing hers.

The Princess does not herself possess her own feelings. She cannot bring
herself to accept the Duke, even when everything in her life and the constant instruction of court example counsel her to do so. She cannot forget that it was the
Duke de Nemours who was the occasion for the death of the husband whom she
did not love, but rather admired as a man of many virtues. Nor can she ever trust
someone whose vocation is—or at least has been—seduction, no matter how
strongly she finds herself aroused by him. She makes a life of isolation for herself
now, this old woman, this still beautiful woman, of eighteen, spending half the
year at a convent and half at her estates. The Duke is left in his own kind of isolation, "as overwhelmed by grief as a man can be when he loses all possible hope

of ever seeing again a woman he loved with a passion the most ardent, the most natural, and the best founded that ever was." As for the Princess, she "so lived that there was little possibility of her ever returning."[14]

The Princess de Clèves has achieved one of the great freedoms, for which so many modern women yearn—she has herself to herself. She is her own tutor now, her own model, her own tyrant or benevolent dictator. What she cannot be—for all the acts of "inimitable virtue" that the dry last sentence of the tale tells us she performs—is attached to another human being. Her instinctive life has been underground too long. Her feeling and intellect have been forcibly separated. The collective scene in which she was so skillfully nurtured has been too strong. What she has come to understand with her head about "men's insecurity, their deceit, and their faithlessness," she is not able to put aside with her heart. Though she herself is a woman of incomparable sincerity, honesty, and good faith, she is not available for relationship.

In one version of "The Twelve Dancing Princesses," the king opposes his daughters' dancing, suggesting that not only is there no feminine life in the dominant cultural consciousness, but even the possibility of the feminine is viewed with suspicion. The father may be projecting onto his daughters his own neglected and mistrusted anima. Even though mistrusted and misunderstood, the feminine is still missed and looked for. The king wants to know what is happening to his daughters and wants somehow to rescue them, to draw them back into life. For the natural flow of things has halted. The girls will not marry nor even meet suitors in any serious way. Instead, each anima-girl reacts as an agent of bewitchment who makes her own and her suitors' vitality disappear. Without feminine activity, present and lived as a conscious female ego-identity, serious holes occur in the lives of individual women; susceptibility to dissociation increases, and serious gaps arise in the culture around them. The male-female relationship breaks down, masculine determination disappears, and a general attitude of suspicion and tension arises, directed toward women.

Furthermore, in this situation it is not enough for a man or men to be connected to the feminine. The rescuing prince or gardener's helper knows a valuable, lift-promoting guidance that he has gleaned from the unconscious, particularly from association with a good feminine archetypal figure. Why not leave it at that and let the male carry the connection to the feminine? After all, this life-promoting understanding will lead the prince to rescue the princess and to marry her. But that will not be enough. In other words, the male with a well functioning anima connection does not himself concretize the feminine in the world, but rather he needs and seeks a complementary female partner, suggesting that the helpful anima heightens a man's masculine ego-identity so that he may find his complementary opposite. He cannot simply replace it with anima projections.

One interpretation of the compulsive womanizing of the Duke de Nemours in *La Princesse de Clèves* might well be that he, like many of the other players in the love games at the French court, was looking wildly all around him for his complementary female partner. When he seems finally to have found her in the Princesse de Clèves, he must learn that he has at the same time lost her. Almost certainly there will not be another like her for him. The games he has played, though perhaps necessary for him and certainly inevitable in that environment, have defeated him as much as they have debased her. It is essential to know the desire for what it is, and to bring desire and understanding together so that when one meets one's matching partner, one can prepare everything—oneself, one's world, and the other—to accept the match.

In one version of the tale of the dancing princesses, the youngest princess is named Hyacinth, which recalls the Greek mythological figure Hyacinthus, who was loved by both the sun god Apollo and the wind god Zephyr. When the youth chooses Apollo, Zephyr is so hurt and angry, he blows a raging wind against the discus that the two are playing with and so strikes Hyacinthus dead. From the youth's blood, the distraught Apollo causes a flower to grow which he calls "Hyacinth." This sweet-smelling flower of early spring, associated at its appearance at Easter-time with natural and supernatural rebirth, hints at the theme of love in changed form. The rivalry of Apollo and Zephyr tells of envy and the determination to despoil the good of another. The result of their rivalry is the destruction of the beloved good object, Hyacinthus, who can now live only in symbolic form. Thus in a collective culture that lacks adequate feminine representation, we learn to expect a heightened preciosity in relations between men, a sweetness that hides savage emotions of envy, hostile mistrust, and revenge. A metamorphosis of the loved object into a symbolic form takes place. We touch here on a critical difference between the vital femininity of a woman, and its paler reflection in the anima of the male personality. In a culture without sufficient feminine presence, we might expect homosexual love to increase, both to thwart the emergence of the feminine *per se* and to amass enough anima intensity to provide at least a diluted version of the missing feminine.

We think of our time as unusually preoccupied with the nature of femininity and its place in society. The tales of the dancing princesses, of Goethe and of Joyce, the modern drama, and Madame de La Fayette all point to a concern for the meaning of the feminine that reaches back to the primordial roots of sexual identity. Perhaps what we are able to do now is to read the fairy tale, the epic verse drama, the novel, and the modern play with a greater understanding, because of the discoveries and speculations of depth psychology. We know now, with an even greater urgency than our forbears did, the need of the feminine. We know that it must be rescued when it goes into hiding, when it is so dazzlingly bewitched. It must be rescued from the witch. It must be rescued from itself.

For us, the largest meaning of bewitchment is the occasion it presents to see how the unconscious may be severed from life, or brought back to consciousness and connected to life again. The rescuing prince is not a cardboard figure, a remnant of cloud-cuckoo-land fantasy kept alive by dreamers out of touch with reality. He is a necessary symbol. His struggle is the incarnation in dream, literature, and myth of the combat from which woman emerges with all her resources—or fails to do so. And, need we add, her failure to emerge is only too clearly mirrored in the male's matching distance from consciousness and from clear identity.

The pathos of the situation is suggested by that plaintive refrain of the Victorian mourning the fall of a maiden: "No mother to guide her!" As we have seen several times suggested in these pages, the model that the mother-figure provides is vital to the identity-seeking young girl. Such a figure does not exist in the tale of the princesses, except, ironically enough, as a guide for the rescuing prince. Enter the witch, the one-sided female, herself bewitched by her formidable powers. She is an agent, in effect, of the intellect separated from feeling; she spins the web that catches the unprepared dancers, as all the figures of sorcery catch Faust for a while, as Bella Cohen whips Leopold Bloom and Stephen Dedalus into her bordello circus-ring fantasies, as the Princesse de Clèves's mother tries, with the enchantment of worldly counsel, to do for her daughter. But the dancers—the young girls or the unhappy older men separated from their anima lives—can be rescued. If we accept the terms of these extraordinary narratives, we must believe they *will* be rescued.

When woman is rescued in the tales of bewitchment, it is always because she has reached out from her captivity to her prince. The rescuer must have his powers called into being by the rescued. At its most elaborate, this is the great pilgrimage of a Faust, which ends with the clearest proclamation in our literature of an anima-directed destiny. At its most subtle and frustrating, this is the great uncertainty of a Princesse de Clèves, who cannot be rescued because the identity of her rescuer is not clearly enough defined. At its most satisfactory, in many ways, this is the tale of the dancing princesses, whose spinning in and out of bewitchment has the moral stature of a great affirmation of life. Their love of the dance brings the love of the unconscious into full consciousness, with the result that the natural energy and fascination of the life of the psyche is released to be lived. That is the fitting end of bewitchment.

IV The Hag: Wise Woman Manquée

The Image

The witch as hag evokes a vivid image: a female no longer youthful, badly dressed, with stringy hair, spindly legs, and claw-like fingers. She mutters things to herself in a cackling voice. Black whiskers sprout from her chin. A wart bedecks her nose. Everything about her rasps. She exhibits a phallic capacity to rise and descend on her broomstick. Like the Baba Yaga, she messes about with her mortar and pestle. She is ugly, unmotherly, sexually unemployed. Yet she exerts a fascination as soothsayer, healer, wise counselor. She possesses uncanny knowledge; she is mistress of guile. Powers collect about her. She exudes a magic atmosphere, an eerie one. She is unpredictable: raging, gleeful, suddenly withdrawn. Her attacks keep her intended victims off balance. She hops on one foot, she does a jig. She smolders with revenge, she screeches with laughter. She refuses to speak, only glares balefully. Ungiving and ungiven, she is not in possession of herself, but is yanked this way and that by gusts of emotion, hostile intents, and lavish gestures, reaching others out of the mixture of fullness and vacuity within her.

The world treats the hag badly, and she is vulnerable in her misery to the world's attacks. Others' rejection of her aggravates her own failure to accept herself. Society constantly puts her on trial. Feared and accused of fearsome powers, she is a candidate for torture and death. The death may be a living one of humiliation and ridicule as a demented old crone full of intolerable absurdity and folly.[1] Consigned to these extremes of persecution or trivialization, she finds no way back through others to accepting herself. She lives remote and lonely on the borders of human community, unable or unwilling to enter into a shared existence with others.

The very word "hag" lives at the edges of language, moving obliquely into modern English from the Old English *haga* and Old High German *hag,* meaning hedge, fence, enclosure, grove, or woods, as it continues to mean in modern German. The word came generally to describe demons, ghosts, and evil spirits, especially in their nighttime manifestations, and was particularized in the person of the demonic hedge-woman, the ugly wood- or wild-woman. The reach of the word extends to *haw,* as in hawthorn (hedge-thorn), hawfinch (the common grosbeak), and to the more obvious hagberry and haggard. In every case, by denotation and connotation, it brings us to boundary lines, to figures of hedge-life.[2]

The borderline life of the hag is reflected in images so extreme, so disparate, that we often fail to recognize the figure being depicted. For most of us, the hag is that hapless, toothless creature we have been describing, advanced in years beyond clear identification except perhaps in terms of decades—we think of her as fiftyish, sixtyish, seventyish, a hundred. What hairs she has are borderline sexual symbols, often seen as bearding or mustaching the poor woman, dressing her into a maculate masculinity. Her head reaches back into a grotesque femininity, generally crowned as it is by a frightwig, oddments of hair reaching wildly into the atmosphere, with no hope of conquest by comb or brush and certainly no interest on the part of the hag in subduing the witch's brew that surmounts her. Entertaining or frightening or beyond our interest, this picture of the hag is but a caricature. It fails to account for the extraordinary person whose life has been reduced to such ugliness on the surface—if in fact that is the surface that presents itself to us.

"She is ugly, unmotherly, sexually unemployed. Yet she exerts a fascination as soothsayer, healer, wise counselor. She possesses uncanny knowledge. . ." (Dürer)

The hag as we see her is actually a much more variable creature than the bedraggled curiosity just described. Her psychology has fascinated a remarkable range of chroniclers and depicters, from the ancients through medieval and Renaissance dwellers on human types, to reach a kind of apogee in the portraits of middle-aged and older women of Racine in the seventeenth century and of Ibsen, Giraudoux, and Shaw in the nineteenth and twentieth. She is a central figure in operas from Mozart to Verdi, Wagner, and Richard Strauss. She is a gathering force for the contradictions and challenges, the frustrations and powers of a large part of womankind, which when neglected lead not only the women themselves into a life of suspension at the best and of terror at the worst, but deprive all the world of major resources for understanding and defining the human character.

Think of the grandes dames of Dürer, Cranach, and Rembrandt, with their residual meditative force written graphically on their faces. Think of the reserves of power and wisdom, even when put to nefarious purpose, in the great witches of literature. These are women drawn from life, from fantasy, from the archetypal wells, like the splendid portrait of the witch of Dovne in Selma Lagerlöf's *Gösta Berling*:

> She was powerful. She didn't bend to anyone. She could call down hail and guide the lightning. She could lead the herds off the roads and set the wolves on the sheep. She could do little good but much evil. It was best to be on good terms with her. If she should ever beg for your only goat and a whole pound of wool, give it to her; if you don't, your horse will slip and fall, the house will burn, or the cow sicken, or a child will die.
>
> . . . Evil signs went with her: the army worms appeared, foxes and owls howled and hooted in the twilight; red and black serpents, which were venomous, crawled out of the wood up to the very doorsill.
>
> She could sing charms and brew potions. She knew all herbs. Everybody was afraid when they saw her, but the strong daughter of the wilderness went calmly on her way among them, protected by their dread. The exploits of her sort were not forgotten, nor were her own. Just as the cat trusts its claws, so she trusted in her wisdom and in the strength of her divine prophecies. No king is more sure of his power than she of the kingdom of fear in which she ruled.[3]

Concentrating on such an image of the hag gives us access to a precious dimension of human experience where the archetypes instruct our fears and extricate us from our bewilderments. D. W. Winnicott, who spent so much of his distinguished career working with children, suggests that only through such primordial images as the witch can we grasp our presentiment of life's dreadful impacts, for otherwise ". . . the deepest unconscious material is indescribable. . . . Society offers names, verbalisation, fairy story and myth to the child to help him or her to deal with the unnamed fears that belong to the unnameable."[4] These names, these images, these stories and myths belong to us as adults, too, and for similar purposes, for the hag's qualities and frightening aspects can be found in ordinary women, too, not simply in the bizarre figures of archetypal fantasy. We need to find ways to assimilate the experience whenever and however it comes to us. The hag is one central gathering-place of what an ordinary woman must come to terms with if she would possess all of herself, and what the rest of us must come to understand as we live out our lives with women.

The hag is usually a woman who has lost her bewitching sexual powers. She no longer can lure victims with voluptuous delights into unconscious thralldom. She has entered those dangerous years when, in frenzied desperation, a woman feels she must seize what powers remain to her, however deeply buried they may be, and rouse them into life or lose them forever, and with them any command over her own fortunes. The hag image depicts a woman's fear that she will be used up without ever having really been used or having been able herself to make use of anything significant in herself or her world. Unlike the female fear about her fertility—whether she can conceive, grow life within herself, and bring forth into the world a healthy baby, or symbolically, any living creation—the hag's dread centers on spiritual and emotional creativity; her power is not to conceive new flesh, but to produce in her old self something substantial and to put it into the world. She fears a barrenness of spirit, not of belly. She dreads drying up psychically, dreads the withering of her capacity to present herself effectively to others, and a potential lost because never lived. Finally, she fears she will be left with only the urge to make her mark negatively, to do evil, if need be, rather than to do nothing at all—to make herself noticed through her violent reactions, through her assaults on what constrains her, through a drama of nagging, of backbiting, of emotional and spiritual violence. Society misunderstands her, eclipses her, persecutes her, stops her everywhere. Will she use up all her energy in hurling herself against walls of rejection and incomprehension, with her energies turned bitter, her passions resentful?

The hag image focuses for us a special part of a larger witch constellation. It brings us to the primordial intellectual and spiritual powers that a woman in these straits needs to claim, and that we need to claim through her. The intellectual and spiritual power that we are talking about shows in a hag-woman's intense concentration on finding purpose, in her fierce concentration of gaze to see what is hidden, to uncover it, to disclose it, to make room in her and our awareness for the great unseen forces to which she has been introduced. She gathers them and draws them into focus in herself, determined to reveal them. She draws aside great, thick veils to give utterance to truths—harshly spoken, perhaps, but truths all the same.

The hag shows us the primitive force of the female as she knows it in herself, the drive to be her own self, independent of others, with her own purposes to effect, her own resources to pull from, her own deep wells to draw materials from, right to the surface. With this hag power, a woman can unearth original insights, singular ideas, fresh responses to ancient problems, and can contribute to the spiritual well-being of whole communities of women and men.[5] Women need to face the hag in themselves, to know this archetypal witch-power as it lives in them. Without it, a woman can easily be overrun, giving herself away to others in all the ways of the so-called feminine virtues, disappearing, for example, into her nurturing roles, whether for children, husband, friends, colleagues, whomever. And when she is overrun, so is the world around her. Jung describes the effect a woman has on others when she fails to claim her hag potential and to deliberately channel it where it belongs.

> . . . She would descend to the animal world; she would be a witch. One could say that a witch resembles an intellectual woman. . . . It is nature's wisdom speaking through her, not her own. It speaks through her in the way of the serpent, a most dubious and insinuating way, and helps things along that should not be helped. It touches upon people's sore spots, it cleverly says things which should not be said. Yet if she touches upon sore spots at all, she should never do so without preamble; she should be very careful in introducing the whole matter . . . so that the person to whom she is speaking will be aware that she is conscious of what she is doing. . . . If she simply blurts things out without knowing what she is doing, it means she is in a witch-like state, and it has a blinding, confusing effect; it is like working black magic. . . . Knowledge means power, and if

that knowledge remains unconscious, it operates as nature does and nature is cruel, absolutely regardless of the human being.
. . . [A] witch creates illusions that lead people onto wrong tracks. There seems to be no evil intention, but it is as if her words became twisted in the air, or as if one heard something other than what was said.[6]

The hapless hag sounds themes that reverberate through all of witchdom: the reversal of the flow of life-energies, the making of nothing where there was something, effecting absence where there was presence. Instead of feeding children, this witch eats them to feed herself. Instead of caring for others, she sucks their life's blood from them to augment her own. A bewitching female of any age caught this way, instead of opening to her partner and to her own desires, closes down around her partner's potency and lures him to a land of sterile fantasy. The older woman who is the hag rouses herself to her own great pitches of excitement, but her energies are never discharged into life. She knows things. She schemes; she plots. She lusts after power; she promises herself endless potency. But the plots and schemes and the multiple fantasies in which they are housed never get lived. The tremendous instinctual energies amassed in the hag-unconscious find no ego-portal through which to be realized and satisfied. All the energy crashes back upon her in intense anguish, disappointment, and rage, so aptly symbolized in the image of the hag gnashing her teeth and making terrible, bitter sounds, like a wounded bear.

Many women know this experience. It is not a fairy tale for them, with vague personal associations, but is an acute form of psychic suffering. One woman described it as being "possessed"; another as being "diseased." Women experience a chaotic stirring up of their instinctual and spiritual energies, the terrible tension of unbroken expectation, of undelivered release, of fantasies of all this energy being transformed into fulfilling self-expression. But nothing happens. They may get a job, but it turns out to be just a job, not a vocation that gives expression to their inmost being. They may run a house, but they merely exist in it; it is not a home for them, a place of warming fires. They may join a church, but it does not quicken the spirit. There is no probing the depths; they just endure day by day, their lives unrolling but still left unspent. They feel frustrated, angry, dissipated, deeply let down.

If this experience repeats itself too often, frustration mounts to furious despair at somehow being cheated by somebody, by life itself. Hag-women feel they "cannot get out," as one woman put it, as if a pane of thick glass divides them from the world, blocking energy from flowing into action, keeping fantasy from becoming live imagination. They come to people, to events, to analytic sessions time and again with the hope that this time it will come out right—this job, this man, this project, this idea, this event, this meeting will work—only to go away again, all expectations dashed. They feel happily expanded, bursting with excited anticipation. For example: "This time I will be recognized as a person of impact"; "Now I will connect to others in a way that unmistakably feels significant"; "At last I will make a real contribution entirely out of myself." Yet all this excited expectation is quickly pricked by the reality that fails. Instead of all the good, there is sudden deflation, collapse.

They feel betrayed. Bitter, unable to communicate or connect with other people, to be heard or to hear any word that makes a difference, they attack others with a nasty hostility, lashing out, creating a villain who can be held responsible for the defeat of their hopes. Miserable, confused, they feel their best efforts meet only misunderstanding, lack of reception. Doomed to struggle for the most meager satisfactions, they feel selected by a villainous fate for endless obstacles and illusory success. Above all, they feel their "power" has been stolen from them. All capacity to create themselves has mysteriously vanished. They feel deprived of being.

The witch symbol has long been connected to evil. Here we see the ironic nexus: She makes nothing where something was. Like an illustration of the Christian doctrine of *privatio boni,* the witch's power is an active force that not only deprives one of the being with which one has been endowed, but wipes out the possibility of any being at all.[7] It is the privation that precedes total deprivation. The hag cuts right down to the roots so nothing can grow again.

If a woman fails to reckon with the hag force constellated within her psyche, she may risk being ground to bits, may see her substance declining into nothingness. For the hag personifies the woman of undischarged excitement that produces the woman of unlived life. The hag is a woman of repeated fantasies that never develop into symbols with their own spiritual meaning. She is the woman who has not accepted all of the being that belongs to her, not gathered her masculine animus into her feminine identity. The witch-hag presents an image of archetypal female power, of spirit and intellect, of the phallic potency within the female psyche that a woman must house within her feminine identity. Unhoused, unlived, this power exerts a witch's spell, bent on making nothing of whatever something there may be in a woman.

Wise Woman Manquée

What the hag shows us is the primordial feminine force of intellect and spirit which the animus mediates to the ego. Integrated, this force builds an unmistakable female strength. Unintegrated, it combats her identity and she appears to have become a man-woman. What is compelling about the hag image is its depiction in primordial and unadapted form of a feminine way of being masculine; it is not a man's way at all. Though clearly female, the witch bodies forth a potency usually associated with the masculine. But the hag rarely houses her great power. The resulting conflict of the masculine and feminine parts of herself shows in everything, even in her appearance. She seems masculinized, or at the very least androgynous. She shuns conventional feminine attention to dress or beauty. Yet she exerts fascination through her fierce determination to achieve her own ends, to proceed in her own way. Something wild and undaunted clings to her, something unattainable unless she chooses to offer it. In the sense of the masculine as "knowing what one wants and doing what is necessary to achieve it," the hag's absorption in her own powers depicts a masculine potency within a feminine psyche.[8] She goes right after her goals. Where the bewitching female accents the power of sexuality, the hag stresses the power of a knowledge that can, when integrated, mean wisdom.

The hag is a wise woman manquée because she has yet to recognize her unconscious power and house it in her ego. Instead she identifies with it, carried away in the orgies of using it, puffed up, dashed down, finally depleted. Her animus does not mediate this power to her consciousness, but rather stands stiffly in front of her ego. Instead of receiving her power and using it, she falls into identification with it, displaying the figure of the archetypal animus-ridden woman caught in her own spells.

The wise woman hidden beneath the hag possesses fearsome powers to lay things open, to go inward to focus with concentrated energy, to present truths for others to examine and receive. She plunges further and further, to unearth, to unveil, to exhibit. From this inward place, she instructs, she counsels, she summons. Her power stands ready to flow into the human community. Yet, unlike the frustrated hag, she holds her penetrating power comfortably within her being. She houses its wholeness within herself. It is not a shield or a weapon, but a living force in her personality. And unlike the undifferentiated hag, she holds in her caring the particularity of the human beings with whom she meets, knowing their needs, their hopes, their frailties. She intercedes. She heals. The wise woman accomplishes the task set before the hag: to bring together into harmony the masculine part in her feminine identity. She brews the right mixtures; the disconnected witch does not. In the witch-woman all the parts go unrecognized and remain unassimilated to human concerns. Intellect is not lived into life; instead, the hag uses her knowledge constantly to gain an upper hand in a relationship. Fantasy does not feed the ego-imagination, but sucks it into a fixated, monotonous, ultimately deadening cycle. Her animus does not serve her ego, but simply substitutes unconscious, impersonal slogans for genuine ideas, unfocused power drives for the sustained strength that comes from commitment to value. Values are swamped by a frustrated self-expression, are caught in a destructive power process: power over others' intellects; power over others' sexuality; power always to work on others, never to work with them; power to complain, to protest, to wreak havoc, to envy, to despoil.

The task set before the hag is to know what she knows, and to assimilate the powerful spirit within her. Left unassimilated, her neglected potency draws her energies into remote, inhuman, archetypal worlds. She loses her own personal reality and violates that of others. She becomes inaccessible to reason and develops endless refractory resources.

The incomparable examples of this perversity in the hag-witch, which moves from protest to every kind of violence, and almost always ends in disaster, are the older women of Racine. The first of these, Andromache in the play of the same name, is not knowingly destructive, except in the way she inveigles Pyrrhus, the son of Achilles, into a marriage that cannot possibly end in anything but death, for her love is forever given to her heroic husband Hector, who was slain at the end of the Trojan war by Pyrrhus's father. She is made to understand that she must accept Pyrrhus or lose her son to the Greeks. Around her, crossed loves and defeated majesty go to their deaths. They are not directly her victims, but are hypnotized and made powerless by her unshakable devotion. They are lost to consciousness or blocked from rationality by her acting out of her role as guardian of the heroic masculine image, of Hector's image, which she must keep alive in herself and in her son Astyanax.

Agrippina, mother of Nero in Racine's *Britannicus*, is her son's instructor in tyranny and in all the channels of imperial Roman evil. She is both a model on which to found the baneful empire, and an obstacle to be overcome to achieve that high-low ground. Her scheming to bring Nero's half-brother Britannicus and the lady Junia together and to keep Nero from marrying her, because she fears the power that will pass to Junia from Nero, is splendidly managed. But nothing so thoroughly exposes her drive to power, oedipal and trans-oedipal, as the great speeches of Act IV. There she outlines in morbidly fascinating detail her plotting to put Nero on the throne; there she puts her complaint to him that his gratitude to her lasted a mere six months. She knows him to be a monster of "feigned caresses," a too well tutored protégé—in a word, her son. "Remorse, fear, perils, nothing," she explains, has stopped her. It says more about her than about Nero, her inevitable lover and enemy, when he ends this exchange in a short speech that begins:

> . . . madam, I wish my gratitude henceforth
> To engrave your power upon the hearts of all;
> And I already bless that happy coldness
> Which will relight the warmth of our affection.

The complexity of characterization of Athalie, the eponymous figure of Racine's Biblical drama, defies flattening into any of the commonplaces of evil to which one may be tempted to reduce things from moment to moment in the progress of Racine's last play from lesser to greater violences. Athalie is another Queen of the Night, daughter of the murdered Ahab and Jezebel, votary of Baal, an idolater of power and at the same time a kind of doting grandmother who is at first bemused and then altogether caught up in the vision of the godly future that the child holds forth, this "innocent," this "treasure": "The sweetness of his voice, his childlike ways, His grace. . . . Could I be moved by pity?" She who "stifled a mother's tenderness," and a grandmother's as well, in arranging to have all the children of her son killed in order to bring an end to the line of David as vengeance for her father's and mother's and brother's deaths, she can hate only so long and so deeply. Finally, her masculine and feminine potencies come brilliantly, if violently, together, and she must use the power earlier employed to end the house of David, in an effort to preserve in it what looks to be its most treasurable prince, her grandson.[9]

The most considerable of all of Racine's women, Phèdre, is not exactly confused by any mixture or conflict of feelings. In her passion for her stepson, Hippolyte, she knows only the desire for that all-enveloping darkness—the sun and the light are her utmost enemies—in which every moral constraint and all possible difficulties of time and place, custom and conditioning, will be effaced. For a moment the widowhood of sexual fantasy, in which her husband Thésée ceases to be an obstacle, becomes a widowhood of fact with the news (false, as it turns out) that Thésée is dead. But she does not need this or any other mere mechanics of collaboration from the gods. Her passion is aimed straightway at Hippolyte and herself. She cannot stand aside from it. Only a light of supernatural dimension would permit her to acknowledge the intensity of feeling that flays her, inside and out.

Phèdre's family line is a guarantor of such a confluence of the violent and the sacred. She is a descendant of Zeus and Europa through her father Minos, and of the sun through her mother Pasiphae. The Minotaur is her brother. But her feet are planted in an unreceptive earth, where only the energy of her imagination can achieve the heights that everything inside her demands and nothing outside her can fulfill. The merely human cannot provide assuagement to such incompleteness. What Phèdre hunts—and her words hang again and again on metaphors of the chase—is an end to all feeling, all ache, everything that stands in the way of—of what?—of anything. She fears the terrifying divinity on her father's side; she recoils from the revealing light on her mother's side. She cannot accept such an intensity of feeling in herself. She is a witch-hag caught in her own prodigious inherited process. When she makes her tortured, triumphant, daring, unspeakable confession to Hippolyte, she can at last ask for nothing but her own destruction. Punish me, she says, for *"un odieux amour."* Free the universe, she urges Hippolyte, from a monster. The extraordinary erotic point of this most confronting scene in the drama of woman's sexuality is her baring of her breast. *"Voilà mon coeur,"* she says; take your hand, strike it. I can feel my heart coming to meet your arm. If that is too much for you, if I am unworthy of *"un supplice si doux"* (so sweet a torture), then give me your sword in place of your arm.[10]

It is too easy to reduce *Phèdre* to the conventions of literary tragedy, either the classical Greek or neo-classical French, or to look into Racine's lines to find the convolutions of his struggle with Jansenistic theology. One says almost nothing about the convulsions stirred in the woman herself, and so often aroused again in readers and viewers, by taking her outside herself and losing her in the bright, destructive chatter of literary analysis. She is not a literary commonplace, any more than she is a psychoanalytical commonplace. She is an archetypal figure, but not one who fits neatly into well-lit categories. She will not look at herself until it is too late, will not expose herself to the light until there is no light left for her. Her life is in the shadows, and her conflict is the unresolved one of a sexuality so much at war with itself that it can do nothing but obliterate itself.

The hag's task, or that of any woman when she is touched by this particular archetypal image, as most women are sooner or later (even if not with the intensity of a Phèdre) is to be willing to see the fierce masculine potency within her and connect it up to her revealing feminine identity. The animus, acting like a bridge, mediates images of this potency to her consciousness. A woman must receive and ground and hold her animus within her feminine development, rather than *become* her animus and let it substitute for her feminine identity. This requires step-by-step collecting into consciousness of the animus parts that are particular ways in which the primordial potency presents itself to a woman's ego. It means risking full exposure to herself, such as a Phèdre will not or cannot do.

A woman facing the hag must carry her masculinity within her in a feminine way, rather than replace her femininity by trying to turn into a kind of mock male. Unlike Freud, Melanie Klein stresses the primary desire of a little girl to receive a penis, over her secondary desire to possess a penis of her own. This determination to receive a penis precedes any envy of the male organ. In Klein's system, "penis" carries large symbolic weight, representing both a vital connection between a girl and her father, and between a girl's ego and her superego capacity to put good things into the world, to repair damage done by herself or others by actively begetting the necessary creative ingredient out of which new life is made. Penis-envy occurs in a girl only after her first desire to receive into herself the valued organ, symbolically endowed as an agent of gratification, of reparation, and of creative production, is frustrated.[11]

A little girl's wish to possess a penis of her own not only expresses her inherent bisexuality, as does a boy's wish to have breasts and to produce babies, but also expresses her identification with the internalized imaginary penis of her father. When her wish to receive the male organ, and all that it represents as creative force to put good things into the world, fails, she comes to identify with it, that is, to incorporate it into herself imaginatively, in place of the real object; it becomes what the jargon calls an internalized object. The girl's relation to the masculine works itself out in the relation between these two impulses—the one to receive, the other to identify with the male organ. With luck she makes room for both impulses, thus losing neither her feminine desire to receive nor her masculine drive to implant, but keeping both capacities at her disposal. This drama between child and father makes up what Klein calls the girl's "male position." The joining of this male identification with a girl's "female position," where her primary identification is with her mother, produces a woman's final ease with all the parts of herself that go to make up a satisfying female identity.

Karen Horney makes the same point about male breast and womb envy. A man needs to integrate his experience of the female capacity to create and nurture being, in both modes of response, wanting to be a recipient of it from a

woman and wanting to replace the woman and to possess these capacities himself. Failing that integration, he will stay caught in the envying position, unconsciously identifying with and repudiating the female he so admires.[12]

The hag, though clearly no divinity, does possess an uncanny, all but supernatural quality, as if she were speaking from a perspective outside and beyond the ego and its human values. Her jolting, eerie effect is due in part to her mixing of masculine and feminine characteristics. Erich Neumann's remarks about the "masculine principle as an unconscious aspect of the mother" apply here. This is the mother with a phallus, the phallic woman, but as Melanie Klein stresses, this is a female figure, in effect, with the father's penis inside her, not a woman turned male nor even an androgynous person, but an unmistakable woman, with her female organs intact, surrounding and containing a male organ. Neumann writes, "the formative principle that is active in her is associated with the world of the masculine. It is symbolically masculine because it intervenes actively, directs, determines, guides and violates, but also because it tries consciously to establish the order indispensable to a rational spiritual world."[13]

A major part of the formative principle long associated with the masculine is the primordial power of spirit and intellect. It is presented strongly to us in the hag image. She embodies a crude, deep knowledge that can cut like a knife, without regard for human feelings or needs.[14] Here, knowledge is not yet assimilated for human use; it is up above her and us in her head, pointed and sharp, unhoused by feminine capacities to conceive and contain. A little boy of seven, a patient of Winnicott's, drew a witch with "a big hat because that is where she keeps all her magic books."[15]

Jung writes of this part of a woman's psychology as the "natural mind." It ". . . has mana. It comes from natural sources, rather than from opinions in books; it wells up from the earth like a spring, bringing with it the peculiar wisdom of nature, which often fits situations so exactly that it really has a magic effect." This natural mind ". . . says absolutely straight and ruthless things." Jung associates this natural mind with spirit, which he describes as a special attitude, in which one speaks,

> for example, of doing something in a certain spirit, or of being moved by a certain spirit, meaning a sort of general idea or archetype. But it is not made by man; . . . when a natural spiritual attitude is present, it works immediately. . . .
> To fight convention by futile arguments and attacks upon society only leads us into a new convention worse than the one before. . . . The only thing that may break conventions is the spirit. To oppose convention for a whim or a fad is nothing but foolish destruction, if we succeed at all. But for the spirit it is something else. Spirit is constructive; out of spirit something can come, because it is a living thing and a fertilizing thing . . . always creative. You can find this psychology in the Epistles of St. Paul; everything that I am saying here he has already said.

The power of this "mind" or "spirit" also reaches beyond sexual distinctions. Thus the hag appears as a woman who is also mannish: "the natural mind is no longer subject to the sexual point of view, it is neither a man's nor a woman's point of view, it is the point of view just beyond, and that accounts for its divinity."[16]

This large-spirited component of the female personality is often depicted for us in bodily terms by the primitive layers of our unconscious, as we frequently see, for example, in a young child's fantasy-image of the mother, great in possessing both penis and vagina. It is understandable, with such echoes of childhood impressions in our unconscious, that we should fear women, or even hate them. The well-known female fear of success and the male fear of successful women springs from this unconscious apprehension of a woman with double potencies, those of fertility and creativity. With her capacity to take in, conceive, and bring new life forth out of herself, she possesses the ability to thrust into the world the seeds of new thought, new words, new deeds. Housing all this large possibility and living it effectively into life and relationship with others is the task the hag sets before many women today.

No more precise example of this kind of confounding, demanding, alternately positive and negative woman exists than the intriguing figure of the Queen of the Night in Mozart's *The Magic Flute*. Conceived by the librettists Schikaneder and Giesecke out of an apparent amalgam of Freemasonry, eighteenth-century ideas of freedom of spirit, and bits and pieces of their own unconscious careening wildly into operatic place, the Queen achieves her fleshly majesty in Mozart's music. She is perplexing to many, a failure of characterization to some, a confusing mixture of good and evil explained, perhaps, by a change of conception in midstream, which turned a personification of goodness into one of evil. Several commentators agree that she is finally nothing less than a representation of the Austrian Queen Maria Theresa—tyrannical, self-righteous, a hater of Masons, a kind of anti-Enlightenment model. But this portrait misses the elements of the goddess in the Queen of the Night, the qualities of Isis in and out of Masonic lore, the reach into the firmament of a divinity who touches the moon and the stars and, with whatever motivation or conviction, is the agent of the central love plot, bringing her daughter Pamina and Prince Tamino together and acting as both foil for and collaborator with the priest, Sarastro. He in turn is both her dedicated enemy and her enchanted lover of old. She is, in psychological and musical fact, a gathering place for all the contradictions and reconciliations of this most fanciful of Mozart's works, in which what begins as a cloud-cuckoo fantasy becomes a journey to the underworld of the utmost seriousness, where the resources of human interiority are paraded before us for meditation, even if sometimes the parade is just on the edge of burlesque.

The Magic Flute is an opera of edges which keep cutting into each other. Pamina is tied to her Queen-mother by custom and duty, but also because, in the deepest sense of the music, at least, she is meant to represent what she says to Sarastro: "*Mir klingt der Muttername süsse*" ("The sweet name of mother compels me"). Sarastro's rejoinder, that she is "a proud woman [*Weib*]," is just as properly concluded with his insistence to the young girl that a man must guide her heart. Her relationship with Tamino will spare her the life of vengeance, despair, and death which the Queen of the Night sums up in chilling coloratura measures in her famous aria. She is a perfect example of the woman whose femininity just barely complements a piercing masculinity of the kind we would expect in a tragic military figure, a Coriolanus, a Mark Antony, one who will bring down a kingdom rather than suffer any abridgement of feeling. It is unthinkable to her that Pamina could remain her daughter unless Sarastro is destroyed, and destroyed by Pamina. Unless that happens, she promises, every natural tie will be broken: *"Hört, Rachegötter, hört der Mutter Schwur!"* ("Hear this, O gods of vengeance, hear this mother's curse!").[17]

There is almost too much in this incredible woman to be managed on a stage, even the most wildly melodramatic operatic stage. She symbolizes endless power, for good or evil. She knows, with a precise inversion of the proprieties, that her kind of potency is defeated by conventional order, sacramental structures, anything that stands in the way of her unresolved dual sexuality. But she is not a monster any more than she is the mutation fantasy of some science-fiction zealot. Made larger than life by the extraordinary music assigned her in the most penetrating and violent moments in the opera, she is a fair representation of a vital part of life as it is lived by women whose formative principle is masculine. And so, though her schemes of vengeance must be defeated, her potency must be used, not so very differently from the way a man's must be. In her bringing together of the strategies of generalship and maternity, we see some of the residual powers of the wise woman lurking beneath the hag. The conventional sexual order is not reversed, but deepened. Being is renewed, at least symbolically. In his handling of the bewitching Queen of the Night, Mozart transformed the near-comic textures of his libretto into a work of archetypal splendor.

V The Hag Complex: Origins

Origins: Mother

The hag complex, like any other, shows a loosely organized cluster of energies, emotional and behavioral reactions, and images. It enjoys an all but autonomous life in a person's psyche, arranging things, influencing attitudes, even at times determining a person's moods, outbursts of emotion, or reactions to others. A useful picture of a complex suggests layers of response organized in a series of concentric circles. The outermost rim is a gathering of personal influences in one's life, a reflection of family members and immediate associations in one's hometown, city, school, and the like. The next circle shows the influence of what Jung calls the personal unconscious—all those repressed but still lively emotions, impulses, experiences of others, and responses to them that are not in easy accord with one's conscious outlook and posture presented to the world. The following circle reflects the collective influences of one's culture and time in history, in ways also not readily accessible to consciousness, ways that afford Marx and Freud their "interpretation of suspicion," as Ricoeur calls it.[1] These things— scraps of conversation, bits of radio, television and film, newspaper writing, books, song lyrics, political slogans—are the billboards and placards of the psyche, and go far to determine our view of the world and value systems. At the center of the circles lies the archetype whose energy fuels the whole complex. It takes the form of an irrepressible readiness to respond in a distinct way, manifesting itself in symbolic images that fix our emotions and actions in precise patterns. We experience the archetype as an urge to react to things in a patterned way; our personal and collective histories, both conscious and unconscious, fill in the specific contents of the patterns.

To examine the witch archetype is to explore its universal relevance to human experience in many different times and cultures. Only specific human experience can actualize this archetype in a person's life. Only those experiences that mark us as who we are in our own family and society, in our immediate social setting and larger collective context, can have this effect. For the hag, such marking experiences usually occur in times of transition from dependence to independence, from undifferentiation to a differentiated identity.

Witches as a species arise in the popular imagination in the archetypal role of the bad mother.[2] The witch emerges again in childhood, youth, and even later, in many ways, in many guises, but especially as a hag in moments of major transition, when women try to claim all their power. These are the solemn moments that some like to call rites of passage, when, for example, school begins or puberty makes its claim; these are the times of marriage and childbirth, divorce, illness, change of job, of discovering a major vocation, times of retirement, of facing death. Society's inflamed consciousness of witches and its persecution of them flare up in times of collective rites of passage, of upheaval and transition.[3]

We can examine how the witch archetype originates in early childhood by studying the case of the hag. In the witch species as a whole or the hag in particular, it arises from three sources: ruthless instinctual experience, radical splitting of good from bad, and the reversal of roles of child and mother. The witch or hag image appears in a child's fantasy elaboration of instinctual experiences of an unsparing intensity, where the infant seeks gratification without concern for or awareness of its effect on its mother or itself.[4] Ruthlessness is part of the experience of the witch archetype. It turns up now in the witch, now in those who hunt her, now in the child, now in the mother. Winnicott takes the mythological figure of Lilith as an image of the "early ruthless object relationship" between mother and child that is common in early childhood, and links it to the mother: "The normal child enjoys a ruthless relation to his mother, mostly showing in play, and he needs his mother because only she can be expected to tolerate his ruthless relation to her even in play, because this really hurts her and wears her out. Without this play with her he can only hide a ruthless self and give it life in a state of dissociation."[5]

Most mothers know only too well the unsparing side of their young children, who, apparently without mercy, will not acknowledge that their mothers also must sleep, eat, go to the bathroom, and have a life of their own separate from their children. Women know what it means to be "eaten alive" by their babies, a painful knowledge that makes a child's first recognition of its mother as a person in her own right all the more thrilling and welcome when it comes.

If a mother-child couple fails to house these angry, unyielding aspects of instinct, the child will dissociate from the ruthlessness. For example, the child greedily bites at her mother's breast and insists on her unbroken presence. The mother reacts by being deeply hurt, withdrawing, or getting angry. Such reactions communicate to the child that ruthlessness is bad, not allowed. Those reactions usually spring up in the mother because she has not been able to make room for her own ruthless qualities of response. So it is that ruthlessness is outlawed and symbolized, whether in child or mother, as a witchy part. An adult woman, for example, felt that if people knew about her witchy moods, they would be appalled and would completely disown her as friend or relative, for the moods made strong claims on her. When rushing to catch a train, she would mutter nastily, "Get out of my way!" Or, more boldly, "Look out lady, I'm going to run you over!" The witch leaped out in her. She wanted to shove and push, to get on her way without regard for anyone else. Equally strong was the anger she felt when kept waiting for a restaurant table. Again there was the impulse to shout, "Get out of my way! I need to eat! I'm tired! You wait! Make way for me! Everybody, everything for me!" She had no thought for anyone else's fatigue or hunger. That, to her, was the witch essence.

Witch-hunting arises in large part from the outburst of just such dissociated ruthlessness erupting in those who go after the witches. Long repressed, and hence unmodified by reality testing, the ruthlessness springs up in primitive forms in reactions to women whom the hunters fear as being too powerful. It is an ironic series, for the hunters consciously or unconsciously see the witches as mothers who have refused to acknowledge their children's—that is, the hunters' —powers. Now grown up on the outside, but still infants on the inside, the hunters, under the guise of righteous principle, seek to gratify their repressed ruthlessness in ways that are a grisly match for any child's primitive fantasies.⁶ The women who are persecuted are actually guilty of nothing more than their own all-too-human dissociation from their own ruthlessness, but it is enough to attract to them the projections of persons similarly dissociated and eager to act out their own split-off sides.

Our major resource against this invasion of repressed instincts is to house their ruthlessness within our consciousness, to undo the dissociation and find ways to accept, and hence to modify, this angry, demanding quality of our experience. Another resource is to secure recognition of the mother or the child as a person in her own right. It is a process involving the sorting out of good from bad, in oneself and in others. At best, it starts very early as an infant comes to separate instinctual oral impulses to devour, bite, and suck dry its mother's breast, from contrary impulses to drink in, to mouth tenderly and gratefully hold onto the breast. The infant begins to distinguish early anal impulses to push out as well as to hoard, to burn or stuff full its mother's body, all of which feel violently aggressive to the child, as against its quieter instincts to let go, to give, or just to hold on contentedly. The infant is imaginatively dividing bad from good emotions within itself, and, in the world outside itself, a bad from a good mother. This splitting, held within reasonable limits, helps the child to differentiate emotions and objects into good and bad ones.⁷ The infant's nascent ego can then safely identify with a good object. This is a process that lays a rudimentary foundation for belief in the power of goodness as something stronger than badness, in both the inside and outside worlds.

What eventually results from the sorting process is the formation of an imago, a psychic entity either of good or ill. The imago of goodness is comprised of an infant's good experience of its mother and the warm emotions and fantasy elaborations of satisfaction that the experience generates. Goodness is experienced as a psychic reality that draws on outer and inner worlds, on both fact and fantasy. When the infant ego identifies with the imago of goodness, it forms a core of growing self-confidence in personal being. The imago of badness is similarly made up of experiences with the mother that are frustrating and disappointing, hurtful and rage-filled, alongside the child's inner impulses to destroy and repudiate. All these bad feelings combine in an infant to form an image of the destructive powers of evil—like an archetypal bad breast that poisons as it invades the psyche, that acts to suffocate or dry up the child's interior life, arousing it alternately to furious aggression and angry despair.

Although initially an infant needs to keep imagos of good and evil separate in order to make elementary differentiations and to gain confidence that the good will not succumb to the bad, eventually it must face the task of integrating its split imagos into one unmistakable whole. The child must recognize and accept that it is the same self that feels bad and good responses, and the same mother that does bad and good things. Parts of the good and bad imagos also go to form the kernel of the superego. As the child comes to unite the initially opposed good and bad imagos into a whole psychic reality, the superego reflects this fusion of life (good) and death (bad) instincts in its own moderating character.

The witch image is a very satisfactory fantasy elaboration of a child's experiences of badness, both in its own emotions and in relation to its mother. The identifying mark of the witch here is her reversal of the natural flow of life. She dries up milk instead of giving it. She is absent instead of present. She is the invader, hexing, rejecting, poisoning, turning away, and bursting forth, always with angry noise, howling her disappointment. The witch comes to personify the combined inner and outer badness with which the child feels confronted, in a figure very different from the image of the mother whom the child loves. Melanie Klein writes of a five-year old boy who obtained a witch figure "by division of the mother imago." He split off this "second female figure . . . from his beloved mother, in order to maintain her as she is. . . ." Moreover, as we have suggested so often happens with the witch, and especially the hag, this little boy saw his witch as "the woman with the penis. . . ."[8]

The witch figure obtained from the sharp splitting of good and bad resides in the personal unconscious. The "bad" part of the mother and the child's "bad" urges toward the mother are repressed into what is in effect a storehouse of personal material in the unconscious. In addition, a more fearsome, because more archaic witch-image looms up from the objective psyche. In this realm of unconscious life, where Jung postulates that all of the history of the human psyche is somehow present, contents are not derived from personal experience and repression, but rather arise to meet our personal experience out of an antecedent archetypal seedbed. Thus adverse reactions to negative mother experiences activate in the infant and the mother alike an unconscious readiness to endow the parent-child interaction with a witchiness that is larger than life. The personal conflict of mother and child thus brings direct experience of a tension between our morality and an uncanny female potency that seems almost more than mortal. The tension develops in the fantasies of both mother and child a sharper awareness of the reality of their conflict. For example, a child may perceive her mother as who she really is, yet also see her as possessed of evil, magical powers, able to cast spells merely with her bad moods. Or a teen-age daughter may imagine that her mother's strictness about dating is a malevolent attempt to paralyze her budding sexuality. On her side, the mother may feel invaded by something that is spoiling even her best intents.

From the archetypal point of view, the witch mother personifies aspects of our own unconscious, especially its regressive pull away from consciousness, just as the good mother symbolizes those aspects of the unconscious psyche that promote and support the growth of consciousness, and with it the flowering of the whole personality. The good-bad mother comes close to the dual-mother lineaments of the hero who is born of an earthly mother, and then reborn of a symbolic mother who is more than mortal. The hero's ordinary earthly existence is then imbued with outstanding elements drawn from the archetypal realm: "He who stems from two mothers is the hero: the first birth makes him a mortal man, the second an immortal half-god."[9]

For the woman who must wrestle with the witch inside her, the heroic life has an added lure, a specifically feminine one. For the female is not just pulled, as a man might be, toward the devouring witch force of the psyche; the female also becomes the witch. She knows the witch's power as part of her own female identity. To face and accept and integrate the fact of the witch presence within her is to experience the archetypal feminine flowing through her. She does not feel possessed by it; that would be to identify with it. But it does abide in her psyche. To face its negativity is also to reap positive effects, as we shall see.

In some people the witch archetype is more active than in others and may come to pose a serious problem. This is when sorting out takes on a savage force, so that what results is not imagos of good separated from bad, but a radical splitting into an extreme goodness on the one hand, and a persecuting badness on the other. Whereas normal sorting out promotes ego differentiation, a radical splitting leaves the ego feeling too small to house the good and bad imagos. All it can do is toss itself back and forth between them. Normal splitting leads to what Klein defined as the depressive position. In it, a child finally combines the good and bad inside itself to make up a new whole, accepting the good and bad mother outside itself as another whole. But in the case of radical splitting, integration is short-circuited. Radical splitting prevents any reconciliation of good and bad, either in the self or in the object. The gap between good and bad has grown too great. The fusion of good and bad instinctual forces falls apart. The destructive, death-dealing forces remain unchecked by the constructive, life-supporting ones. Fantasy figures of destructive force assume terrifying proportions, arousing intolerable anxiety in the person, who then defends herself, as Klein says, by relegating them "to the deeper layers of the unconscious,"[10] there to exist "in a separate area of the mind in the deep unconscious, split off from both the ego and the super-ego, where they remain unintegrated and unmodified by normal processes of growth."[11] In crisis situations, these monstrous unconscious figures can threaten to break into consciousness. These are the kinds of figures that were projected onto women who were hunted down and tortured as witches, leaving them helpless and at the mercy of their persecutors' projections, while the persecutors were terrified of these women whom they themselves had endowed with their own deepest and most appalling fantasies of persecutory power.

Winnicott gives an example of the same outsized terror in the face of a witch force that was making a child's mother actually seem to vanish. A boy, who still suffered from his mother's having frequently fallen into acute depression when he was an infant, drew a picture for Winnicott of a woman holding a baby, with her eyes all "smudged." Winnicott speculated that that was what the mother had looked like to her infant son when she was deeply depressed. Though present, she had gone out of focus, slipped into the unconscious, fallen asleep. The boy remembered a terrifying dream about what seemed like annihilating powers: "You can't be seen and you can't see yourself." These powers attacked both his mother and himself. ". . . [T]he witch came when the mother shut her eyes. I just screamed. I saw the witch. Mummy saw the witch."[12]

An adolescent girl records a similar recognition of a disintegrating force taking over her mother and menacing her whole family's existence. With all the attendant ambivalence between seeing her mother as a victim overcome by an evil force and as a villain exerting the force, she said: "My mother would be sitting at the kitchen table, obviously having been there for several hours before we had been awakened for school. She looked sallow and teary, but would struggle to smile and force the tears back as she asked what I wanted for breakfast. My reaction was anger, and I would attack with something like, 'Mommy you better stop before the kids or Daddy see you like this,' or I would plead, 'Mommy why can't you get better; . . . all you have to do is be.' . . . I felt something absolutely dreadful was going to happen to me. . . . I was angry that she was like this, yet I sensed that there was nothing she could do about it. I felt helpless, and hopeless that she could ever act as 'mother' again. . . . There was an enemy, an imminent danger lurking in the background, but I could not grasp it. . . . I was afraid of someone or something disappearing."

The domination of the witch archetype in a woman's psychology does not derive just from the experience of ruthless instinct or from radical splits in a child's fantasy. It also arises from peculiar conditions in the relation between child and mother. Again, what stands out is the reversal of the ordinary flow of energy in the couple: the child becomes mother to the mother. The image of the witch ensnaring children to make slaves of them or eat them offers a vivid example of what in real life accumulates in infinitely subtle ways in the bewitched psyche.

A mother falling under a witch's spell fails to adapt in appropriately sensitive ways to her child's gestures of communication. Instead, she substitutes gestures of her own which compel the child to adapt to her. Such a mother runs to her crying baby, but does not ask, "What's the trouble? Are you wet? Is a pin sticking you somewhere?" Instead she demands, "What have *I* done wrong?" She reverses the communication system. She takes the baby's cries to evaluate her own mothering acts, rather than as a message from the infant about its own experiences and needs. Thus, witch-like, she eats at her infant, annihilating its independent existence. As we shall see later, the mother is living on precarious ground, in constant danger herself of feeling annihilated. Thus she clings to her infant as a small raft of affirmation of her worth in a sea of anxiety. The mother makes the baby into a measure of her success or failure as a mother.

Edith Weigert writes about communication-reversal as the factor in a mother that can engender psychosis in a child. Alice Miller sees the reversal as a deep wound to a child's narcissism. For Winnicott, the reversal is the source of the false self.[13] A mother falling under the spell of this reversal fails to adapt to her baby's spontaneous gestures, which might usefully confirm in the child a temporary sense of omnipotence, as it sees its wishes correspond to results in reality. This correspondence is necessary to build a lively, trustful connection between self and reality. Instead of offering this support, the mother substitutes her own gesture for the child's, thus demanding compliance from the child. The roles reverse: the child now confirms the mother and becomes parent to the parent at the expense of its own childhood. The child then experiences reality as impingement, not confirmation, and must divert its energies to construct a false compliant self that can adapt to imposed demands. The spontaneous gesture is destroyed at the source, because the mother has failed to confirm its reality by responding to it. As a result, the child may never develop its spontaneous gestures into a capacity to use the symbols of communication with those gestures and images that assure psychological survival. What results from a mother's reversal of the communication system—the impoverishment or loss of the symbolic experience of life—is disastrous for the child, and often enough for many others as well, those who must live with the child in later life.

We have not had to wait for depth psychology to learn about the disasters caused by mothers reversing their children's communications. In a very few scenes—a masterpiece of dramatic economy—Shakespeare draws a portrait of such a mother in *Coriolanus*. Volumnia's name is a pun on the volumes of fantasy with which she endows her son Caius Marcius, named Coriolanus after his military triumph at Corioli, where he defeated Aufidius and the Volscians for Rome. In Act I, scene iii, speaking to her daughter-in-law, she explains her conception of motherhood:

> When yet he was but tender-bodied, and the only son of my womb; when youth with comeliness plucked all gaze his way; when, for a day of king's entreaties, a mother should not sell him an hour from her beholding; I, considering how honour should become such a person—that it was no better than picturelike to hang by the wall if renown made it not stir—was pleased to let him seek danger where he was like to find fame. To a cruel war I sent him, from whence he returned, his brows bound with oak. I tell thee, daughter, I sprang not more in joy at first hearing he was a man-child than now in first seeing he had proved himself a man.

"But," her son's wife interrupts, "had he died in the business, madam? How then?"

Then his good report should have been my son; I therein would have found issue. Hear me profess sincerely: had I a dozen sons, each in my love alike, and none less dear than thine and my good Marcius, I had rather had eleven die nobly for their country than one voluptuously surfeit out of action.

Volumnia's martial fantasy feeds on blood, the blood of her son's victims, the blood of her son. Reproved by her daughter-in-law for exulting over the image of Coriolanus's "bloody brow," she blasts away with the force of a cannon:

> Away, you fool! it more becomes a man
> Than gilt his trophy: the breasts of Hecuba,
> When she did suckle Hector, look'd not lovelier
> Than Hector's forehead when it spit forth blood
> At Grecian swords contending.

Volumnia is her son's goad, and more, his impossibly masculine military self where he most needs the nurturing of a mother's femininity. She has seized his gestures as her own, made herself a greater general than he in spite of his unmistakable prowess. It is a process, as she is only too happy to say, that started in infancy. His wife comes too late, in Shakespeare's chronology of the psyche, to bring her countervailing femininity to support Coriolanus. His mother's bloodsoaked witchiness and the feverish conflict of castes and classes in Rome make inevitable Coriolanus's fall from power and public esteem. Banished from all his worlds and wombs, he seeks a dangerous alliance with his old enemy Aufidius, only to be talked out of it by his mother, once more reversing the gestures and words of her son. If you conquer Rome for the Volscians, she warns him,

> the benefit
> Which thou shalt thereby reap is such a name,
> Whose repetition will be dogg'd with curses. . . .

She dogs him with a mother's—a martial mother's—ironies:

> There is no man in the world
> More bound to his mother; yet there he lets me
> Like one i' the stocks. Thou hast never in thy life
> Show'd thy dear mother any courtesy;
> When she—poor hen—fond of no second brood,
> Has cluck'd thee to the wars, and safely home,
> Loaden with honour.

She mocks his attempts to hold off from war:

> He turns away:
> Down, ladies; let us shame him with our knees.

She twists his only too accessible feeling with a picture of a ruined Rome; but even that burning appeal is edged with irony:

> I am hush'd until our city be afire,
> And then I'll speak a little.

Coriolanus knows what effect Volumnia has had upon him. The gods laugh, he says, at "this unnatural scene." A victory for Rome, perhaps, but not for him: "Most dangerously," he tells his mother, you have "prevailed" with your son, "If not most mortal to him." He knows his communication system has been turned upside down, but he is helpless to do anything about it.

Coriolanus's final words in this scene both conceal and reveal his impossible state:

> Ladies, you deserve
> To have a temple built you; all the swords
> In Italy, and her confederate arms,
> Could not have made this peace.

The point is, of course, that this peace cannot be made at all, not with swords, not with words, not with nations, not with the sons of such mothers. Aufidius, jealous and frightened of his antagonist-turned-confederate, accuses Coriolanus of treason to the Volscians, of having "given up, For certain drops of salt, your city Rome—I say your city—to his wife and mother." He draws his sword, and with his fellow-conspirators kills the great Roman. "Yet," the Volscian says of Coriolanus, in the concluding line of the play, "he shall have a noble memory."[14]

But the memory, like the life, is the mother's. She fed him her milk to make in him her blood, not his, to build in him such strength as should permit him to fight for her, to bleed for her, to kill for her, to die for her. What makes her believable, and not simply a one-dimensional Roman witch, is the psychic energy that enters into her few but always compelling eruptions in the drama. The false self she has created in her child is not a small one. Coriolanus is a figure of tragic stature, not merely a doomed general. The Volumnias of the world must not be underestimated, Shakespeare is telling us. They cry havoc and they wreak havoc, but with grandeur. And often their progeny, direct and indirect, have such nobility that we must bow to them while at the same time we weep for them. In revealing to the Volumnia-type the terror of her ways, we are not simply arresting a troublesome neurosis or establishing some ease of adjustment for the bedeviled woman; we are fighting our own fight to save for civilization what could be a great positive nurturing force.

A softer, more subtle way in which a mother exerts witchy powers is in her seeming anticipation of her child's every need without reliance on the child's signalling of need. Mother always knows best. Her perfect helpfulness smothers her child's initiative. Her oversolicitous concern denies existence to any attempt on the child's part to communicate out of its own existence. She removes all need for communication, extending the unconscious umbilical cord into her child's life long after it should have been cut. Winnicott describes such a mother.

> The creative gesture, the cry, the protest, all the little signs that are supposed to produce what the mother does, all these little things are missing, because the mother has already met the need just as if the infant were still merged with

her and she with the infant. In this way the mother, by being a seemingly good mother, does something worse than castrate the infant. The latter is left with two alternatives: either being in a permanent state of regression and of being merged with the mother, or else staging a total rejection of the mother, even of the seemingly good mother.

For the child, the mother who "knows their needs in advance . . . is dangerous, a witch."[15]

The difference between a good enough mother, in Winnicott's terms, who can adapt to her infant, and the mother who invades her infant, rests on recognition of the infant's otherness.[16] It is a distinction that applies to many other situations besides the literal mother-child relationship. It applies to all those professionals who draw on maternal functions to do their jobs: to teachers, for example, and to clergy, and to psychoanalysts, too, in so far as they draw upon mothering capacities in their work and are thus subject to witchy reversals where they feed off those they should be nourishing, using their patients to aggrandize their own starving selves. The first kind of mother, or helping professional, understands her infant on the basis of something in the infant that signals its needs or wish for playful communication. The infant is the other who communicates. The second kind of mother, or professional, appropriates the infant's experience for herself, thus canceling the infant's need to communicate its otherness.

Lest we condemn the mother, or helping professional, as simply a villain, which is a move typical of the scapegoating mentality that we easily adopt when confronted with overwhelmingly fearsome forces, we must recognize our own need to see that the reversal that the mother imposes on her child is no more than a repetition of the reversal that was earlier imposed upon her. She has been invaded by so many cancelings of her own being, and givings over of it to accommodate others, that she has quite fallen under a witch's spell, a fact that a child often recognizes consciously or unconsciously and capitalizes upon.

Origins: Father

Although we associate the witch archetype almost entirely with mothers, fathers also play decisive roles in generating the complex that goes with it, in particular the hag variation. If the mother acts in an omnipresent, negative way, the father is exactly the opposite in this archetypal realm: he is positively omniabsent. Often, in the actual lives of women afflicted by a witch complex, their fathers stand out as powerful men, with distinct identities, holding effective jobs, often in high places in the world. In every way they seem positive personalities, and their daughters usually view them positively. But they lead their powerful lives at a great distance from their young daughters. Theirs is the distance of unrelatedness to the feminine, of withdrawn feelings, of open scorn for things female, of sexual disconnectedness. The result for the daughter is that what the father represents for her always hangs in the distance, far from comfortable realization and enjoyment. He may be a strong man, but he is weak in relation to the feminine. His child cannot get inside herself what he symbolizes to her, to be lived in her own way in her own life. She is left discontent, unfulfilled, yearning for the power he stands for.

Such a father's omniabsence takes many forms. A typical one results from a daughter looking to find in her father the mothering she lacked in her mother. The father, made to act as mother, must then withdraw from whatever shadowy father role he has been playing. A child is dependent on its mother, or mother-substitute, for containment, holding, mirroring, for tender and adapted affirmation, for reception of her instinctive energies. When frustrated, all that is transferred to the father, whether or not he consciously offers himself as a substitute for the mother. In either case, the child does not grow slowly out of relation to the mother into relation with the father, but shifts to it abruptly, displacing one with the other, with all the characteristics of disjointedness that are so painfully typical of borderline disorders.[17] The child's linkings to either parent are short-circuited; substitution replaces gradual maturation; switching from one parent to the other replaces an enlarging confidence fostered in a facilitating environment provided by both parents. Primary-process, nondirected thinking does not—as it should—undergird a process of conscious, secondary-process, directed thinking. Instead, they rapidly alternate, with the unconscious dominating. Words get hypercathected. Symbolic equations persist at the expense of the construction of symbols. Primitive representations do not differentiate into expressive images to give the child a sense of a rich inner life and the power to express it.

Prematurely transferring to a father the frustrated dependency on a mother condenses the pre-oedipal and oedipal phases of a child's growth. The child's pre-oedipal aggression towards its mother now falls onto the oedipal relation with the father, with severe consequences. A daughter's oral-aggressive conflicts with her mother invade her oedipal longings, desires, and ambitions, blowing up the feared maternal rival into terrifying proportions, and evoking in her savage superego prohibitions against all genital sexuality. As Kernberg points out, such displacement in girls of pregenital aggression toward their mother reinforces masochistic tendencies in their later relations with men.[18] Adult relationships with men do not work out easily or well for them. Either they put up with far too much negativity in their partners, or they simply never get a partner at all. Deep down, they feel they simply have no right to a male lover: "It just isn't my fate," they say, or, "There must be something wrong with me."

An attractive and successful young woman illustrates this problem and its murky underpinnings. Though she had risen to a vice-presidential position in her business, and enjoyed good friends and a fullness of literary and charitable activities, she constantly bemoaned her failure to make a durable, loving relationship with a man. It was puzzling. She was endowed with good looks, kindness, and the zest to be an appealing mate to a variety of men. What came clear on inspection was an accompanying conviction that she was "too much" for men, that she really could not have a man of her own because it would make her feel too guilty before her mother, who seemed to her to have had so much less from life than she did. The roots of this conviction grew deep and strong. Her own childhood was marked by great negativity from her mother, who insisted not only on rigid control of her daughter's actions, but of her thoughts as well. Her mother's despotic behavior resulted in flaming fights with her husband, who frequently absented himself from the family on business trips. Nonetheless, he, the father, tried to act the good mother to his daughter, always kind and supportive. Glad as the daughter was for this warm feeling, it left her feeling she had stolen her father from her mother, and therefore she could not once again steal him away through his surrogates, the men who promised to be her happy sexual partners. Her mother had nothing—no real husband, no sexual partner, no good motherly relation to her daughter.

This daughter got her mother in her father, thus stealing her mother's maternal function away from her. Could she also then get her father as a sexual object? No, for then she would lose the only mother she had ever had—in him—and leave her mother utterly bereft, while she, the daughter, would have everything. Having everything led to the strong conviction in her that she was simply "too much" for men—a typical hag fear. Besides her many gifts and her passion for life, the unconscious meaning of "too much" meant not only greedily getting everything at the expense of her mother, who withheld everything, but also the terrible fear that *au fond* she was just like her mother. While growing up, she thought of her mother as witchy because of the countless scenes of destruction that took place nightly at the dinner table—her arguing and then slamming off to her room, her constant attitude of critical attack, and her insatiable appetite for getting things just so, so that nothing the daughter did was ever enough. But the daughter feared she too was a witch—full of bile, ill-will, and repressed rage at her mother. If a man ever got really close to her, really came to know her, the witch in her would leap out. Not having a man in her life served a double purpose: to keep her from the guilt of impoverishing her mother still more, and from exposing the witch that lurked within herself. What men she did link up with sexually usually belonged to someone else. The condensation of oedipal and pre-oedipal stages into one stage played itself out in sex as theft, sex as abandonment of mother, sex as grasped only from a distance, sex with no permanent relationship, in order to keep the inner witch locked up and secret.

Feeling herself to be secretly harboring a witch, an adult woman tends to project too much of the good outside herself, idealizing the object of love as a defense against her unworked-through, primitive rage. The rage must sooner or later break through, either in a rapid breakdown of the idealization into its opposite or in a continuous shifting back and forth between idealized and persecutory images both of the love object and the self. A woman might, for instance, get a crush on a man, and when the relationship fails to bloom, fall victim to self-attacking doubt and repudiation. One woman in her fifties, for example, found a man whose nurturing love, like the qualities of a good mother, made her feel, for the first time in her life, loved and cherished for her own unique self. But she also suffered attacks of life-threatening rage toward the same man when he took on for her the withholding qualities of her earliest experiences with her mother. She felt not only angry and hurt, but also threatened with what looked like a life-and-death struggle. The fury she suffered took on true hag proportions, exploding with passion in dramatic scenes that accurately expressed her distress, but also exhausted her lover and herself.

The specific hag component of such attacks of rage is worth pausing over, for every borderline personality that is given to explosive anger is not necessarily also caught up in a hag complex. The reverse is more likely to be true: those who suffer a hag complex are likely to show borderline features in their personalities. Hag rage shows fascinating mixtures of the merely awful and of the profoundly truthful. A woman caught in such a state would turn her lover into a toad or worse if she could, so great is her outrage at his refusal to join her in her way of seeing things, so huge is her desolation at the gap between them. But she also perceives essential truths about him, and somewhere he knows this and knows it to be true. That accounts in large part for his not just quitting the scene forever, glad to be rid of her, when she explodes. She is not just a mistress of melodrama. She is also a seer who might point the way for him to move his own capacity-to-be into a larger terrain, released from his own narrow, stereotyped vision. Sometimes he is in thrall to a negative wife-mother, tied to her by chains of guilt and cowardice. As he rescues the hag woman from her own negative mothering, she in turn may rescue him. The problem they share is that neither of them is housing the hag dynamism, and so it is driven to exhibit itself in a disruptive way. Its positive force in the woman, however, is what holds the man to her, that germ of uncanny insight into his true self and into the true nature of what matters in life. She holds a tight line to it and remains fiercely loyal to it. Through her he sees the promise of finding a way to the self.

There are many ways, then, of losing a father in the maelstrom of the mothering function, and many consequences of the resultant flowing together of oedipal and pre-oedipal strivings. The mother and father images condense into one set, an apparent unity that is not really one at all, but only a gathering of partial aspects of both parents and a child's relations to the two.[19] In addition, the child's unworked-through and now outsized love and rage toward both parents succeed each other in rapid alternation, so that from the very beginning the relation of woman to man never stabilizes, never rests. Frenzy lurks constantly at the edges; agitation is ready to explode at any moment. Neither the object nor the self feels reliable, for each must constantly prove itself. From the man's point of view, witchy elements infuse such a woman, threatening to suck out all his energies. She exudes a hag intensity which, as one man put it, "exhausts me—she just sets too many tests for me to pass. Who needs it?" The woman's combination of childlike vulnerability to the slightest hurt, with primitive attacking rage when that hurt occurs, makes relationship very risky, both for her and her partner. For each, it is like trying to find the other in a mine field.

Another biting experience of the mother-in-the-father is that of a grown-up woman who eagerly marries a motherly male, and then comes to hold him in contempt as a negligible wimp. She now scorns the very virtue which drew her to him. She has found a home in him, with much needed warm support for herself. But she has not found a home for her aggression, which eventually must break out in ugly raids on his or her self-esteem. In her agony, she often attacks herself as unreasonable and uncharitable toward her mate, finding herself inexplicably hard to satisfy, for she shuns the macho type of man she is berating her husband for failing to be. The unconscious reasons for her attacks of scorn—toward her husband's softness, toward the opposite hard kind of male, and above all toward herself for being caught up in chronic dissatisfaction—crouch beneath her unworked-through aggression. She has lost all connection with the lavish love which drew her into the relationship to begin with. The two feelings—of lavish love and of aggression—alternate as idealization and negativity. Her intense sensitivity and vulnerability, fluctuating between love and hate, make her feel only tentatively alive. She cannot find any housing in her marriage for her aggressiveness and power. They stay with her in a primitive form of rage, but neither she nor her mate can house it as attack or as defense. For he is a mother, not a man to her, a mother who in serene moments nourishes her, then in anger withholds his nurture. The jousting, wrestling, building thrusts of her once-glowing aggression fall outside the relationship. All she can do is to project the problem into her mate, who is not unaware of it himself, as she accuses him of not owning his own power, calling him weak, wet, foolish, unalive, unassertive, never able to lay hold of life. She feels too powerful for him, knows herself to be a nag, a bitch, animus-ridden in the most negative sense. Toward herself, she feels a loathing for being so difficult, chronically discontent, poisonously apart.[20]

She finds no place with him to put and to rediscover the masculine. In fact, of course, she married him mainly to find the feminine, but she has found no way now to house the masculine part of her own feminine identity. If she goes after a more masculine male, she usually finds a man altogether out of touch with the feminine, and so the opposite consequence develops—she has nowhere to house the feminine in her, and thus the masculine hag takes over. The parts do not fit. The result is war.

Another origin of this disjunction of parts arises from a father who is absent to his daughter's more aggressive sides. Because he is not in touch with his own feeling, he cannot touch hers. One woman reported that as a girl she simply did not know her father, had no idea at all who he was. He remained a benign background presence. In her late teens she made a conscious decision to try to get to know her father. She set about it systematically, by joining him in his gardening, learning about his kind of job, getting him to talk about his life. It worked. They became close, even loving, but it had all been her doing. It meant laying aside

"[S]he has nowhere to house the feminine in her and thus the masculine hag takes over. The parts do not fit. The result is war." (Francesco Parmigianino)

her own intensity in order softly to reach her father's withdrawn and undeveloped feeling. She became the parent to him. She had to find his terms, articulate them, and then meet him there, in his words, in his life. A mutual exchange that could include disagreements, noisy opinions, spontaneous assertions, and impulsive behavior was not available. Her efforts yielded a warm, close connection to her father, but one which excluded her own fire, her own holding forth, her own crude aggression. All that was laid aside and continued to live mainly outside their relationship, rather than being woven through it and gradually differentiated.

Even a strong father presents problems to his daughter when he is absent to the feminine in himself, for his strength comes from such a distance. The girl can find no way to incorporate it into her female identity. The father represents the spirit, as Jung says, "whose function it is to oppose pure instinctuality. That is his archetypal role, which falls to him regardless of his personal qualities." He exerts influence on his daughter's "mind or spirit . . . by increasing her intellectuality. . . . ," and there the problem arises. Even if he does not exert influence to what Jung calls a "pathological degree," creating in his daughter a kind of "animus possession," his way of receiving his daughter lacks sufficient appreciation of her increasingly womanly ways.[21] The defect follows from his own estrangement from the feminine within himself. He does not work out of his own anima, or hear its counsel in dealing with his daughter. What he will show is strong awareness of her intellectual capabilities, expecting much from them and teaching her to expect much of herself, perhaps too much, thus encouraging his daughter's spiritual and mental development in an unwomanly style. She will then imitate him and learn to relate to him as male to male. His absence from the feminine within himself will foster a similar absence in her. She will then identify with the animus in her, becoming his son, as it were, living at a great distance from her own femininity. Her mother will happily support this scheme, because it reduces the power of the daughter as a rival on the oedipal scene. The daughter is her father's mental companion; all the more reason to keep her from becoming his sexual one. She does develop her mental and spiritual gifts, but they remain unhoused in any recognizably feminine womanly identity.

In some cases, such a father will actively discourage his daughter's sexuality in favor of certain skills, intellectual or otherwise, thus furthering the split between those two sides of her self. Ibsen's Hedda Gabler is a brilliant example of the split. She relies on her seductive siren side to lure men, but once she has them—new husband, old lover, hopeful wooer—she can do nothing with them. They cannot provide her with the military coolness, the masculine domination which she possesses far more than they do. They cannot even die with the virile elegance that she seeks, and so she must at last demonstrate what she means by taking her own life with one of the pistols of her late father, General Gabler.[22]

In extreme forms, such a father may scorn the very intellectual and spiritual development he is promoting in his daughter, ridiculing her attempts at eloquence, treating with sarcasm her fledgling attempts at serious analysis of ideas, blighting the feeling she brings to her intellectual flights. To protect her feeling, she may cling to what she sees as "rationality," "objectivity," or "logic," severing them from the felt impact of what she thinks, from the longings of her spirit, from the intuitive connections she senses between what she thinks and how she lives. Her father's own distance from the feminine and its values within himself infects his daughter's style of using her mind and spirit, setting the example of an autonomous intellectual-spiritual power, disembodied, unembedded in the flesh of ordinary events and felt values.

Men who have persecuted women, whether in the past as witches or in the present through less open discrimination, show in striking degree this absence of feeling for the feminine. They abstract it; they know no concrete experience of it; they do not meet their daughters or wives as persons. These most intimate companions in their lives are not persons, not women really, but types. Their socializing and psychological failure is to generalize the female wherever they meet it as a type which quickly becomes a stereotype, for these men lack all access to the archetypes that could act as resources against stereotyping. Here absence takes on an active presence in a persecutory form: these men work hard at keeping the female absent from their world.

The result, for the daughter of such a father, is a severe case of an animus split into warring factions.[23] One part, the masculine, is exaggerated quite out of focus, while the female identity that should house it dwindles. Instead of one being carried within the other, at the service of the other, the parts fall into competition. The father gives his daughter a model for splitting her identity, for devaluing her femininity, instead of allowing her to appreciate it herself, to feel it appreciated by the male.

This sad result can come about even from a more positive interaction between a daughter and her father, in which the latter's energetic masculinity, divorced from its contrasexual connections, assures hagdom for the former. A father's archetypal role as procreator may make him for his daughter a person who gets things done, who has work that powerfully absorbs his energies as he creates something in the world. She sees him then as a person who belongs, who has a place in the big scheme of things, and contributes in significant ways to a life beyond himself. He acts as a model for her own outlets of energy and spiritual power, but a male model, not one housed in femaleness. So even great success may breed disjointedness. She may grow up with the unconscious conviction that success in the world will cost her her life as a woman or vice versa. No picture exists of how they can exist together harmoniously, in a successful woman who is unmistakably feminine, in a thoroughly feminine woman who can strive for a place in the world without sacrificing her femininity, a Rebecca West, a Mary Cassatt, a Selma Lagerlöf.

If a mother works, her daughter often sees her wrestling with the tasks of combining work and family, children with creative products of an abstract nature.

Such a life presents a picture of mess, of few clean lines, of little elegance. The tug of war between conflicting duties—the crisis that can instantaneously blow up if the school bus is late, or if sudden illness descends on the child, which means being late to work and on all through the day until the mother drops into bed at night exhausted—shows the struggles of embeddedness. A father's distance, either literal or figurative, from these daily chores can seem attractive to his daughter, can show him shining, more focused, not split-off, handsomely simple instead of full of the strife of competing demands. But the father of the future hag achieves this elegance at the cost of being out of touch with the feminine, putting it at a distance. Hence he hands his daughter bogus material upon which to model her life.

One must add to this the general cultural depreciation of the feminine as a valid mode of symbolizing human experience in both sexes. The hag daughter will look in vain for support to bring her own masculine and feminine parts together. She is either handed the old-fashioned models—"Be a real woman; forget all that masculine stuff; get married; devote your energies to your family"—or she is confronted with the more recent stereotypes of militant feminism or androgyny. The new feminist stereotyping in its extreme form seems to be the opposite of the old one with its stern injunction to shun men entirely and eschew all traditional female roles and values: "Liberate your consciousness. Achieve and assert. Go after your own fulfillment and do not be stopped by all those false claims of the feminine." Androgyny, in its turn, recommends a neither-nor sexuality, to send one beyond male and female categories to personhood. All these commands and enjoinings ignore the essential task for women of coming to terms with their actual bodies. All reduce cultural conditioning to a pitifully narrow reading of gender identity. They bring back, however covertly, the despotic conditioning of the world of the substitute-mother, in which the father is a false female or an exaggerated male in his surrogate role. The substitution of cause or group for mother is simply another version of a paternal maternity, and it has exactly the same effect on women as the old model—they are deeply estranged from their femininity.[24]

In witch trials, the insanity of the male inquisitors raises this estrangement from the feminine to psychotic proportions. Such persons' projective identifications onto women assume delusional power. Their own disowned feminine parts are thrust upon and identified with women. They are flooded with primitive sadistic and sexual fantasies that they repudiate in themselves and fix upon actual women through projection. They identify those fantasies totally with the women on trial, seeing the women as their absolute authors. We see here the social consequences of being fixated at the level of symbolic equations: these women really were a dangerous, demonic feminine force to their prosecutors. They did not stand for that force or represent it or symbolize it; they were the force, fully equated with it. Therefore, to vanquish the evil that the force represented, those actual female persons had to be destroyed. Flooding into this criminally narrow fixed equation are the undifferentiated unconscious levels of infantile fantasies and sexual and aggressive drives. The infantile fantasies—of burning, crushing, chopping up into pieces—are now actually lived out with real victims. A terrible gap exists between the civilized accomplishments of such men and their ancient grounding in their own feminine earth. When we are offended by the violence of women's anger and want to protest against its excesses, we should remember that it is women who fall into this gap, women who are the victims of men's failure to develop relationship to the feminine within themselves.

VI The Hag Complex: Suffering

Undischarged Excitement and Unlived Life

A hag's power to make someone or something disappear is reflected again and again in women's experiences when they are caught in the hag complex. Suddenly, inexplicably, a woman is absent instead of present. Without warning, she falls apart, she fails to cohere and hold herself in being. She is no longer able to contain her own feelings. One woman described it as positive feelings of "energetic joy that built up and up until I couldn't stand it. There was nowhere to put them, no way to live them. They just dissolved. I lost them. I went out of existence."

A woman dealing with the hag archetype is faced with an ego that cannot house the instinctual energies that belong to her. As a child, she did not know a reliable mother, one who held onto her and saw her needs while she was still dependent and her ego was forming. She could not introject and identify with the image that such a mother might have provided; she could not adapt to and respond to her own instinctive experiences. Instead, she will in most cases have taken in and identified with the reverse image, that of a mother who disappears, falls apart, leaves; a mother who never saw who she was, but rather forced a personality upon her, one that the mother wanted for herself or needed her daughter to become. As an adult, the hag-woman's ego functions in the same way toward her own psychic experience. She does not receive the spontaneous communication of her instincts that might connect her to the life she lives in her own body. Instead, she experiences such a signal as a threat to her stability and self-esteem, or as a judgment of her self-management. So, as with the woman described above, even intense joy leaves her feeling inadequate, because she does not see how she can handle it, hold it, allow herself to feel it. The ego-house is too small, too shaky to accommodate her instincts. There is no easy way to live them. Instead, the instincts amass an undischarged excitement that has nowhere to go, that in the end consumes her.

In *Ivanov*, Chekhov describes a similar plight in his first major dramatic figure's despair at being "overexcited" to the point where he has lost all inspiration and feeling.[1] Freud says that in an anxiety attack, we flee our libido as if it were external to us, not ours at all.[2] Winnicott describes the greatly dependent state of early infancy, where id events are experienced at first by the infant as external to the ego, as outside happenings, alien and nonpersonal, as he puts it, like a "thunder-clap." His simile suggests the frightening sound that heralds the approach of

107

an entirely new epoch, as, for example, Joyce seats it in the collective unconscious in *Finnegan's Wake*, with his hundred-letter crescendo of thunder.[3] In
good health, these experiences of instinctual excitement are gathered into the
ego's domain and experienced as "ego strengtheners." Gradually, the infant can
link up body events to a growing sense of person. But for the woman caught up
in a hag-complex, such instinctive experiences remain frightening thunder claps,
assaulting her from the outside, not connecting her to her own vital energy, but
bombarding her with threats of separation. The attack creates great anxiety. Under its mounting pressure, it is as if the ego cannot hold; it has not grown sturdy
enough to house in potential form what could later develop into a rich actualization. No channels for the energy exist, and so the ego floods with its distress and
feels unable to do anything; it is simply stunned—or worse, paralyzed—as if
caught in a witch's spell.

Lacking an ego-space in which to sort out what is happening, such a person
makes frantic efforts at self-protection and survival. She severs all connections to
get away from the invading instinctive energies, reliving ancient terrors, trying to
lift the drawbridge to flee to the depths of the forest, to hide in the bottom-most
parts of the sea. Here the borderline features of the hag-complex are most evident. Instead of housing the instincts, the woman, as she breaks connections,
splits everything apart in the most extreme ways. She is the person that Kernberg
writes about, who "cuts off emotional links between what otherwise would be
chaotic, contradictory, highly frustrating and frightening emotional experiences
with significant others in his [or her] immediate environment."[4] She is at war
with herself, and everything about her shows it. One can see it in her face, in her
movements, as that brilliant hag-woman of the modern dance, Mary Wigman, so
often demonstrated in her performances. In her *Face of Night*, for example, part
of a 1929 cycle called *Shifting Landscape*, she dealt with her reactions to a visit to
a German soldiers' cemetery in the Vosges mountains in France, a "place of invio-
lable silence and limitless forlornness." The effect on the living woman is "the
ghastly terror of ultimate aloneness." One sees it in the pictures of the dance in
her book *The Language of the Dance*, not only in *Face of Night*, but in many
other works—the sharp contortions of her body, shrouded in black, partly covered, partly exposed; the bleak image, hands upthrust, eyes widened in horror;
the war of opposing emotions, face open, face masked. She speaks, as in her
Song of Fate, for the woman of frightening affect, the person who, no matter
what her ultimate destiny, must for some of the time feel "an unbearable tension"
in her "entire being."[5]

The person we are talking about is set adrift, is left in limbo. As one woman
put it, "After all my hard effort, no progress, back to square one. . . . Everything I
try to do is thwarted. I'm frustrated. I'm left out. I cannot connect. I cannot share.
I cannot know. I am not living at all. I must find my life!" With startling similarity
to an ancient image of a witch with fiery red eyes, this woman says to herself,
"The energy that burns through my eyes is love. Love of life? Love of self? But

where can this love go? No channels. Can't let go. It's my life, the life I want. It is a primal urge. I'm the victim of this fire. I'm the sacrificial pig on the spit. . . . There is no life for me. . . . I burn with envy and fear."

Inside the woman everything falls apart. The meeting and uniting of good and evil splits into opposites once again. Just as the mother image of early childhood split into radical opposing elements, so now the good achieves an idealized fairy-godmother perfection, too perfect to survive experience, and the bad looms as an impossibly negative witch, too evil to be endured. Life amounts to nothing but struggle. The instincts toward life and their opposing destructive forces split apart, leaving the ego no secure footing. Under the slightest stress, everything will slip away.

The witch's spell again sounds the persistent theme of reversal. The ego cannot master the instincts. It is exactly the other way around: the animal overruns the human; the princess is transmogrified into a frog or bear or goat; water dries up or floods; the civilized world regresses to the bestial; conscious and unconscious divide; action disintegrates into a chaos of conflicting instinctual demands. In such an experience, one's ego feels assaulted by one's every instinctual reaction, rather than filled by it. Hence one feels simultaneously stuffed and starved, besieged and bereft, bombarded by instinctive reactions one cannot manage, and then left hungry for any kind of nourishment that will make one feel alive, in possession of being. One lives in a perpetual frenzy. For example, one woman found herself in the grip of eating attacks that she altogether disapproved of but could not disavow. Her feeling of being out of control regarding what kind of food she would put into her mouth and the amount of it terrified her. The attacks came punctually every afternoon, when after a full day's work in a demanding profession she fetched her children from the school bus, gave them their snacks, helped them with their homework, and finally put dinner before them, at which point she had to go out again to her job's evening meetings. The witch lurked in those hours. She felt that everyone was receiving some mothering and time off—everyone but herself. Her feelings of rage alarmed her, and she ate voraciously to squash them. Her feelings of need were bottomless. She had to eat madly to fill them up. But all that aggressive energy turned against her in the form of resentment of her properly fed children and in self-loathing as she contemplated her burgeoning weight. Yet all that need remained unsatisfied, buried beneath all the poundage, the opposite physically of the ever-stringy figure of the witch who never got fed, but psychologically identical with its thinness.[6]

Eating attacks are just one example of the way instincts may bombard a hagwoman's ego. Some women deny themselves the experience of sexual orgasm because of its "disintegrating" impact on the ego, as one woman put it. Others feel charged with energy to a manic intensity, and just as suddenly suffer its complete loss, leaving them overcome by inertia. Some women can sleep for hours without ever gaining refreshment, attacked by the need to sleep, only to awake to feelings of depletion and humiliation. As all the examples show, a particular suffering of the hag complex is that instinctive impulses do not get housed, sorted through, and channeled by the ego. Rather, they reverse and back up in the woman's psyche. They live alongside the ego, like an impregnable armor, or invade and desert the ego like tumbling waters that rush in and rush out. The woman feels she must always cope with, regulate, react to, or just suffer her impulses. The physical and psychical tension that result can make a woman a candidate for serious illness—high blood pressure, chronic constipation, tense muscles, colitis, coronary attacks.

The undischarged excitement that produces a chronic tension of the body that can find no release leaves a woman unable to rest in a truly restorative way. Alternating rhythms of rest and instinctual excitement, release, and rest, fail to establish themselves. Instead, disjointed tempos establish a side-by-side existence. One woman's pattern was to work compulsively, with mounting excitement and exhaustion, for half a year, and then to fall ill and take to her bed for the other half. She suffered her opposite rhythms, endlessly stuck together, rather than looking to see them mutually benefitting each other, easing the pace of work and combatting the long bouts of illness. Another woman suffered what she called periods of "careening," where she felt her sexual energies to be out of control. This could suddenly switch into its opposite state, what she called "juicelessness." The sexual feelings did not feed her ego, but just took it over or left it empty and dry. The inner space that a resting ego finds, where a person is not doing anything for specific results, but rather sheds everything but a generalized purposiveness to simply wander happily, is just what a woman caught in a hag complex lacks. That accounts for a lot of her agitation, her sense of always having to struggle—with herself, with her unconscious, with everything and everyone.

The disjointed tempo afflicts the hag-woman's psyche on all sides. She shares with the clown the experience of constant bombardment by strong physical sensations, from within and without, and a sense of chronic vulnerability to them. She deals with her plight differently from the clown. Where he tries to patch the bits into the appearance of a whole functioning ego in a unified, coherent world, a witch's rhythm is jerky, slapping opposites any which way onto each other. For example, a hag-woman suffers acutely the hunger for a sense of meaning and lived connection to the depth of things. Despite the melodramatic trappings, her hunger is real. One woman complained of an empty void within herself, a "nothing-place" where no feeling could grow, no thought take root. Yet she would gulp whole the ideas of someone else, anyone she could hold up to herself as an "authority." She never chewed over these ideas, never digested them. She swallowed them like great hard chunks of food, that inevitably would then drag her down from the inside, in a weighty indigestion, instead of feeding her.

Thus there develops an inner emptiness, built around an idealized object or person.[7] Idea or person, the idealized object is magnified out of all proportion as the answer to a great hunger of soul. This psychical transaction may coincide with a powerful projection of a woman's animus onto a man. She endows him with the power to connect her to her deepest self, thereby not only bringing her truly to life, but also anchoring her in an ego-transcending world. Such a projection leaves a woman a sitting duck for a man's manipulations. She is easily seducible, often betrayed, or as one woman put it, "delivered into Hades." More often than not, the man's betrayal is unwitting, or at least not fully intentional, for he has no inkling of the power the woman has put into his hands. She has delivered herself to him to mediate her own ego-self connection, a function that her own animus would ordinarily perform.

A woman caught up in the opposite strains of yawning voids and gulped-down solutions finds herself compelled to look for global answers, always to her distress. Every problem must be fully solved; a partial solution amounts to nothing. Analysis proves particularly frustrating to this attitude. Under its sway, one woman found her analytic sessions vexing, then enraging. Regardless of the work accomplished in any given hour, it always failed to produce the looked-for "final" answer for all her conflicts, all her hopes. For a period of time she came to hate her analysis and her analyst, too. She returned each time, as she described her feelings, "with mounting excitement, expecting something that was never given," and went away furiously disappointed, feeling "bitter, cheated, betrayed." Unused power dissolved into power struggles between controlling and being controlled. In the dashing of her hopes and in her fury, this woman ineluctably would undo the constructive connections made in the sessions, dismiss insights she had reached, reject the nurturant links to the analyst that she had earlier felt.

The witch is known, as we have noted, for her stringy figure and voracious appetite. She shows the ravaging effects of the lack of an interceding ego to mediate between her deep hunger and what is offered to feed it. She is a picture of primitive, oral gulping, a receptivity as yet undifferentiated from aggression. Desires to receive and actively take things in mix with aggressive fantasies of robbing, gobbling, annihilating the object of her hunger. As yet no ego-ability exists to take nourishment from the experiences offered, either from within, from her own instincts and images, or from without, through other people. So she is immersed in her hungry rage, driving anyone away who might want to give anything to her, for no matter what is given it is never enough and as a result she will never appear grateful. One woman describes the pain of such experience. "I want to feed on this book I'm reading and I can't. As I was eating dinner I became most upset. A picture of this group I belong to came to mind, and I hated them. They sit there, mute and unresponsive, uncaring, unrelated, never aware of my pain. I want to scream at them and tell them I am there. Why don't they see me, understand my pain! But then as I raged at them I realized I was raging at everything in my life—my longing to be out of this life because it is all a joke. . . . I cannot reach people and they seem unable to reach me. I can love them in the abstract, but individually I dislike them. I try to give and am rejected. . . . There is no way, no form for my energy, so I might as well not have it."

A last effect of the witch reversal, a fitting addition to her undischarged excitement, splitting, and inability to rest, is a predatory, if unearned guilt. Such fury as just described—where a woman in effect tears to bits her own good resources and makes nothing of her own hard work in an analytical session, undoing any effort on the part of others to reach her—almost inevitably stirs up guilt. The woman feels the effect of so much destructive aggression. But the hungry and underfed ego cannot contain this guilt any more than it can contain instinctual excitement. Hence the guilt is felt as an extreme assault on the ego, an attack from an external agent who intends to make the ego feel as bad as possible. Melanie Klein sums this up very well: "If premature guilt is experienced by an ego not yet capable of bearing it, guilt is felt as persecution and the object that rouses guilt is turned into a persecutor."[8]

Such guilt goes all the way back to early relations with the mother. A mother who turns away from her child—whether from indifference, malice, or mental or physical illness, or from too many other stresses in her life, such as the illness of another child or her husband, the unceasing strain of poverty, or unremitting hard work—fails to mediate to her child the size of the child's own existence and the reality of the outside world. Where a child should see its own face reflected, encouraging the growth of its own ego, it sees instead nothing. It confronts unbroken gaps, holes, empty spaces with no one looking back, no one showing recognition, an awful void. It is this empty nothingness that the child introjects as a central part of its personality structure. As a result, the ego cannot achieve a proper balance or foundation for itself. Rather it is like a floor with a hole in the center that reaches down into a black emptiness stretching endlessly beneath the ego-structure. The child's dependency needs, which normally would find an outlet in a trusted mother who is symbolic of the child's own secure possibilities to grow up and be independent, go untended and unchanneled. These are rampant, undirected, clamorous needs that cannot now be satisfied by the mother, and the child comes dimly to perceive this as a grim fact of its existence. But the needs do not as a result go away, and their persistent pressure makes a child feel guilty from two directions. Because the child cannot turn these needs off and thus avoid repeated rejections by the parent, it feels guilty before its mother, as if, with its insistent demands for things the mother cannot deliver, the child itself was the cause of her failure to be a good mother. And yet the child cannot satisfy these needs itself, and so feels guilty now for its failure to satisfy these starving instincts itself.

In such a situation, the only recourse may be to try to build an ego-structure *over* these unsatisfied needs, pushing them under the floorboards, so to speak, into that bottomless hole of existence. Where there should be a sense of one's personal continuity of being, going all the way back to birth, there is instead, when such a child becomes an adult, a gap or series of gaps in its ego-structure. Through the gaps, the archaic unconscious processes that seem so alien, so uncanny to our egos can always rush in.

Just as undischarged excitement leads not to lived but to unlived life, so this sort of premature guilt leads not to remorse and reparation, but to anger and retaliation. The fairy-tale witch is famous for her addiction to vengeance. Rather than softening the heart and arousing impulses to make amends, such guilt—"persecutory guilt," for we feel others fully intend us to suffer—hardens the heart into still more aggressiveness, to defend and protect the faltering ego. We want to pay back, to get even, to really "show" our persecutors.

This is the sort of guilt that infects social and political climates. Political demands for reparation payments, for example, may produce exactly the opposite of what was intended. Instead of repairing a damaged trust between peoples, they may set the stage for gigantic retaliation. Germany's economic depression after World War I, in the face of imposed reparation payments which were experienced as forced humiliation, contributed immeasurably to its readiness to swallow, whole and without digestion, in the manner of a witch's feeding, the compensating fantasy of "master race" that led to the Holocaust and World War II. And so it must be with any affirmation that is built so perilously on negative aggression. Collective ego-structures need as much attentive mothering as individual ones. They need the security that a trustworthy symbolization will provide, certainty of their possibility to grow and become independent. The hag complex can attack a whole civilization deprived of its essential maternal supports, as we have seen so often in this century.

Parody Symbolization

Just as a woman afflicted with a hag complex does not have the ego-capacity to house her body's instincts, so she lacks an ego-container to house her spirit. The budding fantasies and images that accompany instinctive experience, which grow into symbols through the processes of introjection and projection, imaginative reflection and spiritual elaboration, often get stuck here, or short-circuited and fixated in their twisted connections. The witch constantly acts out this psychic melodrama in her repetitive gestures and obsessive incantations, working endless variations on the theme of reversal.

Reversal runs all through a witch's activities. It exerts a lethal effect on a woman's fantasy life and her capacity to form symbols. In fighting symbol-formation, it works against the basic orderings of nature. The natural sequence of an infant's spontaneous gestures, when met by a mother's adaptive responses, gives a child an illusion of effective connection with reality. Wish and reality fit each other. Repeated experience of this fitting together builds a child's confidence in a benevolent and exciting world to be explored in play. What is needed can be found and the child can create it. Play plants the root of symbol-formation.[9] In the reversal so characteristic of the witch experience, the mother fails to see and respond to her child's gestures, and substitutes movements of her own to which the child must adapt. Thus begins the child's false compliance with its mother's gestures rather than with its own. It comes to reject its own fresh discoveries and elaborations of them in fantasy. As a result, a false self is constructed, geared to meet another person's expectations, rather than a true self expressed in honest personal gestures toward the world.[10] There is no experience in such a child of reality corresponding to its personal needs. Instead, reality is felt as alien, quite outside one's self. No symbolic connection can be built to it.

Examples of this poignant reversal and loss of honest, trustworthy symbolization may be found at all ages. The child who learns all too soon to hide personal reactions behind opaque facial expressions, who scans a parent's face to forecast coming moods, has sacrificed personal spontaneity for much needed parental love. The adolescent who looks anxiously at boy- or girlfriend's face, at every twist and turn of the body, to see what he or she is expected to do next, has perpetuated that war against instinctive behavior and unpremeditated honesty of feeling that started in childhood. The child who constantly feels burdened by anxiety over meeting others' expectations in order to win their acceptance knows the cost of such agitation and wildly pitched nervous alertness, knows the great diminution of psychic energies it effects.

The witch-effect in the world of play is a macabre drama, complete with fright-wigs and resonating cackles, that looks like fun and games but is in fact a series of warnings to the psyche. Do not play unless you mean it, the hag-complex tells us. Plan it to the last hop, skip, and laugh. Watch yourself! No enjoyment, unless it has been planned for in all its "carefree" details. We cannot ignore the witch's anti-play ministrations. Even in caricature, as in "Hansel and Gretel," she has the skill to turn us away from spontaneous pleasure. The chilling caution works. What is lost to both child and adult as a result is the very ability to play, either physically, with blocks or trucks or stuffed animals or dolls in a child's case, or with fantasies and images in an adult's case. In either case, play is inhibited because personal spontaneity must be monitored so carefully to meet outer expectations. The effects of this inhibition are many and serious.

One extraordinary effect of the loss of play as a connecting link between fantasy and reality is that fantasy becomes reality. Fantasy no longer stands for something as symbol or sign, nor does it represent the meeting of reality and image. Neither does it enrich a real experience with an imaginative amplification of it. Instead, fantasy simply repeats itself in obsessive compulsive repetition. We lose fantasy as fantasy. Its range of meanings collapses into univocal flatness. Fantasy becomes a literal-minded activity as it comes to substitute itself for reality, trapping us in a repetitive rehearsal of the same sequences of imagery, the same sexual imaginings, for decades, each time buzzing noisily through our awareness like a radio or television commercial.

Images do not mean anything, no matter how often we see them. They do not point to anything, do not lead anywhere; they are just themselves, a closed room of pictures in which we circle round and round as if trapped in a witch's cage. One woman obsessed by the need to "gain power" over her life reviewed her frustrating fantasy life. Constant ruminating about jobs she might get, salaries she might command, did not lead to applying for actual positions, but instead left her feeling more powerless and more impoverished in her pictured projections. There was no exit from fantasy to reality. The images of power excited her, tensed her. Up, up, up she went until, exhausted, she sought relief in unconsciousness through sleep, drink, or pills. Another woman's fantasies would catch her just before a social engagement. With mounting excitement, she would anticipate a party, caught in vaguely defined but stirring images of connecting to others who would be there in a "real way." Hidden in this agitated expectation was all the hope of spontaneous connection of her own real self to others as they really were, in contrast to her pattern of hiding who she was in compliance with what she perceived to be others' expectations. But in reality, as the party convenes, all falls flat. She feels let down. Conversations with others occur, but no real meeting takes place. Reality does not match fantasy. She feels frustrated, disappointed, humiliated. Her fantasy seems exposed now as just that—a childish fantasy, even a stupid one. Reality itself seems hostile and cold, distant from what goes on inside her. Her world falls into two disparate parts marked "inside" and "outside," "I" and "they," revealing to her imaginings that are unrealistic and a reality that is unimaginative.

Another woman compulsively fantasized, while she paced up and down her apartment and smoked, that her boss would propose marriage to her. The boss was nothing like any of the fantasy that she projected onto him. He could offer her no hope for a different way of life. The boss was the boss was the boss, no more than that, and possibly less. The boss of fantasy was not the man she really worked for. The layers of fantasy fixation almost completely obscured the actual man. Thus she lost both fantasy and reality, and suffered double impoverishment. The fantasy man who might have personified parts of herself seeking to connect to her consciousness was not accessible to her, nor was the real person with whom she had an actual working relationship.

When fantasy becomes a fixity, substituting itself for reality, we may lose both fantasy and reality. We live reality as if it were a chapter in our fantasy. Acting out the same plot with successive sexual partners, rehearsing with our children the conflicts we suffered with our parents, feeling ineluctably drawn into the same deadening conclusions regardless of where we began our reasoning, our reality shrinks to the constricting dimensions of our trapped fantasies. We become "guilty creatures at a play," as Bernard Shaw described Ibsen's audience, but the play is our own, and the lines we are condemned to repeat over and over again do not provide the heightening effect of a great playwright's eloquence.

Ibsen's Mrs. Alving is a poignant example of fixation in fantasy, made bearable for us by a splendid set of lines. Her play is *Ghosts*, and everything about her life has the quality of obsession with the phantasms of her past. Her marriage with her late husband, Captain Alving, was a series of fantasies covering up his gross infidelities—sexual, economic, human. She has all but exiled her son Oswald from her home to keep him from being infected by what she sees as her husband's communicable moral disease, but she continues to play out her fantasies after his death. She uses Alving's considerable fortune to build an orphan asylum which is destined to keep his reputation clear, if not holy. Fixed in her fantasy, she believes that somehow she can make all things right again. But the venereal disease, which Ibsen's and the late nineteenth century's defective biology diagnosed as inevitably inherited from the father, remains alive in the son. Perhaps even more seriously afflicted with the knowledge of his father's true character than with the syphilitic strain, the son begins to duplicate his father's behavior. He attempts a sexual relationship with a house servant, who is in fact his bastard half-sister, and he finally brings himself to tell his mother that he is being ravaged by his father's disease. He pleads with his mother to poison him, to free him from his compulsive condition. "Never to be able to work again! To be dead, yet alive! Can you imagine anything more horrible?"[11]

It is Mrs. Alving who is most fully described by her son's words, not Oswald. She is, as Michael Meyer has suggested, "not unlike a portrait of what Nora [in *A Doll's House*] might have become had she decided to stay with her husband and children. . . ." She is not, however, simply a woman "strangled by convention and a misplaced sense of duty," as Meyer says, however strong these elements may be in such a person's motivation for life.[12] She is that stunning summation of flatness in the life of a woman of undischarged energies that a first-rate dramatist can provide. She has lived through a series of anxieties over meeting the expectations of others, which have obliterated her own expectations, whatever they once might have been. All she cares about is to follow her hag complex where it leads, to have a plan for everything, and thus at least to make things seem right. She is the willing collaborator in endless deceits—her husband's when alive, her husband's when dead, and perhaps most tellingly those of the churchman she really loves, Pastor Manders. Like so many of these women who are determined to exert some unmistakable power over their own lives, even if only in a monstrous deceit, she is locked forever in impotence. Her response to her son's cry for help at the end of the play is no response. Her helplessness is real enough at that point. Who would poison her own son? But on the other hand, what else has she to offer? The tableau of mother and son that provides the curtain for *Ghosts* is the symbolic enactment of death in life, the polluted blood still flowing—just barely. Stasis. Stop.

Ibsen's play was attacked on its publication in 1881 as "a repulsive pathological phenomenon," for which "complete silence would . . . be the most fitting reception." A Norwegian poet described Ibsen as the bearer of "an evil stench of corruption." The play's supporters declared it to be "the noblest deed in [Ibsen's] literary career," and even more, "the greatest work of art which he, or indeed our whole dramatic literature, has produced." And yet a century later, *Ghosts* seems dated to many. It is not much produced. It no longer has the allure it once had for actresses like Alla Nazimova, who found in Mrs. Alving a vehicle to carry them well into their late years. Because it was condemned and praised in terms that reduced that centerpiece, Mrs. Alving, to a small-scale revelation of the victimizing power of convention, it never quite made its enduring point about the ulcerative—or, if one prefers, syphilitic—power of undischarged psychic energies. But the point remains. It is piercing in this play because it is at the center of events, a fixation not of any of the characters but of Ibsen's. His dramas have too often been seen as works crusading for social reform, or perhaps more subtly, as attacks on the simplifications and tyrannies of the reformers, but have not often enough been examined for the dilemmas of the psyche that they represent. The later Ibsen has a whole gallery of women related to Mrs. Alving—Gina Ekdal in *The Wild Duck*, Rebecca West in *Rosmersholm*, Ellida in *The Lady from the Sea*, the extraordinary old sisters who contend almost beyond life for the title character in *John Gabriel Borkman*, the other-worldly sculptor's model, Irene, on whose discharge of energies Ibsen's last play, *When We Dead Awaken*, depends for its compelling power. With whatever degree of consciousness, Ibsen had found his way to the center of conflict in the women around him—young, middle-aged, old—and had discovered a series of plots with which to dramatize the deadness to which so many of them had surrendered. And in that splendidly paradoxical way of art, that deadness brought—and still brings—a continuing life to his plays.[13]

In this sort of drama, which Ibsen did not contribute to life but lifted from it, we act out our fantasies in place of reality, and lose reality as a consequence. No surprises, only repeated blows. We come increasingly to experience ourselves as victims. The same bad record spins in our damaged psyches over and over again, and we are powerless to change it. The serious consequences of such fantasy fixation for society are writ large in the deranged dramas of both conscious and unconscious terrorists. We see it in the barbaric behavior of hostage-takers smashing a helpless serviceman's face, breaking his bones, throwing his body out of a plane. We see it in the sniper in a Texas tower shooting innocent people below who have utterly lost their own discrete realities in the sniper's eyes. All these victims are stand-ins for fantasy persecutors who must be destroyed. The unhoused fantasy bursts out into paranoia. Under the assault of the fantasy, the hag-woman, like Mrs. Alving, becomes its accomplice—and its scapegoat. She conspires with anyone who is available, such as Oswald Alving, to keep the fantasy alive. And then she herself becomes its most obvious victim, as all her hag-life she has been promising to do. No one is a better candidate for persecution than a hag. She is a model victim.

It is the primordial drama. On the one hand, we lose touch with reality when caught in a fixating fantasy. On the other, the spontaneous images arising from the unconscious have nowhere to go. As a result, fantasy stays at primitive levels and regresses to more archaic forms.[14] Images from the deeper collective layer of the unconscious are mobilized without benefit of modification by contact with reality. Nothing checks the fantasy or helps to personalize it. It gets more and more fantastic and fearsome. We feel we are sitting on a time bomb. Some

"Here we find the worst images of the hag — the one who remorselessly plots the utter destruction of human kindness . . . who does not hesitate for a moment to make the human form hideous if she is defied." (Dürer)

terrible force will come crashing through to swamp our fragile consciousness. This threat only makes us cling more tightly to the fixating fantasy; its rigidity must stave off a mounting flood of unconscious material. Needless to say, our tension only increases with this course of action. When it reaches an unbearable pitch, something must happen to break it. That is our ironic comfort: It must break, for archaic images at a great distance from personal experience have no clear place to go, and our more and more meager and deadening personal experience has created a situation for us where there is no container to house the archetypal imagery that must sooner or later burst forth in its most primitive forms. Here we find the worst images of the hag—the one who remorselessly plots the utter destruction of human kindness, vowing to make our hearts dry up to a mere seed, who laughs insanely when human values are crushed, who does not hesitate for a moment to make the human form hideous if she is defied. Here is the real destruction of the human heart, which all those transmutations of princes and princesses into frogs and ravens and boars signify.

However, the worst effect of all of the witch's reversal of life energies is the blighting of the human capacity for symbol-formation and for the enlarging transformation of the imagination, for which it stands. A child's play, which releases instinctive energy and elaborates fantasies about making connections with the world, naturally leads to the development of symbols. A child's first beloved toy possesses all the power and presence of a totem animal. This "transitional object," to use Winnicott's memorable term for it, acts as the first symbolic bridge between the child's self and the world, which at this point is still represented primarily by its mother.[15] For a child, a favorite bear is both created out of imagination and yet found there already, firmly existing in its world. The bear effects transition between child and reality, between hallucination and external object, between self and mother. A favorite animal fills the gap created as the child gradually differentiates itself from mother and from the unconscious to find its own independent ego-identity. Into that widening space within, a child puts play and the creations of fantasy that come to stand for the child's experience of the unity of self and other. What in illness forms a gap, a threatening dissociation of self and world, in health effects a widening out of self-in-relation-to-world, which quickly gets filled with richly elaborated toys, tunes, and ritual actions, imaginative communications that express felt connections between self and reality.

In the inner space of the child, symbols grow. These symbols enable a new self to develop to achieve that precious sense of being alive as a person in the world. Winnicott holds that in adults, this enabling space is filled with culture, art, and religion. Here we find an engaging paradox. We bring the world alive for ourselves with the meaning that we put into it, and then we discover that meaning there already, waiting for us to find it. This is Karl Popper's "third world," populated with Cassirer's "spiritual organs of reality" and Jung's archetypes.[16] Without this world of symbol and sign we do not feel alive and real. It is right there, in that delicate yet necessary space of imaginative activity, that the hag stuns us with her spell. The effect is like that of the poisoned spindle of the crone in "Sleeping Beauty." We are transfixed, held fast in the unconscious. It is then that we lose the freedom of the inner space, where we play around with our impulses and let fantasy be fantasy without the penalty of action, where we can combine and recombine conflicting tendencies and give free reign to hostile impulses. There, when all is well, the body discharges its excitement in a child's destruction of a tower of blocks or sinking of a great naval fleet. There energy is fully lived by an adult who lets himself or herself go by dancing, or running, or working crossword puzzles. There the ego gets a chance to rest from holding together the conscious and unconscious pulls of real responsibility and dream fantasy. There we can relax from the tension we have felt from trying to keep congruent the contrary pulls toward neighbor and self and contradictory impulses to love and to hate.

In this space we rest from all ego-work: We go to the movies; we go window shopping; we sit in the sun; we eat ice cream; we speculate on God's existence. In fantasy, we concoct our revenge on an enemy or focus desires on a friend. We try on new ideas and new hairdos; we exchange our personality for another. We imagine what it might be like to exist as a panda, or an astronaut, or someone of the opposite sex. We take walks in the woods and watch green shoots push through winter leaves or falling snow cover great evergreens. We sit fishing in our lives, delighted when a new image thrusts to the surface. In this fertile soil of wildly different constituents, symbols may grow to combine all the parts—the physical, spiritual, emotional, and mental, the immediate and the distant, belonging to self and reaching far beyond self. In the hag complex, this space is lost to us; no real symbols can grow, only parodies of symbols that falsify transformation. The caricature of freedom that meticulously planned play produces in us carries all before it. As spontaneity, the great enemy of hagdom, is crushed, the imagination withers, nature turns sour, and we can live only at the most terrifying literal level. With the loss of inner space, outer space constricts. There are only surfaces. Nothing exists inside things, and worst of all, we are not even sure anything is alive within us.

A hag cannot get her own fantasies into life, and derives no satisfaction from them. An impregnable barrier is erected between fantasy and reality. She symbolizes the arrest of symbol-making and the way life falls apart as a result. Physical excitement stays merely physical; it is never transformed into spiritual forms. She is arrested at the plane of first objects, and cannot substitute any other objects for them. So it is that a woman, damaged by her mother's failure to provide empathic response, may spend half her life looking for a new mother who will respond properly to her. Though she needs it more than ever, all growth in relationships halts. Her symbols have failed to combine her personal fantasies with what actually exists in the world, so that though she retains her symbols, they are too private, too fantastic, too cut off from others to be shared. She does keep alive something of an inner world, but at the expense of life with others. The hag is known for mooning about her own secret places, hovering over her brewing pots, but she lives so fearfully alone that she is inevitably thought by everyone to be crazy and threatening. So it is with her symbols. They are private to the point of being bizarre, without communal meaning, and, for some, menacing. If her symbols are more rational, they still fail to include that spontaneous physical excitement that makes them seem alive and immediate to her or to others. Her symbols are, in effect, dead or dying, with little quickening power.

All these unhappy possibilities are the results of damage to the symbol-making function. That is why in fairy tales we often see that the way to beat the hag arises out of a prior series of exciting fantasies that galvanize into action the energies of the imagination. Thus Gretel plays—that is the necessary word, plays —with schemes to save Hansel from being eaten by the old witch. Substituting a chicken bone for Hansel's finger, in order to fool the witch into thinking that he still is too scrawny to eat, must precede her bold move to trick the witch into the oven. Gretel is appealing to the hag's greed for a still more plump boy, reaching to the hag's know-it-all, plan-for-all vanity to demonstrate that the stove is in fact big enough to cook the boy. Gretel could not stimulate the witch's aggressive hunger and pride into lustful life without first reaching those energies in herself. Sweetness gets her nowhere; helplessness moves the hag to gleeful laughter. Only the fantasy that feeds action with an aim, that symbolizes a way altogether other than the hag's—a way that is equally intense but far more imaginative—can triumph over the hag in the end.

The severance of fantasy and reality and the failure of the imagination that the hag complex effects also blunts the ego-self connection. Self-energies find no access to reach the ego, because the symbols that might channel those energies get bogged down in symbolic equations.[17] Literalism prevails, whereby *this* actually is *that*, instead of this merely standing for that. What we must see is that the hag herself can be a powerful symbol, one that can aid our psychic growth if we are not caught in identification with her. With her images of destruction, she shows us the nondiscursive elements of suffering that do not yield to explanations. She makes visible the hate that we cannot ourselves express, the knowledge that exerts power, the tension that seeks to be lived. Her isolation and unrelieved agitation, her lack of ability to rest and re-create, her repetitious fantasies that spell the same plot of revenge, power, and frustration again and again—all these portray what it means for an ego to be cut off from a self, to be left stranded in one's own little squirrel cage, with no exit. There we go, round and round, always the same way, without change, held fast, fixated, arrested in our obsessions, defended in our little prison against the large outside world and the even larger collective unconscious, yet totally vulnerable to its impact, and liable to be swept right off our perch at any time.

When the effects of a barrier between ego and self in an individual person make their way into a collective society, the results can be frightening. Whole crowds may succumb to the welling-up of undischarged excitement that afflicts an immature ego. That is the way mobs are formed and brought to act. Witnesses to such action know that "bewitchment" is not a strong enough word to describe the demonic seizure of the crowd. The inner, undischarged tension, with no personal ego to integrate and quiet it, meets us as an outer event, sweeping us up into the rampaging crowd. The fantasy that has been blocked and has regressed to archaic form now moves boldly, unchecked, into the crowd's actions. The most primitive kinds of projected images get activated and circulated. Crude "Us/Them" lines are drawn. Small actions take on tremendous significance that incite a howling, passionate response.

All the guilt that should have been gathered up by a personal ego, but which instead has been felt as inflicted from the outside, as a more intensified form of persecution, now seeks its revenge and surges through the crowd, looking to find a target, a scapegoat who will stand still, concretely, clearly identified, for the conscience that has so mercilessly attacked the mob. In a tempest of emotionality, it is as if a witch's curse has set people aflame with madness. In this experience, we can all become frogs and toads, boars and ravens. Robert Musil gives a breathtaking description of such collective frenzy in volume two of *The Man Without Qualities*. With that splendid irony of which Musil is a master, a scene of spectacular disarray is brought on as a protest against the "continual disorders" of the dying Austro-Hungarian empire just before World War I. The terms of the situation are summed up in an all but unanimous "grave supplementary comment that it was high time for *something* to be done, even though nobody volunteered to state clearly *what*." The event is filtered through one man's, Walter's, sensibility, which in its immaturity and walled-off ego is made to order for the impressions that follow.

> And the further he went in this way, the more often he noticed on the faces into which he glanced a look of something irrational and overbrimming, overflowing the bounds of reason. By now it seemed to have become a matter of general indifference what was happening at the place whither they were all being drawn. The mere fact that something unusual was going on seemed indeed to be enough to work them into a frenzy; and although the term 'frenzy' must be understood only in a weak figurative sense, indicating a very ordinary degree of mild excitement, there was nevertheless something to be felt in it as a more remote kinship with long-forgotten states of ecstasy and transfiguration, as it were a growing unconscious readiness, in all of these people, to jump out of their clothes and indeed out of their skins.

Writing some years before the full-fledged advent of Nazism, Musil shows how an Austrian crowd, moved by anti-German sentiment and its own witchery, turns into the kind of mob that gives holocausts their necessary musculature:

> . . . people felt indignation or fear, pugnacity or the pressure of a moral imperative, and now began to thrust forward in a mood in which they were guided by thoroughly ordinary emotions, which took on different form in each of them but which, in spite of their dominant position in the individual's consciousness, had so little intellectual significance that they combined into one single vital energy,

turning all these people into one single vast body and exerting more influence on the muscles than on the brain.

Walter is caught up in the bewitching movement and is "soon in an over-stimulated, empty state . . . rather like an early stage of drunkenness." What works to change a protest against disorder into such a fine, frenzied example of organized chaos? Probably, says Musil in one of his characteristic essays in the great novel, the crowd's lack of "an outlet for its emotions," and the fact that "those who set the example and lead the way will always be those who are the most excitable, most sensitive and least capable of withstanding pressure. . . ." But they are merely conveyors; "the shout . . . is uttered through them more than . . . by them. . . ." Stones, like words, "somehow" fall into their hands. Emotions burst. The excitement reaches an "unendurable pitch" and a mob-action ensues "which is felt by all to be something that is half compulsion and half liberation."

Musil's wistful conclusion to both the essay and the scene is that "if everything were as it should be where the meaning of life is concerned, then so it would be too with all that is meaningless, senseless, in life; and this negative side would not necessarily be accompanied by symptoms of mental deficiency." That is what interests Musil: not what stands behind the immediate "discharge" of violence, but rather "the whole problem of what causes the readiness to get into such a state at all."[18] Our answer, conjectural though it may be, is that the bewitched world we have been describing, where fantasy has become reality and the imagination has been ripped from its moorings, is deeply involved.

Split-Animus and the Persecution of Women

A woman caught in a hag complex finds her body excitement blunted. She discovers no discharge in the play of fantasy; a spiritual deadening has occurred. Symbols remain mere signs. Sensation substitutes for spiritual perception. Sex is an empty physical affair, with no meeting of souls. The disembodied spirit splits away from any human connection to self or community. Work is a drab expediency, with no sense of vocation to lighten or enlarge it. Wishes and hopes are squashed with flat questions: So what? What good will that do? What difference will it make? The woman feels confined in a witch's cage, left to rot, to be trapped as her captor's slave year after year, not even able to imagine getting free. Rescue must come from outside herself. In such situations the ego's natural connection to the self is thwarted, and we cease to unfold and to grow. The witch stands firm, a barrier between ego and self, blighting, spoiling, cursing, paralyzing.

Just as the ego caught in the hag complex cannot house the instincts nor the fantasies that would grow into symbols and open onto the spiritual life, just so does it split away from the animus. The animus normally functions to mediate contrasexual unconscious content to consciousness, thus bringing the ego to the threshold of the self and making possible a rich unfolding of the person. When she is in the possession of the hag complex, the animus bridge breaks down in even the most apparently self-possessed woman.[19] That self is illusory; the connections that the animus looks to effect simply cannot be made. The unfolding of the person has stopped.

Bernard Shaw makes much of such a ceasing to unfold in his play *Getting Married*. None of the women in that remarkable dramatic discourse on the strengths and weaknesses of marriage has fully discharged her energies—sexual, spiritual, political, whatever. All have a stature that, one way or another, stands over their men, defeats their men, and yet supports their men. But a greater defeat confronts them—their own, at their own hands as well as at their men's. They stand ready to make the great, bridging connection from ego to self—and they themselves, caught in the hag-complex, frustrate it. As Shaw grew older, he was more and more fascinated with older women who have a power bordering on Napoleon's and a sensitivity bordering on Mozart's, but he never in his plays quite runs to earth this confounding, ingratiating, baffled, and baffling kind of woman, the prototype for whom was surely his own mother. However, he does provide us with the ciphers for analysis, especially in his portrait of the lady Mayoress of Chelsea in 1908 London.

> Mrs. George is every inch a Mayoress in point of stylish dressing; and she does it very well indeed. There is nothing quiet about Mrs. George; she is not afraid of colours, and knows how to make the most of them. Not at all a lady in Lesbia's use of the term as a class label, she proclaims herself to the first glance as the triumphant, pampered, wilful, intensely alive woman who has always been rich among poor people. In a historical museum she would explain Edward the Fourth's taste for shopkeeper's wives. Her age, which is certainly 40, and might be 50, is carried off by her vitality, her resilient figure, and her confident marriage. So far, a remarkably well-preserved woman. But her beauty is wrecked, like an ageless landscape ravaged by long and fierce war. Her eyes are alive, arresting, and haunting; and there is still a turn of delicate beauty and pride in her indomitable chin; but her cheeks are wasted and lined, her mouth writhen and piteous. The whole face is a battle-field of the passions, quite deplorable until she speaks, when an alert sense of fun rejuvenates her in a moment, and makes her company irresistible.

Mrs. George herself knows what she has been, what she is, what she might be. When St. John Hotchkiss, the amiable dandy of the drama, pays her court, her first response is encouraging—and honest in its self-appraisal:

> Oh, if you could restore to this wasted exhausted heart one ray of the passion that once welled up at the glance—at the touch of a lover! It's you who would scream then, young man. Do you see this face, once fresh and rosy like your own, now scarred and riven by a hundred burnt-out fires?

She tells Hotchkiss that he may come and see her if he will promise to amuse her husband. "Do you love this absurd coal merchant?" he asks her.

> Oh, I don't know that I love him. He's my husband, you know. But if I got anxious about George's health, and I thought it would nourish him, I would fry you

with onions for his breakfast and think nothing of it. George and I are good friends. George belongs to me. Other men may come and go; but George goes on forever.

Mrs. George's insistence on Hotchkiss's making some sort of friendship with her husband quite disarms him. The play ends on the quivering note this exchange provides.

> *Hotchkiss*: To disbelieve in marriage is easy; to love a married woman is easy; but to betray a comrade, to be disloyal to a host, to break the covenant of bread and salt, is impossible. You may take me home with you, Polly; you have nothing to fear.
> *Mrs. George*: And nothing to hope?
> *Hotchkiss*: Since you put it in that more than kind way, Polly, absolutely nothing.
> *Mrs. George*: Hm! Like most men, you think you know everything a woman wants, don't you? But the thing one wants most has nothing to do with marriage at all. Perhaps Anthony here [indicating an Anglican clergyman] has a glimmering of it. Eh, Anthony?
> *Soames*: Christian fellowship?
> *Mrs. George*: You call it that, do you?
> *Soames*: What do you call it?[20]

There is no clear answer that Shaw has for the question of the deeply disabled woman, and he makes none except by an amusing and purposefully unsettling indirection. He brings the play to an end by leading the Lady Mayoress offstage, where she is about to perform a marriage, with the ceremonial words of a beadle: "Make way there, gentlemen, please. Way for the worshipful the Mayoress." At one performance, the first, the beadle was played by Shaw himself —fittingly. For that is as far as he can go, to make way for the Mrs. Georges of the world, knowing their great strengths, their great sensitivities, and their great frustrations.[21] Confined in what really are the witches' cages of the twentieth century, they look for rescue, they find what seems to be deliverance, and then they recognize, for all their powers, their inability to ride to the rescue. The rescuer must be turned away. They have ceased to unfold.

A hag like Mrs. George shows us a picture of a woman at odds with herself, a woman of potential greatness who has come to a deadening stop. She has fallen victim to the power of her own gifts and to the cruel persecution that comes with other people's misunderstanding and fear of her. The masculine part of herself wages war against her feminine identity; her feminine ego cannot hold all the rich potential for knowledge and power that belongs to her. We see instead a woman—Mrs. George or any other of the species—go way off in tangential reasoning that verges on the crackpot. We see a woman consumed by unfocused fury or a woman burning up with unlived ambition. Such images catch the poignant and powerful suffering of the persecuted state of the hag. She gnashes her iron teeth; she twists her claw-like fingers; she glares out of a ravaged face. As a result, others fear her, ostracize her, imprison her, burn her. Feeling herself to be the eternal victim, she gathers her energies to play the eternal persecutor. In her fury and misery, she vows eternal revenge.

Caught in the hag complex, a woman's ego feels insecure in her female identity and cannot house the animus part of herself. She cannot make any room for it anywhere. The unhoused animus responds by making the masculine seem disgusting, distorted, a caricature of whatever contents it would mediate to her ego. The great witch theme of reversal sounds again. Instead of animus serving the ego, making a bridge for it to the self, it breaks down and its bridge goes with it. Instead of serving its proper function, the animus comes to substitute for her ego.[22] The hag-woman is now dominated by whatever particular contents her specific animus would bring. They take over. In this turmoil of the hag, we can see the part of ourselves that the animus would mediate to us in a dissociated state. It becomes unacceptable to us, then—ugly and undesirable. The masculine, properly housed within the feminine, is feminine. The masculine, unaccepted by the feminine, unbridged, in constant turmoil, becomes an ugly caricature of the masculine.

We see many examples of this roiling complex in women and in those who persecute women. Many modern women have at least a piece of the hag problem in their psychologies, the result of not knowing how to put together the masculine parts of themselves with their feminine egos. How does one get the mixture right? The ego cannot hold it all. Most important, it cannot hold together the instinctive and spiritual aspects of a hag-ridden woman's personality. Thus a woman may fall violently in love with a man who is not really available. He may be married to someone else or submerged in problems of his own. Relationship with him cannot unfold naturally. Yet she may feel, as many women have, that she has glimpsed within him an essential spiritual connectedness of the kind that makes life worth living. But other people do not see it this way. They greet her with pat explanations, thin ones, rejecting ones. It is just sex, they say, or her way of avoiding real relationship; it is simply the repetition of her desire for her father, or the mechanical projection onto a man of her own missing spiritual component, which she somehow must retrieve and integrate.

And in a way they are right. All of these things do apply. But they miss the point—her point. She has seen a true way to live, a way connected in everyday life to spiritual truth. Others' misunderstanding may reduce her to feeling like a talkative fool, a hag muttering to herself. She feels enraged by the arrogant assumption of her friends that her experience can be reduced to a stereotyped pathology. Do they see her as a crazy hag? She will respond like one! She wreaks her revenge. She quits their company. In talk, in action, she cuts them off all the time; she is openly angry. But inside herself, such a woman cannot escape persecution and confusion so easily, for she feels for this man a bursting emotion that threatens, as she sees it, to put her in "his power." She experiences her strong emotion as an assault, and must use her aggression to check its outpouring, to calculate when to let it free, for how long, and to what intensity. She knows well enough the unsuitability of this man for her. She senses in her bones that he would drop her cold if he guessed the tremendous intensity of her desire and need for him. So she must hold her excitement in check, and not allow herself to discharge any part of it. Her bodily and emotional responses now play a persecutory role, vying with her self-control for full possession of her. She feels forced into a complicated power game, seeking to hold his interest while hiding her own true feelings. But the pressure of her frustration is to let these emotions show. She comes to feel her emotions assaulting her in a persecutory way in which the man she thinks she loves acts as the agent of her torture.

A matching struggle of the hag that afflicts many modern women is to bring together the capacity to *do* with the capacity to *be*.[23] Melanie Klein writes vividly about the little girl whose identity as a woman rests on two related experiences: as a little girl on the wish to receive the penis; as an older one on the wish to have a penis of her own.[24] These two wishes reflect her identification with both her mother and her father. Identification with her mother comes in the recognition of her own potentiality to create babies, and in time comes to symbolize her capacity to create and carry life within her own person. This way she knows her capacity to be and to house being, both in literal fact and in imagination. Her later identification with her father, and the introjection of his genital reality, act within her superego as symbols of the aspiration to create being outside herself by putting good things into the world. That power to put good things into the world may be her unconscious way of identifying with her father's body, seeing his genital self as part of herself. The girl's double identification, her bisexuality, sets before her the task of integrating two kinds of power—to be and to do, to house being and to produce being, to embrace a being which is not her own and to assert her own being. In intimate relations later on, with husband and children and friends, a woman needs to get the mixture right, not to be so preoccupied with nurturing and housing others that she loses her own identity, not to be so anxious about her own identity that she loses her ability to give herself to others.

One can surmise the drama of being and doing and the conflict that underlies it in the life of the Russian poet Marina Tsvetayeva, who killed herself just one month before she would have been 49. The drama presents itself again and again in her greatly moving poetry. She feels persecuted; she feels in control. She yields to a man and wants to yield. She asks for everything to be given to her; she will give everything that needs to be given. At 17, in a poem called "Prayer," she asks to die while everything that exists opens "like a book for me."

> I want all things: the soul of gypsies—
> To walk with songs and rob someone.
> To hurt for all midst organ-playing.
> To rush to war—an Amazon.[25]

Her life was an impossible shuttle between opposite ends. She was physically, politically, and poetically suspended between being and doing, between what she did or did not do and what was done to her. Her talent was as large as Anna Akhmatova, the other great Russian woman poet of this century, recognized it to be in her poem "There are four of us," the title designating herself and Tsvetayeva, Osip Mandelshtam, and Boris Pasternak. Mandelshtam was beguiled by her, was perhaps at some point in love with her. Pasternak, picking up a book of hers in 1922, was stunned by the almost direct movement of experience into verse in her poems. She was an emigrée married to an emigré in Paris, but her husband became, in spite of his White Army past, a Soviet agent. He returned to Russia in 1937 and, like so many returning agents of the government, was possessed of unwholesome secrets. He was arrested and killed. She, the most enterprising and open of poets, the most firmly attached to ancient traditions of freedom, also returned to the Soviet Union. She went with her teen-age son in 1939 into a perilous life as a translator, working with poems that did not interest her in languages that she did not know. Her daughter, who had returned just before Tsvetayeva's husband, and her sister, who had never left Russia, were held in detention camps by 1941. She herself had been dispatched from Moscow to a small town in the Tartar Republic, miles from any life that could be of interest to her. She had looked for help from the well-placed critic Ilya Ehrenburg in Moscow. She also sought help, it is believed by some, from another writer in good favor with the government, who was established not far from her small Tartar town. Neither did anything for her. On August 31, 1941, she hanged herself, leaving a note for the second writer, Nikolai Aseyev, asking his help for her son—as uselessly, it turned out, as in her requests for herself.[26]

If Tsvetayeva had thought to cast herself in her poetry as an eternal victim, it would not have been melodramatic exaggeration. But her poetic persona is quite something else—not less dramatic, but more complex; not less anguished or anguishing, but closer to the universal experience of women who love with the frightening intensity of creators who bring children and art into a world not able to appreciate what it is being given. She writes as a specialist in every kind of rejection—of Moscow, the city that Peter the Great rejected and that now rejects her; of insomnia, which leaves her "a homeless and sleepless nun." In saluting Akhmatova in a sequence of poems, she identifies herself as both a beggar and a convict. In another group of verses on "The Poet," she sees herself, "blind and fatherless," asking what she can do as she moves over

> the bridge of my enchanted
> visions, that cannot be weighed, in a
> world that deals only in weights and measures?
>
> What shall I do, singer and first-born, in a
> world where the deepest black is grey
> and inspiration is kept in a thermos?

There are no clichés in her "Attempt at Jealousy," but rather a splendor of questions about how her departed lover feels with "the other one," with "an ordinary woman," "an earthly woman, without a sixth sense." Is your life, she wants to know, "as hard as mine with another man?" The side she sees is the side of rejection, rejection of an unearthly woman possessed of countless senses, and with so many gifts they cannot be measured.

In two moving sets of poems memorializing the break-up of an affair with a White Army officer in Prague, she walks round and round her themes in the geography of her broken love. In the first set, "Poem of the Hill," she describes the hill in Prague where the lovers met in such joy, where her soul "rises" now to "sing of sorrow." She sees a future of suburban life rising on that hill, with acid ironies bringing together her present misery and a future happiness built on that precious site:

> because in outskirts like this they say
> the air is better, and it's easier to live:
> so it will be cut into plots of land,
> and many lines of scaffolding will cross it.

In the second sequence, "Poem of the End," she describes at length the last hours the lovers were together. They walk through Prague. They come to the suburbs—the irony returns:

> Life is   only a suburb:
> so you must build elsewhere.

They walk through past conversations as Tsvetayeva vilifies those who stand against her kind of creativity and love and independence. They move around the Jewish section of Prague, where this apostle of the rejected identifies herself with the Jews:

> Ghetto of the chosen. Beyond this
> ditch. No mercy!
> In this   most Christian of worlds
> all poets   are Jews.

In the last two of the fourteen poems, her lover weeps, and she proclaims male tears as "cruel" and echoes the mockery of three whores who see him cry:

> They laugh at the
>   inappropriate
> disgraceful, male
>
> tears of yours, visible
> through the rain like scars!

Then she, who has been most bitter about the separation, a word she sees as "inhumanly senseless . . . insanely unnatural!" ("Is it a Czech whim, this word. *Sep aration*! To *sep arate*!"), finds the requisite sweetness to compassionate his tears. She had too much capacity for both being and doing, she muses, and not enough distance in either case from which to see and taste and understand the other. In the requiem for the love found and lost in Prague, she identified with fitting distaste the logic of separation that meant that the lovers had "to become single creatures again," they "who had grown into one." Perhaps she had herself become too much a person in herself, incapable of holding on to any of the separate parts that in their (at least temporary) separateness make those separate identities possible without which none of us could ever come together. But her capacity as a poet fits her incapacities as a person, however one chooses to identify them, fits them so well that we have in her poetry an incomparable record of the gifts and tortures of her kind of woman. However, in admiring the poetic achievement and its prose mirrorings, which are almost of equal power, we should not gloss over too quickly the terrible drama which the poetry and prose memorialize. The world of the being-doing dilemma is, as Tsvetayeva suggests, a ghetto, where the identifying tonality is "sep aration."[27]

Identification is the issue. Violently or quietly, but always in some way dramatic, the hag-woman must return to the task of sorting out her double identification, her riddling bisexual pressures, and find some way to integrate the two kinds of power in herself, the power to be and to do. She must house being in her feminine way, and must also produce being in her masculinity. She is impelled to embrace being in others, and to assert her own being. The problems that beset one in this task of getting the right mixture of being and doing, often show up in a woman's confusion of her hunger to be nurtured in her own being with the need to see herself as a powerful agent of change. What results is a game where her power to yield to another is set against her power to control. In the playing out of the game, a woman is often confused and made to stop by the need for nourishment that suddenly wells up in her and utterly obstructs her drive to win the game and thus to shape her own destiny. One woman, for example, had to face the dismal fact that much of the dissatisfaction in her marriage derived from the loss of nurturing with which her husband's behavior constantly confronted her. She complained of feeling powerless, cut off from any nourishment of an emotional or almost any other kind, as he formed his liaisons with other persons and built his base of operations away from home. She felt so hungry for companionship and corroboration as a person, and so without hope of food for her self-esteem, that all she could do was accommodate her time, her energies, and her gifts to fit his plans, his ideas, even his new relationships, rather than ask herself where and how she was dissatisfied with him and what her needs demanded of him or her.

This kind of self-denying adaptation only intensified her low self-esteem and sense of powerlessness. A dream spoke sharply to her of the danger: "I was in my kitchen with my daughters. I sensed menace and turned around to see an enormously fat woman standing in the door blocking my way out of the room. She looked crazy, maniacal, and her face was like my husband's." The unfed part of herself threatens her in the room of nourishment, the kitchen, with the younger part of her own feminine identity, her daughters. The unfed part of herself, the fat woman, wears her husband's face, suggesting not only the danger of his devouring her, but also why she could not stand up to him. Unconsciously, she projected her need onto him and was trying to feed herself by accommodating him. The dream signals the possibility of a shorter route: to recognize and connect directly to her own hunger before it can attack her. All the aggressive energies she gave to accommodating her husband should go into efforts to meet her own needs directly. All the anger focused in self-attack she now redirected to confront him and to stand up for herself.

The vying of male and female parts in this hag drama, and the dominance of animus over ego, can be traced in almost every case to a woman's early relation to an omniabsent father, a figure who all but guarantees the woman's being caught in a hag complex in her later years. The father she introjects as a child, and upon whom she models her aspirations to do, to put out, to go after, to beget value, is a man at a demonstrable distance from the feminine. The model of the masculine that she has introjected pushes her toward an animus-ego split. Finding and identifying with such a model means leaving her own femininity behind. In adult life, she invariably ends up sacrificing her own femininity in order to serve the masculine. She has no presentiment, not even a passing image, of saying to an actual man or to her own masculine energies or to the imago within her, "Come to me; recognize me in my own feminine skin; reckon with me as a woman." All her experience with her absent father has taught her to go out to find the masculine, to cover any distance to reach it, explore any territory to reach him—and in the exploration to deny her own femininity entirely. She has little experience of mutual encounter, of his coming to find her, of meetings alternating between these conducted in feminine terms and those in masculine terms. And so she ends up at best as an adult serving only as an anima link for the males in her life, living her femininity only in service to the male, perhaps aware of her own feminine ambitions and aspirations, but only dimly.[28] The best she can do is to lend the recessive feminine to the dominant masculine.

If this woman takes the other route that clearly presents itself, that of looking for her lost feminine nurture strictly in the male, then the ensuing relationship must become much more parental than sexual. She will be living her femininity at the little-girl level. On the other hand, she may choose to identify with her mate—and her own animus—so that the two of them, both masculine now, join to seek the masculine part, a kind of homosexual relationship, even though between a man and a woman. Her animus may in fact appear in her dreams personified in the form of homosexual men, which is certainly preferable to a scornful, castrating father who ridicules her with his sarcasm. The homosexual animus brings her a more sympathetic contact with the masculine, a male who has also suffered in relation to the masculine and is looking for the right connection to it. With all the benefits he brings, the homosexual figure, whether it is an inner dream figure or an actual person, cannot offer much welcome for her full femininity, which must include her sexuality. In that way, the image that is perpetuated is that of her father, who lived at such a hostile distance from the feminine both in himself and in her. A woman suffering the hag complex is almost always dominated by an animus that reflects her father's mocking influence and utterly turns from welcoming the feminine. That is why it is so hard for her ego to meet, receive, and confront such an animus, to house it and to mix it and her feminine ego in appropriate proportions.

Pain is an identifying texture of the hag complex. Pain is one of its main routes to domination. One woman's experience will serve as an illustration. Efficient, energetic, and persistent in her own career, this woman inadvertently stumbled into a reservoir of undigested pain when one of her superiors confronted her sharply with her characteristic way of evading a conflict. She felt stunned by the discovery, and was left uneasy, as if a well-used and dependable armor had been punctured. In analysis, she was led to look behind the shield. There lay vulnerability, long covered over and neglected by her active doing, her constant coping via a chattering persona. She discovered that she never had really registered her hurt feelings, because she excluded this vulnerability from awareness. Explanations and cheery reasoning about others' needs and schedules prevented any sense of their rejection when they did not include her in their work or their lives. What knocked her over now was the flood of sharp but still undefined pain that came rushing at her through the punctured armor. It was then that she remembered repeated early childhood experiences of her mother's failure to attune to what she felt, and her decision just to cut off all the hurt that bred in her by building a world entirely of her own. Her father, a cheerful enough parent, also kept his distance from her actual experience. She did build a world of her own successfully in the world's terms, but not in her own. For her world was not rooted in all of her being; in her being lurked hidden pain. She felt that if she ever started to cry, she would never stop; she would cry eternally.

Her animus did not mediate this pain to her ego. Instead, it acted like an armor around the ego. Her pain lay there, unrecognized and unassimilated, well beyond armoring. It kept her from being truly intimate, for she did not believe others would respond to her unless she did things for them. To be was not enough. The aggression, the intelligence, the sheer psychic power that she needed to face this suffering, was used instead to cover the pain in a multiplicity of ingenious defensive devices. As a result of this painful rent in her capacity to be, her capacity to do and to use her power and intelligence in the world also was blunted. Efficient and competent though she was, she could never be piercing, to the point, really impressive.

A woman caught in the hag complex almost always finds her anger blunted. Her animus does not mediate the energy, the outrage, the exasperation to the ego, which then can focus all of it and use it to fight. Instead, her anger stands outside the ego. The anger is itself the armor, making her untouchable, or it invades her ego, making her seem possessed, like a screeching hag. Often, the anger turns nastily against her, in wounding bouts of self-attack, instead of forging itself into a sword in the ego's hand with which to attack her enemy, the cause of her anger. One woman dreamt a drug addict plunged a heroin needle into her thigh. In real life, she did in fact drug her chronic anger about her life in bouts of meaningless action, busyness, a constant doing of chores. Another woman used her good intelligence to rise above her angry emotions through fits of rationalization, instead of probing to the bottom of what she felt and finding her own way, creating her own ideas. She dreamt of being stranded on top of a high hill as a tidal wave roiled up from the sea below to threaten the land.

In all these examples, the witch theme of reversal resounds. The animus does not mediate her own unconscious primordial power, intellect, and spirit to a woman's ego, but rather steps in front of the ego and supplants it. She becomes the hag, instead of housing the hag's powers. Instead of using her own gifts, the woman falls victim to them. Her spiritual aspiration is not integrated into her ego. She is left unguided, unbound to either an enriching femininity of her own or to a masculinity which will discover, nurture, and embolden her female personality.

Other people's attitudes in this sort of situation only contribute to the disjunctions within the hag-woman. Their projections onto women, seeing them in stereotyped ways as embodiments of nurture, support, and self-giving, only serve to threaten the hag with ostracism if she dares to develop independence and strength in herself. As she has presented herself, so they treat her, reduced to the small version of herself that she has allowed to surface. She is for them only a part-object, and if she demands to be seen in all her parts, they accuse her of being difficult, or, as she importunes them, nasty. However she presents herself, people come to fear her intensity of emotion and anger. They make a wide circle around her, like another invisible armor, that walls her off from all vigorous interchange with others. She is a hag, permitted to live only at the borders of human community. In her job, the refusal to promote her, to pay her well, to salute her achievements as those of a woman and not just a worker, leave unsupported the connections she may be trying to grow in a less public way between her feminine identity and her masculine side.

Social prejudice against a woman becoming all of herself, a woman showing herself to be capable of being and doing, of nurture and assertion, affiliation and ambition, propagates a split image of the female that reciprocally mirrors and causes her split-animus condition. She must constantly deal with the two images of woman that circulate in the popular imagination. One is of woman as comforter, helpmate, companionable friend, reliably there, always attuned to others' feelings, thoughts, and hopes. The other is of woman as exciting challenge, an electrifying being, arousing sexually, sometimes moving spiritually, occasionally an intellectual stimulant, once in a rare while all three, but always attractive, uncontainable, summoning.

These two images derive in part from early experiences of one's mother. Winnicott calls his paired versions of the two images the "environment" and the "instinct" mother, the "holding" and the "object" mother, the "ego" and the "id" mother, the mother who exists for my needs and the mother who exists in herself.[29] Mythologies, folklore, and popular culture all offer the same variations on the binary theme: woman as virgin and whore, mother and soul-partner, friend and sexual mate, homemaker and lover, comrade and passionate spiritual guide. In each case, the division mirrors an inner psychic splitting between ego and instinct, personal world and archetype, ego and self. Many problems in marriage or love relationships of any kind come down to this split, where one or both of the partners are trying to bring together in themselves and with each other the disjoined capacity for excitement and for living in the diurnal world, looking for a poetic passion and permanency in a prosaic environment. Where one spouse or lover seeks an outside affair, it is often to go in search of the split-off soul part that the relationship seems to exclude, or seems at least to fail to make any effort to discover. We see, then, that what we have called undischarged instinctual excitement reaches into the spiritual realm as well. We see standing before us, even if only in our defeated aspirations for our love relationship, that truth that makes us feel alive, present, connected to the depths, an image of that without which we lose hope. We have, perhaps, lost the capacity *to do* effectively because we have lost the capacity *to be* effectively. If the hag condition has done nothing else for us, it has presented us with the central terms of our existence, even if in the breach.

VII Redemption of the Hag

Inspection

The experience of the hag complex confronts a woman with part of herself which must be recognized and claimed. Otherwise it must live unfulfilled and demanding alongside her feminine identity, leaving her dissociated from it or making awkward, unfitting substitutes for it. She needs to know what the hag represents in herself, and more, to know that she knows it. Therefore she must take up a radical inspection of herself, a serious examination in herself of the hag, seeing with fully open eyes where she really is ugly, loathsome, screeching, venomous, undischarged, without fantasy, where part of her has split off into an animus-ridden crone. She must know, hair by hair, concretely, what all this is in herself and how it lives in her. She will see then that within the hag may lurk a wise woman, one who has at her disposal great primordial power and intellect.

The hag in her hag state represents a split-off, dissociated, masculinized part of the female personality, a caricature man who can wreck a woman's femininity. There she is: a virago, a ball-buster, an icicle, an animus-bitch. But the hag embraced within a female's personality will lead to something well beyond the dismissing epithets, to the discovery of her wise-woman potential. The masculine embraced within the female psyche, held and drawn into the center of her being, produces not a man-woman, not the blurred image of an androgynous woman, not an icicle, but a warm female who is sound and solid all the way down, and with the power to do as well as the capacity to be.

The animus conducts this vibrant power to the woman's ego, but the animus is not itself the power. This power, all by itself, is her female power to do, to be by doing, to stir up, uncover, expose, unearth, pull inward, to probe hidden truths. This is the power to stand fast and direct one's gaze to what is, in sustained awareness. Pointing to what is truly there, she can create in others a capacity for truth as she insists on her own authoritative words about what really exists for her and in her, despite attempts to divert, to digress, or to attack. This power to create by doing contrasts with the power to create by being, though it shares some of the same hidden inner sources from which new being grows until it is ready to be born into the world.

Women struggling to live all of themselves must know this hag part of their personality intimately, and come to terms with it by linking it up with their most unmistakably feminine ways of being and doing. They must recognize, as they undertake this linking task, that it is no good to live only part of oneself, no matter which part it is, no matter how urgent it has been to live a truncated life, identi-fied with some incomplete part of one's being. For some women who have suf-fered damage to their feminine identity, the first step toward finding who they are takes them directly into such identification with the masculine component that the hag symbolizes. They have had to establish themselves in work or career, in some kind of competent doing, as effective agents of their masculine sides be-fore they can risk reentry into a mode of being-for-others, where they must meet again, in reciprocal vulnerability, an area of exposure that had proved to be a lo-cus of nearly fatal suffering to them earlier in their lives.

Young women caught in this identification, who eschew marriage and chil-dren, must not be dismissed as disordered in their femininity, but recognized as connecting and developing a valuable part of themselves which offers value to the world—and to themselves, if they are not arrested at this stage. Equally, older women who seek freedom from grown families to strike out for their own place in the world must not be accused of repudiating their roles as wives and moth-ers, but must be supported as they lay claim to additional parts of themselves which are now to be lived. Women who try to unite their capacities in a life that combines family and work need more than to be recognized and supported. They need to be looked to as guides who suggest to all of us how we might mend the fearful splits between masculine and feminine modalities of being and doing that work themselves out in the frightful divisions between men and women. The hag, with her piercing yells, eerie cacklings, and maniacal curses, shows us the fate of an unlived feminine potency. It goes mad. It destroys. It lets loose into society a prodigious force, which if contained builds depth into a civi-lization, but if uncontained, breeds chaos.

It is not enough to claim this female power; we must also integrate it with female identity. The first move toward it is step-by-step assimilation of each bit of being that the animus conveys to consciousness. To understand this, a fairy tale will be helpful, we think, for as a woman tries to see what the different parts are that the animus would mediate to her consciousness, she is, in effect, con-structing the fable of her life. She inspects her qualities as parts of her tale, and then moves to collect them together and integrate them into the parts of her fem-inine identity that the fable brings together.

The tale "How Six Travelled Through the World" presents its motifis suc-cinctly.[1] Frank, its central figure, is a soldier in the king's army who has saved his king's life in battle, and has then abruptly been dismissed with a mere farthing's pay. Protesting this unjust treatment—for he did not claim any reward for his courage, but certainly did not expect to be persecuted for it—he vows revenge. He will make the king pay him in gold for his heroism. He leaves his sweetheart behind and sets out on his adventure to meet the king. Along the way he encoun-ters a series of fellows with remarkable gifts: a miraculously strong man, an aston-ishing marksman, a man who can make the winds blow, a runner so swift he must occasionally take off one of his legs to rest, and a "Frost Man" who can make the weather turn icily cold.

"The tale 'How Six Travelled Through the World' presents its motifs succinctly."

At every point, the king tries to cheat Frank, and at each treachery one of the men's gifts saves the day. At the king's castle, Frank agrees to compete in a race the king has devised. Whoever can defeat his daughter in running will take her as his bride and inherit the kingdom. Whoever tries and fails will forfeit his life. The swift runner can beat the princess, but his over-confidence nearly costs him the race when he stops to take a nap in the middle of it. The marksman saves the day by shooting a rock out from under the runner's head where he naps, thus awakening him to the danger—the princess is about to overtake him. Frank and his friends together do win the race and go to collect the reward which, characteristically, the king does not want to pay. While serving Frank and his friends a banquet in the "iron room," a chamber of metal walls and floors, the king lights a huge fire under the room, hoping to kill the claimants to his fortune. But the Frost Man cools the fiery furnace room and saves their lives. The king consents then to let Frank take as much gold as any one man can carry. The strong man accordingly lifts all the gold the king owns, to which the irate king responds by sending his soldiers to capture Frank and his friends, in order to put them to death. The man who blows the wind is up to the occasion; he promptly scatters the soldiers far and wide with one great breath. At this point, the princess, seeing all the money going off with Frank, says she will marry him, but Frank just laughs and says, "No thanks; not with my nice sweetheart at home."

We interpret Frank as an animus figure who makes the various parts of the psyche accessible by bringing them and their energies together. Relying on his wits, signified by the remarkable allies he has collected, he defeats the ruling king who unjustly oppresses his subjects. The theme of injustice offers a clue to women combatting discrimination in society, a concern only too easily internalized and left to hobble or to destroy altogether a woman's determination to go after what she needs and wants for herself. Frank and his friends symbolize what women need to have at their command, both to fight oppression and to gain their own individual ends. All the parts need each other to triumph over injustice, the tale says. A collective effort is what is called for—not just the ego's view, not just the animus's view, or society's, but all one's wits. This speaks to all concerns, individual, social, general, and special. It is not just one individual's way that succeeds, but the ways of many individuals, each with his or her own particular perspective and capacity joining the assemblage for effective action against injustice. The traditional feminine role, however sketchily drawn, is filled by Frank's sweetheart, who waits for him to rejoin her after he defeats the king. The tale thus emphasizes the animus task of making accessible a potency that later can be connected to a traditional feminine identity.

To say that a woman must inspect and assimilate her masculine side says little until the details have been specified. This fairy tale brings us to the concrete. Like the strong man, a woman must find and claim her specific strength, her capacity to carry weight in every sense, to lift great burdens and to show herself to be a figure of weight, a substantial authority comfortably carrying her responsibilities. As the tale indicates, these responsibilities concern the redress of injustice in a world run by an autocratic masculine power. Thus a woman bringing all her parts together has immediate effects upon her world. This is not some self-indulgent playing of the game of mental health, but a bringing into being of the resources of humanization that must greatly affect her and her community. Unintegrated, this sort of strength may well express itself in a woman's temptation to live the role of the martyr, where she shoulders everybody's burdens and is buried beneath their weight.

Like the marksman, a woman must find and claim her skill, a far-sighted keenness of focus, and accept her ability to hit her target, even if it is obscure to everyone else. When unintegrated, this visionary focus may lead a woman off her course into foolish by-ways, wasting her energies. Like the fairy-tale character, a woman must find and channel her capacity to make the winds blow, to stir up a gale if need be, to set things in motion. Unintegrated, this capacity may express itself in the temptation to blow off steam, to be endlessly windy in her talk, never getting to the point. Without strength to carry her responsibilities, without the ability to bring her parts together, she will be a light-headed, aimless creature easily taken up into the sky, a natural inhabitant of the thin air where spiritual aims dissolve in the mist and personal life dies for lack of enough oxygen. She will be blown about by every wind of opinion, unable to hold her own against conflicting currents of emotion.

The runner's figure presents us with an image of a woman's need for swiftness in getting where she wants to go, for a pace that is well under her control.

When it is not, this latent capacity may express itself in the familiar woman's complaints of being "run off her feet." Unlike the fairy-tale runner, who can voluntarily rest by literally taking off his leg, a woman's capacity to go quickly may actually run away with her as she runs herself into exhaustion. The runner's complacency that he could easily beat the princess hints at the danger of unconscious inflation that the capacity for swiftness may engender in a woman if she does not consciously and conscientiously deal with it. She may "run around" too much, like our earlier example of the woman careening into promiscuous affairs. But the speed must not be disclaimed, for women need it to come quickly to see where they are going and get on with it. Women's movements resound with this archetypal theme of being on the march, going forward, stepping out.

The Frost Man presents us with an unexpected resource, the power to turn cold when needed. This potential is one that women very much need to assimilate consciously, to avoid its unconscious manifestation at the wrong time and in the wrong place. Sexual frigidity, an inability to respond to children, icy dismissal of anyone who disagrees with one's premises all illustrate a misguided coldness that can blight or altogether stifle the growth of aims, skills, actions, and relationships for a woman. Yet the ability to apply doses of coldness is invaluable in a destructive argument or a heated debate that may die simply because the participants fear its intensity. We need to know how to cool down our ardor about a point we are making that we know is right, but which is going to be rejected if we do not stop heating up the interchange by our own explosive affect. Sometimes we need to know how to turn icily cold against the demands of sentimentality that work to manipulate us by making us feel guilty, fearful of consequences, anxious about our claims on others' affection, or just plain mean.

As shown in the ending of the tale, we need all of these powers acting in concert. Cooling the fires that would consume us may seem to lose us the fires of rage at real injustice in the world that have been burning within us, but if our anger only burns us up, what good will it do? We need to contain our fiery anger, to be fueled by it, not destroyed. We need to take and carry all the treasure that belongs to us, however self-contradictory or confused that may sometimes make us feel, not to be talked or frightened out of it by anything in us or outside us. We suggest that for women, this means taking their place with all their differences and samenesses as women, and not being fobbed off with or positively deceived by appeals to androgyny or unisexuality or a common humanity that once again excludes the distinctive presence of women as women.

We need to blow away all the angry challenges to the claims of womanliness which come from women as well as men, as the power-grabbing, cold princess of the fairy tale illustrates so well. When she finally sees which way the wind blows—with Frank and his friends as they take away the gold—she tries eagerly to get Frank to marry her. Thus she combines the worst perversions of her masculine aims for power with the worst caricatures of the traditional female, expressing her vulnerability through open, bold manipulation. The princess shows us the wrong mixture of masculine and feminine, always changing sides according to who is the established power, using her sexuality for quick gain, knowing neither connection to her feminine strength nor access to her female openness. She has a great future as a hag!

Having won the king's and princess's gold, Frank's goal is to rejoin his resident femininity, his sweetheart. This leads us to the last task of integration: the connecting of the animus function to the female ego-identity. We are now in the realm of mute acceptance, as frightening and entertaining as any fairy-tale world, as tough and good, as straightening and enlarging as our own world at its most rewarding.

Mute Acceptance

Our choice of the word "mute" to describe a woman's radical assessment and necessary acceptance of herself may bother some of our readers. We know —women have remained mute too long. Now they must speak out. Clearly, women must demand to be heard, as they protest their subjugation and proclaim their right to be themselves. We recognize that the word "mute" conjures up some of the worst abuses of women in the past. How often an acquiescent wife was made to swallow her identity with her words, as she was forced to adopt a male vocabulary, one that she was told was the "guarantor" of a "true femininity." How often and how insistently strong women were described in terms of penis envy and retiring ones were accused of poisonous resentment and lack of receptivity when they showed any annoyance at not being asked what they had to say. Women, like children, were to be seen but not heard. In choosing the word "mute," we obviously do not mean to convey this sense of a silent recipient of repressive and destructive labeling. We can understand women objecting and yelling, "Strike that word from the books!" But mute is what we mean, perhaps in part because the word brings with it a legacy of pain and anger so familiar to women. It recalls an intrinsic part of their history which must be knit into the transformation by which they can claim all of themselves including the hag part.

Mute acceptance of all that belongs to her transforms a hag into a wise woman. Because the hag cannot accept what belongs to her, she gets pulled into noisy discontent. The result is that she loses her femininity, and fails as well to own her tremendous power and intellect. All turns queer, bizarre, and eccentric, to the point of grotesquery. Mute acceptance means taking what belongs to oneself without noise, with an absence of speech, in a deeply felt way. In this way, in silence, one achieves full awareness of one's roots, of what really belongs to a woman, for better or worse. Wisdom comes to a woman through what is spoken to her from beyond herself. Thus this muteness acknowledges what is in fact there, rooting the woman in her own earth. Such felt acceptance is not spoken, but out of it comes what a woman speaks if she speaks with her authoritative voice.

In this silence she will find the multiple origins of her own voice; her words, when she speaks, will have an authority that comes from her own special experience of the self. Mute acceptance moves the ego beyond its own borders into the large presence of the self. Like the hag who lives at the edges of human community, a woman's mute acceptance takes her to the boundaries of human discourse and discursive thought, there to perceive the presence of something other than a merely human exchange that addresses the personal ego. Hearing herself addressed by this other voice, that of the self, a woman can begin to trust herself as her ego moves toward her self.[2] This voice differs from noisy protest. It is not an imperious "Listen to me!" It differs from animus-contesting, where a woman fights point for point, man to man, as her animus steps in front of her ego, substituting its primitive, maladapted, male-sounding voice for a strong, related, unmistakably female voice. In mute acceptance, the animus remains silent because it is the authoritative, rooted woman who speaks. The animus then performs its proper function, that of mediating to the woman's ego the contents of her self. The animus is accepted and owned by her, but is itself mute, content to support her female voice.

Thus it is that a woman can speak from all her own parts, as a female embracing the feminine and masculine parts of herself, speaking out of listening, having heard the voice of the self. Others then hear in her words her listening to, and hearing of, the self; in this consists her power and authority. She engenders acceptance in her listeners, who cannot now easily dismiss her as caught up in merely personal causes or problems. They hear otherwise; a word is spoken unto them, into them, that they must deal with and account for.

The new female voice that rises out of mute acceptance cannot be brushed aside as simply parroting clichés. This is a voice that reaches into the substance of inherited opinions and traditional views, if there are any, and beyond the fear of what others may think. This muteness acknowledges what is there, factually, objectively confronting one's ego perspective, the terrain of being that will not go away. It greets one as a given, given oneself to deal with, as we say, for better or worse, inescapably ours. Jung describes it well in his comments on one woman's visions: "As long as an analysis moves on the mental plane nothing happens, you dismiss whatever you please, it makes no difference, but when you strike against something below the surface, then a thought comes up in the form of an experience, and stands before you like an object . . . the word 'object' comes from the Latin *ob-jectum*, which means something thrown against you, opposite to you. When you experience a thing that way, you know instantly that it is a fact. . . ."[3]

The hag knows this summons from the self in a powerful way, but she does not accept it. She protests instead. Her failure points up what a woman needs to do: to accept the summons to deal with this inescapable object that demands her earnest attention and full integration into her life. The hag archetype constellates for women the hard task of accepting all that belongs to them.

Acceptance means simply and toughly to take what is offered—not to ask for a new deal or different cards; not to answer with a "What if" or a "Yes, but," a "Why me?" or a "Why now?" There can be no looking into someone else's hand and envying their cards. We have our own. We must take them. To accept is to take the bit of being and becoming that is offered to us specifically, to receive it as true, to be able to take hold of it, to regard it as appropriate, to undertake responsibility for it, to give admittance to it, to draw it into our mind, and to endure it with consent. That is acceptance.

The drama of acceptance is played out superbly in the novels of Dostoevsky, in the acceptance of themselves by men and by women. The conventional wisdom about those novels is that in them "only the men contend," as Konstantin Mochulsky, one of the most discerning of Russian commentators, puts it. "[M]asculine ideas clash together. Dostoevsky's women do not have their own personal history—they enter the heroes' biography, constitute part of their fate." In *The Brothers Karamazov*, he sees each of the brothers fitted out with "his own complement in a female age." To call it a "female age" is to see much about the women, and is certainly to find appropriate roles in the *Brothers* for Katerina Ivanovna beside Ivan and Liza Khokhlakova beside Alyosha. But to make Grushenka, the most important of the Karamazov women, simply a "part" of Dmitri's "fate" is to miss the extraordinary chronicle of that woman's movements toward self-acceptance, which are loud and noisy to begin with, mute at the end. The transformation gives her a place beside all the brothers, a role almost as large as theirs, as she makes her way into Dostoevskyan hagiology.

Dostoevskyan hags are young. They look young, at least to begin with; they are even, as the meaning of Grushenka's name indicates, "juicy." But they age fast:

> Connoisseurs of Russian beauty could have foretold with certainty that this fresh, still youthful, beauty would lose its harmony by the age of thirty, would "spread"; that the face would become puffy, and that wrinkles would very soon appear upon her forehead and round the eyes; the complexion would grow coarse and red perhaps—in fact, that it was the beauty of the moment, the fleeting beauty which is so often met with in Russian women.

Grushenka does lose some of her beauty, not within years, but in weeks. She falls ill three days after Dmitri is arrested for the murder of his father, who has been his rival for Grushenka's affections. She remains unconscious for a week, then emerges from more than a month of illness. We are told she is "very much changed—thinner and a little sallow. . . ." Alyosha finds her not less but more "attractive." Grushenka has come through. Accepting herself, something which she has not been able to do since her seduction at the age of seventeen, has finally been accomplished at the age of twenty-two. It is an almost miraculous transformation.

> A look of firmness and intelligent purpose had developed in her face. There were signs of spiritual transformation in her, and a steadfast, fine, and humble

determination that nothing could shake could be discerned in her. There was a small vertical line between her brows which gave her charming face a look of concentrated thought, almost austere at the first glance. There was scarcely a trace of her former frivolity.[4]

The change is possible for the Dostoevskyan woman especially because of her author's own journey in sexuality from attachment of a barely pubescent kind to his first wife, through an addiction to a mistress, Polina Suslova, that was as obsessive and compulsive as the gambling fever that accompanied his affair with her, to the fourteen years of sexual, psychological, and spiritual security he knew for the rest of his life with Anna Snitkina, his second wife, his rescuer. Although the change in Grushenka complements Dostoevsky's own development, such that it could be interpreted as simply the result of the writer's sensitivity to anima currents and anima repose, its special eloquence and conviction rest on the openness to feminine elements in Grushenka that Dostoevsky knew can be fully expressed only by a female.

Grushenka accomplishes what those not unrelated women, Nastasya Filippovna in *The Idiot* and Marya Lebyatkina in *The Devils*, cannot. For all her effulgent sexuality, Nastasya, whose name means "resurrection," can only hold forth a supernatural glow to the "idiot," Prince Myshkin. When she is murdered, she leaves him as unfinished as ever, without even the trappings of socially acceptable behavior. Grushenka, on the other hand, becomes Dmitri's inner and outer companion, and clearly will accompany him into exile. Lebyatkina is simpleminded and lost in the fantasies of a sterile relationship with her prince, Stavrogin. She is a moving but truncated embodiment of the feminine principle in Russian tradition, imagining herself to be the mother she could not possibly be. Grushenka, however, can easily be assured of love and can depend on it, for what she receives is in every sense what she gives, and with that love she can be assured of every opening, every fertility, every fullness.[5]

Grushenka's vision of hell, where her feeling finds its understanding of love, involves a lake of fire and an onion. At the center of consciousness she holds a story told to her in childhood of a peasant woman who died without leaving "a single good deed behind." The woman's guardian angel offers her a chance to escape hell if she can remember one good deed. Yes, she says, she did once take an onion from her garden to give to a beggar woman. God allows the angel to extend that onion to the woman, who is caught in the lake of fire. If it holds and the angel can pull her out of the water, she will earn heaven; if it breaks, she must remain in hell-fire. Slowly, carefully, the angel begins to pull her. She is just about out when others in the lake grab hold of her so that they can escape too. But her wickedness is inescapable: "I'm to be pulled out, not you. It's my onion, not yours," she says as she kicks at them. The onion breaks. She falls into the lake "and she is burning there to this day."

With a sweet irony that the English translation misses, it is in the village of Mockroe, meaning a place of "wetness," that Grushenka, the juicy one, yanks her-

self from hell into heaven. At the inn in Mockroe, at a party that Dostoevsky identifies in his chapter title as "Delirium" and describes as "almost an orgy, a feast to
which all were welcome," she leaves behind her attachment to her seducer, to
the world, and to the men that have kept her—to everyone except Dmitri and
herself. "[T]hat first, rightful lover, that fateful figure had vanished, leaving no
trace. The terrible phantom had turned into something so small, so comic; it
had been carried into the bedroom and locked in. It would never return." She
shows in her eyes—her own consciousness tells her so—her love for Dmitri, a
love that can face anything: a false accusation of murder, conviction, disgrace. His
consciousness echoes hers. He asks himself, "Was not one moment of her love
worth all the rest of life, even in the agonies of disgrace?"

The scene leaps with her feeling and his feeling. Feeling, which is Dmitri's
appointed task in the troika of identities which make up the *Brothers*, has not often had such clear or mature articulation. "A falcon flew in, and my heart sank,"
Grushenka explains. "'Fool! that's the man you love!' That was what my heart
whispered to me at once." She asks his forgiveness for tormenting him. "It was
through spite I tormented you all. It was for spite I drove the old man [Dmitri's
father] out of his mind." Earlier she has confessed to Alyosha Karamazov, whom
she had just thrust from her knee on learning that his beloved teacher, Father
Zossima, was dead, that she had wanted to ruin him, and even more tellingly, that
in holding onto her attachment to her first lover and in working out the senti-
ments of an "abject heart," she had grown to love her tears. "Perhaps," she concludes, "I only love my resentment, not him." Nothing can faze her now, no complexities of person or plot. The knotted terror of interwoven debt and inheritance
that stands behind Dmitri's trial, and the working out of the narrative history of
the Karamazovs, can be cut through at one blow by her. Dmitri is worried about
stealing 3,000 rubles from another woman, Katya. No, says Grushenka, you didn't
steal it. "Give it back, take it from me. . . . Why make a fuss? Now everything of
mine is yours. What does money matter? We shall waste it anyway. . . . Folks like
us are bound to waste money. But we'd better go and work the land. I want to
dig the earth with my own hands. . . . I won't be your mistress, I'll be faithful to
you, I'll be your slave, I'll work for you. . . . Take her money and love me. . . .
Don't love her any more. If you love her, I shall strangle her. . . . I'll put out both
her eyes with a needle. . . . I love you. I love only you. I'll love you in Siberia. . . ."[6]

Grushenka's exhausting peroration puts her to sleep for a moment and leads
her to dream of being away from earth. Then she has the great joy, as she tells it,
of waking to find her loved one next to her. She is fully awake now and, as she
has always been, very much of the earth, earthy. Like Alyosha kissing the naked
earth on which Father Zossima's bier rests, she finds her other-worldly lines tied
securely to this world; as a result they are rather more, not less, imbued with
spirit. The facts of life—her life, Dmitri's life, the lives of the man who seduced
her and the men she tempted, of all the trials in this New Testament of trials that

The Brothers Karamazov narrates—are not too much for her. The greatest temptation that she has now found the strength to resist is the temptation to withdraw from the unavoidable, the temptation not to exist, which conquers so many who are faced with such a set of facts. It is her strength that rises, in symbolic majesty, to face the immense fact that brings the party—meaning many parties in the town—to an end minutes after her brief sleep of exhaustion, when the deputy prosecutor arrests Dmitri for the murder of his father.

To reduce Grushenka to a mere complement of her destined man in *The Brothers Karamazov,* to someone who simply is there beside him, is to fail to see and follow in detail her personal history in the book; it is to find only the "masculine ideas," and thus to miss much of the true wisdom in Dostoevsky's writing as it accompanies and emerges from the grace of his enduring love for his second wife. His letters to that blessed woman, Anna, when he had to be away from home, are full of a delighted, unquenchable eroticism and at the same time full of his firm assurance of the lofty sense of their life together. In the first year of his *Diary of a Writer,* as it appeared in the journal called *The Citizen,* one reads his warm words of appreciation for Russian women: "In our women one observes more and more sincerity, perseverance, seriousness and honor, sacrifice and search for truth, and in Russian women all these qualities have always been more pronounced than among the men. . . . The woman lies less, some of the women do not lie at all, whereas of the men who do not lie there are hardly any. . . . The woman is more persistent and patient in work; she seeks, more *seriously* than the man, work for work's sake, and not merely for the sake of *pretending.* Perhaps it is from her that we must expect great help!"[7] He had found such help. He had come to find himself acceptable. In the story of Grushenka, he offered an allegorical tale of such help, of such acceptance. It is so finely made that, like the graces from which it springs, it can almost as easily be misidentified or missed entirely as it can be recognized and accepted.

Jung describes acceptance as the task confronting a woman when she steps inside the mandala, that symbol of the center of the psyche that may appear in a vision when one is bent on finding the true order of one's life, the just order of one's priorities. There she is "caught" in the sense that "the situations that arise now are inescapable and unavoidable, no matter what they are." All of her life is the same now. She is in a "magic circle," where she must "accept" herself and her situation. It does not matter what the situation is—it is compelling, it must be accepted,

> for anything in real life can become an unavoidable fact. You see you can accept a situation in a more or less provisional way, promising yourself that you can get out of it when things become too hot; or you can accept it for good and forever, and then you feel that . . . you are in for it, and that makes all the difference in the world. . . .
>
> . . . [E]ach person has something specific to accept . . . [W]e like to be in doubt because we like to live the 'provisional life'. . . . But that is a mistake, it is

most misleading. You may be sure she had to accept exactly as much as you have to accept, only not the same thing, maybe something quite different. Let us just say that the thing she had to accept is whatever you want to escape.[8]

Acceptance of who one is, where one is, spans the personal and collective aspects of human life. In our time women are being asked to carry this task of acceptance. That is why they as women have come to symbolize its meaning for the human community.[9] Individual women, finding their own strong roots in their female experience, their female tradition, their female bodies, their female symbols, their female groups, put into the world in a fresh, new way the ancient vision summed up in the Christian doctrine of incarnation, which holds that a truth originating beyond personal ego-existence comes into the world through particular human beings who hear it, act on it, embody it, and are redeemed by it. Jung speaks to the point:

> . . . [I]t is redeeming and healing for us to accept ourselves as we are, instead of always wanting things to be different. . . . [W]isdom begins when we take things as they are. . . . Only by agreeing with facts as they are can we live on earth in our bodies, only then can we thrive. . . . First we must accept the fact of ourselves, what we are; then we can develop. In accepting ourselves in our embryonic condition we receive ourselves, as a mother receives a child in her womb where it is fed and develops. If we can really accept ourselves, we can feed and develop ourselves; to expect anything else is like expecting a cast-off child to thrive.[10]

Mute acceptance, then, does not mean passive acquiescence to the status quo, to woman's long-defined subordinate place in society. Rather, it means just the opposite. Mute acceptance grounds a woman's person in the deep soil of collective identity with other women, and portrays her in the rich symbolic colors and textures of the primordial feminine. It gives her the toughness to survive and win out in her struggles to create not merely a more just, but a more *humane* society where women can find affirmation for all of themselves. Through mute acceptance of all that belongs to her—her ego identity acting as a portal for the actualization of a feminine modality of being, her solidarity with other females deepening the roots of her self—she can work at the task of bringing together in herself what is split in the world. In taking all that is given her, she is offering us a fresh version of the ancient command of obedience to God's will. It is one of Jung's most insistent and least ambiguous pronouncements. If we do not accept ourselves, we cannot do God's will. Unaccepting of themselves, people

> are somehow cramped or blighted; they don't really produce themselves so as to express the whole of the creative will which is in them; they assume a better judgement than God himself, assume that man ought to be so and so. In that way they exclude many of their real qualities. . . . What the Lord did for the adulterous woman was to change her system so that she could accept the fact and still feel redeemed. You are not redeemed by repentance, . . . because by repentance you are not changed. . . . It must be a change of the system, an acceptance of the things that were unacceptable before.

From this acceptance grows human community, in which a woman can recognize "that we are all the same, that we all suffer from the same problems; to be no longer isolated but rather to be human among human beings . . . she is accepted, she is mankind, she stands upon the soil that is common to all living things."[11]

Mute acceptance as the soil of human communion allows us to penetrate to a depth antecedent to the traditional dualisms of male and female, good and evil, us and them. Mute acceptance addresses the other tree in the garden of Eden, the tree of life, and directs our attention away from the tree of the knowledge of good and evil with which we have been preoccupied for so many centuries.[12] We look in a new place for a new solution. Here, in a reliving of the ancient tale of original temptation, we can see the frightening dimensions of what women are about in trying to accept themselves and assert themselves in the world. They are working on the primordial split in human identity, that of self over against other, which is so acutely presented in the drama of male domination of the female, the quintessence of otherness. Women are trying their new mixtures with the old ingredients, so that instead of the wrenching choices between the two sides in the competing dualisms, they may find it possible to include both sides; instead of either-or, this-and-that.

Their great task must not be understood in the heroic terms of someone attempting to scale the highest mountain or to conquer the most dangerous jungle. Rather, it must be understood as it comes to us in the small particulars of many women's lives, of different women trying to bring together the opposites they find in themselves, trying to originate a new synthesis of their masculine and feminine parts, receiving through the animus function the unconscious contents that must be integrated into their ego-identities. In the small, ordinary psychological growth of multitudes of vastly different women, this new vision of human being will be put into the world. And it will change the world. God offered the tree of life for our acceptance. Women may teach us, finally, something about how to accept it.

Acceptance of this kind may lack the drama of the heights. It offers something else instead—the grace with which some women accept a scouring of their depths. Examples, usually sentimentalized, abound in the popular arts. There, in film or magazine or newspaper story or television drama or what purports to be realistic drawing or painting, the marvels of motherhood, comfortably settled into, are trumpeted. A wife, though she is anonymous to the outside world, is shown to have the clearest possible identity as she defines the meaning of those ancient rhetorical medals of valor, "the better half," "helpmate," the "power behind the throne." There are elements of truth in these sickly sagas, but they are so covered over with sentimentalizing that for anyone sensitized to the exploitation of women, in fact or in word, they can only convey something offensive. The truth that lies buried in the exaggerations of pop culture does have to be rescued, however, along with the women whose fullness of self-acceptance tells us so much about the textures of the extraordinary that may lie concealed in the ordinary when mute acceptance becomes a central fact of a woman's life.[13]

One example stands out in films: the work of Marie Dressler. This large, awkward woman, whose uncanny resemblance to Tenniel's drawing of the Ugly Duchess for *Alice in Wonderland* ceased only when she smiled, had an early success as a result of her appearance in Mack Sennett's *Tillie's Punctured Romance* in 1914. Her part is often forgotten because of the performance in that film of Mabel Normand. Dressler did not become a significant actress again, at least so far as most audiences were concerned, until 1927. Then, with increasing power and precision over the next seven years of her life, she developed the ease with her own size and clumsiness and general homeliness that made her the famous complement of a similar actor and actress, Wallace Beery and Polly Moran, and a star in the MGM pantheon. In her own way, she possessed the stature of a Greta Garbo or a Jean Harlow, though with rather different attractions. She was as impressive as Garbo was in the film adaptation of O'Neill's *Anna Christie*, and was a fine, wry foil for Harlow in *Dinner at Eight*. She made her penetrating understanding of tough, bedraggled old women in films such as *Min and Bill* (for which she won an Oscar) and *Tugboat Annie* into characterizations that in another culture, one less given to maintaining a clear divide between entertainment and "serious" art than the United States was in the 1930s, would have earned her the kind of praise that actors in long-lived classical dramas were used to.

Dressler's major years in film coincided almost exactly with her years of suffering with cancer, and one is tempted to discover some precise cause-and-effect relationship between the illness and the performances. The connection need neither be stressed nor relinquished. Clearly, Marie Dressler knew pain, physical and psychological, and knew how to articulate the range of interior resources with which a woman faces pain, especially a woman without any exterior beauty or obvious sexual attraction. What gives her work such conviction is that wonderful sense she conveys of resting at ease, all but fully content with herself and with her roles, on the screen as in life. With her loud noises and broad gestures and in her quiet, knowing bearing, she represents the triumph of mute acceptance over mere stoicism.

Mae West personified a noisier version of that unmistakably unstoical grace. Like Dressler, in her late years she was the embodiment of the hag turned wise woman. She had done all the cackling and worn all the fright wigs and whalebone corsetings associated with a harridan sexuality. She had taken her stand against a kind of censorship that showed discrimination only in its refusal to allow a woman to present her own lubriciousness for her own purposes, not simply in response to men's manipulations. Moved to the Hollywood screen from the clamorous rituals of her burlesque bacchanales on the New York stage, she showed a dignity and grace that few could have expected from such a loud and shopworn voluptuary. As foil to the young Cary Grant and the old W. C. Fields, she proclaimed the kind of assured authority that comes from gesture and mien rather than words, from step-by-step inspection that has concluded in the most eloquent mute acceptance.[14]

Opera provides what may may seem at first to be a dim and very distant example of such acceptance, in the role of the Marschallin in Hugo von Hoffmansthal's masterful libretto for Richard Strauss's *Der Rosenkavalier*. For one thing, the Marschallin, Princess Werdenberg, the wife of a Field Marshal in the time of Maria Theresa of Austria, is only in her early thirties. For another, she is constantly aware of the encroachments of age and close to bitterness as younger women supplant her in the sexual wars. But this is the eighteenth century, and she is by its standards no longer a young woman. Her consciousness of age is not simply a series of complaints; it is the means by which she comes to accept the inevitable with an ironic good grace that sometimes almost approaches a Mae Westian kind of coarse good cheer. In the first act she sings, "serenely" according to the stage direction, of her astonishment at having lost so thoroughly in herself the convent girl commanded to marry her noble husband.

> Where is she now? Yes,
> look for the snows of yesteryear!
> I say that calmly.

Once she was "little Resi"; soon, perhaps, she will be "an old woman, the old Marschallin." How does the dear Lord do all of this to her when she is still the same woman, and why does he make it so unmistakably clear to her? Why doesn't he conceal it from her?

> It is all a mystery, so much a mystery.
> And we are here to put up with it.
> And in the "how"
> lies all the difference.

She confides her feelings to her young lover, Octavian, cast as a mezzo-soprano, which gives the part not so much a Lesbian overtone as an oblique mirroring relationship to the Marschallin. She explains that she feels intensely aware of the ephemeral nature of everything on earth—the way nothing can be held onto, nothing really hugged tight. Everything eludes us, everything we reach out for vanishes like a dream. And so she goes off to church, and then goes to see, with the most obvious sort of symbolism, her old and crippled Uncle Greifenklau ("gripping claw"). She and Octavian part, and she suddenly realizes that she did not kiss him even once. She sends her footman after him, but he has gone too quickly. All things slip away from us. Nothing holds.

By the end of *Rosenkavalier*, the Marschallin has come to accept Octavian's dalliance with a much younger woman, and can say to herself, as she becomes the linking force that brings the lovers together,

> Today or tomorrow or the day after,
> Didn't I tell myself?
> That everything comes to a stop for every woman.
> Didn't I know it all?
> Didn't I say with all my heart that
> I would bear it calmly. . . .

The repetition of the first line of her monologue then follows, with a suggestion of the self-mockery of Saint Augustine remembering his youthful prayer, "Oh Lord, make me chaste, but not yet!" She will bear it calmly, "Today or tomorrow or the day after." We see in her and hear in her, with the shrewd underlining of meaning that Strauss's motif-laden music delivers, an accommodation to herself that has the good grace of mute acceptance about it. Shortly before the end of the opera, Octavian confides to her some uncertainty about his affair and some real certainty about her goodness ("Marie Theres', how good you are. Marie Theres', I just don't know anything—"). She answers, "I also know nothing, absolutely nothing," but we know better. It is no shock to hear her say to herself, "I chose to love him in exactly the right way, so that I would even love his love for someone else!" Dressler or West could have said such a line convincingly. The Marschallin reflects that when you first come to hear about most things in the world, they are not believable, but when you live through them yourself, you believe—even if you do not know why. She accepts Octavian's affair. She accepts herself. She can bless the lovers' coming together with a clear "*In Gottes Namen,*" saying Amen to their love. She comes and goes, on and off stage, through the lovers' duet that brings the opera to an end, and thus misses the facile references to dream made by both young people: "It's a dream, it can't really be true that we are together forever!" "Everything else slips through my mind like a dream." But *we* do not miss the prescient lines. We hear the echo of the Marschallin explaining her feelings to Octavian in the first act: Everything eludes us, everything we reach out for vanishes like a dream—except, she might add now, whatever we possess of ourselves and fully accept in ourselves. It is she whom we remember, not the young lovers; it is her accepting wisdom that abides, not their eager clinches or mistrustful musings.[15]

The full acceptance of age and hagdom is one of the delights of Jean Giraudoux's play, *The Madwoman of Chaillot.* Written during the German occupation of France, the drama can be seen as an ingenious allegory of revolt in which the powerless, played by the least significant figures in modern society, triumph over the powerful, a brilliantly generalized collection of industrial plenipotentiaries. Giraudoux sees his presidents, chairmen, prospectors, investors and lobbyists as a world of pimps. His little people are all but unnoticeable in a big city: a street singer, a flower-girl, a king of the sewers, young lovers, a deaf-mute, a seller of shoe laces, a ragpicker. They are led—and this is the enduring strength of the dramatic fable—by four madwomen, *les folles* of Passy, of the Place de la Concorde, of Saint-Sulpice, and of Chaillot. It is the last-named "madwoman" who wears her title, the play's title, with unmistakable nobility. She gives the terrors of occupation a meaning in the drama that extends well beyond the creeping invasion of every hole and corner, every last underground holding of the poor and the deprived, by corporate pimpdom. It ever extends beyond the Germans' tyrannizing of Paris, which the pimps of high finance allegorize. Dressed in a mélange of ancient and modern fashions, madly pinned together, with lorgnette, cameo, basket, and dinner bell, she achieves her triumph in an elegance of self-conception that is much more grand than her triumph in dispatching the pimps to their chosen Paradise at the end of the drama, to death in the ultimate sewers deep down below the visible sewers.

The madwoman of Chaillot is a presence throughout the play, in gestures, in postures, in commanding her army of nonentities. She is the spokeswoman for presence, the configuration of presence, a lordly female force risen against invaders and occupiers. She speaks for all of Giraudoux's extraordinary women, for all lordly ladies—Electra, Judith, Alcmene, Florence in *The Song of Songs*, Leah in *Sodom and Gomorrah*. She speaks madly, articulately, elegantly, determined to see things as they are. Though finally hers is only a too-well-made play, with a facile ending that life does not in any way confirm, she herself rings true. She tells us in the fullness of her dramatic being that the only refuge we have against the relentless pimps of occupation-army modernity is an unmistakable aura of mute acceptance, perhaps a wildness of dress like hers, a fullness of hag-and-crone appearance, an individuality from within that is so eccentric that no pimp could ever dream of trading it. That is our secret weapon against invasion.[16]

An archetypal image that depicts in stark symbolic form the power of resistance to all invaders of women's words is the figure of the sibyl.[17] She is the stone-faced guardian of the precincts of mute acceptance. Unlike the compassionate Virgin Mary, who takes the babe on her lap and intercedes for souls in misery, the sibyl simply stands at the gates of Virgil's hell, a figure in a multiplicity of pre-Christian last judgments, remote, it would seem, from the maternal virtues. The sibyl shows us another side of the female: her power, her intellect, and the weight these gifts exert and exact. The sibyl stands between the worlds, a bridge between the human and the divine, mythologically presented, uttering prophecies of what is, of what will be or can be for those who seek her wisdom. She speaks of the unknown as it breaks into the known world, opening the way into the underworld for Virgil's Aeneas, proclaiming the coming of the Messiah in the same poet's fourth eclogue. She is the authority cited alongside King David for the apocalyptic melting of the world into ashes in the monumental prophecies of the medieval *Dies Irae*. She is the worthy companion of the prophets in the gallery of wise old men and women with which Michelangelo supports the drama of creation on the Sistine Chapel ceiling, sibyl matching prophet, portrait for portrait, across the great decorated space. She is the philosopical and spiritual being who is the force behind the sexual strivings of Goethe's *Faust*, the eternal feminine without whom there can be no significant masculinity, earthly or heavenly.[18]

The sibyl's words, when she speaks, always point to something far beyond. With unflinching determination and stamina, she defines the territory of being and becoming, of what is and what as a result shall be. Those who hear her words must wrestle with them, appropriate them in human terms to discover their meaning. If they fail, the words fall on them like an inexorable judgment. If they succeed, they are given the power of knowledge.

The sibyl shows us in the symbolic form of the wise old woman what happens when women synthesize the masculine and feminine in themselves, look at the results, accept them with silent fervor. Such women are indeed wise, strong, capable of uttering an authoritative word from some unknown depth in themselves which will prove useful to the human community, or of saying nothing and accomplishing everything that way. Out of wrestling with the task of personal integration, of bringing together the opposites within themselves, an army of vastly different women, spread throughout greatly differing societies, join sybilline parturition to more conventional kinds of childbirth in the healing work of reconciliation. That is where mute acceptance leads for women, where the hag's wisdom is no longer *manquée*.

A Crucial Tale

The first step a woman takes in resolving a hag complex is to inspect herself with special attention to the unhoused masculinity it represents. In her second step, the woman integrates that piece of unlived life into her feminine identity. We need every resource of the imagination to understand what is involved here —another fairy tale, perhaps, one that is remarkably apposite.

In "Old Gally Mander," a stringy hag lives in a tiny hut, feeding on ash cakes and water, hoarding her money.[19] She sends her son to fetch a young woman to work for her. When the girl shows up, the crone tells her her duties, with one vehement prohibition: she must never look up into the chimney shaft, for that, as we know (but the girl does not), is the hiding place for the hag's sack of gold. Then the witch leaves. Of course, the girl inevitably inspects the chimney. With a long pole, she pushes and pokes her way up in it and soon dislodges the sack of gold. She flees with it. As she escapes, she passes a cow heavy with milk who beseeches the girl to milk her, an old horse with a sore back and tired limbs who begs the girl to bathe her, and a tree bowed down to the breaking point with ripe peaches that entreats the girl to relieve it of its fruits. The young woman refuses all; she must hurry to escape with her treasure. The witch returns, gnashes her teeth ritualistically, and takes off after the fugitive. The cow, horse, and peach tree point out the route of the girl's escape. The witch overtakes her and throws her into the sea.

This sequence then repeats itself with a second young woman. But a third one makes very different decisions. When she meets the beseeching cow, horse, and tree, she consents each time to what they ask. She milks the cow, bathes the horse's tired limbs, and picks peaches. The tree repays her by telling her to hide in its branches from the pursuing witch. When the hag comes running after her, the cow and horse say that the girl had passed by such a long time ago that she must already have escaped, right across the sea. The witch gives up and returns home, resigned to living alone. As for the young woman, she reaches her home with her treasure.

Step by step this tale tells us how a woman may unite her primordial power and intellect with her capacity to nurture. The hag owns wealth, but cannot spend it; hiding her wealth, she lives in deep poverty, with hardly enough to eat. This shows us a clear picture of the hag complex: rich energies undischarged, hunger unsatisfied. The hag lives as if in the worst poverty, feeding on a caricature of food and drink, ash cakes and water. She lives alone in a small place, frightened of being robbed. That is the life of the barricaded ego, unable to make space for its instinctive life, for the play of fantasy, for the imaginative engendering of ways to live energy into life. But there is hope, for the hag does reach out. She sends her son out. In the terms of our interpretation, she dispatches an animus agent to find a feminine ego to help her to restore her house. Thus it is that the dammed-up, undeveloped, and largely unconscious hag complex signals, through the agency of the animus, to the female ego for help. The means of the appeal are significant.

The reader must not imagine that the hag makes her appeal in a friendly way, or in any way reveals her own dependence. Not at all. She makes her appeal under the cover of open domination of her situation. I will give you a job, she says. You owe me this and more—how dare you not give me what I want? In other words, she hides her appeal under a rhetoric of attack. This detail is important, for this is the precise style of communication of a woman beset by the hag complex. Any of us who may be such a woman, or to whom such a woman speaks, need urgently to listen to the unvoiced, desperate need hiding behind the truculent demands. In the tale, the cry for help is heard, and a girl comes, which is to say the cry for help is heeded.

The fact that the one who comes is a girl need not deter anyone, even the oldest of us, from finding a model in her figure. For women caught in a hag complex, the feminine ego is always young, no matter what the actual age of the woman. Their sense of themselves as women still has much growing to do. That is why they cannot reach through the hag complex to the wise-woman potential behind it. The hag-woman's feminine ego is too immature to house this great power, intellect, and spirit. So it remains undischarged, unlived, under all the agitation and isolation of the hag constellation.

By negative example, which is a device typical of the witch's effect upon the female ego, the hag points out where her treasure is hidden. This is the way the hag complex works, not by declaration, but by prohibition, which is a way guaranteed to arouse curiosity. The witch always goes right to the center of the female capacity to rise to a challenge, especially when the female reacts with anything more than paralysis and fear. Here she teases the girl's desire to know exactly what can be there. Equally, the hag inspires the girl's courage to act—she rushes to find out; she goes right up into the chimney shaft.

The hiding place is worth pausing over. The treasure is not in any of the usual fairy-tale places, not in the ground, or a cave, or a locked box, and thus not linked to the symbols usually associated with feminine depths, whether we take the Freudian equations of bowl-like containers with female genitalia or the Jungian interpretation of the unconscious as matrix. Here, instead, the treasure hangs in the air, in a vertical shaft suited for fire, a fire that the hag never lights for herself, contenting herself instead with the ashes of burnt-out fires. A chimney functions to conduct fire upward, to give it a place in the home for its beneficial effects without any of its destructive power. The symbolism of fire is central, for it remains present, even if not actualized, just as the gold stays present though it is unused for human purposes. The gold hangs in the place of the fire, suggesting an interchangeable relationship between them, at least *in potentia*. Both are unused; both are precious; both are related through color; both reflect the life-giving capacities of the sun.

The fire symbolism gives a special accent to the meaning of what the girl finds. Fire acts as a major sign of transformation and regeneration. In its association with the light and warmth of the sun, it is connected with the life energies of instinct and eroticism on the one hand, and with ceremonies of purification, sublimation, and a rising up into spiritual strength on the other. The fire is associated also with the descent of the Holy Ghost in tongues of flame at Pentecost, and with all the enabling strengths with which the disciples could take up and speak the various tongues of their time, with what Jung calls a primitive logos.[20] The chimney is the shaft where the hearth of earth, the ashes, can ascend into the airy realm of spirit, reversing the Pentecost descent, and it is there, in a sort of phallic container, that the feminine ego finds its potentiating treasure. For with the fiery force of the gold she can leave the witch's employ, set up her own household, pursue her own aims. Once the ego gains the hag energy, it will no longer be dominated by the hag complex. The hag's noisy prohibitions are overt disclosures of the hiding place of a treasure she desperately needs to get into life, as much as she wants to go on hiding it. Ambivalence characterizes the hag complex. A hag-woman constantly sends out opposite signals, catching the person to whom she is signaling in the same maddening double-bind situation in which she is herself caught. Anyone in or near a hag complex, in self or other, needs forewarning that no matter what action or nonaction she elects, it will be spurned as inadequate, off the point, or plain wrong.

The fairy-tale girl shows us the right response to this: Take the money and run. The treasure is held by a phallic woman in a phallic place, and so the girl must get to it by poking at it with a pole. All this signals a directed aggression to find the store of wealth awaiting her. In the very act of stealing the treasure, she is already exercising some of its potential. That is the witch's positive effect upon the female ego. The witch's reversal is reversed. The witch now moves the woman to gather her strength together and use it. In terms of mute acceptance, the feminine ego simply takes what is offered silently, confidently. "Takes" is an active verb here, to describe an active, accepting ego, for acceptance, and especially mute acceptance, can be bold and vigorous.

At this point in the tale, the story could end. The girl defies the witch's power, steals the treasure, and escapes. In psychological terms, we can think of this action as finding the energy trapped in the hag complex and returning it to life. But there is another point here. It is not enough to find the energy; we must have an adequate ego-carrier with which to bring the energy into life. A moral factor also enters at this point. This young woman of the tale, or any other woman, cannot get what she needs for herself except by doing for others. Doing for others, she gets things for herself. In intrapsychic terms, she cannot use masculine power except by housing it firmly, clearly in her feminine identity. In interpersonal terms, the split between self and others must be healed by a new mixing together of the constituent elements; self and other are no longer in an either-or separation, but rather in a both-and conjunction. In social terms, self-interest and social concern cooperate, acting as each other's enablers. This is more than a solution to an age-old split. It is an arresting exposé, uncovering the deep interconnectedness of the split elements. In the tale we see the opposites come together. Either both will be canceled, or both will be lived. The choice is not between life and life—between private and public life, life with self or life with others, masculine or feminine life—but between life and death.

The cow, the horse, and the peach tree symbolize archetypal feminine capacities, each of which must be heard and responded to while the girl is still in possession of the precious treasure of life's energies. She must hold the phallic energy while she attends to all the other designated functions, thus suggesting that the route back into life for her newly won potency lies in her connecting it with what we think of as the traditional feminine capacities to receive. Her danger lies in trying to escape with the treasure at the expense of her true femininity. She faces the threat here of animus domination, that excruciating experience that occurs when a woman's animus function steps in front of her ego, substituting for it in a major dislocation of her womanly person. An equal danger is that the girl could lose the treasure altogether in her arduous efforts to help the cow, the horse, and the tree. Here we see another too familiar pattern: a woman holding onto a traditional nurturant femininity which, with the loss of her own unique potency, degenerates into a stereotyped performance or is lost in the travails of collective roles. The worst of all is the third alternative: The girl could lose both her potency and her capacity to nurture, neither doing for others nor for herself. The first two hired girls suffer this fate—symbolized by being tosed into the sea, which is to say, they become unconscious, having neither ego nor animus.

The third female in the tale demonstrates the risk women undergo in trying to combine their masculine and feminine sides. In begetting a new synthesis, they risk the worst of fires. The whole enterprise may blow up in their faces in sudden combustion, and they may face a life broken into pieces. This fear is real. One woman in middle age left her marriage and her business, where she was utterly hagridden, in order to find herself. Not only was her way arduous, but she lived with the constant fear that she had overthrown her life for nothing. Another woman thought she had failed in her attempts to knit together the different sides of her nature, so that she would have to settle for a divided life, one lived in compartments—living now as a married woman who had entirely left behind her job in an office, now as, in effect, a single woman entirely separated from any relationships except those that took shape around her work. The pressures to throw over one side altogether or to live each side by itself, entirely separated from the other, are enormous.

The third girl of the tale faces all the risks involved in including all sides of herself. She must hold the treasure—not lose it, not misplace it, not reject it, not assign it to a separate compartment, not run off with it—while she attends to the nurturing side of her personality. The holding operation requires a sturdy ego that can cling to things as necessary and keep in readiness its reserves of energy, aggression, and riches, at the same time that it is meeting the demands made by the other sides of her nature. In other words, knitting together the various sides of herself means keeping simultaneous awareness of all of them. This awareness will protect her from being dragged into identification with any one part to the exclusion of the others, which is a constant danger that faces women of substance, women of many parts. The undoing of the hag complex focuses precisely on reversing the hag's plight. The once too-small ego now enlarges through this new awareness of the opposing aspects of a woman's psyche.

The cow in the tale represents an elemental aspect of the feminine, from its obvious association with a mother's milk to its more remote reference to the lunar goddess with cow horns on her head. Hindu tradition is useful here.[21] As Vac, the feminine aspect of Brahma, known both as the "melodious cow," which relates to the world's creation out of sound, and as the "Cow of Abundance" that nourishes the whole milky way with her milk, the cow can be said to ask the young woman to relate to this primordial life-giving aspect, to bring nourishing milk into the world. Here we see the breaking down of the block that had afflicted the hag, forcing her instincts to stay outside her ego, amassing frightening pressure on an already fragile ego. The cow can be taken to represent the female body instincts that in the hag remained an undischarged excitement, resulting in an unlived life. Clearly, the cow stands for the maternal instincts at all times, in each stage. The girl consenting to the cow's request may then be interpreted as finding a way to open her ego to these maternal instincts and a way to house them. This does not necessarily mean that the girl will become a mother. The crucial process may not occur until long after the child-bearing years. It means only that a woman has come to claim her instincts and her lifegiving potential, at whatever age, and will find a place for them in her consciousness. Her great strength is that she now can choose how she might or might not fulfill these instincts in action and attitude.

The horse is an ancient symbol for primordial powers. Neptune lashes his horses to rise up out of the waves, suggesting thereby that horses depict cosmic forces that surge out of the depths, configuring the intense desires and blind instinctual forces of primordial chaos. Horses are dedicated to Mars, the god of war in Greek mythology, and thus associated with aggressiveness and attack. Eliade traces the horse's direct connection to burial rites in chthonic cults, and for centuries the black-caparisoned horse was the natural companion of cadaver, coffin, or catafalque in funeral processions. In Plato's *Phaedrus*, the black and white horses represent the earthly and spiritual aspects of the human soul, as well as the contrasting appeals of reason and of the passions. Horses find association with the astrological sign of the Gemini, the twins that represent life and death. Horses associate with the natural, instinctive understanding—one's horse sense —that guides action.[22] In our tale, the horse begs the girl to wash its tired limbs, which suffer the effects of age, fatigue, or approaching death. Can the female who claims the riches of her own potency still hold them in the face of inevitable aging and death? Is her grasp tough enough to survive this inevitable weakening? Or will she, by denying the horse's request, give up before she really begins, thus denying her awareness of the surge and decline of these wild horses, the soul powers that so urgently need her care?

The horse's role in the tale relates specifically to the dilemmas of older women who are past the issue of choosing between career and childbearing, or between career and idleness. What does such an older woman do with the rich treasures of insight, experience, and authority accumulated over the years, a bounty which utterly belongs to her and which the world so desperately needs? How can she hold the opposite sides of that precious energy together with her declining physical powers and fading beauty, when she is within sounding distance of the approach of death? Her ego is the place where these forces of life and death meet. In her time of intensified awareness, they will either be knit together or dissociated. Only by holding together these opposite forces of life and death, linking the ambivalent emotions of satisfaction of self and service to others, can the guilt which so persecutes the hag be allayed and the woman find a way to repair the damage, to see her faith in life survive the fact of death. In the face of great psychic forces and the nagging fatigue that accompanies them, she must find her way through alternating rhythms of exertion and enervation. Energies are not immortal. They too age and die. The female ego must see that fact clearly, accept it courageously, and make do even with sagging energies, unlike the hag who is first possessed by these forces and then left entirely without them.

In the meeting of the small personal ego with the great primitive forces of the unconscious, tense and depotentiating as it may be, patterns of interaction can develop that will supply their own energies. When that occurs, space is made for a rich world of fantasies in which to weave possibilities of how to rest and how to act, how to tame the horses and how to let them go free, how to care for the old nag and how not to forget the ancient energies the tired horse once knew so well. Unlike the hag, whose fantasies fixate in repetitive obsessions, the female ego now houses fantasies that can grow into joyous symbols for the inexpressible spirit that the horse brings up from the bottom of the sea, that the psyche snatches from the far side of death, that the soul brings back from its ascent to heavenly spheres. For the woman knows, in her ego, in her self, that only by helping the horse, the psyche, the soul, can she return to the world to spend and share these previous insights.

The peach tree is a natural phenomenon, not a man-made one. It grows organically out of its own center to ripen and put forth fruit.[23] It stands for the maturational forces of life, with special reference to female sexuality, which extends well beyond those youthful aspects so grossly overemphasized in our culture. Symbolically, a peach is equivalent to an egg, with its seed at the center presenting the biological originating point of life. But the seed pit, unlike the egg, is hard, well protected, an image of the adamantine strength of the self at the center of a woman's psyche, something not easily destroyed. It may fall by the wayside, perhaps, like a discarded peach pit, but it might also then throw up a tree in a ditch beside the road, one of astonishing beauty, wonder, and strength. The life it produces is to be picked and eaten, intimating a sexual life of vigor, fertility, and resourcefulness. Rooted in the environment, dependent upon it, yet unfolding out of its own center, the tree stands for the nexus of human lives, both given and found, both creating and created. The fruit it produces really is to be picked, to be eaten, to be taken in by others; there are no signs on it of interdiction or punishment. Quite the contrary. The fruit symbolizes sexual ripeness, the readiness to be enjoyed. What is left unpicked is a burden: the tree is bowed down to the breaking point, suggesting the despair of a woman who feels unwanted sexually. The pit-centered fruit of the tree seems to signify the sexual life that satisfies almost every set of values when it is linked with the demands and the ways of the central self. In the tale as in so much of life, the sexual pleasure represented by the peaches is linked with self-giving to others for their nourishment and delight.

These images set the task of how to live the fullness of one's life-giving energies into the world, without any loss of the parallel claims of the ego to be independent, self-supporting, and self-directing. This is not just a young woman's problem, but one that women of middle and old age know, too, for the capacity for passion often deepens into a new ripening with age. How does one connect this self-giving juiciness to feed others with the contrary urge to take the treasure and run? Read figuratively, the tale suggests that a woman must make room in her closely inspected self-awareness for her own unfolding sexuality, and not leave it to fall carelessly to the ground or to rot unnoticed on the limb. Fruit is designed to nourish life and repeatedly, in cycles. The tale also focuses, then, on impersonal pressures of sexual instinct to serve the species, and on the desire to channel that force in more personally satisfying ways. The point is not a prescribed way for women to live out their sexuality, which always must await some personal choice, but rather hangs on the acceptance of the fact of desire and the need for some loving. A woman's ego must house these forces. Otherwise, like the hag, she lives split off from every aspect of her femininity—from her reproductive cycle, from her sexual desires, from her longing to pour herself out to another.

The girl does as the tree bids, and then the tree hides her from the pursuing witch. It can be read as suggesting that her own sexual desire rooted in the self will give her refuge from an animus-possession run wild. This does not mean that the girl identifies with her sexuality, for she still holds safely the potent treasure she has stolen from the hag. A woman need not give up her unique power when she finds her sexual nature. It need not be the either-or choice of effective power or receptive sexuality. The girl keeps both because she can hold both simultaneously in her awareness, knowing that both belong to her and that she can live both. Unlike the situation of the hag, where animus opposes ego, here animus serves to connect ego to the treasure of the self. Thus the woman who seeks self-development and potent achievement need not be de-sexed in the process, nor need the woman who enjoys the deep restfulness of an intimate sexual relationship renounce achievement in the world. The tale ends with the girl returning to her own country, for which read the world of daily life, to live and spend the energy taken from the hag, and to dispense it with the fullness of her female capacities, giving milk, holding life in death and death in life, unfolding sexually and spiritually.

When a girl's ego unfolds in awareness of such opposite pulls in life and in her own nature, we can expect the experience of that great positive tension out of which symbols are born. Unlike the hag's impoverishment, which is the result of the opposites falling apart in her and symbols being reduced to flat univocal meaning, here there is a palpable plenty, the result of the interweaving of the personal and the archetypal dimensions of being, symbolized by the cow, horse, and tree, and a lively interplay between hag and girl. Out of these mixtures and the girl's synthesis of the masculine and feminine parts of her nature, new symbols of a burgeoning life will arise. Neither word nor gesture is needed. Mute acceptance is enough.

Thus does the hag occasion a woman's transformation. The hag can go now. It is time for new symbols, to be imaged and uttered and lived by this woman, to be lived and imaged and spoken by that one, each begetting her own word, each offering her own construction of what it means to be wise and to be a woman, to be a wise woman.

VIII The Witch in Men

The Bewitched Man

Men do not escape the witch's spell. In fairy tales, she menaces them by making them into beasts, by confounding them with paralyzing silences, by enslaving them, by picking at their bones. She all but eats them up, her appetite having progressed beyond children and women. Men's dread of the witch's power takes famous and infamous forms. A man concocts his countermagic. He raises his fists, flexes his muscles. He flees the witch's realm and secrets. He projects her onto real women and tortures them to death as her surrogates, pretending to be rescuing their souls from witchdom. In many men's lives the power of this primordial female makes itself known in dreams and fantasies, in relation both to women and to their own souls' reality. Consider these examples.

A man gets swamped by his emotions when he tries to speak about them to anyone. He goes "numb," he says. He rambles; he cannot get the experience into focus. His ego seems too small for the task, impossibly vulnerable, unable to speak for itself. He is overcome by the experience, frightened, in the grip of something that rules him. A dream comes. It describes perfectly the state of being that afflicts him. The dream goes further and shows him fighting back, despite his weakness. He is in a house like his grandmother's. Its depressing atmosphere exudes an "unhealthy life, a dusty one turned sour, unrelated to anything or anyone, not the fulfillment of old age but its oppressive reduction." Little furniture stands in the dream room, except a piano that reminds the dreamer of his mother's playing and her vow never to play again because her children were such a burden. He feels it was his fault that she could not express herself. "Making music," he says, "*is* feeling." The dream continues. "A baby girl tries to crawl to the piano, but a witch keeps stopping her, will not allow her to get to the piano. It is awful! Now I have this witch on my back, and she is digging into me in an excruciatingly painful way with her claws. I feel her bony, clawing hands digging into the back of my hand, into my back, into my body. At the same time I hold her appalling hand in my hand, and to stop her I crush her hand in mine. It is awful, terrifying, and I don't understand how this fearful feminine power can do this. I cry out to her, 'Let me live!' And, then, referring to the female baby on the floor, 'Let her live!' All I want to do is to get her claws out of my body and to stop her wicked killing of this baby on the floor. It is terrifying!"

A second example is of a man in middle age suddenly sprung loose from a long marriage he had labored hard to keep together. His wife had walked out. Then he suddenly saw what all that labor had cost him, how much his energies had gone to feed the marriage, to keep it alive, all the water in his soul constantly feeding a subterranean stream in her, in himself, between them. But it went nowhere, watered no new life into being. His creative powers, which were considerable, flowed away from life, not into it. Once his wife left him, he began to produce again. Creative work poured out of him into finished products that reached the public eye. They existed in reality. All that had been sucked underground now found a channel into life. He saw that his wife was right to leave, more correct than even she knew, so that when she wanted to walk back into his life, he refused. He had thought he was feeding their marriage by the devotion of his energy to it. Now he saw another meaning to his old efforts: He had been trying extravagantly to please, to placate, to keep in being a connection that was not real enough to survive on its own. Once free, he never wanted to go back to that false route and its devilish tensions again. In his worst moments he felt as if he were bewitched by her, pulled into a nether world to spin himself dry. In his best moments, he knew the bewitchment came from within himself. He was feeding his fantasy image of his wife which only bolstered her fantasies about herself. Distance from her broke the spell. He saw it was his own bewitchment that he kept alive by endowing his wife with unlived parts of himself. Once those parts began to live, there was no going back into fantasy, only forward into life lived realistically.

The third example is from the ongoing analytic work of a man, himself an analyst. During one period of his work, he dreamt of himself as an adolescent in his old bedroom. There a beautiful woman turned out to be a witch. She was biting him. They fought furiously. What stood out vividly in the dream and lingered long afterwards in his mind was her impenetrability: "Her skin seemed elastic and unhurtable. I struggled and fought and grew very angry, but couldn't hurt her. I was angry and frightened." This figure was to recur in many different guises. A dream of a year later shows how much his attitude had changed. The witch was no longer simply an enemy to be feared, to be fought, hurt, and defeated. The dream shows the dreamer to be no longer so sure he wants to kill what belongs to the witch. He dreamt he was "some sort of 'hero' who was to 'free' a village from being tyrannized by an animal of some kind." Though he takes a few stabs at what looks like a longmaned horse, nothing really happens. "Then a tiny goat appears and all the villagers yell, 'This is the monster!' I attacked the seemingly helpless goat, which apparently was the servant of a witch. The outcome was in doubt—whether I would kill it or even wanted to, for it seemed so small and helpless. But everyone seemed convinced of its malevolence."

He associated the goat to the god Pan and to his own panicky attacks of anxiety. These had made him resort to a mechanical lust devoid of real feeling in his sexual responses to women. His ambivalence in the dream about killing the goat suggested to him that he could somehow rescue the goat from service to the witch and take care of it himself. Its helplessness touched him. He would do this despite popular opinion and collective panic. His dream shows him finally able to relate to his own anxiety and to undo its power to separate him from feeling. The witch will no longer make him into a lusty old goat. He has found redemptive resources in his own spirit.

For all their frightfulness, these images of a witch's power—a bony hand and lethal clawing, a sucking of life from a man through fantasy, an impenetrable panic-making presence—also give access to the large reality for which she stands. What is sharply and directly expressed by these dream witches is the fearsome power and intellect of the primordial feminine, for images offer a shorter route to the primordial than orderly diagnosis of conceptual categories. We could take the persons in these examples, and in the ones that will follow, and describe their psychic conditions in terms of schizoid disorders, inadequate personality, and the like, and no doubt be correct in doing so. But those terms, with their scientific patina, are too far removed from the experiences they describe. For all the commendable distance they achieve from the disorder, they also build a wall against our understanding it. They do so by imputations of judgment and by thrusting the whole issue into the ego-realm alone, thus falsifying it while seeming to make sense of it. From the ego's point of view, the attack that comes from the unconscious—the bony hand clawing at the back—can be safely distanced by framing it in a concept. At the same time, however, the ego is wounded when the label of sickness is attached to it, so that its strength is sapped at the very moment that its safety is apparently secured.

This is the ambivalence inherent in analysis. At worst, by using diagnostic labels, an analyst is merely cataloguing a patient's ills while keeping himself or herself on the safe side of the health-sickness line. Aside from expressing contempt, this mental attitude is disloyal to the patient, as any working analyst knows. The line that separates health and illness moves uncomfortably back and forth between patient and analyst, and is never clearly defined. At best, the labeling of a condition can provide a needed distance from its turbulence, as long as one does not get fixated there at that distance from the situation. The label is useful only as a resting point, a raft in the sea from which one will plunge in to swim again. We jump in when we take the images seriously enough to work well within them. Then we are engaged, fully caught up in our feeling responses and our ethical tasks.

Through wrestling with images, transformations occur. The dream of the witch's goat showed the dreamer a possible way other than his usual panic and splitting-off from his own feeling. The goat was helpless, and in effect called out for his care. It touched him, showed him a concrete way in which a caring response could be made. This was not simply an idea; the dreamer was moved to care for the goat, to care for himself. He had a choice now. Would he take it? Could he?

The dream of the overwhelming thrust of the clawed hand that snuffed out music and threatened the little girl, and through her the beginning of feminine life, showed its dreamer a way to combat his terror, to move and to act in spite of the forces arrayed against him. He fought for the infant girl, and thus saved himself. This was no foolish melodrama, but a tutoring dream. The man who saw his compulsion to feed a false fantasy as a bewitching spell also saw that he could wake up from it and turn all his withdrawn energy back into useful life. Dream images move us, reach beneath and beyond our concepts. If we understand them, they are the real thing, the coin of life, not just ideas about life. Entering their realm gives us space to move in threatening territory, and to find a stance in our own power. We enter the life of the problem, and get enough room in which to grow toward its resolution. A concept describes the problem, thus providing some useful orientation, but at a considerable remove from our living experience. Ideally, we should use both approaches. Unfortunately, we usually avoid images just because they *are* life.

With images, we support not only our own struggles in the dream territory, but also those of others. With concepts, we benefit from scholars' refinements —for example, of what exactly constitutes a borderline position. That is not a small benefit; it is not to be undervalued. But the images of men wrestling with witches—in fairy tales, in literature and myth and religion, in clinical accounts —bring us into a community of sufferers, strugglers, and conquerors, of those, for example, who have come to victorious terms with the magnificent figure of the female that the witch represents.[1] Thus in what follows we must look closely at the kinds of struggle the witch in men inflicts and the concrete ways men develop to house and relate to her.

Bondage of the Ego

Typological maps of the big and sprawling terrain of the psyche never exhaust the idiosyncratic possibilities of the human, but nonetheless we do need the markers they provide, especially in dealing with the witch, whose brand of feminine power and intellect can altogether transform a man's personality and thus his life. One mapping is structural. We will examine the way a witch captures a man's ego, possesses his anima and holds it prisoner, and how interior identifications of witch with ego or anima change the man himself into a bewitching presence, or make him a victimizer of the women onto whom he has projected the witch force that has invaded him.

Another of our mappings is imagistic. What particular aspect of the witch do we see invade the man? Her devouring hunger? Her sexual spells? Her wise words, unspoken but somehow understood? Is it as cannibalistic mother, canny hag, or bedeviling sexual partner that she gets her hooks into him? The grid constructed from the intersections of concept and image gives access to the witch in men and the ways of redemption for both.

First a witch will attack a man through his ego. In fairy tales, she simply knocks his ego out. He falls mute; he turns to stone. He falls asleep; he is cooked alive to serve as her meal. She drugs him with potions; pins him down, lifeless, in underground caverns. She steals his potency, saps his determination, unmans him. She may even take over his whole ego-identity, so that he himself becomes a kind of witch or witch doctor, an *ersatz* shaman. She reduces him to an object, a contemptible dolt, foolish, empty, impotent. No longer possessed of ego-identity, no longer a man, in fact, he hops around and croaks his protests as a wet frog, or subsides into the condition of a flapping bird.

To feel one's ego threatened—or worse, captured—is truly frightening. It mobilizes the most primitive and ruthless defenses for what a man feels is a life-and-death struggle. The struggle may be over his sanity or his masculinity, his ability to speak or to act, but in all our examples we will see that the man feels invaded by a powerful, cunning female presence that threatens to change him in the most fundamental way, so that he cannot be himself anymore. How can such a threat not fill him with terror? In each case, we see the witch's mark. She reverses the natural flow of energy into life by sucking it into the unconscious. She marks the man by breaking his connection to life—through his body, through his emotions, through his values. Those parts will be split off, pushed out of reach, sometimes utterly lost. Ungrounded in his own matrix of human resources, he can draw on no resources of strength, but must fall, weak and impotent, into the witch's hands.

Here is a typical example, which appears at first to be mild, until one actually experiences it. A man falls asleep when he should be awake and present to everything going on. In group therapy, one man dozed off periodically, lapsed right into unconsciousness, disappeared before the group's eyes. He felt gripped, he explained, by an irresistible pull toward oblivion, despite his wanting "to stay in the room," listen to others, and respond to them. He created rage in the group when he fell asleep on them. They felt dismissed with unmistakable hostility, as if whatever they said or felt was negligible, too trivial for the man's attention. Hence they in turn moved to attack him, to retaliate with their own hostility and dismissal, which left him feeling sabotaged, pulled down into a hole from inside, scorned from outside. After all, what had he done? He had just fallen asleep, under a spell, against all his intentions and conscious wishes.

Only much painstaking work unraveled the sequence of events that caused these lapses from consciousness. Just before a sleep attack hit him, the man felt a great need for others to pay close attention to him. But one thought cut off that feeling of need—the thought that it was childish, that a mature adult should not need this. And so he would resolve to act maturely, to give, listen, respond, and resist the need to sit and have others feed their attention to him. At that precise juncture he would fall asleep. Failing to allow the child in him to be fed resulted in the child part feeding upon him. He even said it was like being swallowed, or as if a spell had tricked him into a witch's cauldron. The witch's disguise here was to be adult and mature, to rise well above childish needs, but then she gobbled up the man from below, snatching at just that hungry part that needed to be fed. Behind the disguise lurked the witch's voraciousness, ready to gulp down his ability to stay conscious, severing him from the care of his childish feelings, making him feel scorned and dismissed by others, just as she herself is. The witch is properly feared for the tremendous strength of her hunger.[2] Instead of feeling the support that comes with nourishment from the matrix of the unconscious, this man experienced a cannibalistic mother who ate him up.

A variation of the gobbling theme comes in sexual guise, even though a man may feel the threat to his ego-identity more than to his sexual functioning. He dreads ego-dissolution, and will resist surrender of his ego in a sexual experience—surrender to his own pleasure and emotions, surrender in any way to his partner. He feels invaded by a terror that he will be pulled into outer space, off the earth, left "ungrounded," as one man put it. He fears he will be devoured by the woman, that he will enter her "and never get out again," as another man said. He fears woman as a fetid hole, a primeval swamp, into which he will "sink without a trace," as another man put it. He fears the woman will get her "fish hook" into him and pull him "out to sea," as still another man described it.

Being invaded by such a witch power transforms a man so that he himself comes to exert bewitching effects on others. Women are the principal victims. The man described above who felt pulled into outer space, there to be dissolved and lost, accused his partner of doing this by "disappearing" in their sexual meetings. But, she explained, this only happened when she really responded to him, when she went all soft and open in desire for him. She felt he wanted to turn her into the man, wanted her to pursue him with male initiative and definition. Thus he worked, as she saw it, to unsex her, making her doubt her own responses. She felt rejected sexually, and worse, "driven crazy" by being told that she was feeling and doing the opposite of what she knew herself to be feeling and doing. When she responded, he told her that she was going away, vanishing. When she opened to him, he told her she was stealing his ground from him. When she wanted to give, to yield to him, he accused her of swallowing him up. In his threatened loss of ego, he attacked her ego, her sense of reality, and her self-esteem. To deal with him, she would have to abandon her sexual response and think through what was happening. Thus he demeaned her sexuality and cut off her feeling, doing to her what the witch power did in him.

Another defense frequently used by a man gripped by the witch in the sexual arena is simply to deny himself sexual experience. He does not get in, and so he need not fear getting out. The result is, of course, tremendous frustration in one's sexual life and the suffering that comes from a sense of being permanently damaged in one's virility, with no basis for self-esteem. One man felt this every day, hated it, and yet still withheld himself from physical contact with his wife, for his terror was too great. Only on the rarest of occasions could he allow himself a brief sexual transaction, usually a commercial one, where he could get in and get out without any binding relationship. As his ego became stronger through therapy, the possibility increased of his housing his sexuality and claiming some of the hunger that invaded him as his own, instead of projecting it onto his wife. But meanwhile his bewitchment persecuted his wife, who was made to feel disgustingly insatiable in her appetites, basely motivated, wanting only to devour him for her own pleasure and then to spit him out like so much chewed gristle and bone. The prostitutes he engaged were in fact just that, food bought and sold, taken up and thrown away.

Other men bewitched in this way simply avoid women altogether, choosing the homosexual route as the least dangerous road, not allowing themselves to get into anybody, but only to be touched from a distance in anonymous contacts. Thus the women in these men's lives remain caught in the men's projections. The women are seen as swampy indentations or fish hooks; they are made to feel that they are less than human, just repulsive objects.

A potent form of witch attack on a man's ego comes through silencing his words. He does not fall asleep now, or fear sexual encounter with a woman, but he cannot speak his feelings. They are the point of severance. He just cannot put his feelings into the world, either in word or in gesture. One man caught in this spell said he was made mute by it, was literally unable to find words or say anything. The man of the piano dream also complained of being made numb, going unfocused, losing the thread of his feeling, of being left unable to articulate or act upon the emotions that surged through him.

This paralysis of the ego's voice sets up odd, conflicting reactions in women. They do not want to help. Instead, they want to jibe and tease, like the witch who trapped Hansel in her cage and poked at him through the bars to see if he was plump enough to eat. In therapy groups and in individual analysis, women explain that a man's numbness or muteness sets off resentment in them. They feel they are expected to be his voice, to coax and support him, to pull whatever is missing out of him. But in fact, *they* feel pulled down into the hole where he is trapped, for their efforts never work, never are quite right in his eyes. They feel they have been judged oafish, clumsy, too aggressive or intrusive. They feel he will anwer all their efforts with the accusation of "never enough," a sentiment that will exude from him no matter what actual words he speaks or does not speak. That is, of course, simply a reenactment on the man's part of the attitude of the voracious witch: "Me! Me! Me! I'm starving! You must give me more, more!" Women are maneuvered by the witch in such men to feed them endlessly, support them, understand them, listen devotedly to them, set themselves aside entirely to give all their energies to him. Then the women begin to feel eaten up, and respond by poking the man with bitter sarcasm and refusing to mother him. Enough of carrying a man's inner witch for him! They are fed up!

In reaction to this sucking action of the witch that pulls them into sleep, into a silent outer space, some men are seized by frenzied activity. Two patients resorted to episodes of wild all-night dancing, whirling themselves into exhaustion, as if to sweat the deadening spell out of themselves and to reassure themselves that they really were alive. This resistance to being sucked into the unconscious takes a manic form, which finally fails to convince. The same can be said for great bouts of sexual activity, of drinking, or even of talking. In fact, the frenzied quality just signals that a witch's spell has invaded one. The man feels caught. He makes his partner into an object, a prop for his manic activity, to defend against being made an object himself of the witch's appetite, merely a means to the end of her needs, which are so insatiable that he must end by being eaten up and disappearing. He makes the woman he is with feel the same way, as if she is a means to the end of his satisfaction, which is unreachable. His use of her can go on forever, but she will never be recognized as more than a complaisant object for him. Victims of wife-beating know the horror of looking into their partner's eyes and seeing no recognition of humanness, of who they are as persons. The husband is possessed, and she is simply the means for venting his possession.

The man's fear of losing his entire identity to the witch makes him think he will go out of control, be unable to stop, will himself cease to be human. He betrays his own values when he feels himself to be overtaken by gigantic rage and the need to hurt the woman he loves—or at least wants to love. Emotional violence, roarings in anger, physical beatings, breaking furniture, throwing objects around are painful examples of how this terror extends itself outward to terrorize others. The man feels himself to be in the grip of a part of himself that has taken over the whole and knows no limits. A man described the violent fights he and his wife got into as the result of both of them "harboring a witch inside," each witch going full tilt at the other. He was frightened that he could not control himself. He felt transformed into a savage beast with exposed talons.

In extreme circumstances, a man may literally believe he is fighting for his life—that more than his manliness, his very self is at stake. This can happen when a woman ends the relationship between them. Then nightmares can assault him with grisly images of the female power—a woman in a bear's mask hunting him down, or a woman as a lethal snake rearing her head to strike at him, like a Medusa's head ready to turn him to stone. All the dream women threaten madness. And the real woman makes him feel tricked, confused, stunned. How could he have been so foolish that he did not see, as she danced the dance of the seven veils, that she would move to behead him? It was a failure of his own manliness not to have seen what was going on. Her frozen tones now pierce him. He must explode into hatred. He has fantasies of beating her to a pulp for playing at love with him, for opening him up and then frigidly shutting up against him.

The vision of the feminine sometimes becomes even more primitive. It is imaged as dripping with menstrual blood, as attacking breasts, as a vagina with iron teeth. Here a man feels menaced by a bewitching female who would do anything to him—poison him, devour him, dismember him. Invaded by his terror, he then becomes as dangerous to women as they have seemed to him. His ego is so fragile that he believes his rage to be fully justified. He must save his life. He projects onto women in general the menacing power to reduce him to parts, to stun his ego, to leave him defenseless. History is full of men who have made this projection the central motivation of their lives. Every day our newspapers bring us more examples of such men. Their aim really is to destroy all women, a large task even for the most gifted murderers. Some of them, such as Bluebeard, appropriately become legends. Most of them act out their projections less violently, like the English Jewish family in Harold Pinter's *The Homecoming*, which has lost its *materfamilias*, Jessie, years before the events of the play, but which is only too happy to find a possible successor in the American wife brought home to them by their philosopher son and brother. In her they see all strength, all sexual power, all mother-wit, and thus all hope. At the same time that they plan to make her into a whore who will support them, they bow to her intrinsic sexual force and wisdom. Pinter's parable dramatizes the dilemma of a bewitched masculinity so utterly identified with the women it attacks, and so without its own ego-identity, that it can only resort to every kind of torture, emotional and physical—to burnings, drownings, beatings, sexual maimings, disfigurements and attacks of every kind—as, in turning upon the women they hate and love, they

"He projects onto women in general the menacing power to reduce him to parts, to stun his ego, to leave him defenseless." (Goya)

turn upon themelves, whom they also hate and love. In their versions of the witch-hunt, they are both hunter and hunted, bewitched and bewitcher. They achieve homicide and suicide in the same act.[3]

In some fairy tales, the power of the hag-witch to attack a man's ego through his value system is also dramatized. A witch becomes a man's spiritual connection, his tie to life. In "Melilot," for example, the witch wants controlling power for herself over the life-giving water that irrigates a whole valley. Three brothers refuse to yield to her. She turns them into squishy, slimy frogs. The battle is over values. All the water for me, to do homage to my omnipotence, or water shared with everybody. The witch's aim is clear; she aims to separate the brothers from their feeling for what matters.

A crisis in values is a witch's happy hunting ground. If a man has projected onto the woman he loves and admires large pieces of ideals he holds dear, and the woman, insisting on expressing her own reality in her own way, shows that she differs from his image of her and cannot or will not carry his values for him exactly as he expects her to do, the bewitched man will become as angry now as he was loving before. He will turn upon her in rage, only to discover how his un-thinking anger has hurt her and himself. What goes on here is the loosening of both ideal and identification. The man cannot lodge either in his chosen woman. He must strike out not at the woman or at himself, but at the bewitchment in which he has ensnared both of them. He must take up the task of relating to his values one way in himself, and another way out of himself. All his rage shows an unbounded aggression that needs to be struggled with, an aggression that must lead him to confront his values directly and no longer depend upon their mediation by the female.

At the opposite end of the value spectrum, when a man is still struggling between hedonistic self-gratification and loving others, the witch appears as a temptress promising her male votaries a fine, easy life. In "Peter and the Witch in the Wood," the witch's taste is for lazy, handsome lads. She draws them to her by shrewdly chosen criminal acts in which they must betray what they most value. Then she rewards them with an easy life of honor and riches that they can never earn for themselves. There is only one drawback. It is clear that they have done some evil thing, for the men can never again look up into anyone's face comfortably, frankly. They must hide behind shaded glasses. The witch tempts Peter by her own disguise. She passes herself off as a beautiful maiden held under chains, her face hidden behind a veil. She sets Peter a pseudo-problem and a bogus sacrifice. Only something immensely precious to its owner will cut the chains loose. The witch lures Peter to try to steal what he knows will fulfill the set terms, to take from his poor, hard-working mother the gold coin hanging around her neck, for which she has long labored, that she plans to leave to her beloved son as his legacy. He almost succeeds in stealing it when she is on her deathbed. In the pseudo-logical way characteristic of the moral cheat, he reasons that she will die anyway, so what difference would it make if he were to take it now. But to act in that way would be to deny his own perception of his mother's love for him, to betray his own gratitude for her hard work, to turn away from the chance to see and to seize the good of her love. He would be cut off from all his own feelings for value. At the last moment, in tears, he cannot do it. He goes further in the re-morse he feels for having let his mother work so hard for him. He vows he will now take care of her. Then the veil is torn from the alluring maiden, and Peter can see for himself the witch's "ugly sallow face, with a yawning cavern for a mouth and two black holes for eyes. . . ."[4]

Bondage of the Anima

Fairy-tale witches work in deliberate ways to capture the anima part of a man. Best of all is to prevent it from emerging in the first place. The man re-mains bound to his experience of the feminine as mother, and does not move into experiences of the feminine as peer, as sister, friend, sexual or soul mate, something quite other to him. In "Sleeping Beauty," a pubescent girl is pricked by a crone's spindle and falls into a deathless sleep that cannot be broken until a hundred years have passed, when a timely prince will find his way to her through a thicket of thorns surrounding her and her whole world. The anima, in the thickets of prevention, never differentiates from the unconscious; it just abides and dreams there, unevoked, passive, waiting. All the work of winning through to the anima figure, to wake her up, falls on the male.

Men know this experience well in their own psychologies. Some vital part of them, which holds their sexual and spiritual reactions to women, lies asleep, imprisoned in the parental castle. A major ingredient of their sexuality never comes into play; they do not move into sexual relations with either sex, but live caught in a presexual forest. They have not awakened to the possibility of pene-tration, of opening, of intimacy. A man may also experience this sleeping anima part in projected form, in the kinds of women he avoids, explaining to himself or others that it is just too much to wake them up—too many tests to pass, too much thicket to fight one's way through, too many thorns. She is not really there, he protests, but is just waiting, expecting him to do all the work of relating.

"Snow White" and "Rapunzel" depict the same motifs in tales of girls impris-oned by witches. But now the anima heroine wants to be delivered, and so she flees the witch and uses what resources she has, even if it is only her own hair somehow made into a ladder with which the prince can rescue her from the witch's tower. These tales tell of the perils of an undifferentiated anima held in a negative mother-complex. Snow White's stepmother would murder her if she could.

The negative-mother witch is undisguised fury much of the time. In "The Magic Ball," the witch lures a little girl to a chillingly cold place where she falls asleep, exhausted, against a rock. When she awakes she finds her hair has grown into the rock so that she cannot move her head even a few inches. Around her an invisible wall imprisons her. Caught in a "sickening loneliness," she slowly freezes to death. It is a parable of the way an imprisoned anima turns cold and lifeless, and a man's vital connection to his unconscious life can be buried in a grave of ice.[5] Such language does not much exaggerate the feeling the man himself has of his life failing him, falling from him, of not really being in his life. In some basic way he has remained formless, undifferentiated, unready to engage himself in what matters. Instead, every other kind of subject state dominates; he is left drifting off, perhaps, or drying up in an empty, floating, cold cynicism. He cannot warm to himself, to others, to anything substantial. Women often describe such men as fundamentally absent, as with Gertrude Stein on Los Angeles: "There is no there there."

If the imprisonment of the anima is actively felt by a man there is hope for rescue, for a fight now goes on and a relationship begins. A man may fight, for example, to free his wife from the dominating influence of her own mother. A man may not only feel active dislike of certain kinds of women onto whom he has projected the confining, life-killing witch-spirit that would enslave all budding feeling in him, dry up all emotion, wither all inspiring value, but he will actually do something about what so deeply disturbs him. In fairy stories, the witch will allow the girl we see as the anima-figure to work, usually at mediocre and menial tasks, but she will not let her thrive. She cannot fulfill her ambition, love passionately, or achieve deep devotion to something outside herself. She needs— the man needs—a rescuing prince, or princeliness, to overcome the mediocrity, which is to say the frozen life force.

A pernicious form of anima imprisonment that fairy tales present in remarkably sophisticated narratives is that motivated by sexual envy. The witch now substitutes herself or her daughter for the envied young woman, one always at a nubile peak. The witch wants to be the one who is desired and thought unspeakably beautiful. In "Goose Girl," she pushes an admired princess into a river, kills her magic horse, and becomes queen in her place. In "The Enchanted Cow," as the title makes clear, the witch changes the heroine into a less than enchanting femininity. The hero must seek and rescue his love from her bovine state. A charming irony is at work here—beneath the cow, the tale says, a beautiful girl may be struggling to get out. The point is that the prince must free the maiden. She cannot liberate herself. Unconscious, asleep, frozen in place, imprisoned in a tower, transformed into a cow, she—the beauty, the princess, the archetype of womankind—must be rescued in operations shared between anima and ego. That is the happy collaboration of a Rapunzel devising a ladder from her braids. When the witch takes over or removes the prince, rescue must come from the anima alone. The maiden must do the revolutionary trick herself, which is especially difficult when it is not sexual preferment the witch envies but power, when she wants to rule as queen herself. In "Brother and Sister," the witch suffocates the queen in her bath when she is exhausted after childbirth, and installs her daughter as queen, the falsest of womanly rulers.[6] A contemporary man's dream captures that falsity in the image of a witchy woman he makes love to, one who has been, of all things, Hitler's woman. But in the dream he finds the necessary anima strength to get the woman away from the monstrous shadow part, winning her for himself, and the Hitler figure ends by shooting himself. Even in that most difficult encounter with a witch, rescue remains possible.

Most confusing is the situation wherein a witch takes total possession of the anima, so that all the parts of the man are mixed up beyond identification. It is a complex whereby a witch spirit invades and posesses the anima, and a witch-like anima overtakes his entire ego-identity. He becomes identified with witchy attributes, a bizarre kind of witch-doctor, and his maleness becomes invaded by a caricature of femaleness. A confusion of male and female parts reigns: feminine anima replaces masculine ego; unconscious anima complex rules conscious ego-behavior. For example, a man dreamt that he was on a train, trying to reach a familiar city. As he pulled into sight of the station, the train stopped; the tracks were washed out. A parade came slowly toward him. At the head of it was a man dressed as a witch, distinguished by "a hooked nose, pointed hat, black cape, and a whole pattern of sequins glued to his chin. At his side was a woman companion, a witch." The dreamer felt repelled by the man-turned-witch, by the mix-up of masculine with distorted feminine features, and connected it to his own hidden homosexuality, of which he felt ashamed. He particularly disliked his own "witchy, bitchy" behavior toward his lover, and any trace of effeminacy in other homosexual men.

Heterosexual men can also experience in themselves an uncanny, witchlike femininity, exhibited in a new ability to strike out poisonously at others just where they themelves would be hurt, and with unmistakably female gestures, movements, and locutions. A man in group therapy felt himself attacked by another man, not for anything he had done but for what he was, the way he looked, his actual body, in fact, which clearly could not be changed. And so he felt unjustly attacked, deeply hurt, and decided he must defend himself as swiftly as possible and with all his might. He swore loudly, nastily, calling the other man "a cunt." He was new to the group and did not know the other man was not only homosexual, but felt impotent in his own manliness. So the word cut deep, right to the center of the other's man's wounded state, as it took what was precious in the female and reversed its value into an ugly epithet. Later, on reflection, the accusing man felt his swift retaliation had just shot out of him from some "witchy" place that unconsciously knew what would hurt.

The confusion of just who is the witch and who the bewitched, who is the killer and who is to be killed, can get thoroughly mixed up between people, as well as between parts of one man's psyche. A man dreamt his wife had become "a total witch." She had "completely shaven her head and taken to wearing colored makeup in streaks like a witch doctor. I tried to control her . . . but she leapt around screaming. . . . She looked like a man I knew in the Navy who himself looked like a male witch, with his head shaved as in basic training. When I woke up, the room had a foul odor about it. . . . I could feel the witch in the room cackling and the hair on the back of my head stood up slightly and I felt scared." Outwardly, the witch first takes over his wife, then a man from his past, then lingers in a menacing way to frighten him. Inwardly, a shift of personality occurs: the witch possesses the anima, then a shadow part, then threatens his ego by blurring the distinctions between dream and reality. Male and female parts cross and recross, understandably frightening him. The parts just do not go together; decisive action is impossible.

The theme of the exchangeable witch, passing back and forth between persons, frequently turns up in analysis if a witch-complex is under scrutiny. It will sometimes affect the analyst as much as the patient, though in very different ways. Leopold Stein's early piece on "Loathsome Women" frankly exposes his own besieged state when he took on an unintegrated witch archetype in several of his woman patients' lives.[7] The unconscious bond between them, he found, circled around a phallic god-image—that potency that the witch notoriously vies with and refuses to integrate. All the women Stein describes suffered from failure to integrate the masculine archetype. As body types, they seemed virginal—unpenetrated and ungiven. Developmentally, they had not come to terms with their fathers. Archetypally, they felt fascination and fury with the male as enchanter and overlord. Yet relationally—to fill out the jargon categories—they bound themselves to men of a feminine character who also had not integrated their own masculinity.

Stein felt himself shift toward internal identification with his own femininity; he was afraid these women would reveal some negative aspect of it, which he would then project onto them. The result would be that he would find something "loathsome" in them that was really his own. Or, he thought, he might find himself combatting his fear of their domination by forcing his interpretations on them. He felt each woman wanted his maleness for herself, not to share it with him but to steal it from him. Sometimes he felt himself to be like a shining knight, wanting to liberate the women from their witch's spells. But their unintegrated male sides would stand in front of their egos, making them think in insoluble either-or alternations that blighted the growth of any new insight. When they did finally receive and accept their own power and intellect, feeling penetrated by it and able then to accept it, the strife between analyst and patient subsided; both were more restored to themselves for having better integrated their contrasexual parts.

A countervailing witch's spell cast over a man and his anima will all but cut him off from his feminine part. The loss degrades him, sometimes to bestial forms. We are all familiar with fairy tales where a witch turns a prince into a frog, a rutting stag, a swan, or a raven. She dehumanizes him because he will not consent to her sexual demands, but insists instead on seeking his true princess. In a ferocious bout of sexual envy, the witch says, in effect, "If I can't have you, no one can!" Severed from his humanity, the man can live only in animal form, overtaken by an animal's habits. A man may indeed suffer such transmutation when cut off from the feminine part of himself, which may be his feeling for women or his very sense of connection to life and meaning. When all that falls away, women become fearsome objects to him—either objects of lust devoid of personal feeling, or of competition to see who can dominate, or of total abhorrence, when feminine values have become so alien to him he can only repudiate them to protect himself from their force.

Deliverance from such a cut-off state can only come from outside a man. The princess now must rescue the prince, through her feminine acceptance of the worst in him, so he can again take up his best parts. The princess must search for him in the witch's castle, or sew human clothing for him as a way of transforming his bird wings into human limbs, or let the slimy frog he has turned into eat from her dish and sleep in her bed with her.

Psychologically, this motif of bewitchment, where a man's sexuality is separated from his emotions and his values, correlates to his being captured by a sexual fantasy or changed into a beast by a compelling obsession. He abandons both himself and the personal self of his partner. The pleasure, if there is pleasure, is brutal and spurs him on, like a witch riding on his back. Once climaxed, he feels impossibly spent, pulled out of himself, but in a false way that parodies self-transcendence, for he never really surrenders himself to another person in the sexual act. His bodily experience fails to achieve any psychic elaboration, but remains crudely caught up in the discharge of tension. As Masud Khan describes it, "instead of instinctual gratification or object-cathexis, the pervert remains a deprived person whose only satisfaction has been of pleasurable discharge and intensified ego-interest."[8] This sense of failing to connect, either to himself or to the other, that afflicts a man caught in sexual compulsion, comes full circle again as he re-enacts the alienating ritual in which he seeks to find himself and connection to another, and only makes more complete the disconnection.

Here sexual fantasy is made to carry a man's secret search for experience of himself as a person, while at the same time it seals him up, out of reach, caught in the solitary fantasy game. Through masturbation, or through projection onto another person of the lost bit of self, his fantasy spins out the drama of the imprisoned part of himself, which he hopes the sexual ritual will somehow make available to him, to be claimed at last. But the ritual proves sterile, a parody symbolization, a false transitional object that gets stuck in obsessive repetition. Either he is totally overtaken by his fantasy, which makes him a ruthless animal, acting in total disregard for his own or his partner's self, or he remains dissociated from the experience, locked into the control booth of his ego, where the players, including himself, are manipulated to act out the preordained fantasy drama. And so round and round the desperate process goes, accelerating; the man is caught in a habit that leaves his self in shreds.[9] Acting out a fantasy with a partner is, he thinks, a hopeful possibility, except that the element of play is missing, and each actor begins to manipulate the other to stand in as a character in his or her own psychic drama. As Masud Khan notes, if "each is matching actively from his own explicit need and desire the same fantasy in the other," the danger is that "the result can reach criminal proportions."[10]

Voyeurism becomes another failed resource when a man, unable to acknowledge the feminine adequately in his own life, worships his far-off princess, spying on her through distant windows. The feminine is no longer a person for him, but simply a frightening object to be held at a safe distance, nonhuman, a goddess in her unreachable beauty. The man can only be moved by her from the distance; his sexual release is solitary, autoerotic. Up close, his fear of what the female evokes in him—his intense desire, his dread of her power, his awe of her beauty and otherness—silences him. He can speak no word, make no move. Adoring from afar, he falls dumb and defensive in intimate encounters with a woman, unable to express his own manhood and terrified that she will somehow take it from him. The only way he can relate to the woman is to separate himself from his emotions and just take her sexually. That will prove who has the phallus.

The female undergoes a matching distortion of her reality. For her pathological lover, she becomes goddess-like at a distance and witch-like close up. Beauty and aggression are severed, sexuality and power dissociated. Unable to house the feminine within himself, the man pays his obeisance to her in parody effect, caught in compulsive attachment to his woman or to a sexual habit that has become an addiction. His image of woman splits into greatly simplified good and evil parts. For example, a man dreamt a woman was not allowed to express herself in the school they both attended; nothing feminine in her, no word, no gesture was to be tolerated, especially not her negative feelings in what he called her "witch rage." By the end of the dream she was going to be expelled for even having such emotions. The dream really describes his own psyche. His dilemma is clear. He can show his anger and get expelled—from school in the dream, from life as he knows it—or suppress it and achieve a bogus victory, for the student who passes courses in this witch's school is merely play-acting, conforming to rigorous anti-female restrictions.

Redeeming the Witch in Men

How then does a man free himself from the many spells and guises of the witch, each of which has its own intensely negative effect? The witch can take out his ego, or overpower him with a seemingly limitless rage that makes him a danger to himself and to all women he encounters. She can set him ablaze with sexual lust, rutting till exhaustion, leaving him feeling jaded or degraded, spent, limp, altogether without life energy. She can poison his creative connection to life or sap the spirit he finds in things, turning him listless, pallid, bloodless. Defending against her, he cuts himself off from his feeling, keeps a wary distance from any intensity of feeling, any serious sexual involvement. He banishes passion from his life, from his work, his friendships, wherever he has felt intimate connection. To avoid the witch's menacing form, standing there for him at the border between consciousness and the unconscious, he lies low in both worlds. He makes only surface connections; he takes the safe route of dry theory or a gutless imagining, where earlier he would have acted.

Fearsome as the witch is for such a man, she also intrigues him. She promises fascinating experiences. She calls a man out of himself with her alien beauty. She challenges his courage and wit. She takes him to a new territory that demands new maps, new mixtures of spirit and sex, of body and mind, of female and male. And for all her difference from human conventions, for all her outsized superhuman proportions, hers is a presentation of primordial feminine power and intellect that is fully human and that clearly can deliver a man into the here and now, the concrete natural world. The witch is not a goddess, though she touches unearthly powers. She is not a personification of nature or a natural force like fertility or food, though she brings into human awareness nature's remote places, its secret herbal mixtures that have life-and-death powers. Her function is to take a man across the border into unconscious realms of human experience, to passions of unlimited range.

If a man is to survive her and achieve relation to her, he must find his own ego standpoint and a way to reverse her malevolent reversal of life's energies, so that they flow into his ego and his ego can be fed by them instead of being consumed by the witch's appetites. He must find ways to rescue the anima princess imprisoned by the witch, or even more difficult, to submit to the princess's rescuing him when he is the one whom the witch has seized. He must find ways to inspect the hag force that has come at him, wherein the hag remains unpenetrated by her own masculinity and left always struggling with her own phallic aggression, caught in polarized either-or options that leave her defeated in her creative tasks and frustrated in her loves. Inspecting this hag, he must also accept her, not just adjust her to his terms nor move to suit her to his needs. Her transforming power lies in calling him out beyond his boundaries to meet her otherness, to see and accept where she is different from him.

Redeeming the Ego

For a man, redeeming the witch means recovering his ego and discovering access to his anima and the experience of the self-world that she can show him. It means wrestling with the witch as voracious negative mother, as beguiling bewitcher, as formidable hag.

To redeem his ego, a man must exercise it by the most deliberate and conscious inspection of the effects that a witch can have on his identity—not just the great drama of her paralyzing and stunning him, or turning him to stone or animal form. A man dreamt that he was instructing another man, a younger one, about the witch in himself and in men in general, alerting him to all she could do with her preternatural alertness and deviousness. This sort of recognition of witchery in his own psyche is healing for a man. However little she intends to do so, the witch makes a man keep his wits about him, makes him use his brains, his own trickery, to defeat her wiles. She occasions a new determination in him, despite his fear of her power. He may find himself strong enough to defeat her, as did the man called "Stout Heart" who fought the title character in the story of "The Hungry Old Witch," the hag who exacted yearly tribute of the best animals from a village.[11] Her cheating, stealing, and domination of others may call out heroic impulses in a man, may set him to rescue a people, a maiden, or sometimes even the witch herself. She makes a man of him. She rejects his boyish dependency, laughs in the face of attempts to get her to play the good mother who will make everything all right for him. She makes him bring together and use what he has, coagulating his diffuse anxieties into decisive action, keeping him from surrendering, even to her.

Coming into his own takes two directions for a man emerging from a hag complex. He moves into dark passions, away from his identification with the light side of his experience, and at the same time he moves to take control of the great archetypal emotions that threaten to possess him. In a group-therapy session, for example, a man began to speak about his tendency to cloud up, actually to feel stuffed with sinus congestion, whenever he was overwhelmed by such outsized emotions. As he spoke, he lost the thread of what he was saying, the clouds gathered, and his words trailed off. The reactions of the women in the group, and his subsequent interaction with them, sparked his coming into his own. They made it clear that they felt unsympathetic. No one felt moved to encourage him, to quiet his confusion, or to pull words out of him. Some felt imposed upon; some wanted to jab at him; some got openly angry.

By allowing these reactions to show, by feeling no guilt for being cold to his plight or for making jokes about it, the women encouraged him to go further, to take hold of whatever these gigantic emotions might mean. They refused to substitute themselves as the link for his own connection to what he felt. He had to do that connecting work himself. Through their questioning and teasing, he moved past intense anxiety that if he gave way to what loomed up in him he was doomed. He moved boldly into experiencing a flaming sexual passion. He abandoned his notions of proper behavior, and allowed himself to feel the threat of this passion, however much it might threaten his marriage. He even faced the fact, he said, that it might burn up his whole life. But what exactly did that mean? The women pressed him to be concrete. He reached far to find and describe concrete images for this sexual force, in concrete reactions to specific women. The process gradually reduced what had looked like impossibly gigantic emotions to human proportions, within ego-limits related to his own ego-world. None of this would have happened if the women had resisted their initial witchy reactions and become good mothers to him instead. For then they would have lifted the burden from him—though only very briefly—and kept him small in the face of large archetypal emotions. Allowing themselves their witchy reactions, they were able to get him to allow the raw side of his passion to emerge. The more he experienced it in the human container of the group's support, the more the archetypal largeness was made concrete on a human scale—in image, in feeling-reactions to another, in manageable feelings within himself. The defense of "clouding up," which also made him feel caught in a consciousness-numbing spell over which he had no control, gave way to his housing what he experienced.

In fairy-tale terms, the women refused to take charge of this man's animal instincts, as a witch only too gladly does with a man. The witch's favorite way to get power over a man is to steal his animality from him and paralyze or bewitch it. Then he is powerless to call to it for help, for all that is animal in him is held fast by strands of the witch's hair or frozen beyond recovery.

Sometimes the bewitchment that freezes a man's ego is undone by the hag herself. A splendid allegorical enactment of that process is provided by the figure of Mrs. Gray in Rebecca West's *The Return of the Soldier*. The returning soldier in the midst of World War I is an English infantry captain, suffering from shell shock. He retreats in his mind to the moment of youthful discovery of the reality of a deep love, forsaking any memory of his beautiful but selfish wife and his magnificent but burdensome English estate. Mrs. Gray, his first love, appears to be empty of color, like her name. In her hardworked body and face and her rough hands, she shows the poverty of her dress and house, the toll of eighteen difficult years since she and the soldier had loved each other. But her soul has endured in its youthful strengths. Unenviously, she admires the soldier's wife for her evident youth and beauty and her handsomely restored old house. Gladly she welcomes the soldier's love for her, welcomes all that he wants to remember of his past life. She heals his anguish. Only with her, resting after a walk, can he achieve the release of sleep and a simple happiness in being. She "has gathered the soul of the man into her soul and is keeping it warm in love and peace so that his body can rest quiet for a little time." With her he is protected. "While her spell endured they could not send him back into the hell of war. This wonderful kind woman held his body as safely as she held his soul."

Will he ever be able to return to his present life? Psychiatrists say no. The contrast is too great between the bright reality of the past love and the present shadows, the shocking horrors of war that only make more evident the meaningless life he chose with a superficial wife. Why should he return? How could he cross back into the present? Mrs. Gray, a true hag in her power and wisdom, knows the way, and offers it simply: Through a sufficiently strong memory taken from his present life, of a love—even though a wounded one—that is too deep to ignore, he will remember everything again. She comes upon this possibility by accident, but recognizes it for what it is when she sees a photograph of his little son, who died of a mysterious illness at the age of two. Show him a sign of that terrible event, and he will come back. But then Mrs. Gray hesitates. Why should she free him from his happiness, and lose him again? ". . . I know nothing in the world matters so much as happiness. If anybody's happy you ought to let them be." Yet finally the force of what exists now, in this present, must be honored. The soldier cannot be left in the past: "the truth's the truth, and he must know it." The narrator, the soldier's loving cousin, who is herself not far from a hag, agrees: "I knew quite well that when one is adult one must raise to one's lips the wine of the truth, heedless that it is not sweet like milk but draws the mouth with its strength, and celebrate communion with reality, or else walk forever queer and small like a dwarf." Of such stuff is hag wisdom. Confronted by Mrs. Gray with his dead son's ball, the soldier returns to himself. The ball is a totemesque sign of what the soldier has forsworn and what he must return to—his own self and all its wars.[12]

The hag is a repository of wisdom, even though she may be so entangled in events that she herself contrives to work her own and her loved one's liberation from her spells. It is a situation Rebecca West knows well. In West's novel *The Judge*, Marion Yaverland acts the title's part against her own beloved son Richard. With a hag's ferocity of determination, she seeks to free him from the blinding spell of her all-consuming love for him, so that in his freedom he may turn from her and marry the girl he loves. She contrives things badly. She not only drowns herself, but pulls the others to destruction with her. In a fit of rageful guilt over his mother's death, Richard kills his hated half-brother, who blamed him for their mother's suicide, and then visits upon his own betrothed the pregnancy out of wedlock that had originally caused his mother to bind herself so feverishly to her son. The witch's spell moves on to the next generation.[13]

For an ego to be redeemed, conscious inspection of the witch's spell must be undertaken, whereby one really sees the witch, her power, her magnetic attraction, her ability to penetrate through all obstacles to the truth. Seeing what she is consolidates a man's ego in his psychic stance, which is so different from hers. He is limited, she limitless; he functions with warm human affect, she with cold archetypal emotions; he has goals he must struggle to reach, she has distant ideals. If he sees her, he can hold his own. If he holds to his limited egoposition, the witch force will come into focus and he can relate to it instead of just succumb to it.

Redeeming the Anima

The rescue can go both ways, with the prince freeing the maiden and her liberating him. Then the ego frees the anima and the anima saves the ego. Whichever way the rescue goes, determination, aggressive action, and sustained desire are demanded. To succeed, a rescuer must also inspect who the witch is, and accept her reality as it is and not make her into something she is not. In her operatic melodrama, Gretel is a positive spy. She notes the witch's poor eyesight and her greedy appetite for fat, succulent things to eat, and thus determines how to trick the witch. She gives the witch a bony stick to feel through the bars of Hansel's cage instead of his plump finger, thus making the witch believe he is still too scrawny to eat. Then when she gets the chance, Gretel acts decisively and pops the witch into her own oven. No ambivalence, no dogging guilt slows her aggression. She acts.

The anima as heroine may have to undertake a long journey to rescue her beloved, a journey she herself has brought about. In "East of the Sun and West of the Moon," the princess follows her own determination to see her lover, even though she is goaded by her mother, who keeps reiterating naggingly that she should recognize the fact that her prince is really a troll.[14] She thus defies her lover's warning that the utmost secrecy is necessary to free him from his bewitchment, where by each day he is turned into a bear and each night back into a human. The witch promptly whisks him off to her distant castle. The heroine undertakes a long journey to find him, her own essential journey to gather the help of the winds and the wisdom of an old woman. She finally rescues the prince from marriage to the ghastly daughter of the witch. Rescue requires full consciousness joined to perseverance, the willingness to compete and to win against the witch's formidable powers by beating her out in the final tasks. The competition has an almost athletic tension.

Sometimes the heroine effects the rescue simply through accepting her own deep personal feeling, shorn of all conventional gratifications. She becomes capable of loving a particular man as he is, entirely for himself. Beauty rescues Beast from his animal state only after she sees him as he is, accepts him as he is, in his beastly state, and gives him her love.[15] In grim contrast, the heroine may have to pay the price of submission to the witch's power in order to free the one she loves, damming all her feeling, shutting herself off from the life of affect, like the girl who must not laugh or speak or in any way show joy for six years, thus to liberate her brothers from their imprisonment in swan's bodies.[16] Mastering the urge to spontaneous emotion, learning to suppress the quick pleasure of feeling rising in her, she gives herself to the feeling that endures. Thus she endures, thus she can make the most demanding sacrifice, can face others' misunderstanding equably, and can free her brothers.

An anima-heroine can rescue the man she loves with whatever means lie at hand, with anything that may be lying around, be it a trivial implement, a cat, or a dog. In a bucolic society, simple kindness to animals may be the means of rescue, as it is in "The Hut in the Forest." There, the heroine wins the prince from his bewitchment as an old man not only by cleaning and cooking for him, but also by her close attention to and care of his animals.[17] They are the bewitched form his servants have taken. In psychological terms, this might be read as an allegory of the anima's re-establishment of connection between a man's ego and his instincts, so that he can again enjoy a fully claimed and embodied life, no longer split off into the fragments of a schizoid identity where his ego lives in a separate compartment, disowning his instincts.

Similarly, a hero in such symbolic enactments must free his princess from a witch's lair or from her bewitched shape through his acts of courage, his long journeys, or arduous labors. In getting free of the witch's power, both prince and princess—that is, ego and anima—undergo transformation. He is sprung loose from the male stereotypes, from overidentification with his several roles as provider, sexual performer, and ambitious worker. He is restored to the world of values, to compassion, to the reality of ambiguity, to the fact that everything does not yield to quick-fix approaches. In the witch's domain, the polished role-player has no suasion. In fairy tales it is the innocent, the dumbling, the apparent oaf who prevails, not the egregiously virile figure who leaps into every battle. What wins the day is the ability to wait to see what there is that might help, what might come up, rather than great plans of action proceeding in solemn logic from cause to effect. Another rhythm entirely moves the innocent into action—something organic, tidal, lifted by winds and seasons, not collective prescriptions. The innocent's ego loosens itself from what it is told to be by family, culture, and custom. He makes his own new mixtures of intention and procedure; he finds purpose in purposelessness, fact in metaphor, large symbolic life in unexpected combinations such as talking mirrors, carpets that travel, combs that can create woods or rivers, and handkerchiefs that become trap doors that open onto an entirely other dimension of reality.

The anima is not fixed in its ways. It can change itself and its world at any moment, to unveil a great landscape beyond the handkerchief-trap door. Thus the anima asserts the particularity of her nature against the stereotypes that so often trap women. As the man learns that he does not have to turn to stone in order to survive, nor resort to impotency for protection, nor to its opposite, compulsive sexual performance, his contrasexuality springs free. The anima is differentiated from the maternal that surrounds her and from confinement to the role of helpmeet.[18] The man's dropping down through the trap door not only reveals a new dimension outside himself, but introduces new spaces in his consciousness, spaces of silence in his ego-vocabulary, resources of reverie in the midst of conscious action. Different tempos and different goals accompany the gradual disclosure of specific feminine reality in an anima that really touches his ego with her world and her own values. The archetypal depth of the feminine as it touches him now is alive in him, can take its own shape, changing his bland assumption of control over this part of himself and its value to him. New patterns of mutuality replace old fixations on the poles of dominance and submission. To find and claim his anima, a man must undergo fundamental change. Brought into the witch world by his anima, he cannot return to the ego world the same man. Facing the fact of the witch has transformed him.

Redeeming the Hag

Forging his own relation to the feminine releases a man from the ardors of projecting his anima onto women, and releases women from the force of his projective identification. He enters the hag domain in a new way, with new understanding, able to see that powerful female in her own colors, defined for him in intellect, spirit, and power, not in relation to the male, but in her own feminine terms. By rejecting a man's needs for maternal holding, mirroring, empathy, and support, the hag forces his ego to make its own connection directly to those feminine virtues, rather than perform some devious evasion such as bending a woman to carry those virtues for him and then punishing her if she fails to do so. By refusing to act as his substitute in this function, she shows him what he must connect to: the ancient, uncanny, earth-bound sexual, intellectual, and emotional female power. He can no longer thrust that connective function onto a female. Thus when he finds a woman of affect, who by her very being makes him feel more connected, she will be all the more precious to him, and he will feel deep gratitude for her presence in his life and for her in herself, not for her as a substitute filling in for some part of his damaged self.

A man must take full responsibility for the feminine turned negative in him; he must claim what is damaged in him and not blame it on women. No longer can he use a woman to play object to his subject, to cater to his needs with no recognition from him of her person in its own distinctive otherness. For a man caught in sexual compulsion, where archetypal emotion obliterates human feeling and persons are reduced to fantasy parts, to face that compulsion as his own, to inspect and to claim it, is to be pulled right through its beneficent trap door into that rich world of psychic connections that the compulsion camouflaged. Behind the old revolving fantasy live dissociated and repressed feelings—of rage, humiliation, helplessness, and vengeance—that require his attention, his mirroring, and his empathy, not that of some fantasy mother. He needs to find his own ways to mix the repressed stuff with his own conscious ego-centered values so that they can be knit together to make his life whole again. These are depths the witch leads to; if he follows, all of him will be transformed. The beasts will be recognized, fed, released from their slavery, allowed to live. He takes hold now of the task of wrestling with the opposites within him, to link his delicate personal feelings and sheer lust. He is able now to live with both his suppressed tenderness and his demonic sexuality, the restraints that have held back his fear and his rage. There can be no more dichotomizing reality into a man's world, a tough public life of facts and forces, and a woman's world, a soft private life of values and feelings, or the opposite polarization whereby the woman of the world is the carrier of untamed sex while the man plays stable, trustworthy provider. His struggle now is to be open to and to house all the opposing pulls in himself, not to assign them to the sexes, one for him, one for her, back and forth *ad nauseam*.

The hag shows a man the awful largeness of being. He inspects it. He accepts it. He does not evade it by trying to make her his good mother to life partner or cozy advisor. She remains other to him—her own odd, bold self, intense, alien. Facing up to what she is returns him to the precious values of this human world —and to what he may draw from them, in order to experience a human love big enough to contain the small, funny acts by which the male and female recognize each other, as well as the shocking fact that this familiar feminity is really something other than oneself, independent, free, living from its own mysterious inner core.

IX The Clown Archetype

In sharp contrast to the witch, who so obviously does not give a rap for dependent needs, tender feelings, or anybody's wish to grow, but simply cackles her characteristic cackle and flies off in the face of human concerns, the clown brings color and laughter and the hurly-burly of the circus into the world. The clown gathers feeling into merry bundles. He makes us laugh. He makes us cry. We oohh and aahh with terror as danger stalks him from behind. We howl with relief when he makes his bumbling escape. We sit on the edge of our chairs in anticipation of a terrible event about to occur, and yet thump with glee when disaster befalls. When Laurel and Hardy are moving a piano down a flight of stairs, we know that the piano must fly loose from its moorings and rush down, accompanied by a crashing of keys, a snapping of strings, and a crunching of wood.

In the great Japanese clown tradition associated with the comic interludes of the Noh theater, one man—the comedian—follows another in perambulations around a stage. We tremble with anticipation and delight as we watch the clown mime every movement of the man in front of him, tiptoeing or bowing, walking or running, as the other does so, turning around in perfect mimicry when the first actor turns around, so that the first man never catches even a glimpse of his shadow. The only gesture the clown makes on his own is to put his finger to his mouth as he stares at the audience, thus making sure that he will not be betrayed and signalling everyone's complicity in the action. We acknowledge our willing participation in ancient Japanese clowning or modern American slapstick by the delight we feel, installed in our exalted roles far above the comedy, secure in the knowledge that we alone are aware of what is really going on. Our prescience amounts to something like God's foreknowledge of events. It provides a deep archetypal satisfaction.[1]

The clown arouses our emotions, and emotions of all sorts—sadistic glee when he, rather than any of us, is beaten up; fear and pity when we fully take in his starkly painted, mournful countenance, as if his whitened face, huge mouth, and deeply fixed, encircled eyes prefigure the face of death. We delight in his antics that poke fun at all the established rules; we are grateful for his moving us out of time into the timeless moment where what we feel—where all that *we* feel—matters most. He makes us sad with his poor clothes and wistful eagerness to be included in some game. He makes us lonely when so clearly he is not accepted, and can never be accepted, as one of the group. He shocks us with his rude mimicry of sacred values, his obscene ribaldry that, despite our disapproval, inspires us to laughter. He is altogether a fabulous, funny fellow. Distinct, vivid, unforgettable, the clown stands forth as an immensely potent archetype of human feeling. He makes us feel; he personifies feeling. He enacts feeling; he *is* feeling. What does he tell us with all of this? What is the clown archetype?

The Clown and the Opposites

The word "clown" comes to us from an old Celtic tongue. Originally it designated a farm worker, a boor who seemed funny to townspeople, a lumpish, amusing fellow, a buffoon, a fool. The clown embodies the reverse of what convention holds up as the desirable durable ego, capable of achievement, of placement in harmony with social goals. The clown presents the opposite of well-ordered ego-functioning. He fails. He is weak. He is pitiable. He is anything but master of the situation. Quixotic by temperament, he is sometimes sweet, sometimes good, sometimes malicious, but he is never in command. Even his parading as a self-confident hero debunks all facets of heroism as mere pretense, stupidity, and hubris. He exposes the terrible vulnerability of the human condition, and especially of the person who will not acknowledge it.

"The clown arouses . . . emotions of all sorts— . . . fear and pity when we fully take in his starkly painted, mournful countenance, as if his whitened face, huge mouth, and deeply fixed, encircled eyes prefigure the face of death." (Rouault)

The clown figure presents the direct opposite of the stereotyped heroic male, the opposite of the archetypal masculine principle as embodied in the image of a wise and effective king.[2] In every way, the clown stands against the images and affects with which society has constructed its understanding of what it means to be male. The clown is vulnerable in the extreme. His whole existence is a paradigm of feeling, with tears or laughter painted on his face to make his profession's symbolic association with feeling unmistakably clear. Emotion is always on the ready in the life of the clown, in any situation, in any encounter. Whereas the well-controlled man would at most permit himself a smile, a melancholy adjective, a polite noise of approval or disapproval, the clown will burst forth in roars of laughter or caterwauls of mourning; he will attack others or defend himself in a great, tumultuous display of feeling. No gesture, no posture, no movement is too extreme for the clown engaged in communicating feeling. He himself really *is* feeling—or at least a container for feeling. He carries the feeling that most men in most situations cannot or will not permit themselves, or if they will allow any of it to well up in them, they simply will not acknowledge it publicly.

When feeling is dealt with this way—by ritual and by proxy—it is feeling not felt, feeling pushed aside, feeling condemned and wherever possible extinguished. The clown is man's supreme defense against feeling. Either the clown expresses other men's feeling for them, acting out the feeling they have run away from, or he expresses his own feeling, which remains all the more unacknowledged as he contains it in fixed words or movements, subduing his intensity of pain or pleasure or any of the multiple states of being with which he may be uncomfortable, with a whole gallery of techniques and adornments. And when the inherited apparatus of the clown is not enough, he shows how industrious he can be in the service of the great combat against feeling by inventing new costumes, new machinery, new routines, whole new languages if necessary, to disguise feeling, to mask it.

The modern clown appears in baggy pants, disordered vest, raveled cuffs, a battered hat, and a shabby coat. In ancient times he came dressed as the jester, the harlequin, the multi-colored one of juxtaposed designs, clearly a person altogether other than the one dressed in the solemn, regal robes of the king or high nobleman. The modern clown costume caricatures conventional upper-class dress. In his top hat and black coat, Charlie Chaplin mocks the respectable bourgeois gentleman. Buster Keaton reduces a general to a splendid bedragglement. Inspector Clouseau of the *Pink Panther* films makes hilarious wreckage out of dressing up in one's best clothes to receive a decoration for bravery, catching his sword of state in his tie, which he then manages to get pinned to the official along with the medal he is bestowing on Clouseau; instead of a resplendent occasion, the ensuing mélange of arms, ties, chests, noses, and teeth jumbles together to dissolve dignity into farce.

The clown shows us the missing side of the male personality, the feeling a man finds no room to claim in his conscious adaptation—the passion, the sensitivity, the tears, the vulnerable openness to being. Somehow such feelings are thought to be unmanly, even by the men who feel them; such is the effect of the long and wide repression of the feminine principle. So the clown frequently uses effeminate gestures to make room for these left-out emotions.

We do not allow or want our clowns to be tough. We do not allow our heroic images of the male to betray feeling along with their virility, or our clown figures to show virility with their feelings. Thus the clown is parodying even himself while he gives way to feeling with effeminate gesture or posture. Think of Jack Benny's despairing flip of his hands, palms up, or Bob Hope's sashaying movements around a microphone, coming to a stop finally with his hand flattened on his hip in fine feminine fashion.

In his excessive weeping, the clown, ancient or modern, shows how much contempt he feels for all sentimentality. His exquisite sensitivity to the minutest gesture of emotion is almost always followed quickly with a thumping, bumping chase sequence and a ruthless destruction of property. The barrels burst, the house collapses, the balloon explodes, the platform smashes. The magic moment of feeling communication evaporates.

In archetypal terms, the clown as fool or jester serves to oppose the ruling king, as his symbolic inversion.[3] He is chosen as the king's substitute in ritual assassinations or sacrifices. In any royal hierarchy, he is numbered last; the king, first. In the Tarot deck, the Fool's card is unnumbered, set apart, like the Fool himself, on the fringe of all orders and systems, outside social mobility or psychological transformation. Through his folly he tries to invert the prevailing order; he expresses the duality of all things, saying harsh things kindly and kind things harshly.

In Shakespeare, the role of the fool as countervailing force against king or rich man, against power or convention in almost any form, is crucial. King Lear will trust himself, at least for a moment, with his fool, for the fool, playing clown to the king's unacknowledged or disorganized or unaccepted feelings, speaks the truth for him and makes possible some continuing contact with reality. It is the fool with his unquenchable wit who lightens the terror of the tempest in which Lear is cast adrift at the beginning of Act III. His dry ironies are not enough to soak up the torrential rain, but they make the necessary point: "Good nuncle, in; ask the daughters' blessing: here's a night pities neither wise men nor fools." That is to say, get indoors, no matter what the difficulties, even those of making some sort of peace with your grim children. That small wisdom is wisdom enough, for nature defeats a more pretentious kind of knowledge. The fool has already explained as much to Lear, with his exalted plans to share his kingdom and distribute his goods among his daughters, in the boisterous catechism that ends Act I. "Canst tell how an oyster makes his shell?" the fool asks Lear. "No." "Nor I neither," the fool admits, "but I can tell why a snail has a house." "Why?" "Why, to put his head in; not to give it away to his daughters, and leave his horns without a case." And finally, in sum, "If thou wert my fool, nuncle," the fool says, "I'd have thee beaten for being old before thy time." "How's that?" "Thou shouldst not have been old till thou hadst been wise." To which Lear can only respond, "O, let me be not mad, not mad, sweet heaven!"[4]

Even such small fools, as plot and character development go, as Launcelot Gobbo in *The Merchant of Venice* and Touchstone in *As You Like It* move wittily against the prevailing order in lines that signify the polyvalent nature of their dramas. Both are identified as clowns. Both turn sour comments into sweet wisdom for those willing to step aside from events and look with learned detachment—a fool's distance—at what is happening. Gobbo gives more than passing depth to old saws such as "It is a wise father that knows his old child," in identifying himself to his blind father; and "The sins of the father are to be laid upon the children," in offering Shylock's daughter the only hope he sees for her, "a kind of bastard hope," one that will free her from the taint that must come if she is in physical fact his progeny. But his wisdom, clown's wisdom, is best summed up in his more fervent hope: "Let it be as humours and conceits shall govern." In other words, never be deceived by appearances; let inner meanings rule; the nature of temperaments and of wits is our better nature. And thus it is that with just moments left before the full unraveling of the plot and all the disguises of *As You Like It*, Touchstone establishes himself as a true courtier by his professional knowledge of the art of lying as practiced at court, from the Retort courteous and Quip modest, through the Reply churlish, Reproof valiant, and Countercheck quarrelsome, to the Lie circumstantial and the Lie direct. The precision of his description, his ability to turn things upside down if that is necessary to reveal reality, to say harsh things kindly and kind things harshly, shows him to have earned a higher rank. He need no longer *pretend* to be a fool.[5]

The clown not only presents the opposite side to collective conscious stereotypes of the ideal male, he goes further and embodies in action, pantomime, and word the co-existence of opposite realities in life. He dabbles in these opposites with no attempt to reconcile them; he juggles them and lets the balls fall all round his head with no effort to sustain order. In him opposites are juxtaposed rather than integrated; one flip of his hand, and the sad wandering soul becomes the merry prankster; the gaping, clumsy, dumbshow performer executes a *pas de deux* with astonishing grace. In that most masterful description of a comic mime, Diderot's *The Nephew of Rameau*, the title character is described as a "compound of the highest and the lowest, good sense and folly. The notions of good and evil must be strangely muddled in his head, for the good qualities nature has given him he displays without ostentation, and the bad ones without shame." In his own body, Rameau's nephew presents absolutely opposite aspects of being:

> At times he is thin and gaunt like somebody in the last stages of consumption; you could count his teeth through his cheeks . . . a month later he is sleek and plump. . . . Today, in dirty linen and ragged breeches he slinks along. . . . Tomorrow, powdered, well-shod, . . . beautifully turned out, . . . showing himself off. . . . He lives for the day, gloomy or gay according to circumstances.[6]

The opposites co-exist in the clown figure without any ego holding them together or uniting them. In this way, he presents us with an image of the self—in Jung's terms, that primordial, unconscious wholeness that includes all aspects of life—but without the conscious connection to them that only an ego in relation to self can provide. The clown's presentation of opposites focuses on opposite emotions that are not yet reshaped and gathered into richly changing feelings appropriate to the situation. The clown acts out a succession of opposite emotions of body and of feeling. He is pounded by misfortune, calmed by a moment of beauty; he pampers a bruised knee, hurls himself into big, noisy, and painful leaps. Part of the clown's appeal is his surprise and unpredictability; we never know what will happen next. Anything can happen when an opposing emotion can at any time replace the one presently before us. Opposites quickly alternate with each other, and the quick changes excite us. With all this mobility of libido, nothing sticks. From one moment to the next, who can foresee what happens?

The great clown figures have long been miracles of metamorphosis. They do not themselves know what they will do, who they will be, or how they will feel from moment to moment. Don Quixote, the founding father of one great line of clowns, is certain only of his tutelage in the masterpieces of chivalry as he goes forth on his knightly adventures. His faith is the faith of a believer in books. Knowing where truth has been told, he need only follow the direction of the *Amadis de Gaule* or the countless other fictions from which he has extracted his code of behavior. A coarse village girl can easily become, in such a transformation of libido, the most fragile and beautiful of maidens. Any inanimate object can at any time turn into a wildly moving monster that must be fought to the death. Fantasy takes on the colors and textures of reality for Don Quixote because that is his reality. His is an asceticism of the imagination in which each adventure is a spiritual exercise. He proclaims his sanity a hundred times over, or at least he takes responsibility for what he is doing in a way that with most of us would pass for sanity. "I know who I am!" he insists, as he goes on his clown-knightly way. And yet at the end, on his death-bed, he renounces the world of chivalry, sadly confessing that it is too late for him to change yet again, reading a new set of books "that would enlighten my soul."

Don Quixote is a haunted figure, a magnificent figure, a poignant one. He is the *compleat clown.* In him feeling is gathered to a fullness that should permit all men who need others to act out their feelings for them to feel safe for millennia. But they will not feel safe. They will stand aside. They will feel superior to the cadaverous old soul of honor. They will find their reality better served, many of them, by the literal-mindedness of Sancho Panza and his stubborn assertion of what his senses reflect to him of a gaunt and thankless reality. Instead of anything so grimly logical and unfulfilling, the Don finds his own sublimely mad universe. If they grant Don Quixote his license to adventure, what must they say of their own drab and colorless lives? Who is the more starved for life in all its possibilities, Don Quixote bursting through his tin-plate armor with his deluded passions, or those sedate folk all around him who mock him? Even those whose compassion for him cannot be doubted—his niece, his priest, Bachelor Sampson—live only in his shadow, find color and significance only when their beings are infused for a while with his.[7]

The stunning effect of *Don Quixote* on its first readers, in the two great installments in which it appeared (Book I in 1605, Book II in 1615), was more than matched by the influence it had on the development of the novel. It inspired in writers of a skill not far from Cervantes's own, such as Henry Fielding and Laurence Sterne, an understanding of the role of the clown-figure as surrogate for men with less confidence in their feelings. The understanding was large enough to produce the patriarchal clown of Fielding's *Joseph Andrews*, Parson Abraham

Adams, and Fielding's young clown in the bedroom, Tom Jones. Both are fully human; both are altogether good men, the more convincing for the farce and folly which accompany their adventures. As much again must be said for the prolonged self-examination of the novelist creating character and situation which is Sterne's *Tristam Shandy*. The book positively abounds in Quixotish people, from the shadowy title figure, missing large parts of nose and penis as a result of unfortunately quite plausible misadventure, to his Uncle Toby, his parents, Corporal Trim, Dr. Slop, and the Widow Wadman. Sterne's surrealist imagination is not so congenial as his Spanish progenitor's; it falls much more easily and much more luridly into sexual fantasy. But in its essentials it trusts to the inspiration of the moment, allowing something like an archetypal grandeur to surround those moments when feeling dominates the being of his men and women—and the clown stands larger in the role of noble hero than do the traditional holders of high masculine rank, soldiers, statesmen, and young lovers.[8]

A particularly refreshing variation of this play of opposites, in reality and in fantasy, turns up not only in the slapstick comedy of fifty years ago, but also in such a modern representative of the idiom as Inspector Clouseau. Total destruction and total restitution alternate in rapid sequence in the *Pink Panther* chronicles. Clouseau arranges that when he returns each night to his apartment, his Oriental valet Cato will lie in wait for him, each time hidden in a more ingenious place, ready to spring on his employer to prepare him properly for his Quixotish existence. Each evening they battle to see whose prowess in karate will triumph. Clouseau enters stealthily, eyes alert to the slightest irregularity of furniture that might betray his servant-rival. He looks in the hamper, in the closets, out the window, behind the screen. All this Cato observes from his perch above the canopy of a capacious bed. At the right moment Cato strikes. Yelling his karate cry, he leaps upon the Inspector. With kicks, shoves, whirlings and twirlings, chairs splinter, doors crack, windows shatter, books tumble from shelves. The apartment lies in ruins. But then the phone rings. There is instant peace and accord. The Inspector answers. By tacit agreement a tranquil truce prevails—but not quite. As he speaks on the phone, Clouseau notices a saw cutting a circle around him in the wooden floor on which he stands. He hangs up, and plunges down into the room below, splashing right into a tub of blue paint being used there to redecorate the newly tenanted apartment. It becomes the new scene of destruction. The dripping blue figure of Clouseau squishes against and smears the white walls and freshly upholstered chairs. Cato springs from a corner only to fall flat on a bed, which promptly crumbles under him. The phone is pulled from the wall. Pictures are shattered. The whole place becomes a shocking, glorious mess. Total destruction reigns.

But wait—a miracle! The next night the karate battle resumes in Clouseau's completely reconstituted apartment. All is magically repaired! There is no penalty. No lawsuits are brought by the apartment owners below. No legs have been broken; no one is carted off to the hospital. Somehow the smashed canopy bed will be restored in time for sleep, the dishes will be cleared from the floor, the books will settle back into place on their shelves. No months of repairs, no men tracking through the house to set things right; no trips to the cleaners, no plumbers or electricians or carpenters.

This magical reparation is one great source of the clown's appeal. His antics provide us with a space in which to experience our aggressive impulses to the full, without our having to be responsible for the results. Our egos can rest from the burden of the cause-and-effect sequences we know so well in our diurnal reality. At least for the moment, our egos do not have to hold everything together. We can let go. We can enjoy the wreckage fully, like a child knocking over a tower of blocks or making a great mess of mud. We can enjoy our own truce in tranquillity, not needing to hold our own opposite emotions together. We can indulge vicariously in our impulses to make messes, to let everything fall down, to smash, to rip, to smear—and all without payment of guilt. No need to repair damage done by our hate, because we experience it as totally separate from and unconnected to our love. No sadness or remorse over the damage our destructive impulses may do, because no one has been hurt. In fact as well as in fantasy, it was great fun.[9]

The Clown's Effect on Us

Precisely because the clown embodies qualities entirely opposite to those of the stereotype of the male and of the well-achieving ego, and precisely because the clown dabbles so happily in opposites, he arouses opposite emotions in us. He entertains us and makes us laugh till we cry, diverted from life's more serious responsibilities, work, children, meals, money, everything. He thereby relieves us from the ego-tasks of holding opposites together. He gives our egos a rest, ushering us into a breathing space where without a qualm of guilt we can cheer his being beaten up. It may not be sensible or practical to roar with laughter at the destruction of property, but nonetheless there it is. It is outrageously funny to see all those emblems of success smashed up in a giant car-crash in a Jacques Tati film. In this clown-space, our egos do not have to reconcile all the opposites; we can simply enjoy them to the fullest, each one in isolation from the rest. Tati's brittle walk and gestures convey just a suggestion of diffidence as he goes about his eccentric business. On holiday, at work, investigating the new worlds of modernity, he constantly reassures us, as he crashes into objects and is all but destroyed by them, that we can come through—not unscathed, but enlarged by the experience of going directly where our feelings lead us.

Above all the clown arouses our emotions. He takes us directly to what we feel without the intermediary of words or analysis or a rational sequence of events. The clown is ardent, and awakens in us our own intensity of emotion. He expands our feeling space. He offers us a quick succession of roles with which to identify without having to make any unity of them. Thus we can switch quickly, effortlessly, from being a bumbling fool, to a celebratory triumph over evil, to childlike awe, to sadness beyond words, to an orgy of sadism, to fearful weakness. The clown hands us a great variety of roles and situations in which to try on our feelings—not his, but ours—to be many things, to identify the many paths we might follow now that we have been released from the constraints of reality. He shows us many roles and stimulates in us an attempt to try on different reactions. He enlivens us and makes us expand our identities by dissolving ego-boundaries. Diderot describes the effect of such clowns on other people:

> . . . [T]heir characters contrast sharply with other people's and break the tedious uniformity that our social conventions and set politeness have brought about. If one of them appears in a company of people he is the speck of yeast that leavens the whole, and restores each of us a portion of his natural individuality. He stirs people and gives them a good shaking, makes them take sides, brings out the truth, shows who are really good and unmasks the villains.[10]

Diderot's description was echoed in the experience of the effect of a clown-like man in group therapy. The other members of the group prized him highly. They were drawn, as one said, to his "ardent emotion" that filled the room with feeling for everyone; or as another said, to his amusing ways of presenting his problems, which came through all the more poignantly because of their comic disguise; or, as still another member said, because of the tremendous spark of life in him that counteracted others' gloomy depression. Another person admired this man's great courage in passionately engaging life despite an underlying despair. It seemed an act of heroic courage that this man of great comic disguises could even get up each morning, considering all the chaos that his life faced him with and that he felt so strongly inside himself.

The master of comic disguise in the arena of feeling is the early Anton Chekhov. When as a young medical student he was writing his stories, his vignettes, his wry reflections on the life he saw around him in Moscow, he never missed a chance to combat depression in all its only too accessible forms. His attitude is splendidly summed up in a short article he published in 1885 in a Moscow humor magazine. "Life Is Wonderful" is the title and, after a certain ironic manner, the substance of the piece. "Life is quite an unpleasant business," it begins, "but it is not so very hard to make it wonderful." How? Not by winning a lottery or receiving a high order from the Tsar or marrying a beautiful woman; "these blessings are transitory and liable to become a habit." To find happiness amidst pain and sorrow, he proposes the principle that in any event, things could be worse. He offers such examples as these:

> When your matches suddenly go off in your pocket, rejoice and offer thanks to Heaven that your pocket is not a gunpowder magazine.

> If you get a splinter in your finger, rejoice that it is not in your eye.

Rejoice that you are not a tram-horse, nor a Koch bacillus, nor a trichina, nor a pig, nor an ass, nor a bear led by a gypsy, nor a bug.

If you live in a place not so remote as Siberia, can't you feel pleased at the idea, that by a mere chance you might have been deported there?

If you have pain in one tooth, rejoice that it is not all your teeth that are aching

If your wife has been unfaithful to you, rejoice that she has betrayed merely yourself, and not your country.[11]

The Russians have long been masters at finding clowns' panaceas for their aching souls. They simply indulge their feeling in the clown's manner, thoroughly aware as they do so that their cure-alls will cure almost nothing. What they will do, however, is to provide a tunnel through chaos, a way of dealing with the greater tortures, right up to and including the one that defines and structures all the rest—death. Even with the first of their major writers, Alexander Pushkin, they were indulging themselves in the kind of black humor that can hold off, if not death itself, then the terror it so easily inspires. In Pushkin's story "The Undertaker," Hadrian Prokhorov, the title figure of the story, is consumed with envy when a neighboring shoemaker, and a German at that, is able to give a lavish dinner in celebration of his silver wedding anniversary. Crammed with guests, the shoemaker's affair burgeons into endless toasts, including salutes to all those for whom they toil. It really galls the undertaker when the Finnish nightwatchman turns to him and cries, "Come, old fellow, drink to the health of *your* clients!" He mutters to himself, as he gets home drunk and angry, "After all, in what way is my calling less honorable than others? . . . I had thought of inviting them to my house-warming, giving them a real good time, but I'm blowed if I will now! Tell you what I'll do: invite my clients, the Orthodox dead 'uns." His female assistant is appalled: "The idea of asking corpses to a party!" But he does extend the invitation, and his guests come and cram his quarters with "their blue and yellow faces, their sunken mouths, their dull, half-closed eyes and their pinched noses. . . ." One who had to suffer a pauper's grave stands in a corner, embarrassed by his rags. This is the undertaker's first body, a retired sergeant of the guard reduced now to a small skeleton. He reminds Hadrian that he had passed off a pine coffin on him as solid oak, and them moves to give the undertaker "a bony embrace." Hadrian pushes him away, the sergeant dissolves into dust, and the undertaker loses consciousness. He is very pleased on waking up to discover the whole thing to be a dream.[12]

Chekhov's way of handling the same subject is to arouse an all-purpose orator, who "could make a speech at any time, within seconds of waking, during burning fever, on an empty stomach, or while dead-drunk," to deliver a proper funeral eulogy for an office dignitary who has just died. "The secretary," the orator yawns, "that the one who drinks?" "Yes, he certainly did put it away." And so the orator hastens to catch up with the funeral procession, which is already under way, and quickly produces one of his impromptu miracles. "We have many capable officials," he mourns, "but Prokofi Ossipitch was unique . . . devoted to the honest performance of his duty . . . never spared himself . . . spent sleepless nights . . . was disinterested and incorruptible . . . would distribute his meagre salary to his poorer comrades . . . knew none of the joys of life . . . as you know, he remained single to the end of his mortal span . . . I can see his tragic, clean-shaven features. . . ." The speech is quite up to expectations except for the fact that the dead man's name was Kyril Ivanovitch, had fought all through his life with "his lawful spouse," and "had never shaved in his life." The crowd begins to whisper. Undismayed, the orator goes on: "Prokofi Ossipitch, your features were plain, even ugly, you were aloof and morose, but we all knew that under your skin there beat a true and friendly heart." Even he is forced to stop when he suddenly notices, "with terror in his eyes," that the man he has been eulogizing is alive and standing right there before him. He protests: "I can't take it out." Never mind, he is told, "Go on, go on." When he is finished, the officials who are present laugh: "You buried a living man!" As for Prokofi Ossipitch, he is outraged: "Your speech may have been suitable for a dead man, but for a living one it was sheer mockery, sir! To say such things! Disinterested! Incorruptible! Never take bribes! That can only be said of a living person in mockery! And nobody asked you to make remarks about my face! Plain and ugly it may be, but why say so in public? It's insulting, sir!"[13]

Chekhov and Pushkin had discovered the great comic motif in man's being —perhaps even in the universe's. With a clown's leer fixed in place, they saluted the madness of a constantly changing world "The most profound philosophers," George Santayana says, looking at the comic nature of existence, "deny that any of those things exist which we find existing, and maintain that the only reality is changeless, infinite, and indistinguishable into parts. . . ." The cause of "this obvious folly of theirs" is their humorlessness and their consequent conclusion that the universe is equally humorless. "Yet there is a capital joke in their own systems, which prove that nothing exists so strenuously, that existence laughs aloud in their vociferations and drowns the argument." It is central to Santayana's belief that an existence that is all change and unpredictable happening is "inherently" comic. The incongruity of things is on such a scale that "not only does each thing surprise itself by what it becomes, but is continually astonished and disconcerted by what other things have turned into without its leave. The mishaps, the expedients, the merry solutions of comedy, in which everybody acknowledges himself beaten and deceived, yet is the happier for the unexpected posture of affairs, belong to the very texture of temporal being. . . ." If there are those, he says, who are deeply troubled by these difficulties or are hostile to the implicit answers to the problems which are contained in the very essence of the situation, "it is only because their souls are less plastic and volatile than the general flux of nature."

As Wallace Stevens, a poet much indebted to Santayana, said, we live "in an old chaos of the sun." Quoting Goethe's Mephistopheles, Santayana reminds his reader that "whatever arises deserves to perish." The universe that his comic metaphysics envisions is a "limbo of unheard melodies and uncreated worlds. For anything to emerge from that twilight region is inexplicable and comic, like the popping up of Jack-in-the-Box; and the shock will amuse us, if our wits are as nimble as nature and as quick as time." The secret of the great clowns is to have found their peace in this limbo, in this chaos.[14]

The word "chaos" gives the clue to the disturbing effect of the clown upon us. He evokes in us opposite and ambivalent reactions in rapid succession. We also have opposite reactions to the resting place into which he invites us, where our egos are relieved momentarily of the task of holding together in awareness the tension of ambivalent emotions. We feel uncomfortable, uneasy, with no secure place to stand. The very release from ego-tasks and boundaries introduces us once again to a pre-ego, unconscious stage of chaos where everything blurs together and contradictions co-exist, a state from which we only slowly emerged in those long childhood years in which we constructed or tried to construct durable ego-identities. We are left in an unsettling jumble when opposite emotions collide, with no mediating ego to intercede on behalf of one or the other. We are let loose in a riot of alternating reactions that exhaust us and may even alarm us. Diderot describes this disturbance well in giving his reactions to the multiple roles that Rameau's nephew has acted out:

> As I was listening to him acting the scene of the pimp and the maiden he was procuring, I was torn between opposite impulses and did not know whether to give in to laughter or furious indignation. I felt embarrassed. A score of times a burst of laughter prevented a burst of rage, and a score of times the anger rising in the depths of my heart ended in a burst of laughter. I was dumbfounded at such sagacity and such baseness, such alternately true and false notions, such absolute perversion of feeling and utter turpitude, and yet such uncommon candor. . . .
>
> As for me, I didn't know whether to stay or run away, laugh or to be furious . . . dispel the horror that filled my soul. I was beginning to find irksome the presence of a man who discussed a horrible act, an execrable crime, like a connoisseur of painting or poetry examining the beauties of a work of art. . . .[15]

The clown's disturbing effect upon us may lead us to use him as a scapegoat. Individually, we may saddle him with all the emotions we cannot or will not make room to carry in our own awareness and adaptation. Thus we do not identify with the clown in a feeling of human solidarity. We like his being beaten about. He receives the punishment we secretly fear we ourselves deserve. He breaks the taboos of good taste and decorum, but it is he, not we, who presents a disreputable appearance of unacceptablility. He is the poor, homeless figure, the absolute fool, the dope, the sucker, the weak, stumbling one. We can remain well dressed, under control, respectable, and well behaved in the role of observer. He is a man too gentle to succeed, too sensitive to survive; we can remain tough and realistic and able to cope in the "real" world. He can indulge in obscene gestures, goosing his lady, fondling his friend, wagging his finger slyly, tottering along in variously inebriated states. We remain sober, dignified, "mature" above all. The clown, in Jung's vocabulary, is a handy figure on whom we can park our shadow.

Collectively, the clown may function as the scapegoat for the ills of the group, carrying communal shadow elements to which the dominant mores of society deny a place. He may carry, for example, our wish not to grow up, not to conform, nor even to reach a fixed identity. He may carry those undifferentiated parts of our personalities or those emotions that would challenge the supremacy of the dominant principles of social order and ethical behavior. As a man caught up in compulsive clowning put it, "All those things that are meant to be so right, seem wrong; they bore me."

Archetypally, the clown figure of myths plays this shadow role in a sacrificial way. The jester substitutes for the king as the victim in ritual assassinations concocted to atone for the ills that afflict a given community. He even becomes a Christ figure. One of the major thrusts of early Christianity was identification with clown symbolism. One could be a "fool for Christ." Not only did the clown break all the taboos, he also received all the punishments for it.

The clown as scapegoat is a familiar enough figure in the grease paint and costumes of the circus, in the less than profound but still moving anguish of the central character in the opera *Pagliacci* and in the deeply probing studies of painters. Goya's early depictions of the Spanish people are more good-natured than those that followed upon his torturing deafness, but from the very beginning he sees the victims of society with particular clarity. Old and young, male and female, some recognizably human, others closer to monsters—he sees them all with a bitter sense of humor. The laughter is too quickly suffocated by the horror, but it is there, and remains there, even if only in the rictus of a smile. It reminds us of the speed with which our own amusement can turn to pain or sorrow when we look at or listen to our clowns without any great degree of consciousness.

Rouault's clowns are just the other side of Goya's victims. They are scapegoats, too, carrying the burdens of others. But their misery is more openly accepted. The burdens are not unendurable, because whether taken in a Christian spirit or not, they have purpose. The clowns of Rouault have moved at least as close to Christ on the cross as the good thief.

A similar sense of the clownish spirit, if not of the traditional role of the clown, endows the variously macabre and ironic wit of modern painters as far apart in style as Emile Nolde, the German expressionist, and René Magritte, the Belgian surrealist. In Nolde's "Legend of Maria Aegyptica," the central panel of a 1912 triptych, he shows the desert saint in her days as a whore, altogether given over to the roistering pleasures of the profession. But in the leering clown masks worn by her and those with her, the pleasure is streaked with pain, as it is also in the work of Nolde's Belgian progenitor, James Ensor. The joy depicted in such painting is one step removed from violence. In this, as in other such subjects of Nolde's work, the sacred hangs on a cross of demonic construction.

Magritte's clownishness stretches our understanding of the unconscious with a whole landscape of entertainingly disturbed libidos. The painting called "The Human Condition" turns out to be a canvas of a landscape sitting on an easel before an open window, imposed on the real grass and trees and road that exist behind the painting: Man is condemned to accept appearance rather than reality. It is the function of the clown-artist—i.e., Magritte—to show us what appearance masks. Thus whether on pilgrimage or seeking pleasure, whether thinking or feeling, whether our heads are averted or covered, faces disappear. We live in a ghost-world of ravaging fantasy, as for example in the two versions of "The Rape," Magritte's famous 1934 and 1945 transformations of a woman's face, presumably under the assaulting inspection of a man's eyes, into a pubic mouth, a naval nose, and breasts with erect nipples for eyes. By the second version of the same battle scene, the pubic mouth has lost its hair, the navel has become more vagina-like, and the hair of the brunette has grown longer and turned blond.

Magritte's scapegoat unmistakably seems to be woman. One would not make the same identification in the world of Picasso, especially not in the lengthy series of erotic drawings and etchings that come to something like a climax in the Mougins etchings of 1968. Here the artist occupies the clown's and scape-goat's role, watching others perform. He is sometimes present by proxy figure, sometimes there only in a fillip of interpretation, a lingering trace of frustra-tion—not the frustration of a defeated or impotent sexuality, but rather that which comes from knowing the obstacles involved in getting more than surface sexual-ity into one's work. The artist knows very well what the scapegoat grin looks and feels like; he has been forced into it again and again by the inevitable thwarting of his ambitions as an artist—all the more so if in his dialogues between self and soul he has admitted the near impossibility of getting onto paper or canvas or board even the outlines of his own identity, much less the identities of others.[16]

The clown shows us a glimpse into the life of the self that encompasses all psychic polarities. Without an ego to relate to it, the self left unclaimed can threaten our ego with extinction. Living with all the opposites in a fluid, inter-changeable state presents to our consciousness what the unclaimed self looks like from the perspective of an ego trying to secure its identity. It looks chaotic, other, something to be outlawed or at least placed out there in the circus ring, on the film screen, or in the pages of literature. It can be laughed at, jeered, applauded, or disapproved of, but still it remains out there, not one of us.

The Clown as Outsider

The clown plays the role of "not one of us," the outsider who punctures the illusions we have about our symbolic systems of meaning. What we take as fact, he exposes as fancy; what we hold up as the right way to be, he spears with mockery; what we inflate as the truth, he deflates with ridicule. Take these examples from Rabelais, whose character Panurge attempts to establish with absolute certainty that his future wife will not cuckold him. He seeks counsel from various figures, repositories in different ways of wisdom, among them a sibyl. Poking fun at this archetypally wise woman, he describes her dwelling place as a " . . . straw thatched cottage which was badly built, badly furnished, and filled with smoke. . . ." There "they found the old woman in the chimney corner . . . grim to look at, ill-dressed, ill-nourished, toothless, bleary-eyed, hunchbacked, snotty, and feeble."[17] Hah, we snort—hardly a wise old woman! Thus we make room for an inevitable but usually repressed part of our reactions to any person of gifts that are unmistakably superior to our own.

Erasmus also gibes at all the learned of society, sketching a portrait in joking fashion of what any depth psychologist would label as the affliction of a repressive superego. The scholar is

> a man who wore out his whole boyhood and youth in pursuing the learned disciplines. He wasted the pleasantest time of life in uninterrupted watchings, cares, and studies; and through the remaining part of it he never tasted so much as a tittle of pleasure; always frugal, impecunious, sad, austere; unfair and strict toward himself, morose and unamiable to others; afflicted by pallor, leaness, invalidism, sore eyes, premature age and white hair; dying before his appointed day. By the way, what difference does it make why a man of that sort dies? He has never lived. There you have the clear picture of the wise man.

His parodies of the clergy are even better aimed. These monks who come at last to their maker will only awaken in us pity for God.

> One man will spill out a hundred bushel of hymns . . . another will boast that for sixty years he never touched money, except when his fingers were protected by two pairs of gloves. . . . Another will celebrate the fact that for more than fifty-five years he lived the life of a sponge, always fastened to one spot. Another will show a voice grown hoarse with assiduous chanting; another, a lethargy contracted by living alone; another, a tongue grown dumb under his vow of silence.

And finally there is the preacher: "And this superlative divine had so sweated and toiled on this sermon for the previous eight months that today he is as blind as a mole, all the sharpness of his sight having been exhausted, I fancy, to give edge to his wit."[18]

In his parodies of religious values, the clown approaches the realm of the witch and her black magic, though he never actually enters there. The parody mass conducted on the Feast of Fools, accompanied by generalized merry making where all conventional rules of conduct, sexual circumspection, and orders of rank and privilege were suspended, veered toward the anarchy and disorder associated with the grim revels of hell. This holiday began on the liturgical day of Circumcision and ended on the Day of Epiphany. The Carnival time, on the eve of Ash Wednesday, offers a similar example. Wolfgang Zucker likens the clown to the devil, the Lord of Disorder, tracing the root of Harlequin to *hellekin*, meaning dweller in hell. Order, he writes, "creates, maintains, and protects the social structure in which man is at home, where he knows his way about and where he is, more or less, safe-guarded against the shocking experience of otherness."[19]

The clown plays the outsider and aggressively challenges the protective order. He slips under the fence that safely excludes one from the forbidden danger. Thus the male figure who clowns around sexually, like Tom Jones, makes fun of sober virtue, exposing it as a dreary dullness, the result of a fear of pleasure. He tickles the hidden desire of the laced-in maiden, loosening her bonds to stuffy, life-killing propriety. He moistens the dry maxims of the moralist by unearthing deep wells of wishing and wanting with which to flood his tight little system of do's and don'ts. He promises to return the woman to the earth of her own sensuality, rescuing her from high and dry words and schemes to secure the "right" relationship, the "healthy" balance, a carefully worked-out future. Calculations be damned! Let's live! Awake! Follow your heart, listen to your body, hear life calling to you in the good things of this world. One man, whose playing of the clown veered toward all too many affairs, sought therapy. In trying to describe what impelled him toward his long succession of women, he wrote out his thoughts: "An eye, a thigh, a sigh—even in a woman whose humanity and knowledge I respect —awakes this madness to rub, to rape, to somehow wake myself up—and in this ecstasy arouse, raise us both to that road of existence where hay smells fresh mowed, . . . birds caw, surf surges roar and spray, music echoes from a hundred hidden streets, babies nurse, boys hoop their rings and thumb marbles and become Indians and kings." Feeling helplessly caught in his compulsion, he said, "something happens to me which evokes feeling, and I have no place to put it; so I hurl it at women and have to bed them."

The clown exposes the rebel in all of us who would oppose the system, break the rules, violate the taboos, strike out for freedom from repressive, suffocating, narrow little formulas for living. His clowning parodies the stated norms and values of society, showing up their ridiculous side, their pretension to certainty. He shows the absurdity of a patriotism that breeds war or an ambition that dispatches kings. We are all familiar with the raucous humor that relieves unbearable terror, from the randy speculations of the Porter that follow Macbeth's killing of King Duncan, to all the modern clowns at the war front, from *What Price Glory?* to *M*A*S*H*. Such joking betrays the tremendous strain put on human sanity by an ideology of conquest. The clown mocks our hope for orderly systems of thought and dependable sequences of logic in society. Worst of all, he attacks the principle of logos itself, frequently resorting to silent mime, to dumbshow, to nonverbal dramas that give the lie to words by achieving a high degree of expressive communication. Thus he sabotages language itself and the protective order of rationality that we associate with it.

Socrates, a sort of philosophical clown, takes language and turns it here and twists it there, to reach the opposite intention of his opponent in argument, pulling out of the opponent's own words an unguessed meaning, an unfamiliar, unsuspected rabbit from a familiar hat. Socrates has told us himself in the *Philebus* that the mind constantly experiences "a mixed feeling of pain and pleasure," even, he stresses, at a comedy. When his dialogue-mate, Protarchus, confesses difficulty in understanding this, he moves in his usual catechetical fashion to prove that opposites must go together in the tragedy and comedy of human life. Envy, for example, often induces pleasure at another's misfortunes. An ignorant man, a votary of the inversion of the Delphic oracle's injunction to "Know thyself," may think himself richer than he is, may imagine his soul better than it is, and join "the mass of mankind" in their "interminable disputing and lying about how wise they are." Socrates identifies such behavior as evil, and then further divides "childish envy," with its "curious mixture of pleasure and pain," into two classes of people: "those . . . who are weak and unable to avenge themselves, when they are laughed at, may be truly called ridiculous, but those who can defend themselves may be more truly described as strong and formidable; for ignorance in the powerful is hateful and horrible, because hurtful to others both in reality and in fiction, but powerless ignorance may be reckoned, and in truth is, ridiculous." He goes on to demonstrate that we feel pleasure when we laugh at whatever we find ridiculous in our friends, and then to remind Protarchus that envy is the source of this pleasure, and "envy has been acknowledged by us to be mental pain. . . ." Therefore, pleasing laughter plus painful envy exist side by side— QED. The implications of the ridiculous are serious and painful, and reveal what terrible things society's laughter often really is about.[20]

Rameau's nephew exposes the hideous falsity of social strategems that masquerade as etiquette when he says, "Forgive me Madam . . . I am an unspeakable wretch. It was just an unfortunate moment, for you know I am not given to common sense, and I swear I will never go in for it again for the rest of my life." He does so again when he upbraids himself for not going on with the game: "How can you be such a fool? Couldn't you flatter as well as the next man? Couldn't you manage to lie, swear, perjure, promise, fulfill or back out like anybody else?"[21] In *Waiting for Godot*, Lucky does not speak at all, yet he accomplishes the same brilliant satirical end.[22] And the circus clown returns to image-laden gestures, to affect-rousing impulses that he acts out in a wordless drama more eloquent than volumes of speech.

The Clown's Suffering

All of this rebellion against society's rules—this preference of the outsider's role, the choice of nonverbal ways to express feelings too large for words, the constant challenge to the frailty of collective symbol systems—brings the clown pain. Frequently he presents us with a tragic figure, one who is unable to achieve social acceptance, who is looked down on for his shabby, ill-fitting clothes and shuffling appearance and mocked for his too revealing expressions directed to us without any of the conformist social masque. He is a failure, a fool, likeable but in the end pitiable. He arouses painful and hostile emotions in us. We wonder where the man is behind the constant playing of roles, where the real person can be found among all the masks. Often a person afflicted with the compulsion or the gift of clowning does not know the answer himself. His inner identity mirrors his outer clown's dress: he wears a patch of this and a bit of that, he is a strutting general and a sniveling lackey, fancy socialite and forlorn dustman, a shining success and the pompous fool who slips on the banana peel.

We begin to sense the clown's confusion about himself, about who is really there, when we try to make personal connection to him. He is hard to find; he resists our approach. He turns serious questions aside with a joke. He diverts even himself with his humor, simulating connection to emotion, sometimes achieving it for us even if not for himself. By the time we remember to look for him again, he's off on another skit, another routine, another fable. He never comes all the way over to us to show us *his* feeling. A man caught in a compulsion to clown said sadly of himself: "I've always done half and half: I never really follow the wind, nor real discipline . . . I fear if I bring things off, I'll be superficial . . . I have *genuine* ineptitude. I have to be real, but I'm so inept. I must hold onto my reality."

The clown's principal effect on others is to arouse their emotions so that they fill up with rushes of sadness or remorse or shock or glee. The clown makes us turn around to look at all this emotion suddenly called up in us, pressing us to make room for it, to humanize its primitive bursts into a steady flow of acknowledged feeling. But when we turn to look at the clown, to perceive his feeling, he slips away. We begin to suspect his emphasis on our feeling is the best defense he has against his own feeling. We behold a series of comic defenses, suddenly thrown up like a thick hedge between us and him. We cannot cut through; he alternately hides from us and darts out to us, waving at us over the top of a piece of furniture or a person or an idea, poking his finger through the social scenery, but not emerging clearly before us to be simply there, to remain present, available for contact.

Robert Musil describes the unreality of such a way of being out of contact, with oneself or another, such an inability to be present, in the character of Ulrich, his *Man Without Qualities*, perhaps the greatest of modern literature's intellectual clowns:

> Ulrich went home on foot. The night was fine but dark. . . . In such a night as this it was possible to feel the significance of events as in a theatre. One felt that one was an apparition in this world, something that created the effect of being larger than it really was, something that rang and echoed and, when it passed

across an illuminated background, had its shadow walking with it like some huge, jerking clown, now rising to his full height and at the next instant once more creeping humbly at the walker's heels.

. . . he seemed to himself to be nothing more than some phantom, wandering through the gallery of life, aghast at being unable to find the frame it should slip into. . . .[23]

If this sort of clown mask infects a real man's actual relationships, those who care for him must find him utterly frustrating. He is not there to rely upon emotionally, committed both in time and circumstance to a constant presence, with a firm hold on his feelings and an ability to share them consistently with another in sustained intimacy. In work, he is erratic—enthusiastic to begin with, sometimes inspired, even inspiring, but unable to follow through. He is hypersensitive to criticism, apt to crumple right there before your eyes. If an employer wants to keep him, he must allot much time to prop up the clown-man's wobbly self-esteem. He cannot work as a partner, but hangs on colleagues dependently, like a child.

The person who would reach the clown increasingly suspects that he or she has been had. No room exists in relationship with a clown for one's own feelings, the very feelings so excitingly aroused by the clown-man himself, with so much promise of emotional fulfillment. The promise evaporates with the increasing realization of how much the clown-man needs patience, attention, sustained and extraordinarily kindly interest and encouragement to emerge at all from his masks, to be seen for who he is. Reciprocity does not exist. There is only a one-way street to the clown, paved with quantities of attention—all delivered to him. If we become irritated with the incessant demands of this process, wanting our own moment of attention, requiring however gently that our own feelings emerge, we seem suddenly harsh and insensitive to the charming clown-man, the shy soul in motley. If we bring angry suit against his default of emotional reciprocity, we appear to be labored, stuffy, emotionally contractual. If we insist on our right to intimacy, to be loved and to love in return, his gift of mimicry undoes us, destroying our determination with laughter, but a laughter that quickly becomes manic rather than hearty, because it is based on denial of the validity of our feeling, of our being.

Relationships with others are thus a source of pain to the person playing clown. In symbolic terms, he goes the way of a loner, standing always on the outside, never being part of a friendly group, never at ease in his own home with his own family or friends. In concrete reality, those men overtaken or invaded by the clown archetype suffer the most acute loneliness, never believing that relationship with others can be life-giving, because they suffer a short circuit in relationship with themselves. Such loneliness is compounded by the special suffering that comes from not having an ego that can hold the play of opposites and claim the ardent feelings that are the very essence of a clown's character, the feelings against which he so feverishly defends himself.

The clown's charm and exciting effect are often the result of opposites, as we saw before. But to dabble and to play with opposites is to be dabbled and played with by those opposites, to be shoved to extreme ends, never to find a stable resting place with enough space to embrace what belongs to one. Instead, one always feels cast aside, cast out, poor in the sense of feeling forever deprived, never having arrived. To cover up this inner emptiness, the clown plays roles in a desperate frenzy to maintain the appearance of being alive. As Rameau's nephew describes it: "I am an inexhaustible bag of tricks. At every moment I had some quip ready to make them laugh till they cried. I supplied them with a complete madhouse. . . . I had constantly to play to expectations, to fulfill them, like working a forty-eight hour day."[24]

The Clown's Spiritual Freedom

All is not negative, however. If we can bring ourselves to contemplate the clown archetype in all its complexity, especially those of us who are touched by it in our own psychology, we will find there an extraordinary way to spiritual freedom. The clown is a fool, but often a positive fool who shows us the folly of our human ways when we take them as ultimate values. The fool makes us laugh even at our most sacred notions and beliefs, thus leaving open a space for us in which something beyond our ego-constructions can enter. He leads us through the death of disidentification with various parts of ourselves, to a life of identitiy holding all of the parts in balance.

The clown pokes holes in our universes of meaning. By means of these holes a larger sun may shine through, visions of larger galaxies may be glimpsed. In the true meaning of a sense of humor, a clown may restore our sense of proportion.

What is particularly marvelous about the clown figure is that he throws doors wide open for us to see whole vistas, but he does not whisk us off into airy abstractions divorced from the concrete emotions of human experience. Above all he is particular, and shows us in his pantomine of looking at a rose, for example, that all of being is to be found in this one rose, in its mysterious hiddenness and its folded fragrance, here, now. The way to the truth is through this particular truth given us in this particular, present moment. The way to wisdom is through the folly of this particular pretension to godhood. Perhaps, as Erasmus suggests, God is the ultimate fool, that figure of grace whose light touch punctures our balloons of self-importance, whose enlightening effect reduces our shadowy little systems to rubble, that God who prefers the foolishness of children and donkeys, who prefers doves to eagles, fallen women and fishermen to figures of power.[25]

The clown makes us see what we have by making us feel how and why it matters to us, and then through our laughter making us disidentify with our possessions. Thus he leads us through the particular concrete human possession of self to the other side of possessiveness, where we may detach ourselves from that self to see its relatively small place in the larger scheme of things. To detach is not to leave behind, however, in that kind of schizoid withdrawal that so often pretends to spiritual freedom but in fact masks a dissociation of the spirit. A life lived in accord with reality moves through our personal self, in our own flesh, in this body, in this blood, in the particular relationships that actually belong to us. It is a life we set aside in the sense that we can see through it, so that all that we have hangs loosely on us, not unlike the clown's baggy clothes, not to be taken over-seriously. Only then can we seriously engage life to its depths.

X The Clown Complex: Suffering

Defended Feeling

Themes and roles gather in large assembly in the clown. A major role casts him against male stereotypes and the achieving ego; his joy is to dabble in opposites. As outsider, he has stimulating and disturbing effects upon us, puncturing our illusions, weakening our reliance on the neat, clean structure of logos orientation. He touches us with his gently paraded suffering because he is so clearly a failure, incapable of relationship and yet somehow inclined toward spiritual freedom. Odd roles, strong themes, all saying the same thing: the clown represents feeling in archetypal form. But his is feeling with a difference. His is feeling that is defended against by concentration on just a single feeling, the one that is painted on his face or repeated for us over and over again in a gesture, a catchphrase, a movement of the eyes or hands, an accent, a funny hat, a central, fixed, visible habit of being.

The clown shows us images of feeling and of emotional and behavioral reactions associated with feeling, but his defended feeling is never delivered into personal experience. The clown stays far away in the archetypal world, and will not cross into the world of personal ego-existence. He shows us rubrics of emotion that could become feeling if they were personally accepted. But clowning is a rugged defense; the feeling is not accepted. What the clown displays is unlived feeling, feeling not yet available or arrived, potential feeling not yet collected —affect in shadow, unrealized.

The clown helps us to gather all his themes and roles, which are also our themes and roles, into one image. He holds up a mirror in which we can see our emotions. We look into the mirror and see parts of ourselves. But he only looks away from the mirror; he does not see himself. The clown associates closely with the archetypes of feeling, but for him it is only feeling defended against.

Like the witch, the clown effects reversal, but one entirely his own. Whereas the witch turns the flow of life back on itself, away from others, away from consciousness, away from light into a subterranean darkness, the man caught in identification with the clown archetype reverses things by doing for others what he does not do for himself, evoking in others what he defends against in himself. He wears the mask of feeling to unmask feelings in others. His own feeling is a dodge, a simulation. He never gets the girl, knows no real fulfillment. He is locked into the character of the masker.

The witch absents herself from being. In effect, she holds up to us an empty mirror out of whose unreflecting darkness her hag face peers. She makes us embrace all the more strongly our own very human being. In contrast, the clown holds up a mirror that makes us eager to look. In it, he shows us *our* face, but he is careful to hide his own. He makes us see and feel deeper emotions in ourselves than we had known we possessed, as he mimes us and mocks us and compliments us with laughter and grief and bawdiness and solemnity. He holds up each emotion for our viewing, isolated and unblurred by mixture with other emotions, made large and all but inestimable in his antic gestures and exaggerated drama. Then he offers us a fine stew of mixed emotions—grossly funny moments that quickly become wounding ones filled with poignant sadness. He presents us with the raw materials for a feeling life, pieces of emotion that may become lasting feeling if we can claim them and assimilate them to ego-values and learn to share them and relate them to others.

Feeling always presupposes personal participation. Emotion is more primitive, bursting from the unconscious, laden with undigested affect and instinctive energy that we must sort through and appropriate to consciousness. The clown makes us see these chunks of emotion and, even more, sometimes leads us really to inspect them and to identify with them. Paradoxically, perhaps, the clown's mirroring also permits us to stand back from them and disidentify from them, which is always a necessary step toward consciously claiming them.

Whereas the witch makes us summon all our power to be, and close shut our being against her cold, unfeeling impersonality, the clown makes us open wide to the emotions that move us, in order to welcome what we see and to claim what matters to us. Whereas the witch cuts off our discharge of excitement and body tension, the clown lets it all loose as we rock with laughter, moan over disaster, or shriek at the destruction confronting him, even when we know it is harmless sham.

The clown speaks to us at the most basic preverbal levels, hence his appeal to young children. They—like the child in us—know instinctively that he is bringing down the oversized world of oversized people, adults. It pleases them, and it pleases us, that no one gets hurt, no one gets punished in the disasters wrought by a clown. No one need suffer guilt or anger. A clown's arena is a giant play-space where the unparalleled game of matching inner fantasy and outer reality takes place.[1] He returns to us the building blocks of infancy, now strong enough to support grown-up feelings. He recharges our emotional life with the currents of lost or repressed emotion.

The clown's is a make-believe world; it is not a magical one. It remains human, ordinary even, but opened up to the particular objects and parts of objects that we once found so fascinating, so eliciting of imagination, and that we put away so sadly as we grew up, we thought, to reality. His play-acting with a huge, plump balloon—bigger, bigger, stretched to burst and then . . . bang! it's gone —invites all our childish speculation about being and having, and being and not having.

The clown opens us again to the world of illusion, where objects or parts of objects expressed the meaning of our encounters with them. These were live objects to us, endowed with our inner fantasies, our experience of their separate reality, and our excitement in joining, separating, and recombining the two worlds, inner and outer. These vivid and lively objects connected us directly to our own sense of being alive and uniquely ourselves. For example, for a clown, a chair is not just a chair, as he makes clear in his endlessly frustrated efforts to sit in it. The clown's chair—so near, so funny, so defeating—represents to us our basic struggle with an inanimate reality that suddenly attacks us, whips our legs from under us and throws us to the floor in dishevelment, only then to surprise us by offering us its welcoming lap.

Symbols emerge when we can simultaneously hold in our awareness both fantasy and fact, inner and outer objects, subjective conceptions and objective perceptions; when we can accept difference and similarity as necessary companions. Holding these polarities in our awareness allows us—indeed invites us—to play with them like a clown juggling multi-colored balls. What he is doing is inviting us to try them, first in one pattern and then another. If we drop them all in the process, that is all right too; it is simply another one of life's games. Guntrip's meditation does not take this too far:

> . . . [T]here is a direct link between children's playing and the social and religious rituals of adults. They explore the imponderable reality of human living as personal relationship, a field of reality in which science cannot operate; for when it tries to do so, it only depersonalizes it, as in behavioral psychology.[2]

The clown holds up for our inspection, with whatever degree of consciousness on his part or ours, building blocks of emotion, spaces of illusion, moments of immediate, vital interaction between self and world, all of which comprise the stuff out of which we find and create the symbols that feel alive to us and that make us feel alive. At his best, the clown leads us into the personal dimensions of our surrounding reality by holding up for us the play of opposites that defines the character of the self in relation to which our personal ego-identities emerge. To have these symbols in hand, then, is to experience immediate connection to the self, to feel oneself to be in touch with a life-giving center.[3] If we have lost those symbols, the clown may show us a way back to them by presenting us with the ingredients out of which symbols arise.

Persona Compulsion

The clown mirrors to us for our inspection our emotions and fantasies, in which we may find again the rudiments of a feeling life and its symbols. He himself, however, stays trapped behind the mirror, living on the other side of the glass, looking out. His humor freezes him in his chosen category, making an ego-identity out of an artifact, letting surfaces do the work of the missing interior real-

ity. Clowning substitutes for identity. One of the characteristics of all sorts of people in show business is their nervous shuttling back and forth, trying to find a
surface tag with which to identify themselves—a recognizable theme, a color, a
style that singles them out from the crowd. For Glenn Miller, it was the way he
doubled clarinet and saxophone sounds; for Ted Lewis, a growled question, "Is

"[E]ven a puppet made of steel
would be worn out if you pulled the
string from morning till night . . . "
(John Leech)

everybody happy?," to go with his battered
hat. For Bing Crosby and Perry Como, it was
a manifestly deliberate calm that grew more
and more laid back with the years. Comedians find a nose (Jimmy Durante), a giggle
and a hat (Ed Wynn), clapping hands (Eddie
Cantor) or fluttering ones (Zasu Pitts), something persuasively human, evocative, funny,
and touching enough so that it is not just
boring on repetition.[4]

The person compelled to clown manu-
factures the appearance of feeling to defend
against experiencing his own feelings. He
falls into a persona compulsion, to use Jung's
coinage: The public face he turns to the
world comes to substitute for his own, even
does so perhaps to himself.[5] Playing roles
substitutes for being and owning true self.
Thus all the emotion that would naturally be
transmitted to his ego for sorting and translation into feeling, amasses a change of energy
that fuels the compulsion to wear masks all
the time, getting just the right mask for the
occasion, embellishing it, improving it constantly, expanding upon it.

Diderot's elegant sortie into personal
life, *Rameau's Nephew*, gives poignant expression to this compulsion to wear masks, the
need to play parts rather than be oneself. The
nephew of a composer, a master of mime,
speaks: "And then I thought, God forgive me, that . . . I would never have a minute off, and even a puppet made of steel would be worn out if you pulled the
string from morning till night and night till morning. I have to entertain them,
that is in the bargain. . . ."

After acting out all the parts of an opera, including the musical instruments,
the nephew shows the utter weariness that overtakes such a mask-wearer.

Knocked up with fatigue, like a man coming out of a deep sleep or a long trance,
he stood there motionless, dazed, astonished, looking about him and trying to

recognize his surroundings. . . . Slumped on a seat with his head against the wall, arms hanging limp and eyes half shut, he said: 'I don't know what's the matter with me; when I came here I was fresh and full of life and now I am knocked up and exhausted, as though I had walked thirty miles. . . . I've no go left in me and I've a bit of pain in my chest. I get like this nearly every day, I don't know why.'⁶

Of course a man's heart aches in such a state. It is the result of the great physical tension under which he lives in his compulsion to achieve life for himself by enlivening others, to appear emotional by stirring others' emotions, and even more frighteningly, because the heart of his own being is simply not available to him.

He mounts a frantic campaign to pretend feeling, as a defense against the feeling that makes him so vulnerable. But like all neurotic strategems, the means taken to protect him against the imagined danger inevitably lead him right into the danger. All that miming makes him more vulnerable than ever. We see in such a clown the disarming weakness and the charming softness. We see the sensitivity to the welter of emotions that crowd up from within him, seeking open feeling and communication to others. He shows us our own vulnerability to the objects around us that constantly stimulate reactions and emotions, that both attract us and put us off, that we take in and project upon. The clown shows us our need to be in touch with other persons, and to place ourselves firmly in relation to some large part of what we respond to as the heart of life itself.

To protect himself from such excruciating vulnerability, the clown pretends response, masquerades connection, dramatizes emotion instead of experiencing it. If we could penetrate the clowning mask, we would find raw wounds, a vulnerability so immune to insulation that it can only be blocked off behind masks. But his strategem seals the clown into the outsider's role, divorced from his real feeling for others and theirs for him. Nothing can reach him when he removes his vulnerable heart from being touched. Martin Grotjahn, a neo-Freudian analyst, describes the distressing predicament of the man who clowns through verbal wit or practical jokes as a means of appearing to relate to others:

. . . [H]e lets nobody really come close to him. He fascinates and he charms, but finally alienates people.
. . . [H]ow sick at heart most of them are underneath their witty defenses. They are hostile, lonely, often unloving and unloved; they feel near to tears and suffering.
. . . The life stories of many great clowns give a wealth of clinical evidence of a truly tragic development. . . . Nobody can play with the spirit of incompletely controlled hostility without getting burned himself. Nobody can try to live outside of a group of friends and enemies and still feel that he belongs somewhere. . . . Admiration is not love.⁷

It is that aloneness, that sinking sense of being unloved and, worse, unlovable, that lies at the heart of the clown's vulnerability. If that pain remains defended against, sealed off behind masks, the clown suffers acutely, "helpless in the face of reality," Guntrip says, a man "emotionally alone," no matter what his gifts or skills or intelligence.⁸

Such acute vulnerability and the suffering it brings arise when archetypal energies flood into an unprepared ego. The ego must give way under the impact. If the ego is swept aside entirely, the suffering assumes psychotic proportions and treatment must focus on rebuilding secure ego-boundaries. If the ego is flooded but not destroyed, it tends toward identification with the invading archetype, resulting in inflation or deflation, but not, unfortunately, with any accompanying capacity to make use of those unconscious energies. Treatment then focuses on strengthening the ego, whose permeability is usually traceable to pieces missing in its formation. Recovering these pieces permits a more conscious encounter with the archetype and direct personal engagement in the process of working out relationship to it. In practical terms, an increase of energy occurs, but this energy must be tamed, housed, and adapted to the human purpose and values of conscious ego-existence.

Rational conceptualization and association with related personality disorders are useful resources here, but the essential task is to meet head on the symbols that appear in the unconscious as they turn up in dreams and fantasies, in emotions and in conscious behavior patterns. We must focus on the image that conveys to consciousness the underlying archetypal dynamic. The image touches all our responses—preverbal, in fantasies, in body reactions, in dream experiences, in the life of emotions. The technique for dealing with the image is not to translate it into concept, but to engage it directly like a personal encounter, making it a lived experience of relationship with the clown figure. A man trying to assimilate the clown archetype to his ego-functioning would need to engage in vigorous give-and-take exchanges with the clown images and behavior that beset him, in an effort to get through to the defended feeling behind them.

Both the witch and the clown archetypes direct us back to the primordial, to the crossing over from nonhuman to human dimensions. In the case of the witch, it relates to the way our power and intellect rise in us, especially in the female. In the case of the clown, it relates to the emergence of human feeling out of archaic emotion, especially in the male. Each archetype addresses the early time of childhood, when these fantasy figures of fairy tale and circus make so palpable to a child the humanizing processes involved in coming to terms with the unconscious. Both archetypes address the period of transition from material dependence to the first motions of independent selfhood, where one has some sense of one's own self as separate from parent, sibling, doll, whatever. Characteristically, both archetypes may emerge in our adult lives during a period of crucial transition when we are making our way from dependence to independence, and experiencing vulnerability and excitement in the rite of passage. This is true of the obvious transition-points of puberty, marriage, childbirth, divorce, a person leaving a religious order, or one claiming a sexual identity. It is equally true in moments that are less clearly defined, wherein we are learning to live with our incompleteness, our loneliness, our unfulfilled ambitions, and our need to move on to new ways of leading our lives.

The passage may take one person from reliance on traditional ideas to the discovery of original personal insights; it may take another into the claiming of a distinct personal style of being an artist, an analyst, a doctor, a minister, a husband, a wife, a lover, a mother, or a father, emerging from imitative dependence on one's parents or teachers or other role models. Such a rite may accompany the forsaking of old neurotic patterns, to take up attitudes unencumbered by past suffering. Such a transition may come as we differentiate ourselves from a mother or father complex, an inferiority problem or sexual obsession. Witch and clown images, with their large emotional and behavioral resonances, are apt to appear in our personal psychologies just at those border crossings where personal being comes alive in the struggle to house inherited traditions, or to eject them, or to select intelligently among them.

Ego-Impotence

Unlike the witch, who abandons the human scene to live at a remote distance from human community, a resolve so painfully acted out in the excessive isolation felt by a woman caught in this archetype, the clown plunges himself recklessly into the midst of the human scene. He plays at living with a frenzy. He takes the unconscious energy that animates his creative activity and uses it—but out of context, distorting the symbols of personal being and then imitating them in exaggerated forms. Thus Rameau's nephew plays at being a musician, utterly becomes the instruments themselves, but knows almost nothing of the real activity of creating music. Thus Rabelais's Panurge caricatures a man in search of a faithful wife, but knows nothing of the urge to love another or to give a woman unhesitatingly of himself, to do those things which define fidelity in marriage.[9] The clown plays at ways of being a person within the symbol systems of art and culture and human relations, but never really lives in touch with any of the symbols. He lives only as a role-player, in act after act, without intermission. His ego feels impotent; he cannot create even a bit of being; he is out of touch with real being. He feels overcome with weakness, has a sense of it all being too much for him, of not being able to cope, of being too small, too sick, too ineffectual to manage his life. So he patches together fragmentary appearances of being to cover up the deficit of being, much as he puts together his motley costumes out of bits of this and that. His facial mask is painted on and fixed, yet he easily slips and slides out of his role because it does not grow out of any inner reality, but serves only to cover up his inner emptiness. He feels fixed in a defined position, and at the same time insecure, without stability.

The witch is different from the clown in this—she is a witch through and through. She is in no danger of losing her appearance as a witch; it goes all the way down. Her face can show fury or glee, but it always says "witch." The clown's merriment is only skin-deep, easily dislodged by despondency, anger, despair. His boundless energy quickly collapses, like a balloon that suddenly loses its air.

An actual man, beset by the compulsion to clown and play roles, suffered from the great discrepency between the way he looked and the way he felt. Repeatedly, in his many jobs, he started on a high note of enthusiasm, having used his considerable charm and vitality to win the position. But when it came to producing the actual work, he suddenly recognized his lack of training and of the discipline that comes from repeated performance. He could not translate his aspirations into reality. He could produce only the promise of the goods, not the goods themselves. His energies were invariably diverted to covering up the absence of concrete accomplishment, leading inevitably to unmasking and dismissal. Feeling empty and incompetent, he would then plunge into a frightening depression from which he could only rescue himself by another vaulting leap into the fantasy of accomplishment at yet another new job. He mobilized the energy to take on the new role, always played it well, with humor and animated enthusiasm well beyond the ordinary. His prospective employer almost always was dazzled by his lively presence and touched by his clown's kind of vulnerability and humaneness.

The cycle repeated itself, never apparently to end. For the clown-man, however, the strain grew to terrifying proportions, as he moved from helplessness to compulsive play-acting and back again, like the swing Guntrip describes between passivity and the manic states, where the latter becomes "a desperate attempt to force the whole psyche out of a state of *devitalized passivity*, surrender of the will to live, and regression. The harder the struggle to defeat the passive regressed ego, the more incapable of rest and relaxation the patient becomes. His mind must be kept going non-stop, night and day. . . ."[10] Inside, this clown-man said he felt "dead, numb; my heart is hard. I'm closed up. I can't cry or laugh. I feel like Jonah when the whale closed over him. I feel judged for my appearance, I hate my hands, I feel naked. I give my power away to other people and then I get confused."

His dream showed the same sense of himself as damaged, somehow not working right. In one dream he was in an elevator without power because its wires were twisted. In another dream he was embarked on "an underground journey, but it is a clownish exercise, time-wasting, a fun-house maze, of unnatural fun and emotion." In still another dream he goes into a basement to find "people playing games, screwing girls, loud colors—it's just a waste . . .; boredom." An ensuing dream expressed vividly his sense of inner disease and the strong pull to give up on life: "I live with a leper. All are against him. He is giving up before it is necessary. I try schemes to make him well and urge him to come with me. He wouldn't come." As Winnicott demonstrated in the case of a little boy he treated, the misery that accompanies such role-playing can start at a very early age. Reality for him was "acting a part. . . . On his own he seems to have no identity. . . . he is cut off from being anything and from BEING."[11]

In real life our clown-man felt a deep weariness from all his pushing of himself to go on. At times he broke down into fits of weeping. He thought of suicide.

He felt he was too weak to keep himself in being, to stay alive, to struggle to be a real person while saddled with a part of himself that felt so damaged, so dismal, so lifeless—as he put it, so "juiceless." In his particular case, a pattern of Don Juan sexuality became a compensating compulsion, a pattern not untypical when the clown archetype rules.[12] Though the styles of sexuality may vary, the underlying theme is the same: defense against this sense of being damaged at the center, against the unbearable vulnerability that proclaims an impotence of being, an ego-impotence which feels even more destructive than the sexual variety, and which leads to more and more acting out in the sexual role to compensate for its devastating effects.

Our clown-man was compulsively drawn into transient flirtations and brief affairs, at the same time that he made real attempts to keep his marriage going. He felt, however, that his wife was "asleep," and he himself "dead," and therefore the life promised in secret assignations, the suspense involved in trying to win a new woman, and especially his belief that at least with each new woman he could wake something into life, were irresistible to him: "I wake myself up and raise us both to an existence that is real." Here his clown role seemed a great success. With humor, charm, and gusto, he penetrated a woman's defenses, her codes of morality, her cautious restraints, all in the name of "stirring up life," of "making the juices flow," being alive, immediate, touching. But his sexual pattern gave him no more, finally, than his work pattern. As the simulation took over, reality vanished. The rich beginnings with a woman never led through a middle to an end. It was dazzling, flamboyant, but finally without the substance of relationship.

His dreams reflected this in their reversal of roles. It became less and less clear who was stimulating whom. Consciously, he played the role of a modern Tom Jones character buoyantly offsetting a woman's staid proprieties, opening her to the life flowing through her. Unconsciously, his dreams showed him to be the entrapped one, not the mover but the moved, a mere instrument in the hands of the woman. She may be opened by him or opening herself to him, but he stays closed up tight. In one dream, he forgets the purpose of his train trip as he goes to "shack up with a ravishing chick. . . . But suddenly another girl surges into the room and they both overpower me . . . to torture me by making me satisfy them orally, only to throw cold water on me in return. They offer their bodies seemingly, but always withdraw." In another dream, the man sees a clown figure begin to perform his act by carrying a woman into the ring on his shoulders, seated facing him, thus covering up his face. He is kissing her genitals and she becomes aroused and satisfied, but the man is left to carry her weight as part of the performance. In still another dream, he hides his discovery of a hidden treasure by acting out a "fake love scene with a curvy girl to keep another man from stealing the jewels from me."

Some styles of sexual clowning do not veer toward this Don Juan form at all, but toward a self-deprecating sexuality that is winsome, sweet, apologetic, or funny—anything but forceful and virile. This is a protean style which can move in almost any direction at any time, as masks are taken up and abandoned. Buster Keaton is a splendid example of the type, full of apologies, in manner if not in words, clumsy, retiring, always moving farther backward, until there is no place to go but down on the floor or, frozen, to stand at some great height. Then comes the change of mask—and of body. The "great stone face" has a rubber body. His resilience is astonishing, for far from collapsing in a disconsolate heap, he springs to his feet or leaps as high as necessary in the air. He is in charge of all his personas now, a one-man repertory company of defenses against feeling, parading all sides of his invention before us in rapid succession. By comparison, his late twentieth-century imitator, Woody Allen, offers a drab spectacle indeed, with only the wit and resourcefulness of his cinematographers to make of him and his fables more than just the self-indulgence of languishing neurosis.[13]

Perhaps the best examples we have of the compulsion to adopt whole hosts of personas in succession are those of the surrealists, who work industriously at their curious mixture of craft and compulsion, often with a visible splitting away of the anima exponent. The examples they provide are good, not merely because they illustrate a psychological process, but because in the hands of a poet, a painter, a novelist, or a film director, they become such beguiling, clownish art. The remarkable work of the Frenchman Isidore Ducasse, *Les Chants de Maldoror*, which he began to publish in 1868 at the age of 22, two years before he died, was understandably claimed by the surrealists of the 1920s and 1930s as a model for their kind of exploration of hallucinatory fantasy and the world of the unconscious. Taking the name of Lautréamont, the overbearing protagonist of a Eugene Sue novel, Ducasse develops in his effusive prose a kind of atheism of the sea. The ocean becomes his lord, and man his enemy:

> Man and I, immured in the limits of our intelligence as a lagoon often is within a belt of coral islands, instead of joining our respective forces to defend ourselves against mischance and ill-fortune, move away from one another trembling with hate, and take opposite directions as if each had wounded the other on the point of a dirk!

All things are interchangeable in Lautréamont's oceanic world. Things of similar shape, or with any sort of relationship that the imagination can link, evoke each other—pins and pillars, flies and rhinoceroses, for example. A philosopher laughs to see a donkey eating a fig. Lautréamont sees a fig eating a donkey, and does not laugh but wants to weep: "'Nature! Nature!' I cried out, sobbing, 'The sparrow-hawk rends the sparrow, the fig eats the donkey, and the tapeworm devours man!'" As he says of himself, his personas, and his observations, "I often happen to state, solemnly, the most clownish propositions." That does not provide "a peremptorily sufficient reason for expanding the mouth!" Laugh if you must, he tells us, but let it be melancholy laughter. Laugh and cry at the same time. "If you cannot weep with your eyes, weep with your mouth. If this is still impossible, urinate. But I warn you, some sort of liquid is needed here to atten-

"The Surrealist clown sees with the eyes of the unconscious, and not merely the unconscious but a dozen, a hundred, or a thousand personifications with which he can identify in various ways." (Joan Miró)

uate the drought which sidesplit-pundit laughter carries in her womb." Not for him the laughter of superiority, which for Baudelaire was the "essence" of laughter.[14]

The surrealist clown sees with the eyes of the unconscious, and not merely the unconscious but a dozen, a hundred, or a thousand personifications with which he can identify in various ways. Paul Eluard was a greatly gifted maker of poetic phrases to fit his surrealist images, a particularly felicitous and original love poet, and a friend and close associate of painters, Picasso in particular. His clownish fabrications, like Lautréamont's, bear a heavy melancholy weight. But in the abundant sorrow of his verses, the humor of rapidly changing identities is never lost. We may not find any of the images that sail by at such speed "a peremptorily sufficient reason for expanding the mouth," but the effect is always to arouse some laughter, a smile at least, and to turn a melancholy mood, if not upside down, at least on its side. An "airy icon . . . conjugates itself." There are "Gentle weary builders of churches, gentle builders with temples of pink bricks, with eyes scorched by hope. . . ." There are "Houses more fragile than the eyelids of a dying man. . . ." All this in one beautifully turned prose poem which ends with a handsome permissiveness and a mysterious pronouncement:

> . . . [Y]our gestures are the ladders of your strength, your tears have tarnished the carelessness of your impotent masters, and now you may laugh shamelessly laughter, bouquet of swords, laughter, wind of lust, laughter like rainbows fallen from their scales, like a gigantic fish turning over on itself. Freedom has left your body.[15]

One of the most persistent attempts to penetrate the world of the unconscious by a writer of surrealist inclinations is that of the poet Henri Michaux. He experimented with drugs for half a dozen years, to see if he could "lift the veil from the 'normal,' the unrecognized, unsuspected, incredible, enormous normal." His verse and prose writing about his experiences is hallucinatory in itself, but nowhere quite so convincing as when he associates himself with the urges of mental patients. He reports that "defectives" and so-called "normal" subjects, "during experiments 'diminishing' certain facultires and functions," all felt (if "they were left in peace") that "they lacked *nothing important*"; somehow their "essence" remained "untouched." Michaux defines essence as "what remains when one no longer needs to lower oneself, to keep busy, to function, to become finite, specific, small."[16]

In a volume published ten years earlier, in 1956, Michaux reported somewhat differently on what he called "essenciation." He wondered if anyone could endure its "vertiginous pleasure," its "secret frenzy." He speaks with the authority of a drug-taker about the intensity of feeling narcotized. It is the predicament of those who defend against feeling, rather than know feeling. In such variations on the surrealist mode as Buñuel's early film *L'Age d'Or* or Beckett's *Waiting for Godot*, the "vertiginous pleasure" becomes dizzyingly funny, the "secret frenzy" becomes rich farce. Buñuel's hapless lovers regress from animal-like rolling in the mud to spastic thrusts at each other in a passion so wonderfully inept that they can barely touch the right places or even hold onto each other. Beckett's tramps perform lovely vaudeville turns, with their clothing, with their parodies of pretentious political and academic rhetoric. But in both cases, as in so much of this world of outlawed feeling, the comedy burns, the clown make-up becomes a rictus of pain.[17]

The surrealists bring us a coruscation of images from their voyages to the end of the mind, a tumbling masquerade of interior clowns, but no great sense of peace. Their laughter insists on its resemblance to the sound and look of weeping. Personifications change too swiftly to produce the consoling conviction that nothing important is lacking. The dizziness and frenzy may be dissipated for a moment, but the wholeness does not seem to come this way, either by the route of defensive madness or through the use of drugs. There is about the whole sorrowful comic spectacle too much uncertainty, too fearful a distance from feeling.

In some men's clown routines, female characteristics are made fun of, and more, attacked, revealing multiple uncertainties about feeling and identity. The clown dresses up as a woman, but always in a way that makes it clear that he is really a man. He loses his skirt, or his fake breasts tumble out, or his stockings fall down, revealing muscular male legs. Yet by dressing up as a woman or by using effeminate gestures, he covers up the fact that he is not at all sure he is a man. Male-female distinctions blur to disguise his sense of incompleteness. Grotjahn comments aptly on the covert hostility in this caricature: "The secret joke in the parody of the woman who is no woman points to a different kind of depreciation. The female impersonator seems to proclaim: Women are not women; they are not different; they are no better than men."[18] But there is more going on here than that. The clown playing at being a woman, like our clown-man who felt compelled to wake women to life by stimulating them sexually, points to the missing part in his psychology—a secure connection to the feminine element of his own being, his female capacity to be. Either he plays at it, giving only the appearance of owning it, a sadly inadequate appearance that betrays an identification with a part of himself that he cannot integrate, or he projects it outward onto actual women, hoping that in stimulating them into life he might find his own lost being.

Sexual clowning inevitably meets with defeat, for the problem lies not with an impotent penis but with an impotent ego, displaced by the clown-man onto sexual performance. The clown's garb is bedecked with symbols of impotence. Tassels droop from his cap, his cane collapses, or he wears an emblem of impotence, as Grotjahn points out, such as an "enormous outsized necktie . . . stuffed back into the outrageously large, baggy pants, which again are so big that the contents seem to be ridiculously small and lost. Symbols of the limp, impotent, and ridiculous penis are repeated in many variations."[19] Grotjahn interprets this impotence as symptomatic of the father-son conflict, a point to which we must return. But a more basic problem, in our view, is the inability of the ego to be itself, rather than the sexual failure. Ego-impotence lies beneath the sexual clowning compulsion. Not having a durable ego, the clown is doomed to play the role of outsider; there is nothing and no one sufficiently at home in him to permit him to join the outsiders' group. The dignity of the clown lies in his knowing he is an outsider and why: because of his impotent ego. His courage lies in his trying to cope with this lack, however unhappily. Valiantly, in his misery, he tries to improvise a way of being.

As an archetype of defended feeling, the clown-man holds up to us parts of our psyche that lie outside our conscious identity, parts that undermine our stability because they are more like holes or gaps rather than anything solid at the core of our ego-formation. The sexual symptom in particular expresses the root cause of the persona compulsion, which is a frenzied attempt to simulate the being that is lacking. What is missing is relation to his own feminine capacity to be. Its glaring absence is traceable to an inadequate relation to his mother and a non-existent one to his father. The result is a splitting away of the anima component of the man's personality. We turn now, in detail, to these origins of the clown complex.

XI The Clown Complex: Origins

Mother

As in the witch constellation, a person caught in the clown archetype knows early and sharp damage to his sense of being. While in the witch encounter a child experiences a reversal in the parental relationship—the child acting as mother to the mother, complying with the mother's expectations instead of communicating its own needs and desires, and thereby constructing a false self—in the clown experience the mother is not so much felt as malevolent by the child as she is seen to be ineffective.

The clown's mother has failed to provide a protected space between her infant boy and the stimulating world outside, or room for the stimulating world inside himself of archetypal impulse and image. She does not make available to her child a time and place for contact with these inner and outer realities, in unmistakable attentiveness to his reality. No screening device shields the unprotected infant. There is no warm quilt to wrap up in, no way of withdrawing from a too exciting world, no securely scheduled nap, no regular meal hour, no tranquil lapsitting from which to look out upon an ever-fascinating world, made safe by his mother's shielding arms and watchful eye. Instead, the infant is left painfully exposed to overstimulation, not so much intruded upon by the needs of the mother to get something for herself, as simply bombarded by stimuli against which he has no refuge. He finds no boundaries within which to hold his experience. Thus the grown-up clown roams the circus rings, unconfined, weaving back and forth across the borders that define the spaces for other acts. The clown even goes up into the audience, breaking the continers that separate performer and spectator. Similarly, the clown figure in our entertainment culture is one who disrupts borders and boundaries, bringing chaos to ordered spaces, laughter into realms of sadness, profanity into the precincts of the sacred. This very psychological plight—endless unprotected exposure to the bombardment of the senses— becomes part of the compulsive clowning routine for those suffering its complex, just as it becomes the chosen theme in artistic performance.

The child's perception of this bombarded state is to feel damaged, uncollected at the core, unable to withstand the constant sensations that assault the embryonic ego. His mother offers no model on which to pattern in his nascent ego a capacity to hold the core of his being securely in contact with inner and outer worlds. He knows no calm enjoyment of his being, based on an introjected and imitated model of a mother's holding presence that will alternately present objects to him or screen them out. He finds in her no responsive, gleaming belief in the reality of his experiences. His potency is neither confirmed nor maliciously spiked, just disregarded. It is as if she does not recognize the "hallowed presence" of the self within him,[1] or his work on the growing individuation process, trying to differentiate from the self and to secure an ego with which to relate to it. As a result, he has no sense of the ground plan of his being, no blueprint of its growing core.[2]

The person caught in a clowning complex stays, in effect, within the primal self, juggling its polarities or dropping them all like so many balls in a clown's act, fetching them, throwing them, collapsing under them. But for the clown, the whole does not cohere within those primal boundaries that house the presence of being, a confinement in which one can feel safe. Where the witch splits the polarities of the self wide apart into competing and mutually canceling opposites, the clown remains there in the hurly-burly of all his parts, fixed, disorganized, compulsive.

Irvine Schiffer, the Canadian psychoanalyst, presents valuable data in his book *The Trauma of Time* about the origin of the clowning problem, which afflicted several professional comedians he was treating. He finds one common "developmental denominator" in their self-evaluations:

> . . . [P]art of their infantile 'machinery' was experienced by them as malfunctioning from their earliest years right on through adulthood. They suffered an early deprivation of some crucial aspect of the maternal protection that psychoanalysts now refer to as the holding environment, which strengthens the infant's early reaction to otherwise disturbing stimuli. . . . they were exposed to traumatic stimuli by relatively unprotecting and naive mothers. . . .[3]

This holding environment or holding ego is what Freud eventually called the ego. Jung describes the same capacity in the adult as the unique place of consciousness, where one is capable of holding in awareness opposite polarities of being without losing a central sense of identity to either, expanding one's ego-space instead to make room for both.[4]

The clown's mother, unlike the witch's, is not felt to be vengeful and wicked. Rather, she is unable to do her task. She is not there in any important way to mediate reality, so that as a result reality takes on an attacking quality. One clowning man said of his mother, "She just lost her voice. She could never speak up for herself." The future clown, unlike the future witch, is not nipped in the bud with a poisoned touch and left unable to bring emotion and fantasy into life. The clown makes it into the world, wants to be in the world, but reflecting his experience of his mother, feels ill-equipped, unable to do things. It is a feeling that is easily displaced onto his penis as being too small or somehow defective, a conviction reinforced by society's stereotyped image of virility as invariably Herculean and generously endowed. Again unlike the witch, a clown's method of dealing with this problem does not exude malevolence or resentment at being cheated. Rather it has its own frenzied flavor, an unchanneled excitement that veers toward the manic.

Lacking a wholly present and protective mother, as a model of holding one's experience in hand, to take in and give back as one begins to shape a self, the infant can do nothing but imitate the appearance of a mother without having the real goods inside. Thus many clown-men adopt the role of a good mother toward others, play-acting what they cannot internalize.[5] They settle for the synthetic mother, not out of resentment, but with some bravery in order to make the best of a bad situation.

This courage accounts for the great appeal of clown-men. They evoke our admiration for their valiant struggle with their own vulnerabilities. That is one reason they touch our own wounds without arousing our animosity. We see them suffering more than we do; they are more helpless, overly exposed. With his friendly and kind attitude, the clown-man helps us fashion a tolerant, humorous attitude toward our failures, suggesting that it is all right to be so vulnerable; it is part of the human condition.

The persona compulsion of the clown grows out of early deprivation. Lacking a model in his efforts to hold together and screen out bombarding objects, the child fends off the assaults of the two realities, inner and outer, with the most primitive mechanisms of identification. Those are all he has available to him at his early age. He actually then becomes each object, defending against its impact and struggling to master it. As an adult, the clown-man moves rapidly from role to role, in a series of persona masks that lack real substance because his capacity for sustained internalization of the object has not developed. Inside he feels without "soul," as one man put it, his emptiness concealed in the swift succession of roles with which he is condemned to play at being alive.

Father

The clown-man who has experienced his mother as benignly neglectful responds to his father with outright repudiation. Schiffer notes in all of his comedian patients a sentiment we also found in our clinical research. It is expressed bluntly by one man: "My father is a laughable object."[6] The son dismisses the father as not being worthy of notice, a nonentity, either negligible or worse, altogether "phony." The father is perceived by the son as nothing but a mask, devoid of any inner reality, even the painful kind that the clown man suffers within himself. Moreover, the father has nothing but a lethal effect on the woman closest to him, the clown's mother. His son sees him as a total failure.

One patient referred to his father as never having had a life to lose. He felt his mother had sacrificed her real self to accommodate his father, which simply increased his scorn for him. Another man experienced his father as "not alive," as only posturing at living, masking his inability to be real with an all-out conformity. The son repudiated any identification with his father; such hollow conformity could only quench what little flickering of life he managed to keep going in himself. In his unconscious fantasy, this man saw his father as an enemy to be struck down in order that his own soul could survive. To follow his father's admonitions "to grow up, be responsible, and stop clowning around," would "nail the lid" on his soul's coffin. He too would then be a "phony," like his father. A gruesome dream depicted this view and his conflict about it: "I must saw off my father's leg in order to save my sister. But afterwards it turns out it was not really necessary, and I have to carry my mutilated father on my back, taking him back to town. On the way, I am invited by a girl to an entertainment boat. . . . I put on a cheerleader comedy act that I did not plan on doing. Then suddenly cats converge on me from all directions. I like individual cats in a mild sort of way, but the hordes advancing on me now are frightening." The mutilation (that is, the emasculation) of his father to save his sister (his soul) does not release him from danger, but rather burdens him with a crippled father-image (his father as his sister's predator) that weighs him down. A girl invites him to deal with this burden by playing the clown on an entertainment boat. His improvised comedy act is followed by a letting loose of frightening hordes of cats, familiar enough to us as the animal forms goddesses take, to be interpreted here as signifying an uncontained feminine principle. They mob him, seeking him out in a negative way because he has not met the feminine in any positive way. Masculine paternal authority vies with the feminine—his sister, the girl, the cats—in ways that can only be destructive to the dreamer.

Grotjahn sees a destructive contest as classical to the clown complex. Following the example of Freud's epochal study of humor, Grotjahn focuses on the father-son battle enacted in the clown's pranks. He sees the clown figure as the crippled father, "now depreciated, castrated, and ridiculed," shorn of his former authority and power. The son's conflict with authority is enacted in his subjecting of the clown-father to various humiliations and defeats, all of which the father passively endures. The weaker son now triumphs over the formerly strong father. We in the audience join with the son, venting our repressed rage and envy against all our fathers, personal and social, as well as, in true oedipal fashion, fulfilling our secret wish to become the father by displacing him. Unlike the witch's assaults, however, the clown manages in his to combine humor and kindliness with fiendish jokes. The clown's reach is large in his multiple combinations "of love and aggression, respect and depreciation, of foolishness and wisdom," in which at least "part of the positive relationship between father and son must be saved and expressed in occasional words of wisdom behind the clownish facade. . . ."[7] In contrast to the witch, there is much less defusing of the instincts and warring of opposites with the clown. Love and hate do not totally split apart into isolated states. Conscious and unconscious do not close up against each other. The clown exhibits greater permeability of consciousness to unconscious contents, which accounts in part for the appearance he gives of lively, changing, stimulating affability. He is a less archaic figure than the witch, closer to the human.

Without a mother who means anything to him, a son finds no way to incorporate and identify with the directing principles that the father represents, and so has no means with which to navigate his way through the rules and norms of human behavior. Lacking instruments, he is set adrift in society in a condition of rudderlesness that he displaces onto the issues of phallic potency and ego-potency. His development has been arrested at a frighteningly premature level. Schiffer notes that his comedian-patient "had spurned any meaningful identification" with his father, and with it every kind "of paternal guidance . . . from common sense to homespun philosophy. . . ." Unwilling

> to trade in his mother's ignorance for his father's reality, he was left to his own devices, his distancing from his father leaving him without the traditional values that lead toward some conformity to community standards. While companions became imbued with the burdens of a maturing, oedipally-derived superego, he was left unencumbered as he turned his attentions to his comical antics.[8]

Conflict with the father can occur for some clowning men in less hostile, milder, and sadder forms. One man, for example, did not totally repudiate his father as a fake, but simply judged him inadequate. Despite his father's repeated exhortations to his son to be a man—by playing sports, showing himself to be one of the guys, taking care of his mother and sister—the advice seemed useless, for the son knew his father did not himself feel like a man. The father urged on the son what the father himself could not fulfill. He had hung out with his cronies, was one of the guys, only to come home to his wife's disapproval and more, her disdain, for drinking too much. Moreover, the way the father urged the son to be a man was always in unconvincing clichés, stereotyped images of what men did as jock, buddy, provider. All that totally overlooked who his son really was, including the significant fact of a physical disability that made playing sports impossible. The son did not angrily cast his father aside, but he felt orphaned nonetheless, with little help from anyone in learning how to become his own man.

Our clown-man usually begins life with neither a holding mother on which to model his own ego and manage his growing sense of self, nor with a father to demonstrate guiding principles worthy of identification and action. Without a father to incorporate and identify with, the clown-man sees no way to create his own guiding principles. He finds no model on which to pattern a manly life that is entirely his own. He is not connected, either to something deep down inside himself or to principles that can animate a life in the world. The double lack he suffers, the result of his distance from both parents, leaves the son with his peculiar anima problem. As the witch must receive the masculine part of herself, so the clown must somehow find and be found by the feminine part of himself.

The Anima

In the anima, we allegorize life's own archetype.[9] It is a way of characterizing the psychic function that acts as a bridge connecting the ego to those resources of the unconscious that bring a man to awareness of the center of the whole psyche, the self. This is the connection that confers on a man his sense of feeling alive and real in himself, that makes meaning accessible to him, one might say, at the source. Damage to this anima connection does just the opposite. It leaves a man feeling cut off, drifting, without access to the archetypes that Gaston Bachelard succinctly describes as "reserves of enthusiasm which help us believe in the world, love the world, create our world."[10] The damage must be compensated for. One way to compensate is in the clown's compulsive adoption of persona masks that give the appearance of a lively connection, but behind which are hidden deep feelings of impotence, vulnerability, and confusion about how to put oneself forward.

The anima is first concretized in a man's psychology in his relation to his mother. In later life, a well-functioning anima mediates to a man's ego-consciousness an essential feeling of being in touch with things, whether through a quickening attraction to a woman where the anima is clearly projected, by an igniting thought or conviction whereby the anima is identified with, or by an enlivening image that arises spontaneously from the unconscious, where the ego directly relates to the anima. A second major influence on the shape the anima will take in a man's life comes from his father, and how he does or does not evidence being in touch with this animating principle in his own psychology.

In the clown-man's case, neither parent adequately houses the feminine animating principle. The mother ineffectively manifests the elementary holding capacity of the feminine in her lackluster responses to her own unconscious images and body instincts and the objects which confront her in the world outside herself.[11] She is missing to her son in the essential work of attuning herself to his needs: She does not heed his eager gestures for communication. She thus presents an image of the feminine falling away from the ego, one not there in any basic way. Her absence is less malevolent than the witch's which is an outright refusal to be present. She simply fails to connect in a sustained way, and seems unaware of how important it is to connect. The clown-man's anima is patterned, then, on his mother's falling-away quality. He may exhibit in his adult life a consuming longing for a life-giving connection to a woman, and through her to his own sustained capacity to feel alive. What he actually experiences is an inability to locate either connection with any durability. He will find himself drawn compulsively to women who are absent, withdrawn, elusive, or withheld from him.

The clown's mother has let the world rain down upon her little son without interference. His anima has had a dreary model. It knows no way to bring the contents of his unconscious to his ego. More than likely it will flood his ego with excitement, preparing him for a joyous discharge, then leave him empty, dry, achingly unfulfilled. He feels himself to be all in pieces, a clutter of disconnected parts each going its own way. He gets immersed in objects around him and then, suddenly, is cut off from them. He feels himself unable to hold the pieces together or construct from them an authentic whole.

The specific anima contents of the unconscious are apt to overtake the clown-man so that he falls into active identification with them. Comedians often affect effeminate mannerisms, as we all know. The reasons are not obscure. A man mired in the clown complex tends in his emotional life to become sentimental, maudlin, even weepy, given to melodramatic exaggerations of events. He tends to get hurt easily, all out of proportion to the cause; he is given to sulking, moping, emotional withdrawal. He cannot assert his point of view; like a clown's collapsible cane, it gives way when he leans on it. Or as with the small tie or the big baggy pants, he cannot find a viewpoint of appropriate size, so he steals another's. Placating, appeasing, making a joke covers up this confusion. But he still feels utterly vulnerable, unable to hold his emotions or to cope with them in any way when they sweep over him, unable to find them when they retreat. His clowning routines, so funny to others, are desperate attempts to defend himself from his feeling of helplessness.

His father, the son feels, offers no useful example of a male housing within himself his vulnerability and soul connection. He seems to have extinguished connection altogether and to be busy camouflaging that fact. His father is not really alive in any personal way. He pretends life. He may adopt a cheery persona, in which he imitates connection to life by relentless emphasis on the good, the jolly, the bright side of things, excluding all ambiguous or negative elements. Or he may adopt what looks like righteous conformity to social norms. Whatever his mask, it is a hollow one. What he holds up to the son as the masculine way is a caricature, a soulless life, a picture of an anima snuffed out. Lacking a model, the clown-man's own identity as a male is not at all secure, for he fears it must be purchased at the price of feeling real and alive. Unconsciously, he comes to believe that to be male is to be dead inside. The clown-man's is a labile masculinity, not reliable to anyone, least of all himself. The lively antics of his clowning are an effort to keep alive the anima, while also defending against the vulnerability it has left in him.

The anima-damaged clown-man is a confusing, ambivalent object to the

"The lively antics of his clowning are an effort to keep alive the anima while also defending against the vulnerability it has left in him." (William Makepeace Thackeray)

women in his life. He is in so many ways an attractive man. He seems less locked into male stereotypes, less stiff and stuffy, more flexible and subtle, and certainly more fun than the average man. Even the hag-woman often feels drawn to the clown-man because of his entertaining ways of translating his perception that things are not what they seem, a judgment that matches her own. The clown-man can make her laugh about it instead of just feeling bitter and separated. But when a woman comes too close to the clown-man, he falls apart. He turns cold, he runs away, he cannot receive her. The opposing pushes and pulls from which his anima suffers now afflict the woman. She feels called to, cajoled, jollied, wooed by the clown-man, only to be rebuffed when she responds, or scrutinized coldly, mocked, and finally deserted. She gets from the clown-man the treatment he suffers in his own anima.

The clown-man has lost his way. His anima is unhoused, so he must spend his life looking for that missing bit of feeling, that lost connection. His anima splits away from his ego and provokes entire sets of new problems.[12] He grows out of identification with the anima, which now lives through him rather than being housed in him. He imitates the feminine, rather than relating to it. Her reality is reduced to a shell, a facade that he can put on like a costume, but the anima within him does not comprise an organized personality. It consists simply of clusters of contents, of wandering, conflicting impulses and images. Hence the clown's hodgepodge repertoire, a potpourri of strikingly unharmonious characteristics. He shows grace with clumsiness, sensitivity alongside obtuseness, gentility with obscenity, hilarity on top of despair. He is all opposites, with no ego to hold them together, blend them, humanize them. He is, like Rameau's nephew, a puppet pulled by the strings of the anima.

The clown-man feels bereaved by the loss of the feminine. It is a lack he also feels incompetent to fill or even to ask to have filled. Wistful, poignant, he can only wait and hope some woman will perceive his need, peer behind his masks, and then somehow make up for his losses. One young man, the son of an alcoholic mother whom he experienced as never demonstrating any love for him, felt in his turn unable to demonstrate any love to his girlfriend. His feeling remained inaccessible to him. In fantasy he imagined her peering closely into his face to find the tears behind his smile, eager to fill up the void within him and ease his pain.

The clown-man constantly projects his anima outward, finding it now in one woman, now in another. Lasting, deepening, stable relationships elude him. And so he looks elsewhere to make his anima connections. Large cultural frames attract him—political causes, organized groups of any kind, religious sects, any institutions that promise connection. But as is the case in his relationships with women, there is no inward link to any of this. The man is left dependent on appearances, shells, mimicked feelings. Like a gullible virgin, he is easily seducible by anyone who promises to provide the recognition that he failed to receive from his parents and that he cannot yet give himself. Living at the extremes of seducibility, he compensates by becoming seducer himself.[13]

The clown archetype holds the field with iron determination. As we have tried to demonstrate, to understand the clown we must go back to the period of early deprivation and trace its enduring shadows in clown-men's psychologies. Archetypes are not giant spiders that suddenly drop upon us from trees to ensnare us. They are with us for a lifetime and seem destined to pursue us everywhere. And yet they are not inescapable; they do not follow an inflexible determinism. For it is a happy fact that every boy whose parents failed him does not invariably develop the peculiar dangers and deviltries of the clown constellation.

XII The Clown Complex: Its Deepening Territory

Part-Objects and Identification

The early suffering of persona compulsion and ego-impotence of the man caught in clowning is the merest introduction to the territory. Deeper difficulties await him, where the suffering is more acute because it is more fragmentary. Lacking an attuned feminine presence to mediate the greatly stimulating outer and inner worlds to his nascent ego, the boy overworks the one rudimentary psychic mechanism he has got under some control, identification. He develops a knack for mimicry and caricature. His purpose in identifying with the pieces of external and internal objects that he parodies is not humor, however, but his desperate attempt to get some control over the sensations that come at him from the outside world and the archetypal images and emotions that well up from inside him.

He lives with only parts of things, fragments that alternately assault, excite, service, and overwhelm him. He feels his own self to be divided into parts too, because he has never experienced, never introjected a mother who herself could hold all the pieces together. He has never identified with any holding capacity, and his ego did not develop it for him. He cannot contain his experience. Nor does his anima provide a stable connection that unites unconscious material with conscious awareness. As a result, the clown-man's identity is fixed in successive identifications with whatever impulse, emotion, or image arises from within himself, with people's characteristic ways of talking, moving, or holding themselves in or letting themselves out, with sudden stiffenings of posture or a tone of voice. Anything can catch him as fodder for imitation—the bend of a tree, an opening flower, a gathering wave. Like a professional, a person caught in compulsive clowning fully assumes the mask of these fleeting, partial experiences.[1]

When he plays at being an adult, a role that is far too large for him, the clown-man cuts things down to his size by reductive posturing, role-playing that quickly arouses laughter in others. He likes its effect on others. He sticks with it. He has discovered his capacity to divert, and in so doing to rescue himself. In his clowning antics he appears to be on top of things. In fact, he barely escapes sinking beneath the trappings of his diversions. Everything, as Schiffer writes of one of his patients, "is an attempt to overcome feelings of being damaged, a strategy demanded by an inchoate sense of vulnerability that compelled him to avoid external stimuli that menaced him and to modify internal stimuli that might over-whelm him. . . . Instead of adequately internalizaing, the comics I treated had to 'chop up' what they devoured in an effort to construct a sense of self."[2]

The clown-man wears his mimicry like a fool's motley, like the dominoes and diamonds of *commedia dell'arte* costumes. The parts he plays become his wholes—Harlequin, Columbine, Pierrot. The moon makes him love-sick, and he droops accordingly like Schönberg's *Pierrot Lunaire.* Like Stravinsky's *Petrouchka,* he feigns a consuming passion for a dancing doll. He is quick-witted, foppish, ro-mantic, doltish, a master of any illusion that can be sufficiently reduced and iso-lated to one feeling, one part, at a time.[3]

The clown-man fails to achieve the stage wherein objects become wholes. Neither he himself nor the other comprises a discrete whole. Rather, he is con-fined to perceiving one part at a time. Even without the skills of the great clowns, he falls naturally into their routines. Everything, each object, each sound, is a sig-nal for the mimicry to begin, just as with the development of slapstick panto-mime, the slapping of the bat on the floor served notice that it was time to begin the revels. One moment, the clown acts out anger; the next, pleasure; the next, grief. Never is he the person who feels the emotion, and it is never one emotion consistently, but always a crazily rotating kaleidoscope of changing parts.

This quick succession of roles, this changing identification of self with parts of objects, accounts for the exciting effect of the clown and the complexity of an actual performance of a clown-actor.[4] This is where compulsive aping can turn into art, as a mixture of various part-objects is unified by a dominant symbolic theme. These different parts of objects summon up in the audience multiple sym-bolic associations to comprise a rich and varied feeding. A clown can catch our interest by the reiteration of a device or a theme just as a poet does. T. S. Eliot does this, for example, by the use of anaphora, the repetition of the same word or phrase in successive lines, at the beginning of "Burnt Norton," the first of the *Four Quartets,* and by the insistent content the device brings with it, in this case the nagging presence of time, whether time past or present or future. Similarly, if we can look at a painting in such a way that we can absorb one part at a time, if our eyes are practiced as a clown's are, we can let parts compile themselves into a whole that is all the richer for the detail of lines or blobs of color or planes of light. For example, the pattern of brushstrokes and closely related tints and geo-metrically shaped forms brings us an apple, a dish, a table, a room in a Cézanne still life.[5]

It is not art that results when one is fixated in part-object identification, un-able to bring the parts together into wholes. The man compelled to clown is un-der a great strain. Nothing holds together. Nothing abides. All is a jumble, scat-tered, changing. Everything falls apart. The clown suffers great shame over his inability to bring things together, to cope as others seem to do. He fears being found out and ridiculed. He scrambles madly to defend against his emotions by canceling them quickly with their opposites, turning grief into rowdiness, laughter into tears, making fun of feeling, disavowing it. He cannot hold his emotions, so he mimics them, seeing them only as parts to be taken up and dealt with, one at a time, separated from all others.[6]

In relations with others, the clown-man suffers the same problem of everything being reduced to parts. He cannot see other persons as wholes; he cannot get beyond their parts and what those parts might do for him. They remain "self-objects" for him, never objectively existing in their own right, but only there with reference to his self's needs.[7] In the clown-man's eyes, the other person holds the missing part he so desperately needs. The other is the answer to everything, idealized into an all-perfect state, yielding to the clown's need. There, in the other, is perfect helpfulness, all-giving love, all-knowing answers that will solve the clown-man's problems. But others cast in this impossible role eventually will take offense, feeling used, made into suppliers, connections, never sought out for themselves. The idealization crashes because these others do not supply the missing part, and because they object to being made into self-objects.

The clown-man cannot go all the way out to embrace other persons as they are, in themselves, for themselves, but can only relate to them piecemeal, one part at a time. What can a person feel when he or she is perceived as a series of commodities to serve occasions, to pander to the clown-man's need for talk, for sex, for advice, for security, for power? The clown-man does not live through any time spent with another person in any embodied way, but just plucks out experiences from the persons he mixes with, who then feel cut into pieces, mere parts of themselves. Women today revolt against this part-object view of themselves, where they are advertised as laundry-doers, room-neateners, sexual stimulants, food-dispensers, woman as a gatherer of parts, a hole, never a whole. Women's revolt against part-object status is pivotal in the rescue of the clown-man, as we will see.

Two shattering examples of this sort of reduction of persons to part-objects are to be found in the performances of Evelyn Waugh's character John Beaver, and Anthony Powell's Widmerpool, two of the great, grim comic figures of the modern novel. Both are mother's boys. Both are incapable of taking in more than a piece at a time of the people to whom they react—for talk, for fun, and to the extent to which they can deal with them, for sexual games—in sum, for a parody of relationship. For them persons are parts, for that is all they know of themselves—parts, never themselves as a whole.

John Beaver, in Waugh's *A Handful of Dust,* is a part of his widowed interior decorator mother's establishment. At twenty-five, he has no work, having lost his job as a result of the Depression of the early 1930s: "Since then no one had been able to find anything for him to do. So he got up late and sat near his telephone most of the day, hoping to be called up." His invitations come, when they come at all, as last-moment calls to substitute for missing persons at parties. He is himself a missing person, even when present, but ultimately he has a demon's effect on the world around him. A "joke figure," as that world sees him, he is "suddenly caught . . . among the luminous clouds of deity." Brenda Last is such a shining goddess in early 1930s London. Given to the habits of "any circumspect wife," when Beaver enters her life she suddenly decides on an adventure with her interior decorator's son. The whole thing is, as expressed in that crackling phrase extracted by Waugh from British society's witless conversation, "hard cheese on Tony," Brenda's husband. It is in fact much more than that. It is, however obliquely, the cause of the subsequent falling apart of everything in the life of the aristocratic Tony Last, whose name is emblematic of the kind of nobility—not simply a matter of blood—at which the Beavers of the world so successfully gnaw away. Brenda asks for a divorce after the Lasts' son is killed in an accident, the result of events almost as ridiculously slight as those that throw Brenda into Beaver's arms: ". . . it was several days before Tony fully realized what it meant. He had got into a habit of loving and trusting Brenda."

The trivialization of human contacts that the Beavers of this world represent is not enough to discredit them, even with those most victimized by them, at least not until great damage has been done. Beaver has responded to Brenda as he has to his rescuing phone calls, which summon him at the last moment to fill in for a missing dinner guest, a part-object to play a part. She confesses to him that she had first thought the accident to her son John had actually befallen John Beaver. Until then, she had had no idea that she loved Beaver. Now she does recognize the fact—she loves him. His wooden part-object reply is to note an additional fact: "Well you've said it often enough." Says Brenda: "I'm going to make you understand. You clod." Needless to say, she does not make him understand. She marries someone else and Tony goes off to die in a South American jungle, reading Dickens over and over again to a madman who has captured him, a properly famous ending to Waugh's gothic tale. What must not be forgotten is the role of the gargoyle in the saga—Beaver.[8]

Widmerpool is one of the great comic characterizations of this century. He is Anthony Powell's central figure of evil in his own gothic edifice, the twelve-volume *A Dance to the Music of Time*, which moves from pre-World War I public-school England to the riots and revels of the revolting young that took the place of public-school life in England twenty-five years after the end of World War II. Like Beaver, Widmerpool is a monumental bore, a dismal clown, son of an adoring widowed mother with whom he lives in London at the end of his school years. Not inappropriately for a small Scottish businessman who signalled his joy at marrying above his station by taking his wife's name, his father was a manufacturer of liquid manure, a fact that Widmerpool Jr. is not quick to divulge. Widmerpool is not quick to make known any facts about himself. He drifts in his tubby-figured, sometimes masochistic, often sadistic way from political fashion to political fashion—a faint Marxism, a flirtation with Hitlerism, a pronounced veer to the left, an obsequious bow to big businessmen, involvement with spying, with wars, with rebellious youth and consciousness-raising rituals. He prospers. He becomes a life peer in the House of Lords. He dies ignominiously. He is at best an uncertain sexual partner and at worst a malevolent disaster in bed who is quick to give advice and to spread stories about others. He is a frequent victim, and a deserving one, who never gets the point, as he moves from a lathering with bananas at school to high comic melodrama at a dance in the second volume of Powell's sequence. There his partner, a girl he had every intention of wooing, becomes exasperated at his sour disposition. She explains that he needs "some sweetening" and promptly provides it by emptying a huge sugar dispenser over his head.

The detail gathered by Powell's narrator to make the Widmerpool portrait may seem extravagant, but it is never irrelevant or wrong in tone. Unlike the trimmers, those without the ability to wax hot or cold about anything whom Dante leaves in utter contempt at the gates of hell, Widmerpool does have opinions, does make choices. But they are not real to him, however much they may derange others—as did the entry of that other pallid clown, Beaver, into people's lives. Widmerpool is a modern trimmer-clown. Under the guise of responding to a person, he merely picks some small part from the other on which to grow fat. And when he does not or cannot gain anything from actually using that part-object, which he has selected with such determined trimmer's cynicism and clownly reductiveness, then he can always turn the whole performance around and somehow gain from that. The persistent example in his peregrination through Powell's *Dance* is his treatment of women. Because he cannot respond to them as persons, he cannot in the simplest sexual terms respond to them at all. That failing of his he somehow always employs to his own gain. For example, he becomes a voyeur at his own wife's bed, using her (who is herself a using person) as a valuable part-object, for gratifications both obscure and clear. He lives chained in a dungeon of part-objects, dedicated to bringing as many others as possible to share his imprisonment.[9]

Failed Illusions

If on the outside everything stays in parts for the clown-man, on the inside nothing grows. His illusions do not ripen into values tough enough to survive in the real world. The clown-man is trapped in his transitional space, never making the necessary journey from fantasy to reality, never able to supply himself with lively symbols that might convey the interplay of a self and other.[10] The clown-man is like a child fixed in his play-space with his toys, immersed in his games. The imagination with which a child endows his toys never expands for him, as it does eventually for most children, to sustain linking to the real world. He stays, at first happily, then defensively, with his teddy bears.

An ordinary good-enough mother, attuning herself to our infant needs, will have no trouble fostering the illusions by which reality will be made to correspond to a child's needs and wishes. These are the illusions that build confidence in us, in our ability to make connection to reality. Our omnipotence is confirmed when we need it. We can then gradually relinquish it because we have enjoyed it so thoroughly. As a mother sensitively stops adapting to her child's needs for illusion when it is time to do so, the child comes to know that objects, including mother, exist as subjects in their own right, separate from what we wish them to be or think we need them to be.[11] We vent frustration, anger, and aggression at that fact, and make the remarkable discovery that the objects nonetheless survive. We did not destroy them, and neither did they destroy us, because we are separate from each other.

A good teacher performs a similar service for students, both fostering the illusion that what they have to say and think and create corresponds to reality, and gradually disillusioning them about this as an automatic correspondence. Now the student can take up the work of crafting ideas and insights into words or papers, or eventually striking themes and artistic perceptions that will bring into reality their original fantasy perceptions. This space of recognition between self and other, of their differences and possibilities for being united, widens for the child into the space of play, for the adult into the space of culture. There our fantastic, lavish, all-out loving and hating, our profound hopes and despairs, can be tempered to real dimensions that can be inhabited on a daily basis without losing excitement.

In this transitional space, our inner fantasies do more than elaborate upon the objective reality of objects. They permit us to experiment with different combinations, as do toys with detachable tiny pieces that snap together so we can construct everything from wheel barrows to space rockets, and our micro world can be expanded to the size of the universe. We become at ease with symbols of explosive power. We discover the resources even of toy craft. We learn to steer things, to steer ourselves. We respond to the surging impulses that are rising inside ourselves in the work of powerful objects. In our play, we are forging an identity for ourselves.

It is play, however, and so it can cheerfully accommodate failed transmissions and crashed rockets without shame. Defeat is woven into the pattern. That is how transitional space provides a place of rest. One can experiment without penalty; one can put together and take apart conflicting emotions. One can join and disjoin subjective conceptions with objective perceptions; one need not hold them together or in any way make them consistent with each other. In play, any variation goes. Above all, this is the space for movement in and out of illusion. We move from the more primitive place where our illusions equate with reality, toward the space of possibility, where we can renounce our omnipotent stance. We can now enjoy illusions as open fantasies that enrich rather than substitute for reality. This is how we claim our imagination and find our powers of discrimination. We know we live within finite limits, but we also know how far our dreams can take us. We know the strength of illusion as well as its failures. We know that it will enlarge reality to recognize that it is not reality, except in so far as the imagination is reality. Everything is larger, freer, more open as a result, including ourselves.

The man afflicted with compulsive clowning is not so fortunate. He is still confined to a reality of illusions. What is large and free in him is an addiction to parts. He cannot separate dream from reality. He repeats within himself his parents' failure to support his ego at just that crucial point of making a transition from merged to separate being, from dependence to independence. He does not take the necessary step from illusion to imagination. Just as the mother was absent from him, not sufficiently attuned to her child either to foster the needed temporary illusion or to insist on the permanence of reality and its demands, so he fails to house his own archetypal energies and images. He cannot believe in them or the reality that they in fact support.

We see all of this in the comic situation that the professional clown constructs. He stages scenes in which he proposes illusions that his audience inevitably and necessarily sees through—wonderful, innocent, dreamy nonsense. He sets up a situation in which the audience plays the parts of non-supporting parents and his own non-supporting ego. The audience and the parts they play question the reality-value of his fantasy. We find his purported illusion ridiculous and lovable at the same time, because we know better. We in our omniscience know ahead of time that Don Quixote is spearing nothing but windmills and sheep; that Laurel and Hardy will never get the piano successfully up the stairs, that a crash is inevitable. Whenever possible, we are cast by the clown in the role of Know-It-All, or at least Know-Better, the adult who scoffs at all childish illusions. The coming true of the predictions built into our roles comprises the humor and softens our necessary betrayal of the clown's illusion. But the unmasking retains a hostile tone. It is a contempt-releasing dénouement that in Freud's opinion is one essential element of the joke.[12]

If we transpose the circus clown's comedy into a real man's acute problems, we perceive the abundance of latent suffering. He always falls through the cracks. He does not in fact enjoy the overlapping of illusion and reality provided by a good-enough mother or an ego that, at least initially, wholeheartedly believes in its fantasies. The clown-man quickly enough is fixed in the gap between illusion and reality. His ridiculous clowning reveals a painful discrepancy, not a congruence, between the hoped-for illusion and reality. His is a world of near-misses, prat-falls, floor boards that collapse, chairs and tables that give way, or even more poignantly, jobs that fall through, marriages that do not quite make it, poems that never get finished.

The clown-man, to play on words, is no fool. He does not fully believe in his illusions; he knows that they cannot amount to anything in reality. Yet compulsively he holds onto them in their grandiose forms. He believes and does not believe. What belief he has is a mode of defense. He feels, and mimics what he feels. He wants desperately to actualize his illusions, but has failed so many times that he expects to be rebuffed. He desires but cannot endorse his desires, so again he holds them in defended form, arousing emotions and eager hope in others but not able wholeheartedly to give in to them himself. Never having enjoyed any omnipotence as a child, he cannot as an adult move on to a realistic sense of his own potency. Not having had the germ of a self identified and nurtured by his parents, he cannot build and house one for himself. His illusions stay primitive and grandiose and fall apart easily, never crossing the boundaries to enrich reality.[13] Unlike the witch, who always turns against her illusions in bitter disappointment, he goes on yearning for the realization of his hopes and dreams. He indulges in a wistful, emotion-filled longing for the realization, a sort of primitive feeling-solution, whereas the witch indulges in an excess of power, trying to force others through potions, curses, and spells to realize her ambitions. Each is stuck in illusion, the witch trying to substitute fantasy for reality in an obsessive, repetitive ruminating, the clown endlessly and futilely seeking to touch up reality with the magic and excitement of his illusions. The illusions prove impotent; they do not stand up; they flop around like the baggy clothes of the circus clown and lend force to his compulsion to compensate for ego weakness by sexual prowess. There he is then, a comic Don Juan, declaring that at least something will stand erect.

In extreme instances the illusion may change to delusion if the clown-man retreats into his fantasy through the exclusion of reality. Generally, however, delusion is more the witch's fate, as she withdraws to her miserable hut to eat ashes and bitter brews made from nature's leftovers—newt's eyes, frog's blood, bat's wings, and other such delicacies. She loses the symbolic from her life because she has substituted fantasy for reality, and then loses reality too. The clown, in contrast, goes on with his illusions, but makes a farce of them, thus betraying his growing recognition that they really cannot contribute to reality in any significant way. Immersed in primitive symbolism, unable to link the symbolic and the real, he loses both. Thus does the clown evince a winsome, if pathetic hope, a hope against hope that is sweet but not tough enough to survive. He does not believe that the world can correspond in any significant way to his fantasies about its meaning. He goes on trying to match his personal creativity to reality, but he is like a swimmer who knows he can never reach the opposite shore. He is bogged down in transitional space, with no clear view of either his inner or outer reality. He has only his transitional objects to depend on—child's toys, in effect, part fantasy and part reality and never more than parts. He comes neither to embrace fantasy as fantasy nor real objects as real, and thus loses the advantages of both. Fantasy is hallucination for him; reality, a collection of dead objects. The clown remains in the world of play, but without any fun. Unlike a child's games, the clown's lead nowhere.

With compulsive antics, the clown-man shuttles back and forth between part-objects, playing at being this one and that one but never reaching any conclusion, never producing anything durable. He knows none of the restfulness usually provided by transitional space, but only his frantic efforts to link up spaces, to move across the twin worlds of inner and outer life. His two worlds never join up, however. They pull loose from him, much like a circus clown's rope. Just as the clown fastens the rope at one end of the arena, it works loose at the opposite end. After much huffing and puffing on the clown's part, and elaborate banging of nails to hold the rope down, a stranger wanders by and, finding the rope blocking his way, takes scissors and cuts it!

In this bind, inner fantasy never moves toward the creation of durable symbols that can express a solid experience of reality. The clown-man is not able to use objects to represent the union of his inner and outer worlds. He finds no way to feel personally alive and real in the world. There is no reassurance for him anywhere he turns.

The long quest of Panurge, Rabelais's supreme hunter for reassurance where none can be given, is the classical example of the frenzied clown for whom reality simply cannot take shape. His demeaning fantasy—degrading both to him and to women—is to find a woman who will not betray him. Her fidelity must be guaranteed to him one way or another. He must know it all now, in advance of events, before undertaking marriage. In aid of his quest, he is taken on the great voyage of Book III of *Gargantua and Pantagruel,* from sibyl to magician; from one learned man to another; from friar to philosopher and theologian; from doctor to judge and fool. Neither from the resources of madness nor of sanity can a sure answer be provided. In that bawdiest of jests, Panurge can wear his wife as a ring, slipping her vagina over his finger. He can curb his concupiscence by quantities of wine, by anti-aphrodisiacs, backbreaking work, intense study, or—copulation. He can take heart from the performance of Judge Bridoye (Bridle-goose), that exemplary fool for Christ who never makes a wrong judgment. Even though all his judgments come from throws of dice, his throws are backed by the Providence in which he has such utter faith, except when his eyesight once misleads him. For Bridoye, there is constant reassurance. He will always find the knowledge he needs, though he is the very opposite of a know-it-all.

Panurge can neither emulate Bridoye nor take comfort from the constant reiteration of the facts of relationship. What his wife does will depend, of course, on what he does. If he does not feel alive and real in his world, neither will she, and inevitably, whether through adultery or some other means, she will be unfaithful to him because he is unfaithful to himself and to his world. Rabelais's nostrum for each frenzied clowning is both the simplest and most difficult there is. It is expressed in the rule of the Abbey of Thélème, the house of the will: *Fais-ce que voudras,* do what you will. It comes from the Augustinian prescription, "Love and Do What You Will." The key is the missing word in the Thélème rule—love.[14] What Augustine counsels, and what by every allegorical and symbolic illustration Rabelais supports, is to find in oneself that self-supporting selflessness that rests on a full construction of relationship, human as well as divine, in which there is never any uncertainty about the connection of inner and outer worlds and no racing around for the guarantees that only one's own loving attention can create. Then, when we no longer need such assurance, we have it. We can do what we will. Reality is suddenly revealed to us as benign.

The frenzied clown-man cannot really believe in the existence of a benign external reality. Reality always seems to him an anti-life force, to be defended against rather than turned to with hope. Effective contact with real objects can only be purchased, he thinks, at the price of compliance with expectations alien to the life of his soul, what our clown-man called his "juices." He can somehow get along, succeed in making a living, can get into marriage, but always without feeling really connected to life or those who share it with him. What would such a life be worth? He never sees the riches that reality offers, but only what it will cost. He cannot imagine the nurture a real person might provide him, but only the expectations with which he must comply. His hostile repudiation of reality sets up a tragic conflict in himself, and between himself and society. Power seems forever beyond him. Weakness and disconnection define his life.

Narcissistic Wounds

The clown-man's tragic situation only increases his resistance to facing reality. He cannot renounce his illusory omnipotence nor find symbols for an imaginative, rather than magical, interaction with the world. His illusions can find little outlet in real accomplishment, and tend to regress to more and more inflated forms that are harder and harder to realize in fact. He falls victim to what Heinz Kohut would call narcissistic grandiosity, in his hallucinating a grandiose self and an idealized all-perfect, all-powerful parental imago that can easily be projected onto others. He is, as Kohut says, unable "to regulate self-esteem" or to hold it at a "normal" level. The result is to leave his ego open to "the intrusions of either archaic forms of subject-bound grandiosity or of archaic narcissistically aggrandized self-objects into its realm."[15]

Freud makes a specific connection between the use of humor and the indulgence of narcissism.[16] In humor, the ego that usually must yield to the pleasure-drive, right to the limits of reality, can turn away the confinements that reality insists upon and enjoy to the full a triumphant invulnerability to the real, for which, momentarily at least, it pays no price in guilt. We explode with laughter, and though we may be a bit shocked at a joke or a prank, our laughter almost always overcomes our moral constraint.

Schiffer analyzes one of his comedian-patients' efforts to make up for the loss of a holding mother by contriving his own holding apparatus, one patched together of part-objects. This masquerades as a "rudimentary super-ego" that will sanction his indulgence in narcissism. Schiffer calls the performance a "seduction of the superego," which has the effect of intensifying "the illusion that man can indeed pawn off his narcissism as something other than it is." Schiffer's comedian loses both ego and superego functioning: "his capacity for illusion, for paradox,

"His illusions can find little outlet in real accomplishment and tend to regress to more and more inflated forms that are harder and harder to realize in fact. He falls victim to . . . narcissistic grandiosity. . . ." (George Cruikshank)

and for skewed thinking replaced objectivity and ego performance." His superego was really no more than a "stunted" one filled with "representations of transitional objects," a mixture that, "coupled with a relatively non-performing ego," produced "a caricature effect"—fitting, one might think, for a clown.[17] But clowning routines served only to intensify this man's problems, as invariably they must with men whose difficulties emerge from configurations that are so compelling that they become both problem and solution.

The clown-man offers his fantasies as realities. When they are inevitably rejected, or incapable of realization, usually because they are so out-sized, he suffers once again from not being seen, affirmed, welcomed into the human sphere. In compensation, he pushes himself to even more grandiose schemes, not noticing that his defiance of the principles of reality must inevitably bring failure. His ego is not differentiated from his self.[18] It stays with the self, and therefore knows none of the containing benefits of finitude. Lacking a mirror for his own growing ego that could relate to the self, the clown-man is caught in a constant turmoil, as he tries to find his ego in the mirror of the self's archetypes, which are entirely too big, too unassimilated, to fit human dimensions. Clown routines entertainingly reflect this turmoil, as for example when a performer raising the bucket of water onto the scaffold ignores the laws of gravity and balance. We know what will happen, and happen it does: Great gushes of water inundate him, his scheme, his job.

A patient offers a parallel case. Beset with the clown problem, he does not adequately consider actual obstacles to his ideas and proposals. When he meets up with other people's competitive aggression, he takes it personally, as if it were ruthlessly directed only at him and his thinking. When he offers a piece of work that receives criticism, he cringes, feeling it as the harsh attack of unloving people, never noticing that the work really needs the improvement that the criticism suggests. He teeters between feeling crushed and enraged. He turns to clowning as a defense against both. He is so caught up in extravagances of self because he is so utterly vulnerable at the center of his self. He is not yet validated in his own eyes and remains excruciatingly sensitive to others' opinions of him.[19]

The problem compounds itself in the clown-man's unthinking refusal of what others offer him. He relates to others in a narcissistic fashion, seeing them in terms of what they can supply his wounded self. As we saw in the discussion of part-objects, when real persons are treated as dispensers of commodities, intimacy is impossible. No one, finally, can reach the clown-man. All must constantly adapt to his needs. He is always looking for corroboration of the fact that his self exists and that it is good. Whatever the objective issue, whatever the other person is like, he always returns to the same questions: How did I do? What do you really think of me?

He wants the other to handle his vulnerability all the time, to put up with his angry, noisy rebukes without yelling back, to understand his offensive behavior without protesting or making him feel inadequate in any way. One must be available for closeness when he wants it, but not insist on one's own needs, for they make him feel demanded of. In everyone, he seeks a holding mother; in his employer, his girlfriend, his child, his audience. He wants others to be his connecting anima, to mediate between his ego and self, which, it must be said, can help make therapy successful if worked through in the transference.

Superego Pummeling

Recurrent narcissistic wounds to the clown-man's self-esteem provoke a deepening and dangerous conflict within him, one graphically described in the grand Freudian military metaphor of conflict between a harsh superego and a vulnerable ego.[20] Instead of supporting his ego, the superego condemns it harshly as a failure. A good superego, as Freud defined it, is like a good father—steadily, comfortably behind one, always ready to back one up in difficult times. Such a superego is money in the bank, to be drawn upon for ego projects, to fall back upon in emergencies. Not so the clown-man's superego, which he experiences as a punishing force pounding him with unorganized, contradictory aggressive energies. For him it is indeed like a father, his own bad one—a fake, and unmanly. It deserts him, never provides support, gives him only a hollow example to follow. Instead of feeling respect for superego standards, his ego repudiates them as life-killing values to be disowned, like the father who represents them. Conflict, competition, mutual disregard, and a total lack of mirroring characterize the ego-superego conflict for the clown-man.

In Jung's terms, the self has not become a central content of the clown-man's ego, to be housed, consulted, relied upon, and lived through ego channels into life. The clown-man enters the exhilarating experience of the paradox of self as both father and son to the ego—as a father moving it to obey the self's demands, as a son lifted into the world out of the ego's efforts to realize those demands.[21] Sadly, the clown-man, with his ego tightly merged with his self, merely feels self-inflated, then rejected and self-deflated, constantly made smaller and smaller.

A clown-man in analysis had many dreams that dramatized the self-destructive urges of the species, always directed against his own parts. "A man is pretending to choke another man to death, one he knows so well that it seems he's trying to choke a part of himself to death. It begins casually, almost as a joke. But then it seems that the pretended murder is actually killing someone else, someone dearer, one's own best, softest nature." In another dream he saw himself speeding along on his bike. Fastened next to his handle bars were the handle bars of another man on a bike. The dreamer speeded up and aimed for a narrow break in the traffic where he could squeak through, but the other rider would be smashed against a truck.

In society with others, this clown-man constantly found himself embarked on destructive patterns of behavior. Because he feared that conformity to social standards meant death to his personal self, he sabotaged his chances for success in conventional terms, more often than not by too much clowning around, compulsively failing to meet deadlines, flirting on the job instead of working, or stealing off for some clandestine meeting. Unconsciously, worldly success meant death to his soul, a peril he avoided by deliberate failing. But failure only exposed him to more shame and self-contempt.

The clown-man's defensive antics hurt others as well as himself, as it predictably destroys social atmospheres. A man dreamt that after lengthy negotiations, the two sides of the Middle East conflict were finally to sit down at a table for peace talks. Just as they were gathering, the clown-dreamer tossed in a firecracker as a prank. The signals are clear. The clown-man cannot house the opposing parts, so he lets loose into society his own fragmentation. Sometimes a dream would point to an underlying suicidal theme, inapposite, inadvertent in the circumstances, but no less dangerous for being so. "For cocktail entertainment another guy and I set off army mortars to scare the pants off the guests. But the shells do not explode in the air as they are supposed to; we dive out of the way, only barely missing being torn up by two shells . . . ."

All the support that a helpful superego might provide is converted instead into a punitive judgment of the ego's inadequacy. The vulnerable, needy self is treated as a culprit.[22] This makes maturing impossible and puts the ego under constant pressure just to cope, to stay alive. The amount of tension generated can be staggering, bringing on bodily symptoms of the great strain—aneurysm, hypertension, even cardiac arrest. The greatest danger, the most persistent, is not always so easy to see: It is despair.

Ego-Self Axis

The clown-man who cannot achieve a place in reality falls back time after time to the lonely place where his grandiose fantasies inhabit him, undelivered but for him always present. The symbols they convey to him are both dead and alive in him, real enough but expressive only of lifelessness. He cannot sustain intimacy with others. His ego identifies with whole successions of persona maskings. The future looks very bleak. Time's passing and the process of aging accelerate his anxiety. Feeling that so little of himself has been lived, fearing that still vulnerable place at the center of his being, he panics at the thought of everything passing him by, of being used up, of even this lifeless existence coming to an end. His ego feels impossibly fragile. He experiences his emotions as riotous invaders or as faithless deserters. His clowning, caught in its identifications and defenses against feeling, grows more forced, more thin. His search for the missing link to the self grows more desperate. He resorts often to outbursts against others, accusing them of having failed him, or against himself, feeling that he has failed himself. Bouts of depression, nervous anxiety, and manic laughter assail him. He falls into despair at ever being himself in a shared existence with others.

Jungian metaphors prove to be most useful at this point. The image of the ego being grounded in the larger self and fed by it, provides a way to deal with the deep suffering of the clown-man. We can gather great help from methods that trace the development of the clown's dilemma. We can see step by step, concretely, what has happened to the clown's ego in its disorder. But understanding the etiology of a disorder is not enough. For all its help, it still does not provide a means to a living relationship with which to fill the emptiness left by a past relationship that has foundered. The notion of drawing the ego into close relation with the self envisions the autonomous dynamic of the self-archetype pressing toward completion. If understood and acknowledged, it holds forth an opening to what is alive in the clown-man's circumstances, to see that what was once offered and refused may now be found again and accepted.

Seen this way, healing comes as much from within the psyche as from outside it. This is quite different from the familiar psychoanalytic emphasis on restoring the damaged internalized objects through the offering of new introjects in the analytical relationship. Channels must be found as much inside as outside the psyche, ways through which its archetypal energies can be gathered up and directed toward both new ends and old ends. In effect, we take in what is already there. We claim our damaged parts, our silent parts, even our dead ones. In this perspective, our ordinary daily experience links up to a meaning that transcends each event's particularity. We feel part of a larger whole that encompasses not just the whole of our psyche—every single one of its parts—but also the whole of the human family where we are just one part. Coming to terms with what is really there in our psyche, in whatever condition it may be, is the way we plant our roots in the human community.

In the clown-man's case, his ego is still merged with the self, still immersed in it. No axis of relationship between the two firmly exists as yet. The anima, which must form a bridge between ego and self, is missing, not yet developed, so the two processes of ego and self either jam together in fusion or split apart in dissociation. The clown-man experiences the self as clusters of random parts, archetypal images and emotions that for all their motley condition still have the power to capture him. His ego cannot house this experience and sort it through, but simply falls into identification with each of the component parts. He either puffs up in inflation as a result, or feels forlorn and cast out in deflation. Facing the outside world, he identifies compulsively with whatever is at hand, changing masks as each occasion requires. How can he make connection, how can he bring ego and self together? Where is there secure ground for the clown-man?

The way out is the way of suffering. Through the very vulnerability he defends against, he must find his way into that holding space where ego is ministered to by self. There he can give his ego the rest it so badly needs, and find the time to bring together the parts of his inner and outer worlds in a new wholeness, the first one he will have known. Through the very disconnection of self and ego, which has left him feeling weak, unloved, and alone with his wounds, he may be able to find the means of connection, the joining of ego to self that he so sorely needs. The anima function will prove essential, for he cannot simply switch on "the hallowed presence of the self," as Dorothy Davidson puts it.[23] He needs that inner other to see himself, to claim himself.

XIII The Clown Rescued

Disidentification

The clown-man must take on two worlds in his struggle for survival. Facing the outer world of shared existence, he is caught in identification with a clowning persona that he tries to make into a genuine identity. Facing the world within, he is caught in identification with a weak anima in his effort to defend against the feeling of vulnerability with which even a faltering anima looks to put him in touch. As we saw in Chapter IX, the clown-man presents to the world a fuzzy image of masculinity, the public face of his inner blurring of his masculine ego and feminine anima; he appears as a sort of man-woman. Too soft, to the point of being labeled effeminate; too sensitive, to the point of failing to act decisively; too weak, to the point of seeming nothing but a fool, the clown-man is gifted in many large ways, but hampered by these very gifts as long as they lie beyond his conscious use.

We have seen the clown-man don successive persona maskings (Chapter X), and even deliberately indulge in effeminate gestures to reflect the blurred lines between male and female within him and to disguise the impotence he feels as a man. Even the sexual clowning he takes up as a compulsive Don Juan pattern betrays an anima that is both too close and too far away. Unconsciously identifying with the anima's animating function, the clown-turned-Don Juan feels compelled to wake up successive women to their own femininity. What he is really doing is identifying with what he lacks, compulsively seeking in a woman's awakening a remedy for the deadness in himself.

We have seen the clown-man in earnest pursuit of something or someone to make up for his mother's failure to hold him in being (Chapter XI). We saw him desolate, with no model and no sense of how to house his own being. Playing the good mother to others, he tries to mimic what he so desperately needs and thus to share it with others. He holds before them a mirror in which they can find and feel emotions, but he never finds a mirror of his own to reflect himself. He revenges himself on a strutting shell of a father who, he felt, had sacrificed his soul in his empty dramas of the big man in the big world. With his own clownly strutting, he is mocking his father, pushing through his public mask to the hollowness within. He exposes his father's great secret—that he feels castrated —and thus betrays his own. In this he could identify with his father; he also feels unmanned.

He is left with an anima that performs none of its required tasks, but simply

247

leads him hither and yon as he thrusts his projections onto a whole series of women and situations. He defends his emptiness by identifying with what he lacks. He apes with others the anima function of connecting the ego to defended feelings. The clown-man enlivens others and makes connections for them without ever being able to develop a bridge to his own interiority, leaving him (as we saw in Chapter XI) to suffer in his failed illusions, narcissistic vulnerability, and superego pummeling. Lacking connection, his ego and self both merge and split apart. They cannot find a durable union. The clown-man is left in despair.

There is a way out. It lies in disidentification from the clowning persona on the outside and the anima on the inside. The clown-man, like the woman caught in a hag complex, needs to reverse the reversal to benefit from the archetype to which he has fallen victim. He must now do for himself what he does for other people, must awaken his deepest feelings about himself and his world. He needs to grasp those emotions in their primary colors, all that he arouses in his audi-ences—delight, sorrow, rage, triumph, tenderness, fear, loneliness, rejection, envy, hate, gratitude, hilarity. He needs to see through his own masks, to see that they *are* masks, so that he can take them off as well as put them on, for to disidentify from his clowning role is not necessarily to discard it altogether. The clown can rearrange his relation to any of his roles, moving out of fixation with them as his gifts are brought before him for his conscious disposal. Then he can choose to use clowning and no longer be used by it. The archetype will cease to rule his behavior and emotions. His ego will be able to make room for the ar-chetypal dynamism, and build relation to it.

This double disidentification from persona and anima is a rich exercise in differentiation. The clown-man's blurred masculine-feminine identity moves to-ward a more articulated masculine ego in surer touch with a feminine anima. The anima in turn is set free to do its proper work of mediating to his ego those deep feelings of vulnerability that he had defended against, substituting them for his ego. It is a great gain: direct contact with his vulnerability and a clear place to hold it in his ego. He finds himself enlarging to include both the masculine and feminine aspects of his identity, in place of the ancient blurring.

This disidentification process brings profound changes. Simply being aware of the wounded condition is to make a place for it. An ego takes shape. The clown-man can relinquish his persona life, all those compulsive maskings, and ex-perience the energy that went into those elaborate defenses. All of that is made available for a spacious ego. Now he has his own mirror, the one he failed to find in either his mother or father. The anima functions more distinctly, like a feminine face reflecting back to him who he is in sharp images of what he feels. He can secure access to this feminine part of himself that needs no longer to be either identified with, acted out, or lost in projections. The clown-man's rescue is like that of the hag-woman. She inspects the inner masculine in herself; he finds the inner feminine. Each has a mirror in which to discover accurate pictures of damaged emotions, illusions, vulnerabilities, and the despair that arose from them. The clown's masculine identity is strengthened, not sabotaged, by its new connection to the feminine. All feeling does not have to be defended against by concentration on one masking feeling.

He sees the other as other, instead of as a mere source of supply for his needs. What is more, it is through the very needs that have bedeviled him that he sees the other. The problems with part-objects—the failed illusions, narcissistic vulnerability, and tyrannical self-hatred that brought him to despair—all become the means of transformation. Instead of casting off all his frailties and failures in a headlong retreat from the clown archetype, he claims all that belongs to him as it is mediated to his awareness by his anima. His problems have become the agents of insight not only into his own character, but into the larger world around him. When the clown archetype is set free from the ego's use of it to defend against feeling, the archetype itself is set free to perform its symbolic function; it can show its illuminating character, not simply its problem-making propensity. No longer confined to the constricting view of it that comes through the ego's identification with it, the clown archetype can display its own particular ways of humanizing and freeing the spirit.

"The image of liberation that the clown holds up to us is of a spiritual transformation closely connected to the earth. Abundant pleasures, satisfying emotions, a fulfilling personal life . . . a view of the spirit infused by the feminine principle."

The image of liberation that the clown holds up to us is of a spiritual transformation closely connected to the earth. Abundant pleasures, satisfying emotions, a fulfilling personal life define it. This is a view of the spirit infused by the feminine principle. This is a masculine identity that grows as it actively receives the feminine, just as the witch in her growth becomes more feminine the more she beholds and accepts the masculine within herself. The splits in these major modalities of human being and understanding, so grievously accented in our time, give way here to new mixtures of human sexuality, not the old patterns of mutual exclusion or of androgynous blurring. The contrasexual dynamism, housed within our conscious gender identity, is an unmistakable link to the depths of the unconscious and the mysterious center of the whole psyche, the self, through which we experience God or whatever we choose to call our apprehension of the ultimate and the unknown.

The Rescuing Anima

To be rescued from this defended state, this world of frozen feeling, the clown must reverse field. Instead of masking his wounds, he must welcome them. Instead of looking desperately for another to hold his own gaping openness, he must embrace this place of utter vulnerability himself and hold it in full awareness. Instead of looking indiscriminately to everyone else to tell him that he is a worthwhile someone, he must find this affirmation in himself. Instead of trying to escape his soft places, he must penetrate them, know their hidden crevasses and folds. He must inspect all of himself, positively contemplating everything that defines him positively or negatively, all that is there, all that is missing, all that might be found and rescued in him.

We can imagine a clown-man's rebuke on being handed this set of suggestions, how amusingly he might parody the well-intentioned analyst. He would protest that we recommend precisely what he feels he cannot do. What has he been defending against all these years? How can he go back into that? How can he take hold of himself, see his tender places again and bring them back into consciousness in any validating way? Imagine all this conveyed with a comic forlorn expression, a basset hound's mournful eyes, and a perfectly symmetrical unfolding and draping of the hands.

The clown-man is in fact just like the bewitched princess and must be rescued in just the same way, by instigating the desire to rescue in the rescuer. Whereas the princess was trapped in her secret nether world and could only be freed by the prince she had inspired to find and save her, the clown is imprisoned behind his masks, doomed to a life of endless personifications unless rescue comes from a rescuer whom he himself sets in motion. The rescuer, in his case, must be so "other" to him, so far from him, that he will experience the rescue as originating in an altogether other world. But in fact, the distance from him may not be very great at all. Like the bewitched female who knows the agent of her rescue as a real man or an animus figure or some combination of both, the clown-man may find his rescuing anima in an actual woman, or as an anima part of his own psychology, or in the bewitchings of art, religion, politics, a significant charitable cause, or some combination of all of these.

Heretofore he has simply not wanted to know this anima side of himself. It made the vulnerable feelings he had pushed into his unconscious even more indistinct and painful. It made the donning of masks even more necessary. He has been behaving like the shyest of maidens avoiding self-confrontation. There could be no looking at those parts of himself—small, hidden, unobvious, unmasculine. Like a woman afraid to inspect her own genital parts because they are so concealed and inward-facing, the clown-man has veered away from looking closely into the hidden organs of his feeling, the folded complexities of his sensitivity. Better to stay with all that dwarfs them, the obvious male reactions that stand out visibly like a man's genital parts, clearly seen as what they are, in plain view. But when he disidentifies from his masks, and admits them to be defensive gestures against all his feeling, his anima component begins to emerge from its deep folds in his unconscious and make her own kind of distinct appearance, with her own unmistakable effect.

Whatever form the anima may take in her new appearance, the effect is the same. Like the prince in the tale of bewitchment, she has been inspired to look for and identify the man's true self, and now she calls him to claim it.

We can understand much about the way the anima exerts its rescuing function from an examination of the figure of Scheherazade in *The Arabian Nights*, as she works against the Sultan and his murderous plan to marry a virgin every day and to have her killed the next morning. What she does is to hold him enthralled by her telling of the thousand and one tales that fill the *Nights*.[1] Her fanciful theories create a space in which the Sultan can rest from his compulsive attachment to his bloody vow, a vengeful resolve against all women that arose from his feelings of betrayal by one woman, his first wife. His decision has been to act out his tortured feelings rather than inspect them.[2] He who felt a death blow at the hands of one woman, will now deal death to all women. Rather than feel his hurt, inspect it, and assimilate it, he must defend against it in endless acts of revenge.

Scheherazade voluntarily steps into this dangerous atmosphere by offering to become one of the Sultan's wives and thus a victim in the making. She willingly exposes herself to the violence of his feelings with a shrewd plan to interrupt their enactment. First, the Sultan must allow her sister to sleep in their room on Scheherazade's night with him. Second, Scheherazade instructs her sister to awaken an hour before dawn, the scheduled time for execution, and then to ask her to tell one of her engrossing tales. And so it happens. The Sultan awakes to the sound of Scheherazade recounting a wondrous adventure in her inimitable way, combining great learning and rich imagination. As she finishes one tale, he begs for yet another, each requiring one full night. On and on it goes, another and another and another, until a thousand and one tales are told. With each telling of a tale, execution is postponed.

Scheherazade thus interposes between the Sultan's murderous impulse and his acting upon it stories that arouse his curiosity, his incredulity, his emotions, his unbroken attention. She creates a space in which he can disidentify from his suffering and inspect it, reflect upon it instead of acting it out. She constructs this space out of illusions, fantastic tales about other men's suffering, vulnerability, betrayal, and compassion. The Sultan plays with the images she conjures up. He identifies with the action of Ali Baba going into the forty thieves' cave of gold. He tosses back and forth the opposing emotions that Sinbad's adventures let loose. He protests at the extraordinary denseness of a king who could have believed that his queen gave birth not to children but to a dog, a cat, and a piece of wood, as her jealous sisters claim—a fool of a king who would then banish his queen. No more dense or foolish, answers Scheherazade, than a sultan who vows to kill his bride because of the faithlessness of another woman, a bride who must tell him so many tales to stay her own execution. And there she has him. She has performed her anima task of rescue by making the Sultan aware of his own feelings and forcing him to assimilate them to his consciousness.

Scheherazade turns the Sultan back in upon his own feelings, feelings that he has turned inside-out because he has never looked into them, living only with their outer surfaces of rage and betrayal and generalized vengeance. She reverses his reversal, and thus rescues him from unconsciousness and its theater of enactment. She creates a transitional space where he can play with instinct-backed fantasies of his own in a shared existence with others. The tales are his toys, the illusions of the anima that allow him to take apart and recombine the many facets of his cramped and painful emotions. Scheherazade makes him pause, stop, and wonder, makes him enter that forbidden inner place where, in the reflecting mirror provided by identification with other sultans, emperors, kings, and men of all stations, he can begin to sort himself out.

She creates an equation-by-illusion that makes his story of hurt and betrayal correspond to the pain and suffering of others. She confirms his omnipotence: What he wishes for does in fact happen. But then she shows different ways in and out of the use of power through tales that gradually disencumber him of the conviction that he alone is right in his views. There are other ways to understand what has happened to him. Other facts exist apart from his feelings and needs. She removes from him the delusion that his hurt is his alone, that he alone is unwanted and unloved. She places his isolated feelings in the great arena of other men's suffering, and shows how they perpetuate it by failing to examine their pain, by walling themselves against it, by their extravagant defenses, by their masks of outrage, or bravery, or clowning. She elicits the feeling experience of his suffering through her multiple narrative variations on the theme. She makes space for differentiation. She helps the Sultan enter his wounded feelings at many different points to penetrate to their hidden centers.

Scheherazade rescues the Sultan from his narcissistic vulnerability, not by covering it up, but by going right into it. What had been a fatal wound now becomes the means of identifying with others' hurt, others' sensitivities. What had occasioned his isolation from others, what had made his hurt an all-consuming focus of his life and left him oblivious to the existence of others, now becomes his point of connection with others.

When a man refuses to claim his anima part, he falls victim to his vulnerable feelings, and, as we have seen, to the narcissistic disorder characteristic of the clown-man. There, he yields to a parody anima, unconsciously identified with a female part of himself, as if he had a female sexual organ wide open in him that he was shudderingly avoiding, a place of menace that threatens to suck him into his painful feelings, or that could at any moment be invaded by someone or something else. Denying this vulnerability, he falls right into it and achieves the grandiosity of the narcissist's disorder. He pulls everything that happens to him into this great, gaping openness in himself of which he feels so afraid and ashamed. He relentlessly refers every event back to himself and his prickly sensibility. Grand victim himself, he victimizes everyone around him. Everything gets pulled into his great hole to drown; nothing is held in protective embrace.

The rescuing anima personified by Scheherazade does just the opposite. She holds up for a man's ego a mirror in which to inspect this soft, hidden, interior side of his psyche and everything that arises in it. She brings to his ego awareness of the organ of feeling he has denied. Acknowledging his anima part, a clown-man can disidentify with his impossibly vulnerable feelings, and they can then become the means through which what was a narcissistic condition is transformed into the gift of empathy. What was a cause of excruciating isolation develops into an agent of connection to others. Holding in awareness the vulnerability that his anima shows him, he can perceive the vulnerabilities of others and become sensitive to them. Though not yet integrating his anima as really being his own, the Sultan does feel connected to the feminine world through Scheherazade. He says to her: "You have at length appeased my anger, and I freely revoke in your favor the cruel law I had promulgated. I receive you entirely into my favor, and wish you to be considered the preserver of many ladies, who would, but for you, have been sacrificed to my just resentment."[3]

Through one woman, all women will be protected. Such is the way of the anima when it rescues the clown-man's ego. Her particularity opens him to the feminine in its endless variations. This is borne out in less fanciful experience than Scheherazade's and the Sultan's. A man who trusts the love of one good woman looks kindly on all women, knowing their value, respecting their rights, feeling himself benefited by their presence. A good anima figure will recall the man to his feelings as he sees the place of hurt within himself. She will reflect back to him the vulnerability he has refused to see, has in fact tried to crush by violating others' vulnerabilities, especially those of the women who receive the projections of his unacknowledged anima. She holds his wounds open to him, to enter willingly by lovingly embracing his anima or a real woman who, with courage and skill, has insisted that he claim this part of himself.

Only by going through the narrow door that his anima opens to his own feelings, can he find empathy for others. To find his connecting links to others, to his own feeling, to what matters in life to him, a man must connect to his own anima part—not to one that he would like to have, not to one that he thinks he deserves, just to what is there, to what is his. But before a man can find the anima who comes to find him, he must acknowledge her strengths and yield to them. She can rescue him from a condition from which he cannot save himself. The only appropriate word for what he must do is one so abusively thrown into the teeth of women over the years that it has all but lost its meaning. We must recover the word as it applies here to the man: He must *submit.* He must submit to the anima's authority.

At the end of Mozart's *The Magic Flute,* that feathery clown-man, Papageno, typifies the plight of many clown-men. There the very model of a loathsome old hag presents herself as his intended bride. He recoils. He shudders. He begs to be let off. Not a chance with this anima! When, for all the comic resonances, he submits in terror and trembling and embraces her, in the flash of a great operatic melodrama she changes into his fitting opposite, a feathery female Papagena. The joyous music of their duet echoes the jubilation of lovers everywhere who recognize what they have in each other—not a mate who substitutes for a missing part of themselves, but one who calls them to develop the missing part and so really to become themselves. It is in this sense that Jung writes of the contrasexual archetype, the anima or animus, as acting as the link to the self, the center of the human person.

A man's submission to his anima does not mean he replaces his ego with the anima. What he achieves instead is a reciprocal matching of those two vital centers of his being, point for point, to yield an enlargement of that interior space that heretofore was only associated with the female womb. Perhaps for the first time, he really gains interiority. He has an inner mirror in which to find reflected back to him his experience, an inner space in which to turn over and inspect all that happens to him. He now has an inner other who will talk back to him, through images, moods, and dreams, an other with whom he can enter into dialogue. This is his own particular, concrete anima, not a generalized femininity, not women in general. His anima is not to be generalized, any more than his self is. Erasmus's Folly, so aptly personified as female, laughingly pokes fun at the illusions of feeling that would make this or that specific detail serve symbolically as a lover's paean of praise, but it is those illusions, in their particularity, that are the lifeblood of human relationships. How else except as foolishness can we speak of the

> fellow who kisses the mole of his mistress's neck, or of the other who is delighted by the growth on his little lady's nose, or the father who says of his cross-eyed son that his eyes twinkle? What is all this, I ask you, but sheer folly? . . . Yet this same foolishness both joins friends, and, after joining them, keeps their friendship alive.[4]

In sum, then, the rescuing anima does for the clown-man and helps him to do for himself what before he has done for others. She holds up to him his interior mirror. He is now open to himself for his own inspection. She provides a space between his fearful vulnerability and his defenses against it, so that he can disidentify from the clowning masks on the outside and differentiate from the anima on the inside.

The rescuing anima holds all the fragmentary parts of objects and images together as the clown-man's mother neglected to do, and as his ego cannot yet do. This holding operation gathers the pieces together for the ego's inspection and eventual assimilation, so he can put them together where they belong at the center of his inner life. The anima thus holds out to the clown-man the possibility of carrying his own wounded feelings. No more dumping them onto others; no more hiding from them behind his clowning masks.

The Holding Anima

Clown-men do not always find a woman who will rescue them, or an anima that presents itself in fine, clear-cut personified form as, for example, in the Scheherazade figure. Their rescue must usually be by another route, where deliverance from a compulsion to clown arrives in broken lines and fleeting appearances rather than sustained intimacy. But deliverance is nonetheless available.

Some men find themselves given back to themselves through more impersonal anima carriers, such as the large cultural symbol-systems of art, politics, or religion, or an institution that they have endowed with their emotional life. As with a specific anima figure, their turning point becomes the consciousness that they have endowed with the animating life of their soul—a particular set of values, a school, a business, religious ritual, a cause. Consciousness makes possible disidentification of their ego from those anima contents. Without consciousness, a man continues to live his anima in projected form where it cannot mediate to his ego the specific contents of his own psyche that he is defending against, where he is weak and knows himself to be weak. He retreats from himself. He pours his lifeblood into a cause, a world, an institutionalized defense. Then retirement comes, or illness. He cannot continue.[5] A literal uprooting of his soul takes place. He has let school or business, for example, do the carrying work he should have been doing himself. He has allowed others, people or institutions, to perform the holding function for his ego that should have been his. School, firm, or cause has become the mother he never had. In its life he immerses himself, hoping to find there his protective barrier, a holding ego to support him in inner or outer events. That is what lies behind a wife saying about her husand, "He lives only for his work." His is less a compulsive work habit than it is a determined abiding within the safe confines of a great mother-surrogate. The man has not differentiated for himself an individual anima-connection to life, but has let it be carried for him by the mother or her surrogate. When such a man loses his job, retires, or must resign because of illness, the trauma that comes to light replicates his original loss of his mother.

In working for a cause, say for clean air or clean waters, he feels connected to a central, symbolic goal, to make the world a better place. He feels he is giving his love to others and to the planet itself. But when the air or water is not perfectly cleared, he feels his love has been wasted. He feels impotent unless his animating connection to his goals exists independent of the cause, as well as through it.

In dealing with the world of projection of the clown-man, we can only hope he has not been caught in a tightly bureaucratized institution. What we must look for, what he must find, is the symbolic plane of his experience, where there is a clear chance for consciousness to intervene. In religion, for example, some of the emotion devoted to the figure of the Virgin Mary can be traced to projecting onto her the holding capacity of a mother attuning herself to the child's nascent ego.

When a man moved to such worship becomes aware of this psychological component, that does not necessarily mean he must discard all devotion to the figure of the Virgin Mother. It means he can enter into it, to penetrate its soft side, to disidentify from it, and to hold his own soft vulnerability even as he feels encompassed by the intercessory embrace of Mary. He can fill in the missing side of the clown-man by admitting into his own awareness the openness to feeling that his clowning so successfully awakens in others. That way he will no longer hide behind a facade of feeling. He will stop using his rounds of worship to defend himself from feeling. When he worships now, he will know how small, childish, dependent, and contingent he feels, and face consciously how much he would like to crawl into the protected space of a heavenly mother's arms to find safety. He will carry these feelings into his prayers, rather than unconsciously acting them out as if he were a child instead of a man. Rather than unconsciously identifying with his vulnerability, and expecting some heavenly mother to take care of his childishness, disposing of it like so many dirty diapers, he will consciously take up and hold in his awareness this fragile part of himself, no matter how messy it may be. He will bring it right into his religious ritual, offering it up rather than dumping it there. The figure of Mary will then constellate for him the childish feelings of which he needs so to be conscious. No more acting the part of the motherless waif. He can choose as an adult to house the infant side of himself in his ego and bring it with him into his worship. Devotion replaces addiction, as boy becomes man.

Similarly, in relation to his father, the clown-man finds disidentification by ceasing to perform his compulsive routines of mocking, unmasking, and caricaturing the impotent father who pretends potency. His very sensitivity to the fake, to pompous pronouncements that serve only to hide inner disconnections, may prove to be his surest means of connection to other men. He no longer has to poke fun at fathers, whether they are actual parents or cultural, religious, or political ones. Feeling his own lack of life-enhancing guiding principles, he can feel compassion for a world that is apparently rudderless. He can win through to seeing reflected in his anima not just a longing for the durable or external, but a true sense of it as a motivating force in his ephemeral actings and doings. Thus he can forge a commitment to values that for him bespeak the eternal in the mundane. He shows us a style of living toward the absolute, right here in the relative dimensions of daily life. He sees the transient and patchy nature of things, the clownliness of mortality. But he sees it placed in a larger arena, in the wry sense of humor of creation that mixes the tenderest mercy with a guffaw and a pratfall. The anima mirrors to him through his wounds that nothing is absolutely pure, whole, infallible in judgment or principle. Through the soreness of our wounds and the scrappy ways that we have patched together our principles, we find our rhythm toward eternity. Through the fallible father we find a way to the symbol of the father that endures.

In psychological terms, this process of disidentification promotes the differentiation of the clown-man's ego from the long indulgence of his vulnerability. He suffers awareness of it instead of blindly living it, carries it instead of projecting it. In religious terms, this process of disidentification amounts to a sacrifice. When he offers up the infantile side of himself in his prayers, he is claiming it as his own responsibility and renouncing his unconscious identification with it. In the happiest of ironies, through conscious acceptance of this childish part of himself, a man may free himself to become a fool for God rather than just being foolish. In the language of the gospels, he becomes like a little child, rather than childish. Jesus responded warmly to people who made open fools of themselves out of their intense desire for contact with God. A man cries out in a crowd, and will not be silenced no matter how foolish he appears. A woman insists on receiving food from Jesus, not worrying whether or not she belongs to the right social or religious clan; crumbs are enough—anything rather than nothing. Zacheus climbs a tree in the most awkward way just to get a look at Jesus. That is the foolishness of faith—and of claiming what one is and what one wants, going all out, regardless of embarrassment, or social taboos, or looking a fool. Here is life. One reaches out and takes it. What such a fool seizes is reality.

At the end of his *Decameron,* Giovanni Boccaccio speaks with the voice of faith, faces whatever embarrassment may be involved, and chances making a fool of himself—in worldly terms, at least. In the tenth tale of the tenth day of storytelling, with which a dozen young people have occupied themselves in their self-banishment from plague-ridden Florence, one of the young men tells the story of Patient Griselda. With it he—and Boccaccio—take a bold step into reality, though perhaps not everyone's reality. Griselda is abused as almost no wife in fiction has ever been. She is put aside by her titled husband after she has given birth to two children and begun to rear them. He tells her that they are dead and that he is going to marry another woman. After some time he brings their daughter to the house, introducing her as his new bride, and makes Griselda her handmaid. He sends his wife away, reduced to penury in everything, including her clothing. Finding Griselda endlessly patient under these terrible blows, he brings her back again, with an apology that only a saint could accept. He explains that he has tested her so brutally to teach her—and by her example, others—how to be a wife. For this reason he chanced the outrage of the world at his unjust behavior, as well as to achieve "perpetual quiet," a splendidly equivocal phrase that refers more to the interior disposition he sought than to any outward noiselessness.

Griselda is as much an anima figure as Scheherazade. She is for Boccaccio's marquis what the great tale-teller is to the Sultan. With a resolve that is as moving today as it was when the writer's most admired contemporary, Petrarch, was so caught by the figure, Griselda shows us the holding anima at its most stubborn and most inspired. Having displayed such superhuman patience under affliction, Griselda may "reap the fruits . . . ." She is brought out from her anima obscurity, restored and more than restored to her high position. As the marquis's wife again, she discovers that her children are alive and well and themselves ready for noble roles; her daughter is about to be particularly well married. The marquis, no longer held in contempt, is thought to be a man of some wisdom; his wife is esteemed as "most sage." Who but Griselda, this paragon of virtue, this anima personification, could have endured "the barbarous and unheard proofs" required by her husband? Who could so handsomely have made the move from the humble chemise in which she was turned away to the fine gown in which she was welcomed back?

If we choose to see Griselda in terms of an anima allegory, one need not distort Boccaccio's character to make her fit the terms of psychoanalytical employment. Griselda is the allegorical figure par excellence. She is the personification of the suffering servant, an unmistakable *alter Christus*. Griselda is the way the church is tried. Griselda is the way a man tries his anima and asks everything of it. Her husband, in the medieval and Renaissance fashion of such parables, stands for a higher justice than the worldly sort, a crucifyingly stern justice, as he demands nothing less than a matching charity from his preternaturally patient wife and finally gives, in return for her holding graces, a fullness of love. It is the crowning love that brings to an end a round of tales relating more of foolish love, perverse love, defective love, and catch-as-catch-can bawdiness than of goodness or anything close to charity. It is a world of love played at, snatched at, taunted, love rarely conscious, love almost always beleaguered in a tortured interiority, from which those who are tortured keep looking out for deliverance by means of an agreeable conclusion such as Griselda brings. And yet, in the large allegorical scheme of the *Decameron*'s ten sets of ten tales, it is not simply an agreeable conclusion that brings us Patient Griselda at the end of the series. She represents purposeful folly, the highest wisdom, the most stubborn wisdom, and does so with that special female or anima inflection that Boccaccio gave this gathering of virtue and understanding two centuries before Erasmus cast folly as a woman.[6]

Everything about the great human comedy dramatized by the *Decameron* tales is cast in the persons and purposes of woman, and of what the feminine can represent for men. It is as if Boccaccio were writing an elaborate, witty defense of the contrasexual side of the male, drawing with ingenuity upon the equipment of the male whom he knows best, himself. He opens his story-telling with a long, hopeful explanation to those "gracious ladies" who are his most important readers, asking them not to be offended by his "grisly introduction," the "rugged and steep mountain" he must ask them to climb to get to the "most fair and delightful plain" that lies beyond. The grisly mountain is in fact the plague of 1348, the excuse for his monumental performance.

In the first introduction, Boccaccio pays the feminine some compliments. In the second introduction to the *Decameron,* which opens the Fourth Day, he returns vigorously to the task of pleading his cause. There he defends himself against the accusation that he likes the ladies "overmuch." He has been told that he is too old "to discourse of women or to study to please them." Well, he will put up with calumny, backbiting, and criticism of any kind. Then to make his defense, he will do what he does best: he will tell a tale. A good Florentine named Filippo is left with a son to bring up after his wife's untimely death. He takes the child to live an ascetic Christian life in a hut on a mountain outside the city, where they see no one but each other, where they pray and generally emulate the life of monks. When the boy is eighteen, he asks his father to take him along on one of his trips to Florence. He does so. As they journey, they meet "by chance" a group of attractive young women coming from a wedding. Filippo asks his son to keep custody of the eyes: ". . . look not at them, for they are an ill thing." "How are they called?" "Green geese," says the father, hoping with that description to keep carnality at a proper distance. "Please, Father, get me one of these green geese." "I tell you," the distraught man replies, "they are an ill thing." The son is puzzled that ill things are made so well, "fairer than the painted angels you have shown me." Let us take one back with us, the son proposes, "and I will feed it." "No," says the father; "you do not know on what they feed," and reflects to himself that nature is stronger than his wit. He is sad that he has brought his son into Florence, which for Boccaccio's purposes is the real world. Filippo cannot quite face the female claim on his male child.

Reality at its best is womanly for Boccaccio. He does indeed marvel, he confesses, at the "dainty manners and lovesome beauty and sprightly grace and above all . . . womanly courtesy" of those upon whom he spends his gifts. If they pleased the "hermitling," the "lad without understanding" of his tale, imagine what they bring to a man of his years and experience. It is, no matter what his intention, an adroit tribute to an anima presence. As further support for an older man's understanding, he cites the way women were held in honor by those two great Italian writers, Guido Cavalcanti and Dante Alighieri, "when already stricken in years." All of which leads him, as often in his work he is led to do, to praise the possibilities of fiction and fable, a greater treasury for a poet than worldly goods are for a rich man.[7]

Join fable to women and you get the special wealth of the *Decameron.* The most salacious tales in the collection bring the reader up against the underlying wit, which is much larger and more lasting than the surface humor. For example, there is the famous bit of bawdiness at the end of the third day, in which the monk Rustico teaches a nubile young girl how to become a good Christian, by putting the devil, his penis, into hell, her vagina. The punishment at first offers delights for both, but her delights ultimately turn into his punishment when her appetite becomes far too much for him to assuage. Her indoctrination serves another purpose very well, however. The girl comes away from the desert where she has been leading her interesting version of a hermit's life, brought back against her inclination by a young man. Asked by some women how she had learned to serve God in the desert, she explains by means of words and gestures the ritual of putting the devil into hell. The women tell her not to worry, that that is done in the city, too, and she can be sure her young man "will serve the Lord full well by doing it."

Boccaccio is determined to join all ends of reality together, not the least of them the male and the female. By all means laugh at human folly, at our desperate acts of concupiscence, our self-serving, our multiple betrayals of each other, and the ludicrous strategies by which we attain our ends. But by all means see the wisdom of the human performance, the true charity, the extraordinary wit with which we trap those too cunning for their own or our own good. It is in that balancing of good and evil that Boccaccio so often invokes the importance of women and the consciousness of the feminine in men's lives, and develops alongside his bawdy humor a set of symbols and allegorical tales in which to discover the grammar, logic, and rhetoric of a love that is charitable to oneself and to others. In that service, he also put together the *Lives of Illustrious Women,* 104 of them, to set beside the *Lives of Illustrious Men* of his beloved contemporary, Petrarch. The acts of women, glorious or simply notorious, deserve narration and examination exactly as men's, he says in his Prologue. With delicate irony that is easily overlooked, he points out that "if men with their strength and other worthy ways deserve praise and commendation, how much more ought those women to be praised, who are naturally weak and feeble and with wits not so quick as men's, when they have done so consciously things which would be hard for men to do." He has compiled his volume, he explains, so that women "should not be defrauded" of their accomplishment. What he achieves, less entertainingly in the *De Claris Mulieribus* than the *Decameron* but with related intent, is a firm hold on reality in all its sexual and contrasexual aspects.[8] The anima has its great fourteenth-century troubadour in Giovanni Boccaccio, whether it is putting the devil into hell or preparing our way to heaven with Griselda's patience.

The clown-man who has not been tutored by a Boccaccio has trouble reaching out in any sustained way to his contrasexuality. He has no addiction, foolish or otherwise, to the feminine. He has a hole in his ego, and he feels his ego is in pieces. Without a holding anima, he is a network of wounds with an especially large cavity at the center. But he does have a great positive possession, his clowning procedures, the very ones he uses to cover up his sad, sick, fragmentary life. His endless maskings are, after all, a form of art. In the process of veiling the holes of his being, he points right at them. To veil, as Boccaccio insists so eloquently in his *Genealogy of the Gentile Gods,* is as much to uncover as to cover up. What we acknowledge and assimilate in our veilings is what needs to be revealed. The clown-man's multiple mimickings and personifications may become his *Decameron.* As he tells his tales and plunges into his world of part-objects, he may discover his holding anima, his patient Griselda. The way out is the way through.

When the clown-man finally claims his modest little fragment of an ego, however small, and begins to accept his wounded condition, he discovers what it means to own an imagination and to use it in its own free space. That is what this small but heroic claiming action of the clown-man's amounts to—the discovery of art. He does not feel significantly less beleaguered than heretofore, but he knows he has a place in which to nurture his suffering, a place in which to put all those endless little part-objects, the place of art.

The Holding Arts

It is art now that performs the holding operation that gives the clown's ego its rest from that compulsive artless juggling of parts. It is art, whether he calls it that or not, which permits him to see what he has and use what he has, one piece at a time—even one piece of a piece—and to bring the pieces together, just as we do if we have a tutored eye or ear when we inspect the many segments of a large painting or try to hold together the sections of a long piece of music. In both we see bits and pieces of human experience—part-objects, held within a unified scheme, with dominant symbols—that reflect the informing personality of the artist at least as much as they reveal the world from which he has drawn his scheme and symbols. This is as true of Picasso as it is of Brueghel, of Stravinsky as it is of Mozart, each of whom is an artist whose world at least some of the time reflects some of the textures of the clown-man's. Their work reflects a busy unconscious life, as full of fragments as the clown-man's. They found ways to make space for all the part-objects, the partial representation of a section of feeling—the impulse to rage, for example—that neither denies its existence nor permits it to blow up the whole feeling connection. In contemplating paintings and music we can find space for our bits and pieces, to be held and meditated upon without harm to self or other. Art provides the space of inspection, the time for the essential holding operation that the clown-man's ego must have in which to reflect back parts of himself to himself. The holding and reflecting, however, are slowed down in the stillness of painting or the longstanding line of music, permitting any of us, and especially the clown-man, to appropriate for ourselves the parts we have begun to project onto a painting, a lithograph, a string quartet, an opera.

Adrian Stokes, art critic, painter, and psychoanalytical theorist, writes of the positive effect of entering the great enclosed spaces of cathedrals. He does not offer us any psychoanalytic platitudes. We do not re-enter a womb in search of security. We do not come to feel liberated from an earlier constriction into a new sense of independence. Rather, we find ourselves able to rest from having to synthesize coherences, from having to bring all our parts together. We find we can space out inwardly and return to part-object status. The ego can relax and accept being split into fragments, for the large space of the cathedral performs the necessary holding function. The self is "diluted by the immensity" it has entered, and we feel free as a result and refreshed by the "regression to a part-object relationship."

. . . I believe that part of the refreshment lies in a degree of renunciation or obliteration, not only of this or that aspect of normal mental life but, as a consequence, some reduction of the self as a complicated totality, a reduction that is fused with a part-object re-working to which we can point more easily as we fill a great space with ourselves.[9]

For a clown-man who feels he may be nothing but a bunch of parts, the large spaces of art bring room for all the separate parts to be held within a structural wholeness. In the best sense, he is spaced out. He can accept his condition. Each bit and fragment has its place, and there is enough space overall to look at each one separately. The clown-man is provided with a model through art of a way to hold all together—his fragments of feeling, his bits of mimicry, what he can do, what he cannot do, all that he is. He recognizes that his wholeness depends upon his making a sum of all his parts, and learning to select from those parts as he needs them.

The artist and the viewer of art who really see and take in the large wholenesses in the world around them are clearly marked by an addiction to bits and fragments, to part-objects. What they paint or see, write or read, compose or hear is not wholes. Wholes are too large to take in all at once. They may indeed have whole works in mind as they create or respond to the creation, but they can only come at the large final product by a series of selections. Art is by definition a sequence of objects, even when, as in the case of a miniature painting, for example, we may be able to take the whole thing into our field of vision. We see what we read in chunks, some as large as a group of sentences, some as small as a syllable. We must hear—or read—music in pieces; there is no way of putting it all together in one blast of sound. And almost invariably, as we grow up in the process, we come to inspect paintings, sketches, prints, buildings—anything visual —part by part. This art process is not a limiting one. It is more than a holding of parts in sequence; it is a binding of them together. It gives us space, contemplative distance, a measure from which not only to take in what is in front of us but to deal with it, to see or hear it and perhaps in time to come to understand a good deal about it. The learned and sensitive viewer or listener, like the accomplished artist, returns again and again to the part-objects that are to be found in art, often inspecting one small piece many times. Each time, the piece acquires additional meaning. Each time, whether the piece is being remade by the artist or more penetratingly examined by the viewer, the art process yields a little more of its instructive complexity.

Responding to art at any end of the art-making process is a matter of understanding ambivalence, or better, polyvalence. There is no single value in any genuinely valuable work of art. As with a baby who has learned not to reduce its mother to a good breast (a full, flowing one) or a bad breast (a dry one), the responder to art must come to see a mixture of values and start to give back to art what the baby must return to its mother—complexity, ambiguity—and come to take pleasure in all levels of meaning or truth. This process, what Melanie

Klein calls "reparation" in the case of the baby, delivers the only wholeness that is available to us in this life, that wholeness which is really a great deal more or less than the sum of all its parts, that wholeness that for different persons among us may consist of only a very few of the parts—the part-objects—that make up the whole. The point is that we make the whole, from however many parts; we bind them together and thus discover the reparative or healing powers of art. The clown-man, who is more aware than most of us of the fragmentary nature of the human, has a particular need to find the psychological means to. bring his bits and pieces together.

Precisely because of his need, the clown-man may possess an unusually keen perception of the healing function of the arts. He may find there the holding anima, what Stokes and Klein call the good-breast mother, that he never found in real life. The clown-man's very problem yields a path to its solution. Stokes writes: "The artist sets out for our contemplation a momentous aspect of object-relations, including an attempted restabilization of the good breast that in contemplative experiences is likely to permeate other part-object relationships. This theme of re-establishment, of re-working, characterizes physical health and development . . . ."[10] Parts are no longer frightening, no longer need to be discarded. They can be looked at one at a time, in orderly sequence or in random groups. They hang together. They can be sorted out, recombined, played with in endless combinations, as we bring to their contemplation the insights of criticism, the rigors of scholarship, or just plain enjoyment.

The clown-man in his own private circle and the great clowns of circus, stage, film, and the broadcast media perform their good mothering functions precisely in this way, making a space for us to go back to part-object status and play with putting the pieces of ourselves and our beliefs together again in endlessly new and varied patterns. They give us time out from life, and the constrictions of self, that refreshes us. The clown-man, who could never himself take advantage of what he offered others, may find in art that he can do that necessary turning in upon himself. Grasped in the holding and reflecting embrace of dance, music, painting, or poetry, the clown-man finds himself given back to himself. Not only can he sort through the parts, but modeling his performance on the holding function of the arts, he finds time and space enough slowly to connect his gathering of parts to the small fragment of ego that he accepts now as his own, with all its wounds.[11] His ego begins to grow. He is no less a clown, perhaps, but he is becoming more of a man.

The parts that have never been assimilated gain permission to be. They become the tools of the clown-man's trade, and give him that protean complexity of character that so dazzles the rest of us, who may appear more integrated but are clearly less colorful. Now, instead of being identified with all those parts in a persona compulsion, the clown-man knows in his own ego, however small, free access to his great gallery of parts.

Because of his complexity, his ability now to see himself and his world from so many partial points of view, the clown-man resists better than most of us the temptation to absolutize a part into a whole. His style of perception corrects others' leanings towards literalism, fanaticism, or dogmatism of any kind. What has begun as the affliction of the part-object state may thus be transmuted into a model of a well functioning psyche—anti-reductive, multi-planed, open to the most and the least obvious divagations of the human person. It has its own unmistakable defining rhythm, not always the same one, not necessarily just one at a time, but rhythm or polyrhythms; there is no mistaking its engaging identity.

The clown is like good blues. We look at the way we are looking at the clown, and that is one segment. The clown looks at himself and we look at the clown looking at himself, and that is another. And then we look at ourselves looking at the clown, and that is our conclusion. We summon up consciousness of our proportions and disproportions, in a rhythm of opening and closing up and opening again. We achieve an enlargement of ego-space to make room for all the levels of feeling and understanding at once. We walk around a chair one way (the first four bars); then we walk around a chair the opposite way (the second four bars); then we stand aside to take in and comment on what we have seen (the last four bars).[12] In succeeding choruses, we can take all three statements and play them in and out of each other. The virtuoso jazz musician, like a clown and with much the same kind of humor, can weave the richest of tapestries from the strands of the blues with which he identifies or disidentifies in his improvisations.

Claiming the Parts

The clown leads us firmly into the paradox of disidentifying and identifying. We need to get loose from the masks we wear that hide who we are. We need to shed the persona labels of sexual, racial, historical, or age identity. Taking on a clown's white face and multi-colored features, we lose our own particular face as we have known it; we die to the world and its definitions, so aptly symbolized by the clown's white death mask with its big, circular, dark eyes. We die to fixed definitions of identity, definitions we have chosen or been made to choose, to hide behind. We enter another space, symbolized by the circus arena, that acts like a magic circle, banishing the banalities of the peripheral to focus on the central elements of which identity is constructed.

We return to these basic elements of identity through the clown, as the clown returns to these in himself. A dead identity is resurrected with a new form. No longer is a mask put on from outside. Rather, a real self is expressed from inside, an inside no longer hidden, but recognized as inherently mysterious and indefinable in fixed, final terms. As Jung put it, borrowing from Augustine and Pascal, the self is that mysterious reality, a circle whose center is everywhere and whose circumference is nowhere: "There is little hope of our ever being able to reach even approximate consciousness of the self, since however much we may make conscious there will always exist an indeterminate and indeterminable amount of unconscious material which belongs to the totality of the self."[13] The narcissistic wound that the clown-man suffers exposes him directly to that wide, indefinable reality. As we have seen, his very vulnerability opens him directly to that reality that cannot be summed up in a definition.[14]

The self that is real is possessed of spontaneity and improvisation as expressions of a durable sameness persisting through time. The magic circus-arena circle is no longer a retreat from the real world. It has become a place of origin, from which life can flow into the world. Out of an illusory space come ever new combinations of experience of our inner selves and outer worlds and the ways we put them together. Part-objects are instructive now, rather than destructive.

The part-object lesson is taught negatively by our two greatest masters of stage comedy, Molière and Shakespeare. Both use the clown role as a tutorial instrument. Both do so in complicated ways, which are all the more complicated when the issue seems simple. Both take full advantage of their audiences' inclination to see themselves as superior to the fools on stage. In the manner of the ironic novelists Sterne and Fielding and their great instructors Boccaccio, Rabelais, and Cervantes, they draw us into their mad plots and expose us to their maddened characters, allowing us to convince ourselves that we would never be such misers, pedants, hypochondriacs, intolerant parents, or misanthropes, just to take some of Molière's gallery. Nor would we, of course, permit ourselves such brutality of feeling as Shakespeare's more candid clowns do, nor fall into such indelicacy of expression. The chances are we would not be driven to the extremes of these characters, nor find ourselves in the meshes of such grotesque intrigues. But because we do not see the perils of the part-object any more than we see the virtues when we reduce the world to simple categorical terms, we are, all of us, prone to the imbalances of identification that go with our compulsions, even when they are nice polite compulsions, socially acceptable compulsions, the world's best known and all too easily tolerated compulsions.

Molière absolutizes parts into wholes as his scheme of comedy. He sets tyrannical discipline against freedom of choice through the two brothers of *The School for Husbands,* who are entrusted with bringing up two orphaned sisters. In *The School for Wives,* he produces his own Panurge, a rich older man who cannot marry for fear of being cuckolded, who then behaves like Boccaccio's frightened father, Filippo, and brings up the girl entrusted to his guardianship to be entirely innocent of the ways of sexuality. Molière's all-purpose confidence-man, Tartuffe, and his doctor in spite of himself, Sganarelle, lead his comedy, situation by situation, into the terrors of total identification with such part-objects as money, the role of a gentleman, pedantry, or hypochondria. In each case, each *vrai type,* the immediate victims of the obsessed central figures are their children, who simply cannot be allowed to mate as they choose, even when they choose well. The thickening of plot that develops when obsessive or compulsive parents stand in the way of true love is an old story—it goes back to Roman comedy, in fact. But Molière's modern psychological wit is to make this ancient device hang on the hypnotic fascination of part-objects for parents. He does it in such a way that we in his audience are bound to learn something from the insanity fair that ensues. No matter how superior we may feel to those possessed by part-objects, we come at some level of consciousness to think differently about learning, social status, illness, trust, parenthood, and true love.

If we stay with Molière through the tortures of his version of *Don Juan,* we may come to see impotence as inherent in an excess of sexual display and seduction. We perceive the terror that afflicts such a seducer as he moves incessantly from woman to woman, promises impossible affection, contracts multiple betrothals, and discovers himself to be never satisfied, not by any person, not in any physical act, not in any relationship from that of son and father, through master and servant, to seducer and seduced. Don Juan's servant is the identified clown of the drama, but it is Don Juan himself who acts out the tragicomedy, which ends with the crushing experience of the crumbling of the statue of the Commendatore. The haughty stone guest is the father of one of Don Juan's most unhappy victims; he comes frighteningly to life as he does in the original Tirso de Molina play and Mozart's *Don Giovanni.* On the positive side, Molière's Don is a spokesman for skepticism and for freedom of value and choice. He is also a bitter object lesson in Molière's close scrutiny, in several of his plays, of the effects of the doctrine of impunity, by which one convinces oneself that almost any behavior is somehow acceptable in a broadly permissive society. In modern psychological terms, the lesson is in the use of part-objects, especially the use of human beings as sexual part-objects. It will not work, Molière tells us in his theatrical way. The professional seducer, no matter how generously equipped he may be with the special vocabularies of the skeptic and the libertine, must ultimately become his own worst victim as he locks himself into his role, exactly like the pedant or hypochondriac, miser or would-be gentleman.[15]

With a sufficient sense of the farcical dimensions of such a compulsive part-object sexuality, we can see what is funny about the Don Juans of the world and bring our own sexual fantasies into more useful perspective. We can even laugh, like a liberated clown, at some of our own fantasies, and in the laughter find sexuality more engaging because more in proportion, more a matter of our own reality.

For Shakespeare, always vastly amused and amusing in dealing with men and women caught in the imbroglios of sexuality, there is hope only for those who can achieve a sense of sexual proportion. It is no preacher's balance that he advocates, nor is it the worldly middle way of a Polonius. He shows us with the understandable but ultimately maddening infatuation of a Romeo and Juliet that the exaggerations of pubescent wooing must be fateful—beginning with speaking in sonnets, as Juliet does, and ending with a drug-induced counterfeit death which only too quickly turns into the real thing. He makes even so reflective and indecisive a character as Hamlet into the thoughtless seducer of Ophelia. But equally, in his voluminous fables of vice and its practitioners such as Falstaff and his besotted associates, Cressida and her uncle Pandarus, and the lesser attendants at the sexual revels of his early comedies, he never fails to show the shining complexion of sexuality alongside the scrofulous.[16]

Shakespeare makes the positive case for sexual reality chiefly by indirection, but sometimes also directly, as in his most sustained attack on the Puritan disposition in *Measure for Measure*. There he gives to the clownly voice of Lucio the central truths about human sexuality, setting his scornful rhetoric against the actions of Angelo, the surrogate Mayor of Vienna, who has sentenced Claudio to death for making his fiancée pregnant. In Shakespeare's time this was no significant breach of morality, for betrothal had all but sacramental equality with marriage and provided almost the same sanction for sexual initimacy. Angelo, the great sexual hypocrite of the fiction, promises to carry out the sentence unless Claudio's sister, a convent novice, will allow herself to be bedded. A serio-comic breviary could be compiled from Lucio's ironies in speaking to the man he thinks is a friar, but who is in fact the Duke of Vienna. When Angelo absents himself from this city, the deliberate cause of the bitter drama, Lucio says of him, "A little more lenity in lechery would do no harm to him . . . ." The Duke-as-friar replies, "It is too general a vice, and severity must cure it." Lucio agrees that "the vice is of a great kindred; it is quite well allied: but it is impossible to extirp quite, friar, till eating and drinking be put down." He explains Angelo's case as the likely result of not having been born in the usual "downright way of creation," but rather by having come from two fishes, resulting in his urine being "congealed ice." After some pretentious duelling with the Duke, in which he claims a knowledge of the Duke's habits that he clearly does not possess, Lucio returns to his breviary wisdom to explain the reasons for Claudio's death sentence, translating the sexual act into a series of figures of speech that would do a blues singer proud. What is it good for? Lucio answers:

> Why for filling a bottle with a tun-dish [meaning, to put a funnel into a receptacle, i.e., the female]. I would the duke we speak of were returned again: this ungenitured agent will unpeople the province with contingency; sparrows must not build in his house-eaves because they are lecherous . . . . Marry, this Claudio is condemned for untrussing.[17]

The clownish Parolles in *All's Well That Ends Well*, a companion-piece in time and texture to *Measure for Measure*, speaks with equal bluntness against the unnatural claims of virginity: "It is not politic in the commonwealth of nature to preserve virginity. Loss of virginity is rational increase; and there was never virgin got till virginity was first lost." In this exchange with Helena, the play's central character who develops a wondrous intrigue in her efforts to surrender her virginity to her reluctant husband, Parolles speaks as defender of the sexual faith in opposition to the apologists for celibacy:

> There's little can be said in't; 'tis against the rule of nature. To speak on the part of virginity is to accuse your mothers . . . . He that hangs himself is a virgin; vir-

ginity murders itself; and should be buried in highways, out of all sanctified limit, as a desperate offendress against nature. Virginity breeds mites, much like a cheese; consumes itself to the very paring, and so dies with feeding its own stomach. Besides virginity is peevish, proud, idle, made of self-love which is the most inhibited sin in the canon. Keep it not; you cannot choose but lose by't: out with't! within ten years it will make itself ten, which is a goodly increase; and the principal itself not much the worse: away with it![18]

Helena does eventually trick her unhappy mate—forced to marry her against his will—into bed and, if the play's title (*All's Well That Ends Well*) is not entirely ironic, into a happy marriage as well. Given measure for measure in his play, Angelo the Puritan seducer is seduced into marriage with the woman he originally wooed: Claudio is returned to his proper bed; and his sister, it is clear at the end, will leave her convent pallet for ducal comfort and comforter. The mood in these so-called "problem plays" is bitter-comic, almost as pessimistic about human sexuality as their allied dramas, *Troilus and Cressida* and *Hamlet.*

The doubts never altogether disappear in Shakespeare's dramas, but before the full canon is completed, there are some genuine moments of mature love, tender love, love not altogether suspect. When love triumphs, it is either in the midst of a falling world, as in *Antony and Cleopatra,* or a world that barely survives, as in *Cymbeline,* or after half a lifetime of suspicion, separation, and loneliness, as in *The Winter's Tale,* or as a result of the confluence of magic and faith, shipwreck and reconciliation, as in *The Tempest.* It is real love in each of these cases, love finally triumphant, love finally received and understood and lived in proportion. At that point, the clown persona is ready to be shed. The coarse sexual humor, brilliantly funny as it usually is in Shakespeare, is no longer fitting. There is an answer to the Clown's plaint in Act IV of *The Winter's Tale:* "Is there no manners left among maids? will they wear their plackets where they should bear their faces?" In other words, must women always speak by way of the petticoat openings through which their genitals are to be got at? The answer comes in the last words of the play, when all bawdiness has been abandoned in favor of something even more open. The master of suspicion, Leontes, asks to be led

> from hence; where we may leisurely
> Each one demand, and answer to his part
> Perform'd in this wide gap of time, since first
> We were dissever'd . . . .[19]

When love fills the breach and lovers are no longer "dissever'd," what makes the coming together convincing is the memory of the harshness and rough humor of earlier events and attitudes. The lovers broken apart like the split double-men, double-women, and double men-women of Aristophanes' myth in Plato's *Symposium,* have had to survive all the vicissitudes of history in order to come together. When they do finally unite, it is like the clown-man's bringing together his variously wounded parts. The parts are still there; they may still be wounded.

But they are no longer threatening. They not only can be faced and used again; they have also become agents of health and love, of wholeness.

Among the difficult moments in Shakespeare's histories of the sort of misfortune in love that leads to reconciliation and delight, few have such rhetorical power as that in which Posthumus Leonatus, the all-suspecting center of the plot in *Cymbeline,* denounces not just Imogen, the wife in whose infidelity he has been led to believe, but anything womanly that may exist in himself.

> Could I find out
> The woman's part in me! For there's no motion
> That tends to vice in man but I affirm
> It is the woman's part: be it lying, note it,
> The woman's; flattering, hers; deceiving, hers;
> Lust and rank thoughts, hers, hers; revenges, hers;
> Ambitions, covetings, change of prides, disdain,
> Nice longing, slanders, mutability,
> All faults that have a name, nay, that hell knows,
> Why, hers, in part or all; but rather all;
> For ev'n to vice
> They are not constant, but are changing still
> One vice, but of a minute old, for one
> Not half so old as that. I'll write against them,
> Detest them, curse them.—Yet 'tis greater skill
> In a true hate to pray they have their will:
> The very devils cannot plague them better.[20]

By the end of the play he knows the extent of his bitter credulousness. The condemnation of his own woman's part—his anima—can be faced down in a kind of quick piece of dark comedy within the bleak comic melodrama. The villain who had aroused Posthumus Leonatus's jealousy accuses him of speaking of his wife in a wonderfully funny example of the rhetoric of opposites, as if Diana "had hot dreams." Leonatus accuses himself of even greater villainy in accepting the imputation and acting upon it. His wife, disguised as a page, begs him to wait. What he hears in her speech is scorn for his words; furious, he knocks her down. "O, my lord Posthumus," says his servant, "You ne'er killed Imogen till now." But she recovers quickly enough. Everybody pardons everyone else, and peace comes to settle the war between Britain and Caesar's Rome against which the sexual combat has been played out—a translation of part-objects into people and people into part-objects that matches interior sexual splits with exterior conflict between nations, aggression against the anima with a war against truth and love.

What lifts *Cymbeline* above the early disguise plays and makes the conclusion convincing, even in a reading of Shakespearean psychology that allows for the cynical humors of the problem plays, is the dramatization of a sexuality at war with itself. The play never achieves the high poetry and dramatic terror of *Othello.* But it does permit us to see a man's defenses against his own feeling both raised up and stripped away, and does so at a sufficient pitch of intensity,

and with enough of the contrivances that we have associated with our most ingenious clowns, to make us believe that what we come to at the end is not a mere
resolution of events or a glib last-scene reconciliation of "dissever'd" relationships. It is instead the coming to oneself that follows a full surrender to positive
feeling after a full recognition of negative feeling. It is that opening to interiority
that makes convincing Antony's dying words to Cleopatra:

> I here importune death awhile, until
> Of many thousand kisses the poor last
> I lay upon thy lips.

It also makes equally persuasive Cleopatra's insisting, as she brings the killing
bite of the snake to her bosom, that she hears Antony call to her and that he supports her suicidal pact. For these reasons, she must call out in return:

> Husband, I come:
> Now to that name my courage prove my title![21]

It is more than a fitting of ancient drama to modern purpose to find in
Shakespeare so rich an evidence of anima/animus understanding. Shakespeare
was no Jungian, but he was finely attuned to the interior separations and wound-
ings of the clown-man. He knew, perhaps at first hand, the contrivances of the
man determined to fight all feeling by fixing himself in the mask of one feeling.
That left him, if the progress of the plays is fair witness, to work out a long, difficult, often bitter salvation for the demons of anti-feeling. The play's the thing, we
say, quoting Shakespeare, but in the play the part is the thing—the part as separated interior or exterior object, the part as wounded sensibility, the part as anima, the part as vulnerable man or woman, the part as rejected feeling and recon-
ciled feeling, the part claimed and brought back alive into a world of parts no
longer so hopelessly "dissever'd." For the early Shakespeare, the separated parts,
like the frozen masks of Molière's *vrai types,* are objects of derision. For the middle Shakespeare, like the Molière of *Don Juan,* they are object lessons. For the
late Shakespeare, they are wounds that provide our best opportunities for healing.

XIV The Clown Redeemed

The Integrating Anima

When a clown-man relinquishes his great array of defenses and disidentifies from the clown archetype, his anima emerges in its own distinct colors. He can distinguish between his feelings and his ego. He can face his illusions; he can face disillusionment about his illusions, and be in that perilous place so close to despair. Instead of endless cycles of illusion, each time hoping against hope that somehow a new masking, a new defense will work out, only to be thrust back into another unrewarding fantasy, he can pick and choose in his illusory space. Fantasies are his to adopt or reject, not simply to lose in the dull, dry flatness that so many confuse with maturity. Understandably, the clown-man dreads that sort of sterile manhood in which everything is sacrificed to "adjustment."

The disidentified clown-man can now look boldly into the mirror of illusions that he has been holding up for others. In it, he can see the reflection of his own images, instead of his inspired mirrorings of others. He can perceive his own anima reveries, as Bachelard might call them—dreams that dream him, dreams from which he feels himself to be created—instead of simply fashioning skits, routines, and funny stories to amuse others.[1] The clown-man himself now begins to benefit from his rich gifts.

It is not easy to turn back in upon one's illusions, to find a creative life reflected to the ego, to hold in sharp ego-awareness the fanciful rites of transition. The rescued clown-man accepts these illusions as fantasies in his own play-space; they are images at his disposal, images that he no longer must immediately translate into a working reality. Reality is the opposite shore; the illusions are the water, not the land, not the bridge. He from his side may build a bridge that can be met from reality's side by others building connecting links to him. Illusion is freed to be illusion—to be splashed in, dived into, floated upon, or faced through, but always to remain itself in its own dimension. Illusion accepted becomes support, the ritual resource of the comic against the tragic nature of existence.

How does the clown turn in upon his illusions to accept them for what they are? Perhaps in relation to a loving woman, perhaps with a loving anima-figure, perhaps in relation to the worlds of art—any or all will do. The work of analysis offers another holding space where the identifying bits and pieces of the clown self may be put. The analyst reflects them back to him, permitting him in a slow tempo to disidentify from his defensive clowning, to accept the wounds at the core of his ego-identity, and to allow his illusions to remain illusions so that he can connect his inner life.

One man saw that his joking always turned up automatically when he presented his work to others, as a means of deflecting his own deep emotions. He felt anxiety of a primordial kind, fragmented into many parts. He worried whether others would accept his work with approval or would choose to attack or dismiss it. He felt small and uncertain, and yet always rallied to the occasion with laugh-getting remarks. But more important, he felt he was drawing near, as he presented his work, to large and awesome realities that his work was trying to describe. The realities moved him. He was attempting in his clowning way to talk about the soul and what mattered about people, what was at the heart of things. He felt himself to be in the presence of symbols of the numinous, and he did not know what to do with the feelings they aroused. Disidentifying from his clowning defenses, he was opening himself to primal emotions stirring in him. He submitted to them. He allowed the emotions to flow through him. His presentations deepened; they went better than before, because he stopped joking and deflecting his audience from what he was saying. He could stop there because he had stopped joking in the analytical space, using the time previously given to clowning to tell his analyst his fears and, eventually, how moved he was—then, finally, just feeling it. He allowed himself to depend on the analyst's holding what he brought to the sessions. He did not have to give all his energies to defense. Connection gradually replaced dependence, connection to the analyst, to his emotions, to the numinous symbols. By holding onto the reflecting space of the analytical relationship, he could endure the great light of the numinous that so stirred him.

The analysis and analyst receive the anima-role, to bring to the awareness of the clown-man's ego his unconscious feelings—but only temporarily.[2] In the analytical dialogue there is adumbrated the dialogue that eventually will occur between the ego and the anima that will link the clown to his deeper self.

One troubled man had his clowning defenses break down completely when he was performing a major ritual act in the Christian eucharist, holding up the chalice and then administering it to people receiving communion. Different parts of this action were all jumbled together for him. The way out for this clown-man was to sort through the parts, not to discard them—to inspect them, hold them, to see what thread of meaning moved through them. The parts were many: his anxiety about being looked at and found wanting, his fear of exposure, his feeling small, never adequate. But in the midst of them flowed another fact, a numinous one for him, that the elements and events conjoined: the blood and wine of the eucharist mystery, the communicants and the figure of Christ, the human and the divine. The putting together of parts, the fact that essential elements could come together to make a whole, was the truth before which the clown-man felt his defenses crumble, felt his body literally shake. Putting the parts of his own life together is what he desperately wanted to do and was sure he could not do, and yet here he was, participating in a ritual celebrating the fact that it was done. His sorting through the parts and allowing himself to feel each one in analysis broke through the jumbles and the shaking. The parts could be held now in the space, reflected and allowed to grow together.

These examples illustrate the way the clown-man's plight opens directly into the archetypal world and the mystery of the human. What do we mean when we say "human being"? "Soul"? "The heart of things"? How do our parts unite to make a whole that is clearly more than just the sum of the parts? The clown-man's thin psychological skin makes him permeable to these great questions. His struggle with his problems of feeling brings those around him near to his condition, and with it to those questions. Like the witch whose suffering makes available to others her primordial power and intellect, the clown gives access to the deep mysteries of feeling, binds us more closely together, permits us to claim our jumbled parts, to sort through them, to make space for ourselves as parts grow together into social coherence. The clown-man's riot of disjointed parts and deep-seated ambivalences is transformed into polyvalences of meaning and truth, and not for him alone.

Truth does not come here through the organs of intellection, but rather through a lively relation to the unconscious. Jung, believing so firmly in what he called the objective psyche, stressed that it does not help the patient to translate living unconscious material into conceptual terms. What is needed, what in fact comprises the goal of treatment, is to build a personal relation to the unconscious, not explanations about it. We must accept the unconscious on its own terms as much as we can, and make a large space for the life of images, fantasies, rudimentary symbols—all those fish that swim in our illusions.

What this means in practical terms for the clown-man is having the strength to accept those different jostling, bombarding part-objects that compete for his attention and feeling. He sees his parts as somehow connected within him, and as connecting him to others. He feels the unifying power of the psyche building in him, healing him, bringing him new potentialities and a healing power of his own. He sifts through the parts, examines each one, ceases to be tossed back and forth among their opposing realities like the ball in one of his own clown routines. He is investing his libido, his narcissistic energy, in the linking up of the parts, so that room can be made for all of them.[3] This means, at any given moment or period of time, diverting libido from flowing into archetypal images, such as the absent mother or the elusive anima, and investing it instead in the wobbly, nascent ego which grows from the root of his true self. It may mean turning his libido from its overdetermined feelings of inadequacy toward its appropriate self-judgment, to feel small but not undeserving before the giant symbols of the numinous. Whenever one part is invested to the exclusion of others, a clown-man must withdraw energy and redeploy it to the missing parts. Healing consists in pursuing connections, to join dessicated parts into a living, flowing whole. This means joining all the parts in a man's psyche, and the man himself as a part with others in a transcendent whole, in what has been called a "cosmic narcisism."[4] Thus the clown-man's healing, like his clowning, moves from the ridiculous to the sublime, to find the extraordinary in the ordinary. In the clown as archetype, we see symbolized a spacious arena wherein the opposites can be suffered to live together and cohere, with the clown's performance now taking on transcendent hues. At worst, it produces *Pagliacci*; at its best, the wise fool of Erasmus.

In more mundane terms, when a clown-man makes these links it means he accepts his size as smaller than his grandiose illusions have suggested. He develops a sense of humor about himself and the great tragicomedy he has been creating around his wounds. Humor, as Kohut notes, is one unmistakable sign of a patient having worked through narcissistic grandiosity. The humor "testifies to the fact that the ego can now see in realistic proportions the greatness aspirations of the infantile grandiose self or the former demands for the unlimited perfection and power of the idealized parent image, and that the ego can now contemplate these old configurations with the amusement that is an expression of its freedom."[5]

The clown-man at last gets to enjoy his own humor instead of using it only to arouse others to laughter. The Sultan, after all, was entertained by Scheherazade's thousand and one tales. Such enjoyment increases the clown-man's pleasure in others, too, those whom he can now release from their constricted roles as dispensers of his psychic needs. He no longer need work so assiduously at the good-boy/bad-boy drama, living up to father or rebelling against father. Holding his own wounds, rather than repudiating them as contemptible, his self-hate softens and he learns to respect and care for his sensitivities, learns to acknowledge his responsiveness—all of it, its sweetness, pliability, naiveté, and tenderness. He knows now that this part of him, like a female sexual organ, reacts to the slightest touch and must not be rammed into. He knows, too, that it is his job, not a woman's, not an analyst's, not an institution's, to penetrate that soft spot in himself and to hold it protectingly within him.

What began as despair over his failure to make his illusions come to life may end, then, with the clown-man's acceptance of the impermanence of illusions as being appropriate to their nature. Illusions are necessarily only suggestive and therefore incomplete. They cannot be fully brought into reality. Therein lies their charm. The very impermanence of illusions, from which the clown-man suffered so acutely, unable to give them up and unable to realize them, now gives him insight into the finite nature of human existence. At the risk of repetition, we must underline the point: When he has turned in upon his illusions and allowed himself to experience them fully, the clown-man learns how well their impermanence prepares all of us for the impermanence of all things human. He sees how closely connected with the ability to laugh at oneself this newly acquired wisdom is, to laugh at the disproportion of things that are inherently incomplete, necessarily impermanent, and at least as much worth laughing at as crying over. Kohut affirms the lesson: In persons healed of narcissistic disorders, alongside their newly found humorous attitude, "a modest and limited form of wisdom emerges too which includes the emotional acceptance of the transience of individual existence."[6]

The figure of wisdom in the Old Testament offers in symbolic terms the same intermixture of playful fun, sage counsel, and personification. Wisdom is female, and portrays in archetypal terms the mediating role of the anima to the man's ego, not to achieve perfection, but rather a redeeming imbalance. The clown finds himself constantly discovering, with plentiful feeling, that there are undiscovered feelings still to be found, and large ones at that. In his struggle to open himself to his own feelings, he encounters a wisdom that is both humorous and instructive as it moves to connect our only too human condition to that largest of holding presences, that which we call God. For it is this wisdom, the Biblical scholar Samuel Terrien tells us,

> at once divine and human, who reveals to man the meaning of the universe, with its origin and its end. One should not speak of the "self-revelation of creation." By using the figure of personified wisdom, at once the entertainer of divinity and the educator of humanity, the hymnist hinted at a similarity, perhaps an actual kinship, between the human thirst for knowledge and the childlike freedom of the Godhead.

This is a new play-space for the clown-man, where the exchange with his anima occurs. The mediating figure, art object, or religious image recalls in its presence the exchanges between Yahweh and the female personification of Wisdom, which boldly employ the rhetoric of love: "Then, he sees her and he celebrates her, he embraces her and he penetrates her." As it brings a man's vulnerable feelings into full awareness, the wise anima figure reflects the openness of the divine and the human as each becomes present to the other, and the astonishing pleasure that comes with that intermingling of presences. "The objective delight of Wisdom with God becomes the subjective delight of Wisdom with men. The delight she gives the creator is the delight she receives from the creature. Playful Wisdom is the mediatrix of presence."[7]

In this rich presence, the clown-man penetrates to the archetypal dimension of the clown, well beyond his own personal problems as a clown. It is the cycle of redemption for him. He has come to terms with his compulsive clowning, through disidentification from his elaborate masking defenses. His anima has emerged and brought to his ego a full supply of wounded feelings to be integrated. Enlarging his consciousness, he has brought about a corresponding freeing in the unconscious. The stature of the clown, as symbolic of the human condition and its determination to be free, can now emerge for him to see and for us to contemplate.

The Feminine Within the Masculine

With the freeing of the anima to perform its mediating function, the clown has won half his battle. The anima, he now recognizes, is his rescuer from identification with the clown archetype, and from the accompanying unconscious condition with its identifying symptom, compulsive comic-persona performing. The other half of the battle remains: to integrate his femininity—his anima—into his masculine identity. It is not enough to know the anima. One must live with her, so to speak, and assimilate with conscious adaptation the unconscious feelings of vulnerability that the anima works to communicate to him. As with the witch, these are tasks of recognition and integration of the crucial fact that the whole person is a contrasexual person. Witch or clown, man or woman, we need to see and relate to that part of our psychology that is characterized for us as the opposite sex, our anima or animus.

The woman coming to terms with the witch archetype that represents the primordial power and intellect of the female, mediated to her awareness by the animus function, must thoroughly inspect herself and recognize where she diminishes herself by identifying with this inner witch instead of receiving from it connection to her own potency. She must disidentify from the archetype, and then draw the contents the animus brings into her conscious identity as a woman. It involves a step-by-step claiming of the witch parts that the animus conveys to her. If she fails to do this, she inevitably falls into identification with the witch archetype, and loses not only relation to its power but to her own femininity. She appears then as a man-woman, increasingly overtaken in her conscious adaptation by the unlived masculine part of herself. The animus that she has failed to receive steps in front of her ego and comes to replace her. Once she claims the witch parts of her psyche conveyed to her by the animus, she can proceed to knit them together, holding the masculine where it belongs for her, well within her feminine identity. The result is a strong, soft, tough, yielding, spirited, receptive woman, a rich gathering of contrasting textures of being, symbolized as both masculine and feminine and all the more womanly as a result.

The clown shows the other side of this process. He must steel himself to recognize and accept all of the contents that the anima conveys to his awareness, and assimilate all of them to his masculine identity. Failing to do this results in psychological castration. He falls into identification with his anima contents, and they come to dominate his conscious adaptation where his masculinity should rule. A feminine orientation substitutes for the masculine. Instead of enlarging his consciousness, what he has done—or had done to him, for his ego has been passively overtaken by his unconscious feelings of vulnerability—is to narrow it greatly and turn it right around. Unaware of his anima component, a man confines himself to a one-sided adaptation, loudly proclaiming his maleness while yielding everything to the anima, altogether excluding his masculinity. He becomes a womanish man with access neither to his feelings nor to a clear male identity. He parodies the feelings of a hard-to-get, hard-to-find woman. His feelings must be searched for, teased out, approached with the utmost care, as he or others hunt for that elusive place where he can be touched.

Redeemed from this either/or alternation by an anima brought to consciouss adaptation, the clown discovers conscious identity, firmly male identity. As with the woman who integrates the witch archetype into fully conscious being, the man integrating the clown becomes not effeminate, but more manly. Not castration now for him, but a new sensitivity to the smaller, softer, more vulnerable parts of himself, which, perhaps paradoxically, proves to be a quite masculine undertaking. In penetrating to the center of those parts, and at the same time yielding to them in a feminine way, the clown becomes not androgynous, but virile. He gains profound understanding of his interior self, of the withdrawn and hidden parts of himself that do not hang out to everyone's view.

Claiming and possessing his interiority, the clown-man adds much more to his emotional rhythms than simply up-and-down, in-and-out levels of feeling. Remarkably like the experience of a woman in mute acceptance of herself, which leads her to her own strong voice, he attains a kind of particular interior roundness, a soft, dependable holding space within himself, a circle in which to contain the inconclusive, the partial, the fantasy-laden feelings he must now attest to and ponder within himself. He is free of that disastrous bim-bam, thank-you-ma'am emotional and sexual life, that automatic discharge, that push-pull manipulation of feelings that always leaves one more manipulated than manipulator. He has acquired his own receptacle, a holding one, a mirroring one, in which has own reflection is now clear to him. He is in a place where he can interact with his feelings openly and can appropriate them. They are his personal feelings now, to give or to hold, at his disposal rather than the other way around. He has reversed the original reversal, whereby he was always at the beck and call of archetypal emotional demands.

No fixed pattern exists that he must follow. Endless patterns bubble up in him, spontaneous, fresh, with the characteristics of his own particular space of illusion. Instead of feeling burdened by emotional duties, which do not sustain his feelings but rather annihilate them, he gains a new sense of play, delighting in the dartings of the unexpected. As with the professional clown, almost anything can be material for a new response, a new moment of feeling, a new life.

A man who integrates his anima is great fun to live with. He changes in his constancy. He never gets caught in a rut. He contributes in a major way to that human dream of housing passion in a permanency of openness. He connects repeatedly along different routes to his feeling sources and touches complementary resources in those around him. His constancy is to inspire new combinations of old ingredients. He delights in rescuing others from the emotional treadmills whereon the juices of potentiality are ground out of them. He is altogether himself, and yet through him can be glimpsed images of a spiritual freedom that belongs to everyone.

In clinical terms, disidentification from the clown archetype signifies the emergence of the contrasexual personality. In archetypal terms, the clown has arrived at the level of life of symbol where dichotomies become unities—heaven *and* earth, light *and* dark, masculine *and* feminine, letter *and* spirit, eternity *and* finitude. The clown, like the witch, mixes up new potions.

New Mixtures

In this new form of spiritual freedom we see through the personal to the universal, rather than abstracting from the personal to reach what transcends it. The clown always reminds us of our concrete, particular personal and human reality. He embodies the essentially human. We may fly away above reality on a balloon, but the balloon is always just on the verge of being punctured by a slingshot, a pebble, or a bird's claws, or within seconds of running out of gas. Bang! We land on earth. The clown makes us see our earthly parts and accept them as intrinsic to our life in the spirit. There is no ascetic denial here, though it is unmistakably a spiritual exercise. Comedy is "an art that is dedicated to the telling of the Whole Truth," as Nathan Scott says:

> [W]e are not pure, disembodied essences . . . our health and happiness are contingent upon our facing into the fact that we are finite and conditioned, and therefore subject to all sorts of absurdities, interruptions, inconveniences, embarrassments—and weaknesses. This is, we might say, the courage that the comic vision requires.[8]

There are not many clowns or "comic" men who fully conform to Scott's description, but at least one inspired literary clown of our time comes very close. Berenger, Eugene Ionesco's spokesman in the central sequence of his plays, is such a person. His very limitations make him the best possible representative of the comic man who accepts himself and the Whole Truth of his human world. He feels trapped in a prison only too often, and is embarrassed by the grossest and most absurd expressions of creatureliness—his, ours, everybody's. Who could help but be so embarrassed in the modern world? The fact that he emerges with dignity from the challenge of a rhinoceros-infested universe in the play named after that beast is proof enough of his strength. The fact that he survives the vision he is permitted of an atomic disaster in *The Pedestrian in the Air* is confirmation of his stature. Both situations are holocausts. Of the two, the rhinoceros mania is perhaps the easier to understand.

In *Rhinoceros*, the inhabitants of a small French provincial town are possessed by an insane desire to turn into rhinoceroses, once it is clear that the metamorphosis is the latest fad in their lower-middle-class world. That is Ionesco's way of dramatizing the rise of Nazism and all totalitarian infestations. The plague (as Camus allegorized the Nazi invasion of France in his novel, *La Peste*) is irresistible to the masses, like a hemline change, a fashion in television comedy, an omnipotent, insistently promoted rock singer. What difference does it make if we are overcome by such a hitherto unimaginable madness as giving up our human skins, our two-leggedness, our spiritual values for the life of the horned beast? If mass taste opts for it, then it is clearly right. Berenger argues with the mass-man, Jean:

> *BERENGER*: Well, at any rate, we have our own moral standards which I consider incompatible with the standards of animals.
>
> *JEAN*: Moral standards! I'm sick of moral standards! We need to go beyond moral standards!
>
> *BERENGER*: What would you put in their place?
>
> *JEAN*: Nature!
>
> *BERENGER*: Nature?
>
> *JEAN*: Nature has its own laws. Morality's against Nature.
>
> *BERENGER*: Are you suggesting we replace our moral laws by the law of the jungle?
>
> *JEAN*: It would suit me, suit me fine.
>
> *BERENGER*: You say that. But deep down, no one . . .
>
> *JEAN*: (*interrupting him, pacing up and down*)
> We've got to build our life on new foundations. We must get back to primeval integrity.

Berenger does not agree with Jean and struggles against the rhinoceros holocaust. But it sweeps over everything and everybody in its path, even Berenger's beloved, Daisy. "We are together, aren't we?" he asks her. "No one can separate us. Our love is the only thing that's real. Nobody has the right to stop us from being happy—in fact, nobody could, could they?"

But they can be separated. Ionesco's brilliant translation of the inclinations of the mob into the stampede of a herd of rhinocerosses—and more, into the stampede of masses of people to become rhinoceroses once the politics of fad is established—makes Berenger's kind of love impossible. Daisy thinks, looking at the proliferation of rhinoceros-heads all around her, "Those are the real people. They look happy. [What does a happy rhinoceros look like? One would have to ask a rhinoceros.] They're content to be what they are. They don't look insane. They look very natural. They were right to do what they did." That provokes another declaration of the rights of love from Berenger, and in return the most significant rejection of all from Daisy: "I feel a bit ashamed of what you call love— this morbid feeling, this male weakness. And female, too. It just doesn't compare with the ardour and the tremendous energy emanating from all these creatures around us."

The shaken Berenger brings the drama to an end with a long soliloquy in which he shifts ground a number of times, but ends up where Ionesco always does, in a humanism that achieves its majesty precisely where human beings must—in the flesh, asserted, accepted, even at its most gross, its most imbalanced and incomplete, its most absurd, holding on to itself, just at the point where the whole world seems arranged against it. "Men aren't so bad-looking, you know," Berenger ruminates. "And I'm not a particularly handsome specimen! . . . She didn't even leave a message. That's no way to behave. Now I'm all on my own. But they won't get me. You won't get me! [*He addresses all the rhinoceros heads.*] I'm not joining you; I don't understand you! I'm staying as I am. I'm a human being." But soon enough he sees reason to worry. He is speaking French, he says, but can he be sure? He can call it that and nobody can deny it, because he is the only one left speaking the language. He worries about his looks. He knows he is not good-looking. He suddenly is convinced that he is wrong—it is "they" who are good-looking! He longs for horns: "A smooth brow looks so ugly. I need one or two horns to give my sagging face a lift." He bemoans his limp hands, his slack skin, his white, hairy body: "Oh I'd love to have a hard skin in that wonderful dull green colour—a skin that looks decent naked without any hair on it." He tries his voice at rhinoceros-trumpeting and realizes it is too late to join up now. Now all he can be is a human monster, never a rhinoceros. He is ashamed of the way he looks. He is ugly. "People who try to hang on to their individuality always come to a bad end!" That snaps him out of his mood. Too bad, he sums up. He decides he will take them all on, if necessary, "fight against the lot of them. . . . I'm the last man left, and I'm staying that way until the end. I'm not capitulating."[9] He claims all that he is, funny-looking as he is, imperfect collection of parts that he is, clown that he is. He may also lead us, tutoring by example, to claim all that we are and all that has made us what we are.

The clown calls us to the spirit within creation, planting us firmly in this world as the way through which we go to the next. In the clown's world, unconscious imagery discovers its concrete particularities, vulnerable feelings find their *raison d'être*, human and animal community discover their wholeness in time and history. This is where we find life. The way, we learn, is always through the human, never in spite of it or abstracted from it. Like the witch, the mature clown accepts all that is and embodies a new liveliness in the face of creation that persists in it despite all attacks upon it, as Scott says:

> . . . [T]he comic man is unembarrassed by even the grossest expressions of his creatureliness . . . he has no sense of . . . desperate entrapment within a prison. . . . He does not insist upon life's conforming to his special requirements but consents to take it on the terms of its own created actuality and the art of comedy is devoted to an exhibition of his deep involvement in the world: so it shirks at nothing—none of the irrelevant absurdities, none of the vexatious inconveniences. . . .[10]

The spirit is joyously found in the flesh by the clown. Here below, on earth, we will find heaven and hell mixed with the earth. In the midst of this world of imperfections, we can embrace created goodness whole-heartedly, even if the embrace must come at the end of a long list of denials.

Sometimes it is right there in his most extravagant denials that the clown directs us to the most positive affirmations. Dostoevsky uses that kind of clowning in a crucial scene in *The Devils*, his most earth-centered novel and most persuasive dramatization of the confluence of heaven and hell on earth. The conspirators who fill out the demonic roles in the 1871 drama are meeting at the house of one of them, Virginsky, on the excuse of a name-day party for their host, who has not the slightest intention of conducting the usual sort of celebration of his name and its presumably saintly source. The tone of the psychodrama to be acted out is set by Dostoevsky's description of Mme. Virginsky. She is a greedy midwife who contrives in her professional life to serve only wealthy women. Even for them she makes no effort beyond rudimentary obstetrics. Her special skill is to scare "nervous patients by the most incredible and nihilistic disregard of good manners, or by jeering at 'everything holy,' at the very time when 'everything holy' might [be] most useful." But her method works, in the comic manner of this large episode in the novel. For example, at one moment when a patient was crying out to the Lord in pain and hope, "a free-thinking sally from Anna Prokhorovna [Mme. Virginsky], fired off like a pistol-shot, had so terrifying an effect on the patient that it greatly accelerated her delivery."

Anna Prokhorovna's brother, Shigalyov, enters the story like a pistol-shot at this point—a deadly comic explosion. One of the conspiratorial devils of the title, he is a splendid contradiction in terms, like a midwife sister who enjoys dressing up and confusing guests at christenings, such as the clergy, by her mixture of elegant ritual in handing out champagne and "the most insolent air." But he is not at all one-sided like the midwife or his other sister, "a silent and malevolent creature, with flaxen hair and no eyebrows, who shared her sister's progressive ideas and was an object of terror to Virginsky himself in domestic life." People are not terrified by Shigalyov. He is a clown, a learned fool, to whose sociological fulminations people listen with good humor.

Shigalyov, immediately identifiable by his long ears, steps to the center of events to deliver an oration. His appearance is at first "gloomy and sullen," but as he warms to his subject, his attitude changes. He becomes charged with his message.

> Dedicating my energies to the study of the social organisation which is in the future to replace the present condition of things, I've come to the conviction that all makers of social systems from ancient times up to the present year, 187-, have been dreamers, tellers of fairy-tales, fools who contradicted themselves, who understood nothing of natural science and the strange animal called man.

Let us look then at the very least for consistency, in this analyst of social systems, for whom Plato, Rousseau, and Fourier "are only fit for sparrows." To "avoid further uncertainty," he offers his own "system of world organization" and points to his notebook to establish its full-fledged existence.

> I wanted to expound my views to the meeting in the most concise form possible, but I see that I should need to add a great many verbal explanations, and so the whole exposition would occupy at least ten evenings, one for each of my chapters.

Laughter greets this announcement and its accompanying one, that the system is not yet finished. Then comes the cruel fact.

> I am perplexed by my own data and my conclusion is a direct contradiction of the original idea with which I start. Starting from unlimited freedom, I arrived at unlimited despotism. I will add, however, that there can be no solution of the social problem but mine.

What value has the system, he is asked, if he cannot make it consistent and if he has himself been reduced to despair by it? He admits to the despair, but insists there is no system that can take the place of his. A lame teacher who is present moves to defend the systematizer. He has read Shigalyov's book. In it, mankind is divided into two factions, one-tenth with absolute freedom and unbounded power over the remaining nine-tenths. "The others have to give up all individuality and become, so to speak, a herd." What gives unction to their sacrifice of everything is the promise of achieving "primeval innocence, something like the Garden of Eden." They will have to labor hard to accomplish this great end, but will have Shigalyov's "very remarkable" educational plan to take away their liberty and transform them into a herd, one "founded on the facts of nature and highly logical." The teacher-apologist grants that others might argue with some of the reasoning, but no one could doubt the intelligence or the knowledge of the system builder. Too bad, he concludes, we cannot arrange for him the ten evenings his system needs to be explicated and understood.

Even the pistol-shot midwife is appalled by the clown-sociologist's proposals. "Can you be in earnest, when that man doesn't know what to do with people and so turns nine-tenths of them into slaves? I've suspected him for a long time." Shigalyov is undismayed. What he proposes, he says to a female student who finds his ideas contemptible, is an earthly paradise; "there can be no other on earth." Lyamshin, another of the devils, offers his variation on the system: "For my part, if I didn't know what to do with nine-tenths of mankind, I'd take them and blow them up into the air instead of putting them in paradise. I'd only leave a handful of educated people, who would live happily ever afterwards on scientific principles."

The student cries, "No one but a buffoon can talk like that!" She is right, of course, Mme. Virginsky whispers to her, "but he is of use." Peter Verkhovensky, the leader and animating force of the little demonic circle, calls it all "pretty thorough rot." But he acts upon just such despotic principles, without the clown-man's kind of open avowal. Under his direction, murder and suicide become the rule and one-tenth do in fact turn nine-tenths into slaves. Since 1871, as we all know, Shigalyov's demonic system, developed without any humor, has found hordes of followers only too easily made into slaves. Some might even say that it has conquered nine-tenths of the world.[11]

Dostoevsky's satire is much more than a literary extravaganza in the service of anti-totalitarian politics. It is more accurately described as a kind of psychological hermeneutic, depending upon a clown play for full interpretation and understanding. As in the drama of the Grand Inquisitor in *The Brothers Karamazov*, Dostoevsky is demonstrating the fallacy of systems, all systems, any systems, that pretend to offer total organization as even a possibility. That way lies only one certain totality: slavery for nine-tenths of the world, or whatever part of the world may find itself so "organized." In 1871 it was possible to call such organizers buffoons, but even then it was clear that they had their use, as Mme. Virginsky points out. Today, we either salute our Shigalyovs as grand social thinkers or recognize their deadly buffoonery for what it is.

The clown shows us a way to build up goodness in the face of evil, whether instructing us by intention or not. His great lesson is the Pauline one: not to be overcome by evil, but right up to the end to live by accepting the goodness of being and becoming that we find in ourselves and others. The clown's is not, however, a falsely cheery good humor built on the denial of evil and human tragedy. Sometimes there is about him some of Shigalyov's exemplary befuddlement. Often he is the hungry, the despised, the rejected one persecuted by others. He knows evil at first hand, and out of that knowledge touches the sadness and despair in each of us. Rouault, for whom the clown is a powerful personal symbol, paints his portrait; in every way he is a redeeming figure, the exact parallel in mien and expression of the painter's Christ, a visible *coincidentia oppositorum*. "Their laugh," says Rouault of clowns, "is familiar to me; it reaches the realm of a million stifled sobs."[12]

Sometimes we must depend upon the clown spirit to rescue us from despair; the clown's persistent good humor in the face of tragedy and the abiding presence in that humor of something more dependable and more enduring than the merely human can redeem us from hopelessness. Laughter is our most trustworthy exorcism. It can drive off demons. A sense of humor restores a sense of proportion. It returns us to what really matters and gives us the courage to face our devils, whatever breed afflicts us. All the Jewish jokes, the black jokes, all the comedies set in insane asylums bear witness to the hidden power of the comic within the tragic and of the tragic within the comic. The clown affirms life and quickens that affirmation in us, even in the midst of the worst blows of chance, or the most crushing injustice.

When it is of this scourging sort, the clown's comedy points to a redeeming presence at the center of existence that corresponds to the vulnerability at the core of the human condition. Comedy, says M. C. Hyer,

> presupposes faith in a sacred order, or depth dimension of being, at the same time that it represents a persistent refusal to absolutize it and take it with abso-

lute seriousness. . . . For all its levity and frivolity, it is an affirmation of light rather than darkness at the heart of reality, of meaning rather than absurdity at the center of the mystery of Being. . . . In its own outrageous manner it is an agent of redemption; for in its very opening up of the sacred cosmos to the profane chaos, it bears witness to a faith in the ontological priority of cosmos over chaos.[13]

The laughter elicited by the redeemed clown-man is in the service of values and purposiveness. He knows and helps us to know how to take heart at the edge of defeat. Dying, we rise again in paroxysms of laughter. The inspired clown's performance can be seen as a paradigm of dying and resurrection. "He is indeed the *Doppelgänger*," as S. H. Miller suggests, "the man with two shadows, two worlds, one in the dust, crumpled, embarrassed, shattered, the fool, the failure—the other in the sky, incredibly gay, utterly impossible but never unbelievable. . . ."[14] He touches our deepest, most wounded places and moves us to claim our humanity by infusing his roles with a majesty that would be unendurable in its size and power if it did not come wrapped in laughter. He has found a way to bring us into the presence that the Old Testament warns us must kill us if we look at it directly. He has found the appropriate symbol for that presence.

The Holy Fool

When we are not identified with the clown archetype we can allow it to function symbolically, as the redeemed clown does, to re-present ultimate presence in its most fitting proximate guise, that of Everyman.

Who is Everyman? He who pictures our human condition and interprets for us its subjective meaning. Who is the clown? He who tells us that only through this human life do we know the mystery of being. Only by accepting our humanness can we open ourselves to God.

The redeemed clown chooses a way that is a multiple way, the way of Everyman in disidentification from the powers and pomps of the self-aggrandizing, literal-minded role-players of this world. As William Lynch says, with appropriate solemnity, "The comic is par excellence the great enemy of the univocal mind. . . . [the] mentality [that] wishes to reduce and flatten everything to the terms of its own sameness, since it cannot abide the intractable differences, zigzags and surprises of the actual."[15] Clown wisdom is to accept as inevitable the proliferation of masks, the disguises of people ashamed of their wounds and determined to keep them hidden. The clown, himself no longer ashamed, juggles with the masks, plays happily with them, showing the absurdity, the fear, and the fun that is in them when they are not absolutized but simply accepted as the elaborate defenses they are and seen through. Thus he permits us to accept our wounds, and if not to display them proudly, at least not to hide the feelings that define them. We can say with Rouault, "I saw clearly that the 'clown' was myself, ourselves, almost all of us."[16]

The key is conscious choice, that small but necessary response that makes all the difference between compulsion and freedom. The clown figure enacts acceptance of the human lot in his comedy—all of it, its absurdity, its grotesqueness, its suffering, its tragedy. His acceptance does not strike a gloomy pose. His acceptance is openhearted; his feeling, warm. He is glad to be here in the midst of life.

In the clown's acceptance is enfolded a new experience of time. We step with him out of the ordinary sequence of events into the isolated moment, the transitional space of illusion, the circus arena, the stage, the sacred place where the heart speaks in movements that without words voice a prayer of acceptance. We are in the now. Time has stopped rushing by. We are free to open to the moment that has opened time to us. We come into a deeper presence, which is what it means to come into our own. We are focused on the feeling before us and in us. Giving such attention fills us. There will be plentiful food for us in the future, air enough, time enough—even though time itself now seems so full, no longer open-ended, passing by us, dying. We accomplish everything in such single-minded concentrations of energy as this one. We know in such devoted moments the richness of a past filled up with what we have done and a present with a matching abundance to accomplish. In the midst of time's inevitable arrivals and disappearances, we know the abundance of simultaneity. We hold opposite emotions in easy awareness. We understand something of the archetypal world that lies beneath them. We both claim and reject our defenses. We accept our feelings and hold them in our affection like the juggling clown.

This is where the clown and the Christ figure merge to speak of the goodness and the abundance of life, of the preserving fullness of a tragic world that is also a comic world, a free world that must be both tragic and comic. We see the divine the only way we can, through acceptance of the human. "The motions of comedy," in Nathan Scott's words, "finally lead to joy, but it is a joy that we win only after we have consented to journey through this familiar, actual world of earth which is our home, and, by doing so, have had our faith in its stability and permanence restored."[17] It is a vote of confidence we make in the acceptance of the clown's way, the fool's way, the disguise choosen by the transcendent itself. In that disguise, wisdom becomes folly and man becomes woman in both senses of the word "becomes"—each is more becoming as the result, each is transformed.

The transformed clown disappears, whether we speak of the professional who becomes a master of all roles, from farce to tragedy, or of the clown-man who is no longer required to play any roles. Clowning is absorbed into the whole personality. It is no longer a defense, no longer a substitute for an ego-identity. This identity houses the clowning rather than hides behind it. The clowning is a part, not an evasion of parts, a thread of color that lights up and gives a defining texture to the whole fabric of identity. We know why the fool's is such an exalted place in Scripture.

Erasmus gathers persuasive witnesses to testify to the fullness of scriptural support of the high place of the fool in God's dispensation. Ecclesiastes 1 provides certification of the endless number of fools—"infinite," says the Preacher. When the same wise man says "Vanity of vanities, all is vanity," he means that human life "is nothing but a sport of folly." A deepening of meaning comes from Jeremiah: "Every man is made foolish by his own wisdom." King Solomon calls himself "the most foolish of men." And Paul, the special apostle of folly in the Erasmian sense, tells us with great rhetorical force that he speaks as a fool, that he wants to be received as a fool, that God has chosen the foolish things of this world for his own and to save the world by foolishness.

"The clowning is a part, not an evasion of parts, a thread of color that lights up and gives a defining texture to the whole fabric of identity. We know why the fool's is such an exalted place in Scripture." (Thackeray)

Erasmus proposes nothing less in his elaborate oration *In Praise of Folly* than to save the world by foolishness. All that is negative in the world is made positive by the affirmations of Folly, the daughter, according to ancient myth, of Plutus, a drunken personification of wealth, and a nymph, the personification of youth. Nursed by Drunkenness and Ignorance, Folly is supported, accoutered, and surrounded by Self-Love, Flattery, Forgetfulness, Pleasure, Laziness, Madness, Sensuality, Intemperance, and Sound Sleep. The very creation of life depends upon folly—look at the organ of generation, "that foolish, even silly, part which cannot be named without laughter. . . ." Folly makes life possible; only by listening to its counsels can we put up with the difficulties of existence. Man was given woman as a helpmate, and God knows she is "a stupid animal . . . and a giddy one, yet funny and sweet. . . ." Men endure each other because they admire themselves—what could be more foolish? Who are more foolish than those who pass their lives seeking fame, or than philosophers who believe in their own wisdom? Who are the most happy of men? Morons, fools, and half-wits.

Erasmus is thorough in his satirical excoriation of the folly of churchmen in priding themselves so much on their offices, in their orotund devoutness, in the pomp and ceremony of their lives—true foolishness, but not wise folly. For the Erasmian fool, the one acceptable model is Jesus Christ, who became our kind of fool, a human fool, to save us from our kind of human foolishness. If we follow his example, the world will rightly think us fools: "The happiness of Christians . . . is nothing else but a kind of madness and folly." But that insanity leads to nothing less than eternal happiness, giving us "a foretaste and a glow of the reward to come." That is enough to say, and so Folly stops, with a word of contempt for those who expect her to remember what she has said in a neat summary, and with a lovely disclaimer: "If anything I have said shall seem too saucy or too glib, stop and think: 'tis Folly, and a woman that has spoken."

In the ironies of Folly, we are presented with the *summum bonum* of the clown: self-acknowledgment. This is a larger and more demanding injunction than the Socratic "Know thyself." For here we must not only know who we are, but accept ourselves as we are. In summarizing Erasmus's work, we can easily overlook the fact that his Folly is personified as a woman who comes to praise herself, and who does it quickly, without ceremony or rhetorical flourish. No hiding behind Latin and Greek phrases or the names of philosophers for her: "What great orators elsewhere can hardly bring about in a long, carefully planned speech, I have done in a moment, with nothing but my looks." That is the ultimate yielding to feeling by the clown as a foolish woman, as the very essence of clownly folly, speaking with her own voice and no one else's, claiming her sacred moment, breaking through time to seize her permanent "now."

The model Erasmus proposes is the one we achieve when we come to our own full clownly dignity, announcing with gladsome foolishness, "I am who I am," here and now. If we have any sense of phrases and the history that lies behind them, we will recognize that we are calling ourselves after the name by which God identified himself to Moses: "I am who I am."[18] Our humbleness and our pride, our folly, in a word, lies in the recognition that we do not speak for all being, but just for that small segment of it that has come to rest in us in our sacred moment. In refusing to disguise ourselves or to look to others to provide a cover by their flattery or criticism or their equally disguising neutral descriptions, we begin to measure up to the high role that has been assigned us in having been brought into existence and given human resources with which to meet that existence.

If we face up to our resources, we must acknowledge both our adequacies and our inadequacies, both the comic and the tragic textures of our lives. However we make our acknowledgment, we will make fools of ourselves. But what a marvelous set of examples we have from which to learn the motions of our folly! We have Erasmus's instruction to guide us, and we have those who taught him, the instructors of Scripture: Ecclesiastes and Solomon and Paul, for example, and alongside them Cicero and Augustine, Boccaccio and Rabelais. We have all the courageous clowns of literature. We have Shakespeare and Molière. We have Rousseau, whose *Confessions* show him to be boastful, impotent, endlessly engaged in his several searches for a mother and fame and self-righteousness, and willing to make a fool of himself in each of his quests, and even more of a fool in showing himself a fool. We have all those who have followed his clownly example, epitomized for us in our time by the fumbling peregrination into self of Joyce's Everyman, Leopold Bloom. Bloom is rewarded with all the promised regalia of Folly, not the least of which is his return to his marriage bed and the echo of Folly to be found in Mrs. Bloom, Molly.[19] We have the princely clowns of slapstick film comedy, who endure their suffering with silent mime.

We have, after all the tortures of this century and the inhumanity to which we have so often surrendered our existence, the guidance of that gifted German-

Jewish poet Paul Celan. His way of naming the unnameable name of the God of Judaism is to write a Psalm to *Niemand,* No one. The "No one" who created us out of earth and clay, the "No one" whose praise he hymns, is the God not only of Judaism, but also of Erasmus's Folly and the redeemed clown. In his words, the "No one" whose blessing we seek is the "No one" who confirms us in the folly that gives us wisdom and the nothingness that gives us being:

> Praised be thy name, No one.
> For love of thee
> we will flower
> Towards
> thee.
>
> A nothing
> we were, we are, we will
> remain, flowering—
> the nothing, the
> No-one's-rose.[20]

XV The Clown in Women

The Clowning Woman

When clowning seduces a woman, it will make her many things, striking things, unconventional things, but not seductive things. Clown-women are notable for their wit, their beguiling gestures, their far-ranging use of humor. They are greatly appealing as well as entertaining companions. But that's just it—companions, not intimates, not lovers. Caught in the clown role, they use their clowning to deflect penetration. Other people's feeling does not reach through to their own, and theirs remains invisible to others. Dominated by clowning, a clown-women feels compelled to use mannerisms, poses, masks behind which she languishes unseen, unloved, ungiven into life. She often feels sexually inadequate, despite unusual beauty or bodily presence. Like the male clown, she feels herself to be an outsider, a forlorn one, even a scapegoat.

Psychologically, the problem can be described as the clown archetype invading her animus and then overtaking her ego. The animus fails to function as a mediator of the contents of the objective psyche to her ego.[1] She does not receive the information she needs from the animus; instead it is conscripted into the clowning defense against feeling. Her ego falls into a passive, secondary position in relation to the animus, and as we have seen with its anima counterpart, the animus steps in front of it, displaying the clowning syndrome to the world in place of the ego. She plays the clown instead of being herself. She does not simply use her clowning gifts; she becomes them. What she shows of her feelings of hurt, panic, betrayal, suicidal desolation, and hostility are parodies. She cannot experience or communicate them directly. She plays at feelings, often stirring them in others, but in herself can evoke only bits and pieces. However, when they mount up, they are enough to overwhelm her. She becomes elusive, impenetrable, touchingly closed, prickly, unreachable. She arouses all sorts of emotions —conflicting, sympathetic, lively—in those close to her, but cannot get close to them. She is as a result lonely, poignant, maddening. A man greatly moved by such a woman said, "There is such a sweetness about her, a beautiful, sad sweetness." But these are qualities that usually come in a jumble, so that while they make her interesting, even fascinating sometimes, they also show her to be beset by problems. Charming, witty, sad, enraging, she must be found in her problems to be cured.

The woman caught in clowning does not fit fixed categories, but rather breaks them. Her originality makes her attractive, but also unexpectedly dangerous. Her orphaned air, for example, combines with a skill for the barbed remark or angry joke that pricks her companions with its hostility while simultaneously disarming any angry retaliation because it has been uttered by a waif, a sadly wounded and anxious one. Hostility, even filtered through humor, remains hostile, but the humor is often irresistible. One clown-woman reveals this in a dream involving her former analyst. She is in a restaurant with friends, enjoying "good food and witty, educated talk." She spies her former analyst at the other end of the room, working as a waiter. Though she felt fond of him, "he was not one of us, did not really belong to our little group." She awoke feeling superior to him and grimly amused at having put him in his place through a verbal pun. His name actually meant "waiter" in another language in which the dreamer was fluent. So she put Dr. "Waiter" in his place, both visually and verbally, in the position of waiting on her, with all those satisfying bits of revenge—having to take time for her, to pay court to her, to serve her in countless little ways. It was funny. It also alerted her present analyst to what was in store for her. Did the woman feel the inequality of the analytic relationship so strongly as a master-servant relationship that she needed to revenge herself by dream-fantasy, by making the analyst wait upon her? Yet one must also see that the dream speaks truth. The analyst does wait on the patient in every sense of the word. The sharp humor makes the dream bristle with hostility, and yet the same humor softens the hostility. Thus, in true clown fashion, this dream makes and unmakes the point, mixes up its categories, reverses and maintains its roles, crosses, and recrosses its dividing boundaries.

Clown-women do evince a beguiling mixture of hostility, often sharp in intent, and humor equally sharp in its way. Another clown-woman was kept waiting fifteen minutes by her analyst because of an emergency with a previous patient that the waiting woman could not have known about, of course. She herself was chronically late for her analytical sessions, a habit in which she persisted despite many attempts to sort it out and end it. Rarely was the analyst late, and never before for so long a time. Another person was also in the waiting room, waiting to see the other analyst in the office suite. Impromptu, on the spot, the clown-woman produced a routine, complete with audience effects, to express her anger. She sat and waited—and waited—and waited, posing, mimicking all the gestures and postures of impatient waiting. Then, laughing, she got up, went out the door and came back into the waiting room again, as if just arriving, joking to the other person, her audience, that she clearly was not the favored one. It was pleasingly ambiguous as to just who was or was not favored—the patient in the analyst's office, the other patient in the waiting room, the patient the clown was playing, the one who had just arrived, or herself, the clown, who was first kept waiting.

Often a clowning woman directs her hostility through humor at herself, making nasty, cutting, and yet funny remarks about her own stupidity, dumpiness, silliness, even major physical deformities or speech disorders. The clowning woman's mixing of categories, serious and trivial, entertaining and destructive, goes as far as her experience can take her. The theme running through all the wit and the anger is that she does not fit, does not belong anywhere, possesses no stable definition. She calls out others' compassion by playing the outsider. She never fits into her family, never cleanly belongs to a social class or caste. There she is, wounded, embarrassed, poignant, always with her slip hanging out, or with words slipping out to proclaim her positionless status. At the same time, she defies any effort to bring her into a group, under protection. Nothing can challenge the fact: she really does not fit, by nature. It is no accident; the categories are wrong, both of individual and group, and more wrong still are the boundaries between them.

The clown-woman's determination to defeat others' efforts to help her find her place is total and enraging. It can turn a situation ugly. She is made to order for the role of scapegoat. She arouses every sort of social disturbance, so let her carry all that disturbs us! Though she draws pity in her outcast state, she seems actively to seek it. A woman's dream captures the ambiguity of the clown's plight, though here the dreamer avoids becoming a scapegoat. She dreamt she was part of a group of women taking a special course at a men's university. Some breach of conduct had occurred. The culprits were thought to be women, or at least the dreamer thought they were women. But the accused were actually unknown, marked only by the red caps and white clown-gloves of their version of academic regalia. The accused women were asked to present themselves. If they did not do so they would not become known, even though they were wearing clown's clothing that would seem to identify them. It is as if a ritual confession of identity must be made. Without it, the group is blind to the oddly different clothing that sets the wearers apart, which is to say the oddnesses of character and psychological type that set the clowning woman apart. In other words, if the dreamer does not volunteer for the role of culprit, she will not be selected for it, either.

The Scapegoat

Often these women take on the scapegoat role in their families, cast as the least favored of their mothers' children, or seen as the least cooperative within family rules. Their independence is seen pejoratively as selfishness. In their clowning antics, it is as if they are always jabbing away at customary ways of doing things, and thus exposing, by detaching themselves from fixed customs and patterns of behavior, the implicit power collected in the general assumption that these customs and patterns are the only ways of doing things.

This motif was acted and re-enacted in the analysis of the clowning woman who always came late to her sessions. One strand of meaning in her lateness that was thus uncovered was her challenge to the whole analytic enterprise, to its set times and specific duration of sessions, fixed by the analyst. Though the pattern is workable as it carves out its boundaries of space and time devoted regularly to the interests of specific persons, this woman's lateness constantly brought into question whether this was really so, must be so, could be so. Unexpected things always happened: last-minute phone calls, important matters that delayed her. How could one count on any stability of space or time? Thus she told her story through dramatic acts, articulating her experience of life as a series of fragments not reliably put together, but ever subject to interruption, intrusion, divergence from agreed-upon schedules. She felt unable to order her daily existence, but spoke and acted out her sense of its disorder as part of her illness, one that made her feel on the edge of madness, always threatened by a great tide of material things, of appointments, of chores rushing toward her.

By being late so often, she pulled one part of the analytic relationship loose from the whole—like tearing off one patch of a clown's costume. The patch that came loose was the latent power issue in the conventional structure of the analytic relationship. The analyst fell right in, as tumultuously as in a clowning routine, into the tug of war over who really is in charge of the session, who sets its time, who decides when to begin, when to end. The clowning woman thus exposed in transference how controlled she felt by the conventional patterns of her original family, how she had been made to come to heel like a performing dog, and how she had exerted her own power by mocking and negating those patterns. From her position on the outside, she challenged the whole demarcation of inside and outside roles. She broke her family's boundary between chaos and order, thus threatening it with an invasion of chaos by making a farce of fixed family patterns, of meals at precise times, of exactingly defined behavior. That was what she was re-enacting by challenging the conventions of analysis and its fixed schedules.

The analyst has countertransference reactions to deal with, too. Only too often does he or she feel pulled out of the larger, encompassing analytic concerns, caught in the patches of power struggle. It does not matter what is the issue; it devolves into a wrestling match to see who is going to pull whom across the line. The clowning woman teaches an analyst a lot about the possibilities for crude power struggle woven into the caring work of analysis. Again, as in a clowning routine, the analyst feels as if shot out of a cannon, delivered willy-nilly into the explosive emotions of a gross authoritarianism, willingly or unwillingly filling the role of the analysand's father laying down the law. Under the guise of keeping the analytic frame, the analyst will be boss, the patient will arrive promptly or forfeit the time. The theater of affect becomes almost complete; all that is missing is mustache, cane, and banging fist. Any pose of calm, analytic neutrality, or interpretive stance, disappears. But just as suddenly the humor of the situation may burst through, disrupting the tug of war, exposing to the analyst the fictional nature of the whole analytical endeavor—its story-line, its myth-making, its inherent contingency. Thus does the analyst become the opposite number of the analysand, feeling the despair that one way is no better, is no more certain than another; thus do both welcome the glad liberation from fixation to any one way, the happy opening to the creative imagination of analysis. The patches can be pulled together. One need not sermonize about the sacredness of an infallible method.

Paradoxically, in the experience of analysis with a clowning woman, an analyst is made free to choose to stick to the pattern of a beginning and ending for sessions, and the clowning woman is freed to consent to it, at least for a time. As long as no one believes that this is a pattern etched in stone, as long as the power plays inherent in it are bared for inspection, it can be taken seriously. Analysis and analyst grow under the tutelage of such a clowning woman.

Persona Compulsion

Like the man caught in clowning, the clowning woman feels compelled to find the right mask for the right audience. She too suffers a persona compulsion. The interior relationship between the woman and her own animus is lived outwardly, a substitute inside herself for her ego-adaptation to the reality of those around her. The animus does not function to connect her to her own unconscious; it clowns instead. She is caught in the dynamism of the autonomous archetype, so instead of connecting the emotions of fear, dread, threat, or sorrow in the woman in order to produce a workable insight into the realities of her situation, the animus seals off each experience in clowning gestures. Her ego lies passive and secondary in the face of the animus assault. Instead of receiving or confronting her impulses to perform the pratfall or the beguiling, duping gesture, instead of developing a clear, open point of view, her ego is blank. The clowning routines rush in to fill the ego-vacuum. Rather than a feeling of desperation or humiliation, of failure, what rises in her is the need to improvise, to try to recoup the situation by covering up the feeling, as in the following dream of a clowning woman.

The dream tries to show the dreamer the compulsion to cover up and what lies behind it. In it, the dreamer finds herself "dressed up as a tubby, pillow-stuffed female clown in an old-fashioned white tennis dress with the star-spangled banner of the flag around my waist. I'm trying desperately to be funny, to entertain. Someone like George Plimpton or Andy Warhol is rolling the cameras. Only, nobody is laughing. I can't get any reaction. I am also competitive with a guy on the other side of the net. Suddenly he serves the ball—and he is funny. It lands at my feet, a fatty, yellow chicken carcass—like a helpless, exposed woman, as if to say, 'You are chicken!' I have to improvise all the time. . . . Still desperate for a laugh, I lie down like a W. C. Fields character, or like a chicken, with my white legs up in the air, and then turn a backwards sommersault, showing the ass, being an ass. A man tells me I should be ashamed. . . . Another female comes on, all made up, very phony, very serious, quite lovely. She is dressed in a long Kate Greenaway dress made from the American flag and lies down . . . and all you see of her are her feet and the sparkle of her net underslips—the opposite of my white underpinnings; she's like Miss America, starry-eyed. The effect is very mystical, highly visual, but quite vapid. However, I know that I, the original, have been outdone."

This need to improvise the right mask for an audience can sometimes pervade the entire ego-adaptation of a woman caught in clowning. The first thought for her is not, What do I feel? or What do I think about what is going on? or What do I want to put into this situation or get out of it? but rather, What will the audience like? What will be approved of? The impulse to wear the right mask, the persona required by the situation, operates automatically, and only half consciously. If an analyst presses the clown patient, however, and if the relationship stores a sufficient trust, it often emerges that in fact the woman has prepared various versions in her mind to have ready for the telling of a story or the presenting of a problem. The persona compulsion is both autonomous and contrived, suffered and colluded in by the clowning woman.

Group therapy can prove very helpful in addressing the persona problem of a clowning woman. In a group, there is bound to be someone who will spot the mask. A group provides sufficient people to share the troublesome task of unmasking the painful emotions behind the mask. The concealed emotions usually show a mix of pain and power. The clowning woman wants to retain power, to give up just the snippets she chooses and to keep others out of circulation. She wants power to create effects that will compensate for her pain. She wants the best of both worlds: a stellar place of power in the group constellation, while enjoying the concern that goes with revealing her painful feelings of inferiority. She revels in her power to dazzle and then quickly withdraw, her power above all to keep control. The pain is not easily controlled. It leaps up at her from her outsized emotions, never perfectly masked from their primitive quality in the extremely uneasy relationship she maintains with them. She feels bewildered, threatened by an overwhelming force, like waves rising up from the sea. One woman always prepared in advance what she would say in group sessions, including humorous turns of phrase, detailed conjurings of scenes, and layings out of plot. She always played to an audience. But it all fell flat. The group had gone deeply enough into its analytical work. The whole performance was seen for what it was, an elaborate masking, hiding something very different underneath, most significantly the urge to control the group's reactions. In fact, the general response evoked by the women's prepared presentations was an equally deliberate tuning out or spontaneous rage. The group reacted both to being controlled and to all else that was hidden behind her masks. Their response made the clowning woman feel abandoned and threatened by their anger.

The group's implacable holding to its responses to the clown-woman, neither sweetening them nor attacking her with them, made it clear that she had entered the group already feeling abandoned and enraged. That explained the group's responses. She evoked in others the emotions that she dreaded to face in herself. Courage is demanded to work something like this through, for a clowning woman, like her male counterpart, is shot through with confusion and vulnerability. Members of a group need courage to persist in giving their intensely negative reactions and not appeasing a clown with sweet reassurance. A caring group will strip her of her mask, and she will quickly feel pain. She in turn will need courage to endure the inevitable suffering to which it leads, and trust that it can come to resolution. But before that point there must be still more suffering, as she is made to confront feeling being abandoned, inadequate, and enraged all at once, a frightening congeries of emotions.

True to the clown constellation, such an unmasking will also bring out into the open the problems in others set off by her antics. One member of this group reacted to the controlling motif, the clown-woman's hidden power drives, because the member also had issues of control of deal with. Another in the group reacted to the hidden hostility because of her own ample reservoirs of anger. Another identified with the clown's wounded feelings because it touched his own. Working on issues of their own, members of a group can protect the clown from the terrors of the scapegoat role, which is a constant danger in group treatment of a clown.

The problem both conceals and reveals the cure. The clown-woman rouses primitive emotions in other members that each must face while simultaneously, in a virtuoso juggling, holding and communicating to her how they see her. She herself needs to hold still to hear what they say, while simultaneously feeling the urge to improvise, to slip away, to dart out, to don still another mask to win approval where she is so frightened. The holding still to feel reactions, one's own and others', is to walk the tightrope that connects her masking compulsion on the one side to the safety of open and admitted reality on the other.

Ego-Weakness

The clown-woman's compulsion to win others' approval and to identify herself with the masks she uses hides a deep sense of defect, what is in fact a large ego-weakness. Something feels damaged, not right, not put together, because it is just that. The focus often falls on the sexual area, or other parts of the body, or even on a woman's sense of being. One woman felt she never could win a man whom any other woman was interested in: "Any woman could take a man away from me; they have the stuff and I do not." Yet actually this was a woman of remarkable beauty, whose charm and sweetness attracted many men to her. The problem lay in her own defective vision, her not seeing in her own wounded esteem what she was. She had suffered a real injury to her narcissism. Another woman felt fine about her body sexually, but in other ways it seemed grossly defective to her. She could not rely on its endurance. At any moment her health would break down and she would have to retire to bed, sick, to sleep for days. The basic unreliability of life itself could break in upon her at any moment through her weakened body, sabotaging any security in being that she thought she could maintain.

Another woman suffered wounding to her ego even more severely. For her, the wound came through her sexuality. She entered analysis with a suicide attempt some distance behind her, saying she had felt her life was fundamentally threatened. Thus she had threatened her own life when a boyfriend deserted her. She began treatment because she was again in relationship with a man, and felt vulnerable to the same potential assault. Indeed, her premonitions came true, though this time her rage was uppermost. She gulped pills while listening to her man on the phone expressing his hesitancy about continuing their affair. He and her analyst rushed her to a hospital emergency room, and she was soon out of physical danger. The psychological damage took longer to heal. Indeed the healing took her into marriage and divorce with this same man, a period of great suffering for her. Eventually, she achieved deliverance from her anguish by the painstaking rebuilding of her own inner structure, for which she had initially tried to substitute this man and relationship with him.[2] That had left her at his mercy, utterly dependent on him whom she could not and should not have controlled. The cure came through her facing her own lack of interior connection, making her recognize the animus that connected her to her explosive rage and anguish at feeling so defective. Making this inner connection yielded a great blossoming in her, in both her professional and her personal life. Courageously she left her old work and went after what she had always wanted, a Ph.D. in a new field, which also meant getting into a workable relationship with her lifelong feeling of intellectual inferiority. All was rearranged as she accepted her unmistakable differences, not only from the mind-set of colleagues she had left behind in her former work, but also from her new academic compeers. She found a way to live with her clown's propensities—always taking up things from an odd angle, often a highly original one, which meant not fitting into conventional academic categories. Accepting her originality and all its burdens, she was able gradually to relinquish her compulsive self-judgment of inferiority. She succeeded in taking her degree and in carving out an original use for it, not fitting into a conventional academic career there either. In her personal life she reached to her own large capacity for love, consenting to love a new man and even to marry him, putting her great self-doubts aside. Her rage was harnessed now to support her, where earlier it had sabotaged her life. As she put it, in her own wry clown fashion, "The best revenge is to live well."

Such clown-women's suffering from a sense of ego-weakness strikes deep, whether their pain comes in periods of intense grief and desolation at feeling so precariously knit into life, so basically unlovable, or whether it comes as attacks of physical illness that hide the psyche's anguish by simply forcing sleep or breakdown, or as suicidal impulses.[3] They feel unsupported, unheld in their being, all alone, floating on the wind like a clown's lost balloon. Their ego feels precarious, as indeed it is, because it is not adequately anchored in the depths of self. These women experience the self's energies primarily in the relativization of the ego-world and its purposes and values that nearness to the self always effects. That is the best they can hope for—no alternatives, no windows onto larger, more enduring values opening up. Instead they must live with an ungrounded feeling of being cut loose, of constant treacherous contingency. One could be anywhere or nowhere, could be anyone or no one. When the clowning woman who suffered suicidal attacks won her way through to a self connected to an ego, she gained a large enough space to live her life in its most extravagant demands and fantasies. There was room for all her energies.

Imagination

This particular clowning woman illustrates a quality that belongs to the type as a whole, a strong imagination. Possessed of original ways of looking at things, and the gift of humor, which always places things in proportion, these women can break free of conventional perspectives, can mix up elements of being that are usually separated from each other in severely restricted compartments. They arrive easily at the novel. They share a capacity to develop the original. Their imagination is pervasive in them. It is accessible to them even in moments of stress and suffering, hence their ability to make jokes about their plight or anyone else's. Their perceptions catch what is foolish in what a culture finds wise, what is illusory in what parades itself as reality. Even their homeless outcast quality is useful as it challenges the durability of conventional housings of the real and the valuable. They work to expose us to our interiorities, to being broken in upon by the stream of psychic life that is not captured in conscious categories. They bring with them magical levels of the unconscious, where things merge, mix, oppose, and then become their opposites. When such skills are freed from the defensive use to which the clowning woman constantly feels compelled to divert them, large new creations and perceptions are the result.

Clowning women often work as artists; when they have emerged from their defensive posturings they show remarkable confidence and sureness about the originality of their work. Their anxiety and woundedness may block them from exhibiting their work publicly or allowing themselves to go all out for the career of an artist, but it does not attack their certainty about the quality of their work. Such a woman may be a comedienne, or in a public profession where her clowning will get her into trouble. One way or another, it must emerge to produce, for example, the enchanting performance designed for the outside world by that inspired clown Fanny Brice, while in her private life she moved from one circle of hell to another, never able to find in a man the ingenuity of eye, the exquisite ear, the boldness of clowning adaptation that permitted her to mimic perfectly a witty, galling, precocious child, a Baby Snooks, or a black-draped, all-knee-and-elbow, revolutionary modern dancer, a Martha Graham.[4]

She makes the most engaging companion or the most maddening one, depending on whether her clowning is at her disposal or she at its. In her worst days, the clowning woman who was threatened by suicidal impulses tried to force her first husband's sexual attention, and at the same time expressed her rage at him for not noticing her. All of this, as well as hiding how much she felt damaged and defective as a desirable woman, she expressed by parading stark naked through the room where he would be reading, and true to her clowning instincts, painted all over in different color lipsticks. The shock value of her tactic succeeded in getting his attention, all right, but also provoked annoyance and withdrawal. She was left feeling more frustrated and despairing then ever.

When clowning is not simply a ploy for the clown-woman, its spontaneity and inventiveness embellish situations, not least sexual ones, in surprising ways. People come alive. Laughter and gaiety flourish. A gladness in being is the contribution of such clowns. There is, for example, the woman whose lover was inspired to lick grape jelly off her various parts, happily jumbling together all the stuffy things psychoanalysts might say about oral greed and aggression, regression, and the lifting of repression, making a meal of her in the jubilation of a highly erotic moment. There is the clowning woman who served her friend lunch dressed only in a plate and a few bunches of grapes, in order to distract the friend from a dispiriting bout of the flu. Who was the meal for, anyway? Was there a better way for it to be served?

Treatment

The clown's archetypal image is a mirror for us, in which to see reflected the emotions we avoid, the fragments we stitch together haphazardly, covering instead of connecting the positive contingency that links the boundaries in the universe of becoming. The clown performs this mirroring function by touching our emotions, arousing our bodily reactions, delivering us to a sense of spirit in the flesh of things. Clowning redeems the banality of ordinary events, softens chance, greets being in nature, in children, in things.

A woman whose animus function is arrested in the clown archetype has no mirror in which to find her reflection. She is trapped, looking out of her captivity, feeling unseen. Her animus is taken over by the clown archetype's autonomous dynamism. Her ego falls into animus-identification. Where ego should be, animus prevails. She becomes a depressed version of the clowning woman. Without the lifting rhythm of the unconscious, the animus makes her clowning compulsive. It devolves into dodges, deflecting gestures, jugglings of feeling that fall into snippets, to be tossed away like confetti. Everything she has to say is expressed in a negative rhetoric, a syntax shaped around "not unlike" and "less than" and "not really" and "not at all." By not saying directly what she feels or thinks, but always warding off the living contact of affirmation, she gives others an impression of self-absorption and selfishness. She appears aloof, for she altogether hides the fact that she really has no conviction about what to say or do. Paying a social debt, offering a dinner or party of her own, inspires terror in her that she masks with an elaborate badinage that implies that others are not worth the trouble of a meal or even a drink.

When it comes to analysis or the analyst, masks dominate the scene. The

"Paying a social debt, offering a dinner party of her own, inspires terror in her that she masks with an elaborate badinage that implies that others are not worth the trouble of a meal or even a drink." (Paul Klee)

healing of the clowning defense makes almost impossible demands on both analyst and patient. The major healing move requires the clown-woman to turn as fiercely toward clowning as she has hitherto turned away from it. She must look at it to find her own image in it, even though for her it is like facing the Medusa. Her ego, trapped behind the silenced animus, must reclaim its consciousness. The ego must now actively seek and experience the reactions that her clowning has deflected. She must know them for what they are, feel them in heart, gland, and tissue, think them, respect them. Her ego must become audience to the animus-clown, rousing her to applaud her own experience. The ego can then emerge from its animus domination and disidentify itself from the animus, thus freeing both animus and ego. She can begin to receive, to challenge, to give full response to what the animus conveys to her. The rescue of the ego from animus-identification allows the animus to perform its mediating function in the development of a sense of self, rather than simply pirouetting senselessly in the circus of the clown archetype.

A clown-woman's dream elegantly describes the problem and its resolution. In the dream, the dream-ego, the woman, is at first dominated by the clown, the animus. Then she comes to recognize that she herself is the clown, and moves actively to unite with her clown-self. The dream takes place in a room filled with life-size mechanical dolls. There a male Harlequin-figure sits on "an extremely pale form of a woman. She is so pale that she is almost invisible at first. She has been ravaged by the Harlequin, negated by him . . . I think the Harlequin has ruined the woman by seducing her. Then the dolls come alive; the Harlequin begins to make love to the woman . . . I am both the woman and the Harlequin and become very aroused . . . I want him to desire me, to be his favorite, but I don't think he can care about anyone." The dreamer looked up the meaning of Harlequin and cited it in her associations as not only clown but demon, clearly demonstrated in this dream by his sucking the life out of the dream-ego.[5] The dream shows us a picture of the clown demeaning the woman's ego, sitting on it, ravaging it. But this Harlequin also arouses tremendous sexual response from the woman in the dream. In actuality, her sexuality was quite repressed, and not at all at her disposal. The sexual drama of the dream suggests that the woman needs to engage this Harlequin directly. That will open her ego to feel her own sexuality. When she does so in the dream, she not only is put in touch with her repressed sexuality, but also begins to see the real nature of the Harlequin figure. He does not partake of the feeling-values so precious to the ego-world. His effect on her is to bring into consciousness the repressed sexuality. The dreamer identifies with the Harlequin and thus begins to see and experience the conflict that lives in her, rather than allowing herself to be overrun by it.

Disidentifications, of ego from animus and of animus from absorption in the clown role, must permeate all relationships of the clowning woman, not least her interaction with her analyst. There, in countertransference reactions, the analyst can undergo and sort through another set of mirrors that the patient experiences. Those mirrors will show the great enjoyment that working with a clown-woman brings, and the accompanying danger of wanting to remain there, reveling in the fun of working with such a person. Clown-women really are very funny, witty, imaginative, and entertaining. What a relief to talk with them after the grinding depression of other patients, their suffocating anxiety, their savage hatred! The analyst is in danger of colluding, and not altogether unconsciously, with clowning women's defenses, because they are so pleasing. But that is not the whole story, for the defenses are also in the service of excluding the analyst, often to a serious degree. The mannerisms, the vocal patterns, the relentless logicizing, the galloping tempo of puns and jokes—all deflect interaction or penetration. There is no place to enter. All the clown-woman wants is an audience. She is a virtuoso in displaying the impenetrability of the ego caught in an animus complex. One determined clown-woman simply interrupted her analyst and went right on with her performance. Another waited courteously and then picked up where she had left off when the analyst paused. One particularly adroit clown took portions of what the analyst said and wove them into new routines. Accelerating tempos, fixed mannerisms, noisy chatter, caricatures of emotions flood the analysis. The frustrated analyst may become angry or harsh, in a maddening effort to break through—in collusion again with the defensive masking by demonstrating there really is something to defend against.

In group therapy, it is essential to open channels for the frustration that such a clowning woman builds up in others. She invariably arouses aggression, strong urges just to ram through her routines. The strain can be frightening. Sometimes it produces brilliant counter-moves. One woman had a shrewd rejoinder to an oblique and humorous characterization of herself by a clowning woman. The woman just asked the clown bluntly, persistently, what she meant by her performance. Is all that true? Are you angry at me? Did you really mean to express such hostility? The questioner stuck to her questions in the face of evasions, qualifications, and attempted changes of subject by the clown. Eventually the clown was caught, reeled in, and saved. It was a breakthrough for the clowning woman to say, Yes, I do feel all that, including the anger. She stood still, immediate, there, no longer whirling off, scattering affect. The group could feel her fear of admitting anger and sympathize with her defenses against it, even as she discarded them. She said that to her anger meant being hit the way she had been hit as a child. Facing the anger in herself or her mother meant being "smacked."

The woman who pressed the clown for an answer illustrates what one must endure to reach a clown-woman. It is a whole array of responses repeated countless times in the analyst's countertransference. One feels heavy, plodding, leaden, pedantic, oafish, cruel, aggressive—all the opposites of the airy, imaginative, fetching, subtle, scintillating, clever, kind feelings the clowning seems to deserve in response. Kindness especially defines the trap that the analyst falls into. One feels unkind, and tries to compensate for it by producing its opposite, often achieving no more than a hasty sweetness. The vulnerability of the woman who clowns to protect herself is real enough, her ego fragile enough. Falling under the same spell can catch the analyst in a desolation comparable to the patient's own. One concludes that little or nothing can be done with such a frail creature. At the opposite end of the spectrum, the clowning woman's split-off aggression, controlling events by parading her vulnerability to them, falls over onto the analyst's side. The analyst fails to press the point, stays out of deep waters in the safety of the dry land of interpretive devices. But now the interpretations themselves take on aggressive overtones, communicating the analyst's exasperation, and worse, the conviction that the patient's condition is simply hopeless.

Like the importunate group member, an analyst must be unyielding in making the connection between the clown-woman's ego and her experiences, so that she can look with some calm at her clowning and can inspect what it masks. She must hear again and again what the analyst learns about her clowning antics, must face the fact that when she clowns she is feeling something else that has been pushed aside, hidden, defended against. She may in fact be feeling this right now—face it! The analyst must keep looking into the clowning mirror, seeing and reporting the woman's hidden experiences. Then the woman can come to the mirror herself, can disengage herself from the compulsion always to clown, can take some ease, some pleasure in the disavowed experiences.

Redeeming the Clowning Woman

Pleasantly enough, the clown-woman does not lose her gift of clowning when freed of identification with it. In full scope, from the fun of an original style to the grasp of spirit found in the flesh, the clowning is set free to be used in her work and with those she loves. She can bring into shared existence with others the intimation of a transcendent reality as something accessible, palpable even, in the holes that wait beneath the patches of our comic being.

Animus opens to the self; that is its ultimate purpose. In turning toward her animus and receiving what it mediates to her ego, the clowning woman is moving toward that archetypal interiority, the world of the self. The steps are the same for all, the witch-man, the witch-woman, the clown-man, the clown-woman: to disidentify the ego from the contrasexual part and relate to it. This always means assiduous inspection of that part. Each must ask, How does the opposite sex inhabit me? In image, in associations, in attraction or repulsion to particular images of the opposite sex? What clusters of energy, what symbols of that sex abide in me? Inspecting them this way, we accept them inside ourselves, mutely, without fanfare or clamor. That silent coming together inside enables us outside to be, to become ourselves, and to do so in our own improvised and personal styles of being. These styles act as entry points into the world of archetypes. We experience the archetypes with some real consciousness. They move in us comfortably. Disidentification, inspection, and mute acceptance lead to our housing our opposite sexual parts within our sexual identities, vivifying them, drawing upon them, finding our own femininity or masculinity in their conjoining.

The clown-woman does special things in this arena. She is gifted with a different kind of masculine part, a clown who is not intensely male, who may even be a caricature of masculinity. She gains relief for herself and for others from compulsive clowning identification when she faces her own maleness in the claiming of her femaleness. She moves—and we in some sense can move with her—from fixation on make-up, from closing disguises to open approaches to the archetypal interior. She has been performing on the outside while dodging on the inside, always "on," doing things for an audience, making up for inner anxiety by outer routines. She has been running away from her feelings to the outside world. Redemption is to go back in. Claiming the animus gives her her chance to join others on the outside whom she now sees from the inside. She joins the outside as an insider. For the first time, she can really be part of a group.

The woman who lives in relation to her clowning instead of being possessed by it brings into the world a different kind of masculinity that influences everyone around her. She welcomes the masculine and makes the world welcome it because what she brings is a feeling-toned masculinity, one that has been received by an owning femininity. She houses her maleness, neither identifying with it nor repudiating it.

In welcoming her own masculinity, she makes welcome the masculinity around her; she helps men to be at ease with being men. Often, the men committed to such women speak of how creative they find her, how alive they feel with her, how masculine they are made to feel. Her tone is unmistakable, to the point where some men envy her strength of being, her imagination, her confidence. But with her or against her, there is no mistaking where she has come, her sense of having no regrets, of relinquishing conflict. This, she says, is what I am and should be and wish to be. It feels good; it feels glad.

The enlivening quality of the redeemed clown-woman oozes from her. The archetype of clowning seems to be proclaiming the joy of being set free. It is no longer confined to the dirty work of defense. Now it can weave its way in and out of the crowd, choose to appear or not at an event, produce its fun soberly or cavort in reckless abandonment, openly, happily what it is. As she is set free to use her gift, not to become it—to house it, not abuse it—the clowning gift merrily stretches out through our shared house of community, the constellated archetype of a particular personality, situation, or event, made available through one to many. But the clowning woman no more possesses clowning than she is possessed by it. Gifted with it, infused by its spirit, she shares it with us. We are grateful to her for making this spirit available. In the redeemed clown-woman, we know again what it means to speak of the gift of spirit.

XVI Epilogue

When at any given time we become aware of recurrent motifs in our lives, we begin to bring to consciousness the world of archetypes. It may be our own selves that we are summoning to consciousness, or the selves of others, or the place or places where we find our selves or others find theirs. We may find this new awareness in interior or exterior event, in dream or fantasy, in custom or ceremony. Almost always we find it in a figure with whom we feel close connection, one that greatly supports us or harrasses us, a mother figure or father figure, a lover, a friend, a hated enemy, a figure of beguiling uncertainty, at once a predator and an angelic intermediary in our lives, a witch, a clown.

There is no master list of archetypes, no fixed number, no sure way of discovering or identifying them. And yet we know when we are in their presence or they are in ours. We feel ourselves linked to something primordial in its force, unmistakably authoritative, whether the force and the authority are those of wisdom or of an intelligence best described as cunning. One thing that is clear is that it is a force in our lives, one with which we may absolutely identify ourselves, or from which we know we must struggle to disidentify. So it is with the witch and the clown, figures large in many cultures, alive in many dreams, figures urgent to understand for what they reveal of archetypal process and human identity.

To fail to explore what the witch and the clown represent is to shut ourselves off, we think, from the extraordinary mixtures of the known and the unknown, of the power of the feminine intellect and spirit latent or expressed openly in the witch, and of the soft feeling hidden within the masculine, the experience of spirit in the flesh of feeling that the clown enacts. Most perilously, perhaps, we close ourselves off from the psyche's address to ourselves which makes the whole movement from ego to self possible, and from the sure presence of the spirit which the completion of the journey to selfhood signifies.

There are quantities of recordings of the archetypal witch and clown available to us. High among them and particularly treasured by us are those in which the psyche and spirit invaded by the witch or the clown speak directly to us, whether in analytical session, fable or fairy tale, novel or drama, poem or picture. We have tried here to give those communications of witch and clown their fair share of attention, to urge a quickening of concern for all among us who have been the victims or the beneficiaries of the witch and the clown, and to suggest the ugly consequences of a dereliction of that attention. When attention is not paid to the witch and the clown, we see ourselves as dispossessed of the great strengths of the hag-woman, whose presence is a bedrock necessity for any civi-

305

lized community, and of the clown-man, without whose feelings, reached and let loose, the dual presence of the male and the female is seriously threatened. If we seem here to be doing some special pleading, that is quite intentional. For what we find in the witch and the clown, and hope others will find as well, is a pair of fascinating archetypal figures, endlessly amusing, confounding, difficult, and engaging, who at their best, when brought through great detailed self-inspection to mute self-acceptance, endow all of us with some of the moral stature that is evinced to us in the world of archetypes.

Notes

Epigraph: from C. G. Jung, *The Archetypes of the Collective Unconscious, Collected Works*, Vol. 9:1, tr. R. F. C. Hull (New York: Phantheon, 1959), p. 269 (par. 483).

Chapter I

1. Jung says of archetypes: "Archetypes are, by definition, factors and motifs that arrange the psychic elements into certain images, characterized as archetypal, but in such a way that they can be recognized only from the effects they produce. They exist preconsciously, and presumably they form the structural dominants of the psyche in general. They may be compared to the invisible presence of the crystal lattice in a saturated solution. As *a priori* conditioning factors they represent a special, psychological instance of the biological 'pattern of behavior,' which gives all living organisms their specific qualities. Just as the manifestations of this biological ground plan may change in the course of development, so also can those of the archetype. Empirically considered, however, the archetype did not ever come into existence as a phenomenon of organic life, but entered into the picture with life itself." C. G. Jung, "A Psychological Approach to the Trinity," *Psychology and Religion West and East, Collected Works*, Vol. 11, 45. R. F. C. Hull (New York: Pantheon, 1958), p. 149n.

2. The anthropologist Lucy Mair explains the terms succinctly. "If beliefs about the nightmare witch are found to have much in common all over the world, this is surely to be explained by the fact that the bases of social order are common; respect for life and property and for the rules governing sexual behaviour. The nightmare witch is the being that flouts those rules and in addition disregards the standards of decency that every society, however simple, thinks of as making it 'civilised' in contrast to real or imagined 'savages' outside." The everyday witch, "the person who may actually be living among you, suspected or unsuspected, also embodies an antithesis—this time the antithesis of the kind of person we like our neighbours to be." The nightmare witch is as the name suggests a night prowler; the everyday one, a less hidden, more familiar being. See Lucy Mair, *Witchcraft* (New York: McGraw-Hill, 1969), pp. 36-37.

The etymology of "nightmare" is of more than passing interest. It has Old English, Old High German, Old Norse, and related sources, which bring a series of pejorative associations to rest in the definition of "mare" as "incubus," which is to say an evil spirit that oppresses sleeping persons. The erotic mare as "the inverse of the mother," a figure of devouring sexuality and the proto-Indo-European goddess, is extensively treated in Wendy Doniger O'Flaherty's splendid book *Women, Androgynes, and Other Mythical Beasts* (Chicago: University of Chicago Press, 1980); see especially Chapter 6. A contrary nighttime force of male "good walkers" who rise at night to contend with male witches, literally for the good of the land, to protect crops, is detailed in *The Night Battles: Witchcraft and Agrarian Cults in the Sixteenth and Seventeenth Centuries*, Carlo Ginzburg's celebrated 1966 book only recently translated from the Italian (Baltimore: Johns Hopkins, 1983). If it does nothing else, this examination of the *benandante*-witch demonstrates both the healing power of the dream figure and the aggression he or she has long stirred.

3. For Bodin, see J. C. Baroja, *The World of the Witches*, tr. O. N. V. Glendinning (Chicago: University of Chicago Press, 1975), pp. 113-116. For discussion of Glanvill and

More, see C. A. Hoyt, *Witchcraft* (Carbondale: Southern Illinois University Press, 1981), pp. 4, 64, 65. See also *The Damned Art: Essays in the Literature of Witchcraft*, ed. Sydney Angelo (London: Routledge & Kegan Paul, 1977), especially the essays on Bodin and Reginald Scott.

4. All references to patients and their material, unless otherwise noted, are taken from the analytical practice of Ann Belford Ulanov, with gratitude to those who have given their permission to quote them.

5. It is only too easy to exaggerate the importance of the gods and demi-gods of popular culture, to make the kind of statement "in which the obvious gets locked away in a huge and heavily fortified frame of technical critical reference," as Russell Davies says in his less than enthusiastic summation of the methodology of John Cawelti in *Adventure, Mystery, and Romance* (Chicago: University of Chicago Press, 1976; reviewed in the *Times Literary Supplement*, June 18, 1976, p. 732). The fear of such inflation should not, however, lead us to minimize the contribution of those who triumphed over the formulas of the entertainment arts or of those who attempt to evaluate their achievement. Cawelti speaks to the point near the end of his book when he describes certain efforts of an unmistakable coarseness and simple-mindedness which nonetheless "represent the kind of artistry that can take a popular story formula and present it in such a way that it becomes an expression of a basic pattern of meaning in the consciousness of many members of the audience" (p. 300). See also the chapters on popular culture in Barry Ulanov, *The Two Worlds of American Art: The Private and the Popular* (New York: Macmillan, 1965).

6. Animus is a symbolic concept. Jung used the term to describe the unconscious masculine part of a woman's psyche which shows itself in personified form in images of men or of masculine elements in dream and fantasy. It personifies what Jung calls the logos principle in a woman's psychology, that spirit of truth by which she tries to live. Animus images reflect different levels of influence, extending from the significant males in a woman's personal history—father, brother, etc.—to the dominant cultural images of the masculine in her historical and social context, and to more abiding elemental images of the masculine, such as wind and sun, penetrating light, or masculine deities in mythology and religion. The task facing a woman is to become conscious of the animus images that operate in her, influencing her attitudes and notions of truth as well as her relations with men. The animus needs to become differentiated before it can perform its psychic function of connecting her ego to contrasexual contents in the unconscious.

7. Anima is a symbolic concept. Jung used the word to describe the unconscious feminine part of a man's psyche. Jung calls the anima the archetype of life. It functions to connect a man's ego to contrasexual contents in the unconscious. The anima shows itself in personified form as reflecting several levels of conditioning of the anima image. The influence of significant women in a man's life—mother, sister, aunt, etc.—will be evident, as will the prevalent images of the feminine in his culture and time and the primordial images of the feminine that arise in his psyche in response to specific conscious situations, both personal and collective. A man who takes on the task of differentiating his anima will discover dominant images of women residing in himself, both the positive that immediately attract him and the negative that repel him. These images personify the so-called eros principle of relatedness and will influence his actual relations with women as well as his connection to all life itself.

8. For discussion of anima and animus, see C. G. Jung, *Aion, Collected Works* 9:2, tr. R. F. C. Hull (New York: Pantheon, 1959), pp. 11-23 (par. 20-42). See also Ann Belford Ulanov, "Jung on Male and Female," in *Christian Approaches to Sexuality*, eds. R. T. Barnhouse and U. T. Holmes (New York: Seabury, 1978). See also Katherine Bradway, "Gender Identity and Gender Roles: Their Place in Analytic Practice," in *Jungian Analysis*, ed. Murray Stein (LaSalle: Open Court, 1982), chapter 15.

9. The primordial is not something that can be found in a microscope or in a search through documents. It is in the surviving traces of human beginnings and indeed the beginnings of life itself, all those things and beings we think of as part of the universe. For medieval thinkers, it was the *materia prima*, the *Urstoff*, of creation. For Jung, it was the underlying plane for his inner images (see *Memories, Dreams, Reflections*, New York: Pantheon, 1961, p. 199). For us, it is something that might be described as the unconscious's unconscious.

10. C. G. Jung, *The Visions Seminars*, 2 vol. (Zürich: Spring Publications, 1976), Book 1, pp. 369-370.

11. See William Willeford, *The Fool and His Scepter: A Study in Clowns and Jesters and Their Audience* (Evanston: Northwestern University Press, 1969), Plate 8: "One of Holbein's illustrations to Erasmus' *In Praise of Folly*, showing a fool looking at himself in the mirror." The image, tellingly, sticks its tongue out at the fool.

12. *Ibid.*, p. 234.

13. *Ibid.*, p. 76. See also Ann and Barry Ulanov, *Religion and the Unconscious* (Philadelphia: Westminster Press, 1975), pp. 28-32.

14. For a discussion of hatred of the female, see Ann Belford Ulanov, *Receiving Woman: Studies in the Psychology and Theology of the Feminine* (Philadelphia: Westminster Press, 1981), pp. 85-89.

15. We use that fine word "grimpen" here as T. S. Eliot does in part II of "East Coker," the second of his *Four Quartets*, to suggest the way we can be lost in a witch's morass of deception, a trap which we must face as our own in order to be undeceived. We must recognize, as Eliot says, following Dante, that we are

in a dark wood, in a bramble,
On the edge of a grimpen, where is no secure foothold,
And menaced by monsters, fancy lights,
Risking enchantment.

16. See W. G. Doty, "Hermes, Guide of Souls," *Journal of Analytical Psychology*, Vol. 23, No. 4 (1978), pp. 358-364.

17. See "Laughter," Chapter 12 in Roger Scruton, *The Aesthetic Understanding: Essays in the Philosophy of Art and Culture* (London: Methuen, 1983), p. 163. The essay begins with a provocative statement: "Man is the only animal that laughs, but it seems that laughter belongs also to the immortals."

18. See *Diagnostic and Statistical Manual of Mental Disorders* (DSM III), The American Psychiatric Association, 1981, "Narcissistic Personality Disorder," pp. 315-317; "Borderline Personality Disorder," pp. 321-323.

19. André Green, "The Borderline Concept," in *Borderline Personality Disorders*, ed. Peter Hartcollis (New York: International Universities Press, 1977), pp. 16, 31.

20. In chapter VI on the hag's suffering, we see how the diagnostic outline of the borderline condition sharpens the relevance of the imagery of the witch by translating image into concept, making a firm border around her spell-like effect.

21. Heinz Kohut notes that emptiness, shame, humiliation, and rage characterize a disordered narcissism, along with grandiosity and excessive dependence on others' admiration. See Heinz Kohut, *The Analysis of the Self* (New York: International Universities Press, 1971), pp. 26, 90-91, 114-115, 126-127, 148-149.

22. In Chapters X, XI, and XII we explore this narcissistic wound to being that plagues anyone caught in a compulsion to clown.

23. There is a plethora of books, good and bad, on this subject. To mention but a few: Carol Gilligan, *In a Different Voice, Psychological Theory and Women's Development* (Cambridge: Harvard University Press, 1982); Harold Blum, ed., *Female Sexuality, Contem-*

porary Psychoanalytic Views (New York: International Universities Press, 1977); Jacques Lacan, *Feminine Sexuality*, eds. Juliet Mitchell and Jacqueline Rose, tr. Jacqueline Rose (New York: W. W. Norton, 1982); Robert Stoller, *Sex and Gender*, Vol. 11: *The Transsexual Experiment* (New York: Jason Aronson, 1975); Carol McMillan, *Woman, Reason and Nature: Some Philosophical Problems with Feminism* (Princeton: Princeton University Press, 1982); Thomas B. Hess and Elizabeth C. Baker, eds., *Art and Sexual Politics* (New York: Macmillan, 1973); June Singer, *Androgyny: Toward a New Theory of Sexuality* (New York: Doubleday, 1976); James E. Dittes, *The Male Predicament, On Being a Man Today* (San Francisco: Harper & Row, 1985); Anne Wilson Schaef, *Women's Reality, An Emerging Female System in the White Male Society* (Minneapolis: Winston Press, 1981); Luise Eichenbaum and Susie Orbach, *Outside In, Inside Out Women's Psychology: A Feminist Psychoanalytic Approach* (New York: Penguin, 1982).

24. For a discussion of our inherent, psychic tendency toward abstraction, see J. W. T. Redfearn, "When Are Persons Things and Things Persons?" in *Journal of Analytical Psychology*, Vol. 27, No. 3 (1982), pp. 215-239.

25. The importance of play for the formation of symbols and our experience of ultimate questions about life is discussed in D. W. Winnicott, *Playing and Reality* (London: Tavistock, 1971), pp. 8-19.

26. See Gaston Bachelard, *The Poetics of Reverie*, tr. Daniel Russell (New York: Orion, 1969), p. 1, and Gaston Bachelard, *The Poetics of Space*, tr. Maria Jolas (New York: Orion, 1964), p. xix.

27. For discussion of this point, see Ann Belford Ulanov, "From Image to Imago: Jung and the Study of Religion," in *Essays on Jung and the Study of Religion*, ed. J. Goss and L. H. Martin (Washington: University Press of America, 1985).

28. For an example of this emphasis on splitting, see Andrew Samuels, *Jung and the Post-Jungians* (London: Routledge & Kegan Paul, 1985), chapter 1; see also Nathan Schwartz-Salant's review of *Jungian Analysis*, ed. Murray Stein, *San Francisco Jung Institute Library Journal*, Vol. 5, No. 1, 1984.

29. The same analyst is made over differently by each patient's transference, and each patient's uniqueness is added to by the analyst's countertransference.

30. See C. G. Jung, *Psychological Types, Collected Works*, Vol 6, tr. R. F. C. Hull and H. G. Baynes (Princeton: Princeton University Press, 1971), pp. 473-481 (pars. 814-829). See also Susan K. Deri, *Symbolization and Creativity* (New York: International Universities Press, 1984), pp. 5, 45.

31. See for examples of different approaches to these materials: Robert F. Storey, *Pierrot: A Critical History of a Mask* (Princeton: Princeton University Press, 1978); C. R. Meyer, *How To Be A Clown* (New York: David McKay, 1977); Henry Miller, *The Smile At The Foot of the Ladder* (New York: New Directions, 1948); Henri Bergson, *Laughter* (London: Macmillan, 1911); Stephen Leacock, *Humour: Its Theory and Technique* (London: John Lane, 1935); D. H. Monro, *Argument of Laughter* (Melbourne: Melbourne University Press, 1951); Johan Huizinga, *Homo Ludens* (Boston: Beacon Press, 1950); Bertram Lewin, *The Psychoanalysis of Elation* (New York: Norton, 1950); Francis Connolly, Martin D'Arcy, and Barry Ulanov, *Literature as Christian Comedy* (West Hartford: St. Joseph College, 1962); Norman Cohn, *Europe's Inner Demons, An Enquiry Inspired by the Great Witch-Hunt* (New York: Basic Books, 1975); H. R. Trevor-Roper, *The European Witch Craze of the Sixteenth and Seventeenth Centuries* (New York: Harper & Row, 1969); J. B. Russell, *A History of Witchcraft* (London: Thames and Hudson, 1980); Montague Summers, *The History of Witchcraft* (New York: University Books, 1956); Arkon Daraul, *Witches and Sorcerers* (New York: Citadel, 1969); Chadwick Hansen, *Witchcraft at Salem* (New York: New American Library, 1969); Paul Boyer and Stephen Nissenbaum, *Salem Possessed: The Social Origins of Witchcraft* (Cambridge: Harvard University Press, 1974); G. L. Simons, *The Witch-*

craft World (New York: Barnes & Noble, 1974); Ronald Holmes, *Witchcraft in History* (Secaucus: Citadel, 1977); T. C. Lethbridge, *Witches: Investigating an Ancient Religion* (London: Routledge, 1962); E. E. Evans-Pritchard, *Witchcraft, Oracles, and Magic among the Azande* (Oxford: Clarendon Press, 1976); I. M. Lewis, *Ecstatic Religion: An Anthropological Study of Spirit Possession and Shamanism* (New York: Penguin, 1978).

32. See Hans-Georg Gadamer, *Truth and Method* (New York: Seabury, 1975), p. 23. Gadamer makes his point about history as part of an exploration of "The Significance of the Humanist Tradition."

Chapter II

1. Jung uses the term "objective psyche" to describe our experience of an existence antecedant to any subjective sense of identity: ". . . life and psyche existed for me before I could say 'I,' and when this 'I' disappears, as in sleep or unconsciousness, life and psyche still go on, as our observation of other people and our own dreams inform us." "Basic Postulates of Analytical Psychology" in *The Structure and Dynamics of the Psyche, Collected Works*, vol. 8, tr. R. F. C. Hull (New York: Pantheon, 1960), p. 348 (par. 671). See also C. G. Jung, *The Integration of the Personality*, tr. Stanley Dell (New York: Farrar & Rinehart, 1939), p. 70: "No, the unconscious is anything but a capsulated, personal system; it is the widespread, and objectivity as open as the world. *I* am the object, even the subject of the object, in a complete reversal of my ordinary consciousness, where I am always a subject that has an object."

2. For a discussion of the relevance of "bracketing" to psychological insight, see Ann and Barry Ulanov, *Religion and the Unconscious* (Philadelphia: Westminster Press, 1975), pp. 56, 215-216, 248, 258, 276.

3. Fairy tales have been selected from the Andrew Lang collections (New York: Dover, 1966-68), from *Grimm's Fairy Tales* (New York: Pantheon, 1944) and from the *Let's Pretend* Record Series, distributed by Stereo Dimension Records, New York.

4. Erich Neumann cites Heinrich Zimmer, "Die Indische Weltmutter," Eranos-Jahrbuch, 1938 (Zürich: 1939): "Her devotional image shows her dressed in blood red, standing in a boat floating on a sea of blood." *The Great Mother*, tr. Ralph Manheim (Princeton: Princeton University Press, 1955), p. 152.

5. Ann Ulanov has learned this from women working in analysis with her during the time they have conceived and given birth to children, and from her own experience in having a baby.

6. Geoffrey Parrinder, *Witchcraft: European and African* (London: Faber and Faber, 1963), pp. 20; 45; 50-51; 133-141; and Pennethorne Hughes, *Witchcraft* (London: Longmans, Green and Co., 1952), *passim.*

7. "Everywhere you turn you see it in people's eyes: 'What have we done? Where are we going? Why can't we stop it?' . . . I don't know who the witches are. . . . But even if we can't name them we know they're there, sticking pins in our wax images, muttering spells. Then, before we know what we're doing, we're garrotting men in the dark, disemboweling little children as they sit at school learning their lessons, shooting down half-naked black men in their own villages, or, worse even than that, spreading lies that we know are lies to say that all this is very regrettable but is the only thing a civilized man can do." Thus says Aubrey Menen in his sly, ironic, but not dismissive novel *The Prevalence of Witches* (New York: Scribner's, 1949), pp. 194-195. The wisdom of the book, not unrelated to what we are trying to suggest here, is summed up early in its proceedings: "Don't do anything in a hurry about witches. Things go wrong. Things get back at you." (p. 15)

8. Parrinder, pp. 67-68.

9. Jacques Lacan asserts that "the unconscious is the discourse of the other." Lacan, *The Language of the Self*, tr. Anthony Wilden (Baltimore: Johns Hopkins University Press, 1968), p. 27.

10. Gaston Bachelard, *The Poetics of Reverie*, tr. Daniel Russell (Boston: Beacon Press, 1969), pp. 19, 30, 62-67.

11. *The Cloud of Unknowing*, ed. Dom Justin McCann (London: Burns, Oates and Washbourne, 1936), and Barry Ulanov, "Mysticism and Negative Presence," in *The Gaster Festschrift, The Journal of Ancient Near Eastern Society of Columbia University*, Vol. V (1973), pp. 411-420.

12. Zimmer, cited in Neumann, *The Great Mother*, p. 152.

13. "Wonder Woman" used to be a popular comic book character, and she has been revived in recent years under the influence of the women's liberation movement. She is a comic book and television representation of the archetypal amazon. Daughter of Hippolyta, queen of the Amazons, she fights for justice and truth. She is beautiful, intelligent, talented, and vigorous—a true superwoman.

14. A woman who frequently felt obsessed about ordering her daily chores dreamed of the inhuman quality of her unconscious attitude toward sexual relations. The dream husband may be taken to represent her own animus's approach toward sex. "My husband told me that for the last three months when we are having intercourse he had not entered me but had inserted something mechanical."

Chapter III

1. This quotation is taken from the recorded version of the fairy tale, "The Twelve Dancing Princesses," *Let's Pretend Record Series*, distributed by Stereo Dimension Records, New York. A written version may be found in *The Red Fairy Book*, ed. Andrew Lang (New York: Dover Publications, Inc., 1966). Later references in this chapter are to the same source.

2. Goethe, *Faust*, Pt. II, Act V, sc. 4 (sc. 48 of entire work).

3. *Ibid.*, Act III, scs. 7, 8 (scs. 38, 39 of entire work).

4. C. G. Jung, *The Visions Seminars*, Book 1, p. 141.

5. James Joyce, *Ulysses* (New York: Modern Library, 1946), pp. 515-516, 425, 592-593.

6. D. W. Winnicott, *Through Pediatrics to Psychoanalysis* (New York: Basic Books, 1958), pp. 152-154.

7. See August Strindberg, *To Damascus*, especially the last acts of the three parts of the trilogy, and the final pages of each act of the Chekhov dramas, where the themes of yearning and boredom are reiterated like the themes of a perfectly symmetrical piece of music.

8. Jean Genet, *The Balcony*, trans. Bernard Frechtman (New York: Grove Press, 1958), *passim*.

9. Jean-Paul Sartre, *The Condemned of Altona*, tr. Sylvia and George Leeson (New York: Vintage Books, 1963), especially Franz's addresses to the future in Acts IV, V.

10. R. D. Laing, *The Self and Others* (Chicago: Quadrangle, 1962), pp. 43-44.

11. Vladimir Solovyov, *The Meaning of Love* (London: Geoffrey Bles, 1945), pp. 77, 78, 79-80.

12. Goethe, *Faust*, Pt. II, Act V, sc. 4 (sc. 48 of entire work).

13. Madame de La Fayette, *The Princess of Clèves*, tr. H. Ashton (London: Nonesuch Press, 1943), pp. 13-14.

14. *Ibid.*, pp. 141-142.

Chapter IV

1. Jung writes, "Witchcraft is supposed to be very evil, and also such abstruse and unbelievable nonsense that it seems too stupid to exist." *The Visions Seminars*, Book 2, p. 279.

2. Witchcraft "must be symbolic," Geoffrey Parrinder insists, quoting the anthropologist Margaret Joyce Field. "It is a belief which helps to interpret and canalize the dis-ease of society." To understand the symbolic resonances of the charged vocabulary of the witch-world, however one interprets it, and thus to give it the desired direction, means going to the roots of words, not as an exercise in etymology, but to make some sense of that fertile ground where the figures of our own hedge-life live, the earth of our dreams. See Parrinder, *Witchcraft: European and African*, pp. 204-205.

3. Selma Lagerlöf, *The Story of Gösta Berling*, tr. Robert Bly (New York: New American Library, 1962), pp. 201-202.

4. D. W. Winnicott, *Therapeutic Consultations in Child Psychiatry* (New York: Basic Books, 1971), p. 120.

5. The residual power in women has been much talked about in the decades of feminism, those following World War II, but too often in political or economic terms, making now a claim for recognition, now one for payment—often enough reasonable and just claims, but in the terms in which we are talking about hag power, they are much too meager a set of claims, too little grounded in the reality of woman. There is much to be gained here from what Jose Ortega y Gasset sees as human potential. It is the opposite of completed being, a stone's for example: "When a stone comes into existence, everything that makes up the stone's being or essence or consistency already exists." The stone has no "aspiration to become a stone, but instead is 'all stone' from the moment it begins to exist." But all of us have "the need to be this or that at some future date." We are never completed. Any one of us is "first of all 'someone who is not yet.'" Ours is "the existence of a non-existence." Our way "of being real turns out to be just the opposite of the stone's way." (See Ortega y Gasset, *Historical Reason*, New York: Norton, 1984, p. 93.) Men, we are saying, are at least on occasion aware of their need to know and thus to be able to actualize their potentialities; that is the constant urging, for example, of those who typify fifteenth-century Renaissance accomplishment—Pico della Mirandola, Leon Battista Alberti, Marsiglio Ficino, Leonardo da Vinci. Now, perhaps, it is women's time to do the same, remembering the counsel of St. Augustine, "Love what you are to be" (Sermon CCXVI).

6. Jung, *Visions Seminars*, Book 2, pp. 273-274.

7. The *privatio boni*—the privation of the good—is St. Augustine's understanding of the mystery of evil, and after him that of many others up until our own times. For Augustine, evil has no substance and thus cannot be said to *be*, for being (or substance) is good in itself. Evil exists, but as a privation, a deficiency or defect of something good. It is not a nature, but an absence of it, a deprivation of something that a nature should have. As Augustine says in *The City of God* (XII, 7), "Let no one then look for the efficient cause of an evil will; for it is not efficient but deficient. . . ."

8. C. G. Jung, "Women in Europe," in *Civilization in Transition, Collected Works*, Vol. 10, tr. R. F. C. Hull (New York: Pantheon, 1964), p. 126 (par. 260).

9. See *Brittanicus* and *Athaliah* in Jean Racine, *Five Plays*, tr. Kenneth Muir (New York: Hill & Wang, 1960), pp. 105-106, 252-256.

10. For Racine himself, Phèdre's determination to die rather than to be forced to recognize the intensity of her passion makes her look to the gods to explain her behavior. That is his reasoning in his preface to the play; he is saying in the seventeenth-century fashion that she is an archetypal figure, and never more so than in her confrontation with her stepson—and with her own interiority—at the end of Act II when she so dramatically

bares her breast. Racine's characters meet each other, as the modern playwright Jean Gir-audoux says, "on a footing of awful equality, of physical and moral nudity." (Quoted in Martin Turnell, *The Classical Moment*, London: Hamish Hamilton, 1947, pp. 180-181).

11. See Melanie Klein, "The Oedipus Complex in the Light of Early Anxieties," in *Love, Guilt and Reparation and Other Works 1921-1945* (New York: Delacorte Press/ Seymour Lawrence, 1975), p. 414: "The girl's desire to possess a penis and to be a boy is an expression of her bisexuality and is as inherent a feature in girls as the desire to be a woman is in boys. Her wish to have a penis of her own is secondary to her desire to receive the penis." And on p. 419: "The feminine desire to internalize the penis and to receive a child from her father invariably precedes the wish to possess a penis of her own."

12. Karen Horney makes the same point about the womb and breast envy of men being inherent to their bisexuality. See "The Flight From Womanhood," in Karen Horney, *Feminine Psychology* (New York: Norton, 1967), p. 60.

13. Erich Neumann, *The Child*, tr. Ralph Manheim (New York: Putnam, 1973), pp. 96, 107.

14. See Jung, *Visions Seminars*, Book 2, p. 274.

15. Winnicott, *Therapeutic Consultations*, p. 170.

16. Jung, *Visions Seminars*, Book 2, p. 278; Book 1, pp. 191, 165, 192.

17. The exchange between Pamina and Sarastro takes place in scene 3, the last scene of Act I of *The Magic Flute*; the Queen of the Night's great aria is in Act II, scene 3. In the numbers into which the opera is divided, the exchange is in number 8; the aria, number 14.

Chapter V

1. Paul Ricoeur, *Freud and Philosophy*, tr. Denis Savage (New Haven: Yale University Press, 1970), pp. 32-36.

2. See Erich Neumann, *The Great Mother*, tr. Ralph Manheim (New York: Pantheon, 1955), pp. 38, 67, 148-149; see also M. Pouplier, "Der Archetyp der Hexe," *Analytische Psychologie*, 11:133-152 (1980).

3. See Julio Caro Baroja, *The World of Witches*, tr. O. N. V. Glendinning (Chicago: University of Chicago Press, 1965), pp. xii, xiv.

4. D. W. Winnicott comments that what we share in common is our imaginative elaboration of instinctive experiences and the taking in (introjection) and elimination (projection) of the stuffs of life. (See D. W. Winnicott, "The Depressive Position in Normal Emotional Development," in *Through Paediatrics to Psychoanalysis*, pp. 272-273). Where we differ is in the specific qualities and characteristics of what we introject and project, particularly with regard to whole relationships with other people rather than just parts of them, because people differ in their personalities.

This observation parallels Jung's distinction between the archetypal dimension of experience that we hold in common, and the personal experiences that vary among us. Different mothers, for example, will constellate different aspects of the witch archetype. The witch archetype is not a set content, but is rather a range of images, drive patterns, clusters of emotion that come into play in response to specific personalities in specific situations.

Surprisingly, both Winnicott and Klein offer empirical data from early childhood experience and fantasy that substantiate much of what Jung says in his broader vocabulary about archetypal imagery.

5. Winnicott, "Primitive Emotional Development" in *Through Paediatrics to Psychoanalysis*, p. 154.

6. See G. L. Simons, *The Witchcraft World* (New York: Harper & Row, 1974), chapter 9; see also Mary Daly, *Gyn/ecology, The Metaethics of Radical Feminism* (Boston: Bea-

con Press, 1978), chapter 6; see also J. B. Russell, *A History of Witchcraft*, chapter 4; see also George Mora, "Reification of Evil, Witchcraft, Heresy, and the Scapegoat," in *Evil, Self and Culture*, eds. Marie Coleman Nelson and Michael Eigen (New York: Human Sciences Press, 1984).

7. Melanie Klein discusses this mechanism of splitting at length in Melanie Klein, *op. cit.*, pp. 287-288, 350, 377, 434, 436; see also, Melanie Klein, *Envy and Gratitude and Other Works 1946-1963* (New York: Delacorte Press/Seymour Lawrence, 1975), pp. 6-12, 62, 67, 71, 245, 263, 300, 325.

8. Klein, *Love, Guilt and Reparation*, p. 42.

9. C. G. Jung, *Symbols of Transformation, Collected Works*, Vol. 5, tr. R. F. C. Hull (Princeton: Princeton University Press, 1974), p. 322 (par. 496); see also pp. 328, 330, 370 (pars. 505, 508, 577).

10. Klein, *Envy and Gratitude*, p. 241.

11. *Ibid.*, p. 332.

12. Winnicott, *Therapeutic Consultations*, p. 79.

13. See Edith Weigert, "The Psychotherapy of the Affective Psychoses," in *Psychotherapy of the Psychoses*, ed. Arthur Burton (New York: Basic Books, 1961), p. 357; see also Alice Miller, *Prisoners of Childhood*, tr. Ruth Ward (New York: Basic Books, 1981), p. 35; and "True and False Self," in D. W. Winnicott, *The Maturational Processes and the Facilitating Environment* (New York: International Universities Press, 1965), p. 145.

14. William Shakespeare, *Coriolanus*, Act I, scene iii; Act V, scenes iii and vi.

15. D. W. Winnicott, "Parent-Infant Relationship," in *Maturational Processes*, pp. 51-52. See also Ann and Barry Ulanov, *Cinderella and Her Sisters: The Envied and the Envying* (Philadelphia: Westminster Press, 1983), pp. 27-31, for an example of this intrusive, witchlike mother.

16. See Ann Belford Ulanov, "The Birth of Otherness," in *Receiving Woman*, chapter 5.

17. See Colette Cheland and Serge Lebovici, "Borderline or Prepsychotic Conditions in Childhood—A French Point of View," in *Borderline Personality Disorders*, ed. P. Hartcollis, p. 148.

18. See Otto Kernberg, "The Structural Diagnosis of Borderline Personality Organization," in *ibid.*, pp. 115, 117.

19. *Ibid.*, p. 115.

20. For a discussion of this self-hatred in a woman suffering from a hag-complex, see Polly Young-Eisendrath, *Hags and Heroes: A Feminist Approach to Jungian Psychotherapy with Couples* (Toronto: Inner City Books, 1984), p. 66.

21. C. G. Jung, *Symbols of Transformation, Collected Works* 5, p. 22 (par. 396), 186 (par. 272).

22. See Henrik Ibsen, *Hedda Gabler, passim*, but especially the concluding pages of Act IV, the end of the play, and of Act I, where Hedda says, "Well, there is at least one thing I can amuse myself with. . . ." What, she is asked. "My pistols," she says to her husband, and then with an icy stare, "General Gabler's pistols." Her splitting makes the drama.

23. For discussion of the split-animus condition, see Ann Belford Ulanov, *Receiving Woman*, pp. 129-136.

24. For discussion of these old and new stereotypes, see *ibid.*, chapter 2.

Chapter VI

1. See Anton Chekhov, *Ivanov*, in *Plays by Anton Chekhov*, tr. Elisaveta Fen (Baltimore: Penguin, 1954), p. 88.

2. See Sigmund Freud, *New Introductory Lectures on Psychoanalysis*, tr. James Strachey (New York: Norton, 1965), pp. 82, 84.

3. See D. W. Winnicott, "The Theory of the Parent-Infant Relationship," in *The Maturational Processes and the Facilitating Environment*, p. 40, and James Joyce, *Finnegan's Wake* (New York: Viking, 1958), p. 3, third paragraph, in parentheses, for the first of the many hundred-letter detonations in the book.

4. See Otto Kernberg, *Borderline Conditions and Pathological Narcissism* (New York: Jason Aronson, 1976), p. 165.

5. See Mary Wigman, *The Language of Dance*, tr. Walter Sorell (Middletown: Wesleyan University Press, 1966), pp. 49-51, 74.

6. For discussion of the aggressive factor in eating problems, see Ann Belford Ulanov, "Fatness and the Female" in *Psychological Perspectives*, 10, Fall 1979.

7. Otto Kernberg, *op. cit.*, p. 96.

8. Melanie Klein, "Envy and Gratitude" in *Envy and Gratitude and Other Works*, p. 194.

9. See Melanie Klein, "Personification in the Play of Children," and "The Importance of Symbol-Formation in the Development of the Ego," in *Love, Guilt and Reparation and Other Works*, pp. 199, 221.

10. See D. W. Winnicott, "Ego Distortion in Terms of True and False Self," in *Maturational Processes*, pp. 145ff.

11. Mrs. Alving's fantasy ideals, as Bernard Shaw says, are responsible for driving her husband "to steal his pleasures in secrecy and squalor," bringing "upon him the diseases bred by such conditions"; now the son is the second victim of these ideals. At the end of the play, just "a glance at him shows her that the ideals have claimed their victim, and that the time has come for her to save him from a real horror by sending him from her out of the world, just as she saved him from an imaginary one years before by sending him out of Norway." See *The Quintessence of Ibsenism* (New York: Hill & Wang, 1957), pp. 89, 90.

12. See Michael Meyer, *Ibsen: A Biography* (New York: Doubleday, 1971), p. 490, and for a view closer to our own, Shaw in the passage noted in the footnote above.

13. The intense life of the late Ibsen plays is rediscovered with each new generation of actresses, for it is Ibsen's hag who is the center of his mature dramaturgy, and thus it is that actresses like Alla Nazimova, Peggy Ashcroft, and Ingrid Bergman have been able to bring the hag fully to life, and lesser performers have not. One needs to have something like first-hand experience of the violence of a life of undischarged excitement to act the hag, to make convincing Irene's wild cries of exaltation at the end of *When We Dead Awaken:* "The Sun may look on us. . . ." and "through the mists. And then up, up to the top of our tower where it glows in the sunrise."

14. See C. G. Jung, *Symbols of Transformation*, pp. 28f, 308 (pars. 37, 467); see also D. W. Winnicott, "Primitive Emotional Development" in *Through Paediatrics to Psychoanalysis*, p. 153.

15. See D. W. Winnicott, "Transitional Objects and Transitional Phenomena," in *Playing and Reality*, chapter 1.

16. See Karl Popper, *Unended Quest: An Intellectual Autobiography* (La Salle: Open Court, 1976), pp. 180-187, for a discussion of the "world of statements in themselves"; Ernst Cassirer, *Language and Myth*, tr. Susanne Langer (New York: Dover, 1946), p. 8, and chapter I, footnote 1, for Jungian archetypes.

17. For discussion of symbolic equation, see Melanie Klein, "Symbol-Formation in Ego Development," in Melanie Klein, *Love, Guilt and Reparation and Other Works*, p. 220; see also David Holbrook, *The Masks of Hate* (New York: Pergamon, 1972), p. 162.

18. Robert Musil, *The Man Without Qualities*, two volumes, tr. Eithne Wilkins and Ernest Kaiser (London: Secker & Warburg, 1954), II, p. 405.

19. For discussion of this notion of animus as bridge, see Ann and Barry Ulanov, "The

Archetypal Identity: Anima and Animus," lectures to C. G. Jung Foundation, New York, February 16, 1985. Jung uses this image: "I have defined the anima as a personification of the unconscious in general, and have taken it as a bridge to the unconscious, in other words, as a function of relationship to the unconscious." See his "Commentary on 'The Secret of the Golden Flower,'" *Alchemical Studies, Collected Works* 13, tr. R. F. C. Hull (Princeton: Princeton University Press, 1967), p. 42 (par. 62).

20. See *Getting Married*, in *The Complete Plays of Bernard Shaw* (London: Paul Hamlyn, 1965), pp. 574, 576-577, 588-589.

21. From *Mrs. Warren's Profession* to *Heartbreak House*, Shaw made way for the Mrs. Georges, the great hag-women of his world. He courted them and gave them fitting lines, which was no small achievement for a man, even one so bewitched by hags. In his later plays, even such very different characters in age and background as Saint Joan and the title figure in *The Millionairess* require a touch of the hag to be convincing in performance.

22. See footnote 19 above.

23. For discussion of "being" and "doing" in relation to feminine and masculine, see Harry Guntrip, *Schizoid Phenomena, Object-Relations and the Self* (New York: International Universities Press, 1969), chapter 9.

24. See footnote 7 above; see also Melanie Klein, "Early Stages of the Oedipal Conflict," and "The Oedipus Complex in the Light of Early Anxieties," in *Love, Guilt and Reparation and Other Works*, pp. 192, 401, 409, 413n, 416.

25. Vladimir Markov and Merrill Sparks, *Modern Russian Poetry* (London: MacGibbon & Kee, 1966), pp. 428-429, for the Russian and the English.

26. See Simon Karlinsky, *Marina Cvetaeva, Her Life and Art* (Berkeley: University of California Press, 1966); the biographical and critical materials in the *Selected Poems of Marina Tsvetayeva*, superbly translated by Elaine Feinstein (London: Oxford University Press, 1971), and in Marina Tsvetayeva, *A Captive Spirit: Selected Prose* (London: Virago, 1983).

27. See *Selected Poems* (tr. Feinstein), pp. 12, 18, 24, 25, 41, 64, 90, 91, 94, 88, 89. The great poems of the "Hill" and the "End" are excellently translated into French by Eve Malleret, *Le Poème de la montagne, Le Poème de la fin* (Lausanne: L'Age d'Homme, 1984).

28. Esther Harding discusses this as the "anima woman." See M. Esther Harding, *The Way of All Women* (New York: Longmans, Green & Co., 1936), chapter 1.

29. See D. W. Winnicott, "On Communication," in *Maturational Processes*, pp. 182-183. Otto Rank traces a similar division of women into mothers and hetaeras to the male's creation of an individual self that chooses to relate to the female for pleasure (woman as hetaera), in contrast to a self that exists only as merged into the group where the female's function is viewed as primarily for propagation (woman as mother). See Otto Rank, *Beyond Psychology* (New York: Dover, 1941), chapter 6. From a Jungian perspective, these divisions can be seen as springing from male experience of the feminine as mother and the feminine as anima.

Chapter VII

1. "How Six Travelled Through the World," *Let's Pretend* Records (New York: Tele-General Corporation, 1970); see also "How Six Men Got On In the World," *Grimm's Fairy Tales* (New York: Pantheon, 1944).

2. For discussion of the feminine in relation to the self, see Ann Belford Ulanov, *The Feminine in Jungian Psychology and in Christian Theology*, chapter 9.

3. Jung, *Vision Seminars*, Book 2, pp. 337-338.

4. See Konstantin Mochulsky, *Dostoevsky: His Life and Work*, tr. M. A. Minihan (Princeton: Princeton University Press, 1967), p. 599, and Fyodor Dostoyevsky, *The Brothers Karamazov*, tr. Constance Garnett (New York: Modern Library, 1950), pp. 177, 685.

5. The small details in the portrait of Grushenka in Chapter 1 of Book Four add up, bit by bit, through compassionate smiles, tears, and confidences, to put her at the center of the fullness of psychological events.

6. See *The Brothers Karamazov*, pp. 423-424, 523, 529-532, 428, 535-536.

7. F. M. Dostoievsky, *The Diary of a Writer*, tr. Boris Brasol (New York: Scribner's, 1949), p. 142.

8. Jung, *Vision Seminars*, Book 2, p. 321; see also pp. 333-334.

9. For discussion of this point, see Ann Belford Ulanov, *Receiving Woman*, chapter 7.

10. Jung, *op. cit.*, Book 1, pp. 203-204.

11. *Ibid.*, pp. 134-135.

12. The great spokesman for this address to the tree of life rather than to the fruits of the tree of the knowledge of good and evil is the Russian philosopher Lev Shestov (1866-1938). He is acknowledged often enough as a thinker of central importance to the French existentialists and as a particularly significant influence upon the novelist Albert Camus and the poet Yves Bonnefoy. What is rarely made clear is how far from movements and schools his thought is, how firmly opposed he is to anything that imposes a logic of necessity. As he says in the introduction to his last book, the task he set himself "consists in putting to proof the pretensions to the possession of truth which human reason or speculative philosophy make. Knowledge does not justify being; on the contrary, it is from being that it must obtain its justification. Man wishes to think in the categories in which he lives, and not to live in the categories in which he has become accustomed to think: the tree of knowledge no longer chokes the tree of life." See Lev Shestov, *Athens and Jerusalem*, tr. Bernard Martin (Athens: Ohio University Press, 1966), pp. 65-66.

13. See Chapter I, footnote 5 above.

14. A special blessing of the reworking of popular culture via the video cassette is a new accessibility to the remarkable performances of people like Marie Dressler and Mae West. We urge our readers to see any of the films of these women that may be available; mute acceptance is unmistakable in any extended viewing of their work.

15. The Marschallin's aria "Where is she now?" (*Wo ist die jetzt?*) is the great solo moment of Act I, not long before the curtain; it leads with deceptive smoothness into the exchanges with Octavian. The speculative wisdom of "Today or tomorrow or the day after" (*Heut' oder morgen oder den übernächsten Tag*) stands in the same relation to the final curtain, at the end of Act III. An easily read edition of the libretto is in Hugo von Hofmannsthal, *Selected Plays and Libretti*, Bollingen Series XXXIII.3 (New York: Pantheon, 1963).

16. For *The Madwoman of Chaillot*, tr. Maurice Valency, see Jean Giraudoux, *Four Plays* (New York: Hill and Wang, 1958), Vol. 1. For *The Song of Songs* and *Sodom and Gomorrah*, tr. Herma Briffault, see Barry Ulanov, *Makers of the Modern Theater* (New York: McGraw-Hill, 1961).

17. See C. G. Jung, *Mysterium Coniunctionis, Collected Works*, Vol. 14, tr. R. F. C. Hull (New York: Pantheon, 1963), pp. 211, 213, 226, 227 (pars. 277, 282, 300, 303).

18. To understand the power of the sibylline woman and all her analogues in Goethe's *Faust*, one must give particular attention to Part II, which is unhappily not widely available in full and responsible translation. One version that is satisfactory on all counts is Barker Fairley's, published by the University of Toronto Press in 1970.

19. See "Old Gally Mander," in *Witches, Witches, Witches*, ed. Helen Hoke (New York: Mulberry Books, 1958), pp. 15-19; see also "The Old Witch," in *ibid.*, pp. 80-95.

20. See Jung, *Vision Seminars*, Book 1, p. 131.

21. See J. E. Cirlot, *A Dictionary of Symbols*, tr. Jack Sage (New York: Philosophical Library, 1962), p. 63; see also Jung, *Symbols of Transformation*, *CW* 5, pp. 181, 235, 240, 242, 279n., Plate XXXb (pars. 263, 351, 358, 360, 423n.).

22. See Cirlot, pp. 144-145; see also Jung, *CW* 5, pp. 207, 275, 279, 281, 421 (pars. 302, 421, 423, 427-428, 658).

23. See C. G. Jung, *Alchemical Studies*, *CW* 13, tr. R. F. C. Hull (Princeton: Princeton University Press, 1967), p. 305 (par. 403).

Chapter VIII

1. For example, see Leopold Stein, *Loathsome Women* (London: Weidenfeld and Nicolson, 1959). See also M. Masud Khan, "The Evil Hand" in *Hidden Selves* (New York: International Universities Press, 1983), and Wolfgang Lederer, *The Fear of Women* (New York: Grune and Stratton, 1968).

2. See "The Hungry Old Witch," *Witches, Witches, Witches*, ed. Hoke.

3. See Harold Pinter, *The Homecoming* (New York: Grove Press, 1966), especially the concluding moments of the play, which leave Ruth, the new *materfamilias*, very much in possession, and the surviving men reduced to whimpering or silence.

4. See "Peter and the Witch of the Wood," in Hoke, p. 123.

5. See "The Magic Ball," in Hoke.

6. See "The Goose Girl," in *The Blue Fairy Book*, ed. Andrew Lang (New York: Dover, 1965). For a variation of the same tale, see "The Daughter and the Helper," in Gioia Timpanelli, *Tales From the Roof of the World: Folktales of Tibet* (New York: Viking, 1984). See "The Enchanted Cow" in Hoke. See "Brother and Sister" in *Grimm's Fairy Tales*, ed. Josef Scharl (New York: Pantheon, 1944).

7. See Leopold Stein, "Loathsome Women," *Journal of Analytical Psychology*, Vol. I, No. 1, 1959, pp. 59-79.

8. M. Masud Khan, "Intimacy, Complicity and Mutuality" in *Alienation in Perversions* (New York: International Universities Press, 1979), p. 23.

9. See Alice Miller, *Prisoners of Childhood*, pp. 84-91.

10. M. Masud Khan, *Hidden Selves*, p. 179.

11. See footnote 2 above.

12. Rebecca West, *The Return of the Soldier* (Toronto: Lester & Orpen Dennys, 1982), pp. 144, 147, 178, 182.

13. Rebecca West, *The Judge* (Toronto: Lester & Orpen Dennys, 1981).

14. "East of the Sun and West of the Moon," in *The Blue Fairy Book*.

15. "Beauty and the Beast," in *ibid.*

16. "The Six Swans," in *Grimm's Fairy Tales*.

17. "The Hut in the Forest," in *ibid.*

18. For discussion of the transforming anima, see Ann Belford Ulanov, *The Feminine in Jungian Psychology and in Christian Theology*, pp. 157-162 and chapter 11.

Chapter IX

1. A sense of the place of the clown in ordinary life is conveyed in the *kyogen*, the comic interludes, by the fact that for the most part they are performed without masks, wigs, or costumes.

2. For lack of space, we deal here only with the clown figure as it turns up in male psychology.

3. M. C. Hyers presents an interesting discussion of the jester's function in relation to the sacred values represented by the figure of the king in his "Dialectic of the Sacred and the Comic." See *Holy Laughter*, ed. M. C. Hyers (New York: Seabury, 1969), p. 230.

4. See *King Lear*, I, iv.

5. See *The Merchant of Venice*, II, ii, and III, iv, and *As You Like It*, V, iv.

6. See *Rameau's Nephew* in Denis Diderot, *Rameau's Nephew and D'Alembert's Dream*, tr. L. W. Tracock (Baltimore: Penguin, 1966), pp. 33-34.

7. A sense of the range and intensity of feeling that Don Quixote continues to represent for the Spanish may be gathered in those philosophical masterpieces, Jose Ortega y Gasset's *Meditations on Quixote*, tr. Evelyn Rugg and Diego Marin (New York: Norton, 1961), and Miguel de Unamuno's *Our Lord Don Quixote*, tr. Anthony Kerrigan (Princeton: Princeton University Press, 1967).

8. The "archetypal grandeur" of the clown figure is revealed by few works so insistently as by *Tristram Shandy*. But it is a cumulative effect and requires a full and close reading of the *Life and Opinions* of Tristram, who is both the archetypal clown, and the archetypal writer examining what it means to compose a novel as he does so.

9. See Melanie Klein, *Envy and Gratitude and Other Works*, pp. 61-71. Melanie Klein's description of the "paranoid position" characterizes a very early stage of child development, where good and bad impulses within an infant and good and bad objects outside it are experienced as radically split apart rather than belonging to the same self or to the same object. Destructive impulses are not yet succeeded by guilt at this stage, because the young self does not link them with loving impulses; the "bad" object is not yet recognized as the same object that one loves. Hence one does not feel remorse for having damaged by one's aggression what one also loves.

10. Diderot, p. 35.

11. See Anton Tchekhov, *Literary and Theatrical Reminiscences*, ed. S. S. Koteliansky (London: Routledge, 1927), pp. 231-232.

12. See Alexander Pushkin, "The Undertaker," tr. Walter Morison, in *Russian Humourous Stories*, ed. Janko Lavrin (London: Sylvan Press, 1946), pp. 19, 22, 23.

13. See Anton Chekhov, "The Orator," in Lavrin, pp. 152, 153, 155, 156.

14. See George Santayana, "Carnival," in *Soliloquies in England and Later Soliloquies* (Ann Arbor: Ann Arbor Paperbacks, 1967), pp. 142, 143, 141, 144. See also the preceding and succeeding soliloquies.

15. Diderot, pp. 51, 96.

16. Of all the frustrations an artist feels, few are so daunting as those that accompany the attempt to capture sexual identity in his or her art. For here every defeat can be read as a failure on the part of the artist to express his or her own identity or perhaps even to have laid proper claim to it. That is the kind of thwarting dramatized in Picasso's Mougins etchings.

17. See François Rabelais, *The Histories of Gargantua and Pantagruel*, tr. J. M. Cohen (Baltimore: Penguin, 1955), p. 333.

18. See Desiderius Erasmus, *The Praise of Folly*, tr. H. H. Hudson (Princeton: Princeton University Press, 1941), pp. 51, 87, 90.

19. See Wolfgang Zucker, "The Clown as the Lord of Disorder," in *Holy Laughter*, p. 85.

20. See the *Philebus* in *The Dialogues of Plato*, tr. Benjamin Jowett (New York: Random House, 1937), II, pp. 383-385.

21. Diderot, p. 49.

22. The long stretches of silence by Lucky are loud and clear in *Waiting for Godot*; as with *Tristram Shandy*, the archetypal presence is hard to sample—one must take it all by reading it all.

23. See Robert Musil, *The Man Without Qualities*, II, pp. 432-433.

24. Diderot, pp. 87-88.

25. Erasmus, p. 115.

Chapter X

1. Martin Grotjahn comments in his *Beyond Laughter* (New York: McGraw Hill, 1957), pp. 75-76: "A sense of the comic, its recognition and enjoyment, occurs on a more primitive level than the enjoyment of other forms of humor. While watching the antics of the clown, for instance, the child identifies with his motor effort, activates energy from muscular innervation—but soon realizes that much less energy is needed. This saving of energy intended to be spent on muscular effort is suddenly released in the laughter of superiority."

2. Harry Guntrip, *Schizoid Phenomena, Object-Relations and the Self*, p. 420; see also, D. W. Winnicott, *Through Paediatrics to Psycho-Analysis*, pp. 233-234.

3. Jung's point about defining the ego in relation to the self parallels the interpretation Pinchus Noy gives to Freud's notion of primary-process thinking: "It is obvious that, as the secondary processes are those that are equipped to deal with reality, only the primary ones may serve to maintain the self's sameness and continuity and to integrate new experience with the self." Quoted in Adrian Stokes, *The Game That Must Be Lost* (Cheshire: Carcanet Press, 1973), p. 116; see also Guntrip, *op. cit.*, p. 413.

4. The professional clown's identifying tags may be large, loud, and obvious, but they must also convey something of a sense of calm control, separated from the violences that really do blow up things, a mixture in effect of Durante's nose and Bing Crosby's cool relaxation. "To touch and kindle the mind through laughter demands, more than sprightliness, a most subtle delicacy," George Meredith proclaims in his 1877 "Essay on Comedy," even though it is equally true that "People are ready to surrender themselves to witty thumps on the back, breast, and sides; all except the head. . . ." There is a built-in splitting in the processes of comedy, whether it is the shifting back and forth from thump to delicacy or the persistent "exhibition" of the battles of men and women, to which Meredith also calls our attention, or the fearful responsibility that comes with the conviction that "comedy is the fountain of sound sense; not the less perfectly sound on account of the sparkle. . . ." Here Meredith meets Dante, whose trip to hell, heaven, and purgatory is called *La Commedia* because it ends in paradise, and makes its conclusion a persuasive one for the pilgrimage, the epitome of "sound sense" for the Middle Ages and the Renaissance. See the Meredith essay in *Comedy*, which also includes Bergson's *Laughter* and additional material by Wylie Sypher (New York: Anchor, 1956).

5. See C. G. Jung, *Two Essays in Analytical Psychology, Collected Works*, Vol. 7, tr. R. F. C. Hull (New York: Pantheon, 1966), pp. 157ff. (para. 245-246).

6. Diderot, *Rameau's Nephew and D'Alembert's Dream*, pp. 86, 104, 106.

7. Grotjahn, pp. 46-48.

8. Guntrip, p. 417.

9. Panurge's quest for assurance that there is a wife for him who will not make him a cuckold is the burden of Book III of Rabelais's *Gargantua and Pantagruel*, published in 1546. The most significant of the answers to Panurge's question, which makes a farce of marriage, is Pantagruel's answer to the clown's inquiry about the newly married's ancient exemption from going to war for one year. It is the law of Moses, explains Pantagruel, specifying the aims of producing children where possible, and all the comfort and solace husband and wife could bring to each other before the wars could work their havoc. The precise reference, though Rabelais does not give it in so many words, is Deuteronomy 24:5. Thus does the clown's insecurity make way for a saving grace in Rabelais's bawdy narrative.

10. Guntrip, p. 154.

11. D. W. Winnicott, *Therapeutic Consultations in Child Psychiatry*, pp. 393-394.

12. See Guntrip, p. 154.

13. There is a plenitude of Woody Allen in theaters, television, and video cassettes. Buster Keaton is not so visible, but there are more and more frequent revivals of his films and there is an excellent compilation of sequences of frames from his best-known performances in *The Best of Buster*, ed. R. J. Anobile (New York: Crown, 1976), from which more than a superficial impression of his clowning style can be gathered.

14. See *Lautréamont's Maldoror*, tr. Alexis Lykiard (New York: Crowell, 1972), pp. 112, 115, 116. See also the title essay, tr. Gerard Hopkins, in Charles Baudelaire, *The Essence of Laughter and Other Essays, Journals, and Letters*, ed. Peter Quennell (New York: Meridian, 1956).

15. See Paul Eluard, *Capital of Pain*, tr. R. M. Weisman (New York: Grossman, 1973), p. 109.

16. See Henri Michaux, *The Major Ordeals of the Mind and the Countless Minor Ones*, tr. Richard Howard (New York: Harcourt Brace Jovanovich, 1974), pp. 37-38, and Henri Michaux, *Miserable Miracle*, tr. Louise Varese (San Francisco: City Lights, 1956), p. 73.

17. Outlawed feeling is always present in Buñuel's films. *L'Age d'Or* (1930), which lays out the terms of Buñuel's surrealist cinema, was for the director, who also wrote the screenplay, "a film about passion, *l'amour fou*, the irresistible force that thrusts two people together, and about the impossibility of their ever becoming one." See Luis Buñuel, *My Last Sigh*, tr. Abigail Israel (New York: Knopf, 1983), p. 117.

18. Grotjahn, p. 102.

19. *Ibid.*, p. 92.

Chapter XI

1. See Dorothy Davidson, "Playing and the Growth of the Imagination," *Journal of Analytical Psychology*, Vol. 24, No. 1 (1979), pp. 31-43; see also Michael Fordham, "A Possible Root of Active Imagination," *Journal of Analytical Psychology*, Vol. 22, No. 1 (1977), pp. 317-329.

2. See C. G. Jung, "Conscious, Unconscious, and Individuation," in *The Archetypes of the Collective Unconscious, Collected Works*, 9:1, tr. R. F. C. Hull (New York: Pantheon, 1959), p. 279 (par. 498).

3. Irvine Schiffer, *The Trauma of Time: A Psychoanalytic Investigation* (New York: International Universities Press, 1978), p. 148. Colleagues of Heinz Kohut describe this condition as chronic narcissistic vulnerability: ". . . an individual who suffers a lifelong and at times acutely disabling deficiency in his (ego) capacity to manage internally generated, nonspecific narcissistic tensions and who is at the same time unusually vulnerable to unpredictable and unexpected stimulation from the reality world . . . to suffer from an imbalance between chronic internal tensions, unpredictable stimuli from his object world, and his ego's regulatory capacity. These tensions were diffuse, primitive, and not organized around any particular fantasy; they lacked the qualities of ideational configurations or specific object direction that would suggest they were either predominantly aggressive or libidinal in nature." "Chronic Narcissistic Vulnerability" in *The Psychology of the Self: A Casebook*, ed. Arnold Goldberg, with the collaboration of Heinz Kohut (New York: International Universities Press, 1978), pp. 364-365.

4. "Ego-space" is taken from Ann Belford Ulanov, "The Ego as Space Maker," unpublished paper, 1981.

5. See Grotjahn, *Beyond Laughter*, p. 55.

6. See Schiffer, p. 151.

7. Grotjahn, pp. 93, 97.

8. Schiffer, p. 151.
9. C. G. Jung, "Archetypes of the Collective Unconscious" in *Collected Works*, 9:1, p. 32 (par. 66); see also pp. 2-7 (pars. 57-58).
10. Gaston Bachelard, *The Poetics of Reverie*, p. 124.
11. For a discussion of the elemental feminine, see Ann Belford Ulanov, *The Feminine in Jungian Psychology and in Christian Theology*, pp. 157-158.
12. The "split-anima" (or "split-animus") is a term we used to describe a type of disjunction between the ego and the contrasexual factor in lectures on "The Archetypal Identity: Anima and Animus." See also *Receiving Woman*, chapter 6.
13. See Guntrip, *Schizoid Phenomena*, pp. 422-423.

Chapter XII

1. Jung understands the persona and anima to exist in a compensatory relationship; see C. G. Jung, *Two Essays in Analytical Psychology, Collected Works* 7, pp. 192, 194 (par. 304, 309); see also C. G. Jung, *Psychological Types, Collected Works* 6, p. 465 (par. 800), p. 468 (par. 804). Winnicott makes a similar point in discussing the radical splitting off of a "secret inner life" from the face that one shows to the public, a severe exaggeration of his notion of the "false self," which is like Jung's concept of the persona. See D. W. Winnicott, "Psychosis and Child Care," in *Through Paediatrics to Psycho-Analysis*, p. 225.
2. See Schiffer, *The Trauma of Time*, p. 154; see also Guntrip, *Schizoid Phenomena, Object-Relations and the Self*, p. 422.
3. Pierrot is the very model of a part-object, starting as a servant in *commedia dell'-arte*, ending as a lover: comic, pathetic, now in a large loose hat, now in a dunce cap, his love invariably frustrated, his wholeness resting in his mastery of the part-object role.
4. Schiffer, p. 152. On p. 150 Schiffer comments: "Their vigilant eye and ear for mimicry, a compensatory talent that afforded them a precocious image of a comical and imposturing quality, was described by Freud as the child presenting himself as a serious adult. In later life, this hoaxlike element became disguised by diverting the attention of their audience, a dazzle technique similar to the sleight-of-hand employed by the magician."
5. It is not merely an art class assignment to count the brush strokes in a Cézanne painting and to trace their formal patternings. It is a way to grasp the transformation of form into content and a way to see how a concatenation of parts becomes a whole, in which neither painter nor viewer ever loses sight of the parts.
6. Diderot, p. 54.
7. For discussion of the concept of objects reviewed only with reference to the self's experience of them, see Winnicott's development of the notion of "subjective object" in his *Playing and Reality*, pp. 71, 80, 130; see also Heinz Kohut's use of "selfobject" in his *How Does Analysis Cure?*, ed. Arnold Goldberg and Paul Stepansky (Chicago: University of Chicago Press, 1984), p. 49.
8. See Evelyn Waugh, *A Handful of Dust* (New York: New Directions, 1945), pp. 5, 75, 171, 172, and for the masterpiece of *grand guignol*, reading Dickens in the jungle, pp. 284-302.
9. Anthony Powell's gathering of the parts of twentieth-century Britain into the dozen volumes of his *Dance to the Music of Time* misses none of the arts in its Proust-like peregrination through modern times—from its title, which brings together not only dance and music but painting as well in reference to the Poussin work from which it is taken, to its many characters who are painters, musicians, critics, novelists, film-makers, poets, and actresses. It is an incomparable mosaic, with the part that comes most compellingly alive be-

ing that of the deadly clown Widmerpool, the fullest configuration we have in modern literature of this century's constant fixations on the wrong political part-objects from World War I to the time of the revolting students of the 1960s and 1970s.

10. Winnicott, *Playing and Reality*, chapter 1.

11. See *ibid.*, pp. 10-12. Kohut makes the same point about phase-specific, optimal frustrations furthering the child's transmuting internalization of functions heretofore carried by the parent. See *How Does Analysis Cure?*, pp. 69-72, 99-103.

12. Sigmund Freud, "Humour," *Standard Edition*, Vol. XXI, tr. James Strachey (London: Hogarth Press, 1973), p. 164; see also Sigmund Freud, *Jokes and the Unconscious, SE,* Vol. VIII, pp. 102-105, 201.

13. See Otto Kernberg, *Borderline Conditions and Pathological Narcissism*, p. 266: ". . . this pathological grandiose self compensates for the lack of integration of the normal self concept."

14. See the last chapters of Book I of *Gargantua and Pantagruel*, 52-58, in which every detail is directed to the training and encouragement of good will. The name of the abbey is from the Greek for "will"—*thelema.*

15. Kohut, *The Analysis of the Self*, p. 20; see also pp. 234-235.

16. See Freud, "Humour," *op. cit.*, p. 162.

17. Schiffer, pp. 153, 157.

18. For a discussion of this point about merger of the ego and the self, see Nathan Schwartz-Salant, *Narcissism and Character Transformation, The Psychology of the Narcissistic Character Disorders* (Toronto: Inner City Books, 1982), pp. 66-67; and Kernberg, *op. cit.*, pp. 279, 282-284. Schwartz-Salant makes a useful comparison of Kohut's and Kernberg's views in relation to his own; see *op. cit.*, pp. 19-21.

19. Kohut discusses this narcissistic vulnerability in terms of a person's lack of internal self-structures to adequately supply him with narcissistic energies that can continue to differentiate from their primitive form and achieve mature transformations. Lacking that structure within, such a person depends on others to supply it for him and becomes enraged when they fail to do so. The plight is an anguishing one, tossing the person back and forth between excruciating vulnerability to others' responses to him, and intense rage reactions when they do not conform to his needs. See Heinz Kohut, "Thoughts on Narcissism and Narcissistic Rage," in *The Search for the Self, Selected Writings of Heinz Kohut: 1950-1978*, ed. Paul H. Ornstein (New York: International Universities Press, 1978).

20. This conflict can also be described in Fairbairn's terms of the internal saboteur or anti-libidinal ego attacking the ego, terms which Guntrip adopts. See Ronald W. Fairbairn, *An Object-Relations Theory of the Personality* (New York: Basic Books, 1962), pp. 103, 106-107; see also Harry Guntrip, *Psychoanalytic Theory, Therapy and the Self* (New York: Basic Books, 1973), pp. 97-98.

21. See C. G. Jung, "Transformation Symbolism in the Mass," in *Psychology and Religion: West and East, Collected Works* 11, p. 263 (par. 400).

22. See Guntrip, *Schizoid Phenomena*, p. 187.

23. See Davidson, "Playing and the Growth of the Imagination."

Chapter XIII

1. *The Arabian Nights Entertainments*, illustrated by Louis Rhead (New York: Harpers, 1916), p. 4.

2. For a discussion of the dynamics of acting out, see Judith Hubback, "Acting Out," *Journal of Analytical Psychology*, Vol. 29, No. 3 (1984).

3. *Arabian Nights*, p. 429.

4. Erasmus, *In Praise of Folly*, p. 26.

5. Guntrip gives a poignant example from his own life of the threat he felt when ill health forced his retirement: "I must have felt unconsciously that . . . 'Mother Nature' would at last crush my active self." He discovered that his overdoing compensated for a deep-seated fear that he could not otherwise keep himself going on being. Facing this crisis, he at last, in his seventies, rescued his own anima connection to life from the annihilating effects of his unempathic mother and from his compulsive doing as a defense against her deadening effect on him. Harry Guntrip, "My Analysis with Fairbairn and Winnicott," *International Review of Psychoanalysis*, 1975, 2:145-156.

6. Boccaccio's address to the female is at first mocking in the Proem to the *Decameron*, but as the great work unfolds we see that his is a double irony. When he proposes to recount a "hundred stories or fables or parables or whatever you like," in particular "for the succour and solace of ladies in love (unto others the needle and the spindle and the reel suffice)," he means that his work is for those truly in love, not those who simply follow their appetites. The ladies he has in mind are those of good will, in the Augustinian and Rabelaisian sense.

7. See Giovanni Boccaccio, *The Decameron*, tr. John Payne (New York: Modern Library, n.d.), pp. 298-299, 301-304.

8. See the handsome early-sixteenth-century translation of Boccaccio's *De Claris Mulieribus* by Lord Morley, *Forty-six Lives* (London: Early English Text Society, 1943), pp. 4-5.

9. Adrian Stokes, *op. cit.*, pp. 81-82.

10. *Ibid.*, p. 84.

11. T. S. Eliot, in "Little Gidding," the last section of the last of the *Four Quartets*, describes the holding power of the arts and the particular strength of the ego that has been shaped by it and can now claim its own rights:

> We shall not cease from exploration
> And the end of all our exploring
> Will be to arrive where we started
> And know the place for the first time.

See *The Complete Poems and Plays 1909-1950* (New York: Harcourt Brace, 1952), p. 145.

12. See Barry Ulanov, *A History of Jazz in America* (New York: Viking, 1952), p. 27.

13. See Jung, *Psychology and Alchemy, Collected Works* 12, p. 41 (par. 44), and *Two Essays in Analytical Psychology, Collected Works* 7, p. 177 (par. 274).

14. In his studies of narcissism, Kohut also resists a definitive summation of the self, preferring more inclusive terms that allow for that indefinable experience of the self. Unlike Jung, he does not stress the transcendent aspect of self experience: "My investigation contains hundreds of pages dealing with the psychology of the self—yet it never assigns an inflexible meaning to the term self, it never explains how the essence of the self should be defined. . . . The self, whether conceived within the framework of the psychology of the self in the narrow sense of the term, as a specific structure in the mental apparatus, or, within the framework of the psychology of the self in the broad sense of the term, as the center of the individual's psychological universe, is, like all reality . . . not knowable in its essence. We cannot, by introspection and empathy, penetrate to the self per se; only its introspectively or empathically perceived psychological manifestations are open to us." Heinz Kohut, *The Restoration of the Self* (New York: International Universities Press, 1977), pp. 310-311.

15. As Molière tells it, the Don Juan story is one of impotence, not in the technical sense, for the Don is a ceaseless seducer, but in the spiritual and psychological meaning of the word. Don Juan's dedication to sexual part-objects is altogether without any holding

power; the parts never come together for him; he must end as a burnt-out case, scorched, as he says in his last moments, by an invisible flame, his "whole body . . . a burning firebrand." See *Molière's Comedies*, tr. H. Baker and J. Miller (London: Everyman, 1956), II, p. 50.

16. Even when sexuality is shown in its most empty and betraying exercises, as it is in *Troilus and Cressida*, it is made to glow for moments, just long enough to show its positive strengths, as for example when Cressida proclaims her dedication to Troilus ("the strong base and building of my love / Is as the very center of the earth") in Act IV, scene ii, or when Patroclus, Achilles' homosexual lover, sends him out to fight ("Sweet, rouse yourself . . .") in III, iii. To offer the pitted complexion of sensuality without any of the shine is to make the argument impossibly weak.

17. See *Measure for Measure*, Act III, scene ii.

18. *All's Well That Ends Well*, Act I, scene i.

19. *The Winter's Tale*, Act IV, scene iv; Act V, scene iii.

20. *Cymbeline*, Act II, scene v.

21. *Antony and Cleopatra*, Act IV, scene xv; Act V, scene ii.

Chapter XIV

1. See Gaston Bachelard, *The Poetics of Reverie*, chapter 2.

2. For discussion of an analysand's projection of the anima onto the analyst, see Ann Belford Ulanov, "Transference/Countertransference: A Jungian Perspective" in *Jungian Analysis*, pp. 68-86.

3. For discussion of this linking process, see Rosemary Gordon, "Narcissism and the Self," *Journal of Analytical Psychology*, Vol. 25, No. 3 (1980).

4. See Kohut, *The Analysis of the Self*, pp. 296-321.

5. *Ibid.*, p. 325. See also Heinz Kohut, "Forms and Transformations of Narcissism," in *The Search for Self*, Vol. 1, pp. 446-448, 456-458.

6. Kohut, *The Analysis of the Self*, p. 327; see also p. 328.

7. See Samuel Terrien, *The Elusive Presence* (San Francisco: Harper & Row, 1978), pp. 357, 354, 360, 357.

8. Nathan Scott, "The Bias of Comedy and the Narrow Escape Into Faith," in *Holy Laughter: Essays on Religion in the Comic Perspective*, ed. M. C. Hyer (New York: Seabury, 1969), pp. 52-53.

9. See Eugene Ionesco, *Rhinoceros*, tr. Derek Prouse (New York: Grove Press, 1960), pp. 67, 99.

10. Scott, *op. cit.*, pp. 50-51.

11. See *The Possessed*, which persists as the more frequent translation of the title of Dostoevsky's *The Devils*, tr. Constance Garnett (New York: Modern Library, 1936), pp. 396-397, 408-411.

12. W. A. Dyrness, Rouault, *A Vision of Suffering and Salvation* (Grand Rapids: William B. Eerdmans, 1971), p. 155; see also p. 150.

13. M. C. Hyer, "The Dialectic of the Sacred and the Comic," in Hyer, *op. cit.*, p. 237.

14. Samuel H. Miller, "The Clown in Contemporary Art" in Hyer, p. 101; see also p. 96. And see Henry Miller, *The Smile At the Foot of the Ladder* (New York: New Directions, 1974), p. 46; see also pp. 29, 37-40.

15. William F. Lynch, "The Humanity of Comedy," in Hyer, p. 40.

16. Dyrness, *op. cit.*, pp. 149, 157; see also Lynch, *op. cit.*, pp. 28, 42.

17. Scott, *op. cit.*, p. 58.

18. See Erasmus, *The Praise of Folly*, pp. 106, 108-109, 114-115, 11-14, 23, 29, 31, 47, 119, 124-125.

19. The ironic tone of the penultimate chapter of James Joyce's *Ulysses*, constructed as a mockery of a church catechism in a series of splendidly terse questions and answers, delivers Bloom happily onto and into his wife:

[Q] Womb? Weary?
[A] He rests. He has travelled.

As for Molly, she is the mistress both of an unbecoming foolishness in the famous concluding soliloquy of *Ulysses* and of a handsome folly as she remembers her early, uncompromising acceptance of Bloom: "and first I put my arms around him yes and drew him down to me so he could feel my breasts all perfume yes and his heart was going like mad and yes I said yes I will Yes." See *Ulysses* (New York: Modern Library, 1961), pp. 737, 783.

20. See Paul Celan, *Speech-Grille and Selected Poems* (New York: Dutton, 1971), p. 182.

Chapter XV

1. Emphasizing Jung's notion of the mediating function of anima and animus, we presented in some detail the image of anima and animus as a bridge between the ego and the objective psyche, in lectures on "The Archetypal Identity: Anima and Animus," a portion of a forthcoming work on *Anima and Animus*. See also C. G. Jung, *Alchemical Studies, Collected Works*, Vol. 13, tr. R. F. C. Hull (Princeton: Princeton University Press, 1967), p. 42 (par. 62).

2. For discussion of the substituting of another person for structures within one's own self, see Heinz Kohut, "Narcissism as a Resistance and as a Driving Force in Psychoanalysis," in *The Search for the Self, Selected Writings of Heinz Kohut: 1950-1978*, 2 vols., ed. Paul H. Ornstein (New York: International Universities Press, 1978), vol. 2, pp. 549, 557.

3. For an example of the suffering of a woman caught in the compulsion to clown, see "The Structure of the Grotesque-Comic Sublimation," in Annie Reich, *Psychoanalytic Contributions* (New York: International Universities Press, 1973).

4. Fanny Brice (1891-1951) did not leave enough permanent records of her inspired clowning, but even still-photographs cannot miss altogether the quality of her brilliant mimicking. The recordings that remain of her singing, and her radio performances as Baby Snooks, inadequate as they may be, indicate how much more there was to her than Barbra Streisand at *her* best was able to convey in *Funny Girl* (1968) and *Funny Lady* (1975).

5. William Willeford comments on the Harlequin: "Archaic and magical roots of the deathly aspect of the fool may be seen in the figure of the Harlequin who was once *Herleking* (a form of Wotan), who led a procession of the dead through the night skies . . . the Zuni Koyemci clowns are 'funny' in the sense that they make people laugh, but they are also the most potent and dangerous of the masked dancers." Willeford, *The Fool and His Scepter*, p. 90.

INDEX OF NAMES

INDEX OF SUBJECTS